The Alchemy

From Hermes Trismegistus to Isaac Newton

The Alchemy Reader is a collection of primary source readings on alchemy and hermeticism, which offers readers an informed introduction and background to a complex field through the works of important ancient, medieval and early modern alchemical authors.

Including selections from the legendary Hermes Trismegistus to Robert Boyle and Isaac Newton, the book illustrates basic definitions, conceptions, and varied interests and emphases; and it also illustrates the highly interdisciplinary character of alchemical thought and its links with science and medicine, philosophical and religious currents, the visual arts and iconography and, especially, literary discourse. Like the notable anthologies of alchemical writings published in the sixteenth and seventeenth centuries, it seeks to counter the problem of an acute lack of reliable primary texts and to provide a convenient and accessible point of entry to the field. In addition to newly edited, lightly modernised texts, *The Alchemy Reader* includes a substantial introduction to the subject, head notes to individual selections, annotations, a bibliography, and a glossary.

STANTON J. LINDEN is Professor Emeritus of English, Washington State University, where he taught courses in English Renaissance literature from Shakespeare to Milton. He has published articles on Bacon, Donne, Jonson, Herbert, Milton, Henry Vaughan, Margaret Cavendish, and others, often dealing with alchemical influences or relations between the visual and verbal modes. His recent publications include *Darke Hierogliphicks: Alchemy in English Literature from Chaucer to the Restoration* (1996), *Emblems and Alchemy* (co-editor, 1998), and a critical edition of George Ripley's *Compound of Alchymy* (2001).

The Alchemy Reader

From Hermes Trismegistus to Isaac Newton

EDITED BY

Stanton J. Linden
Washington State University

CAMBRIDGE
UNIVERSITY PRESS

CAMBRIDGE UNIVERSITY PRESS
Cambridge, New York, Melbourne, Madrid, Cape Town, Singapore, São Paulo,
Delhi, Dubai, Tokyo, Mexico City

Cambridge University Press
The Edinburgh Building, Cambridge CB2 8RU, UK

Published in the United States of America by Cambridge University Press, New York

www.cambridge.org
Information on this title: www.cambridge.org/9780521796620

© Stanton J. Linden, 2003

First published 2003
4th printing 2010

Printed in the United Kingdom at the University Press, Cambridge

A catalogue record for this publication is available from the British Library

ISBN 978-0-521-79234-9 Hardback
ISBN 978-0-521-79662-0 Paperback

Contents

Illustrations

Acknowledgments

Preparation of this book has been assisted by a number of individuals and institutions whose contributions I gratefully acknowledge. In order of chronology, if not size of indebtedness, I would like to thank, first of all, the Cambridge University Press for inviting me to submit a proposal for *The Alchemy Reader*, a project I would perhaps not otherwise have undertaken. I am especially grateful to William Davies and Neil de Cort of the Press for their good counsel and unfailingly prompt assistance during the book's planning and production. I am also much indebted to Muriel Hall, my copy-editor, for the intelligence, care and efficiency with which she read the typescript and commented upon it; errors and infelicities that remain are my own. The Department of Special Collections of the University of Glasgow Library has been the primary site for my work, and I would like to extend very special thanks to David Weston and his staff for their kind efforts in my behalf while transcribing texts in the extraordinary Ferguson Collection of Alchemical Books and Manuscripts. The majority of my illustrations are drawn from this collection, and I am grateful for permission to reproduce them here; photographic costs were covered by an earlier award of a Sir William Stirling Maxwell research fellowship from the University of Glasgow. My indebtedness to the Wellcome Trust is also large, the result of a travel grant that enabled further research and writing at the Wellcome Library in London. I am extremely grateful to the editors of *Ambix*, the *Journal of Chemical Education*, the *Journal of the Royal Society of Medicine*, the University of California Press, the Cambridge University Press, and Princeton University Press for permission to reprint materials first published elsewhere; specific acknowledgments are included in the appropriate headnotes. Finally, two colleagues and friends, Professors Nicolas Kiessling of Washington State University and Winfried Schleiner of the University of California, Davis, have generously provided help with textual matters and translations.

Abbreviations

Bibl. Chem.	John Ferguson, *Bibliotheca Chemica*, 2 vols.
Cath. Ency.	*The Catholic Encyclopedia*
DAI	Lyndy Abraham, *A Dictionary of Alchemical Imagery*
DNB	*The Dictionary of National Biography*
DSB	Charles C. Gillispie, ed., *Dictionary of Scientific Biography*
HMES	Lynn Thorndike, *A History of Magic and Experimental Science*
Lexicon	Martin Ruland, *A Lexicon of Alchemy*. Translated by A. E. Waite
OCD	*The Oxford Classical Dictionary*, 2nd edn.
OED	*The Oxford English Dictionary*
TCB	Elias Ashmole, *Theatrum Chemicum Britannicum* (London, 1652)

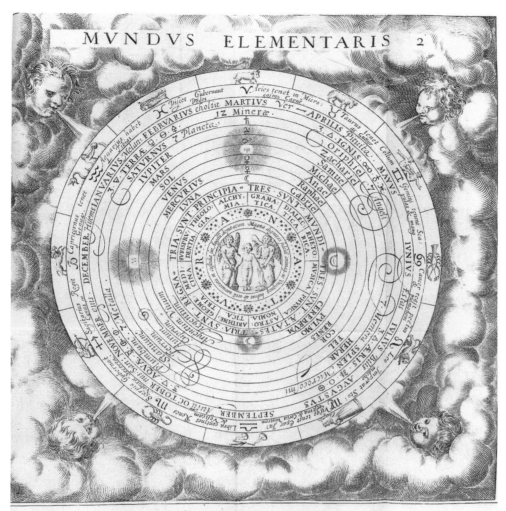

§.1. **D**Eus eſt Ens Æternum, Unitas Infinita, Radicale Rerum omnium Principium: Cujus Eſſentia eſt Lux Immenſa: Poteſtas Omnipotentia: Volun-
tas Bonum Perfectum: Nutus Opus abſolutum.   Plura deſideranti occurrunt ſtupor, Silentium & Abyſſus Gloriæ profundiſſimæ.   §. 2. Mundum ab Æterno in Archetypo ſuo deſcriptum fuiſſe Sapientum plurimi duxerunt: Archetypus autem Ipſe qui Totus Lumen eſt, ante Univerſi Cre-
ationem in ſe complicatus, ceu liber ſibi ſoli illuxit, in Mundi verò productione quaſi parturiens ſe aperuit & explicuit, Opuſq; ſuum in Mente, velut in matri-
ce, prius occultum, quadam ſui Extenſione manifeſtum fecit ac Mundum Idæalem, quaſi duplicatâ Divinitatis Imagine , actualem & materialem eduxit.
Hoc annuit *Triſmegiſtus*, dum Deum formam ſuam mutaſſe ac Univerſa ſubitò revelata & in Lucem converſa fuiſſe refert: Nihil aliud quippe eſt Mundus ,
quàm patens occultæ Divinitatis Imago. Hunc Univerſi ortum intellexiſſe videntur Antiqui per Palladem ſuam è Jovis Cerebro, Vulcani, nempe Ignis ſive
Luminis Divini Ope extractam.   §. 3. Æternus Rerum Parens, non minus in Ordinando Sapiens, quàm in creando potens Organicam Mundi molem in
tam præclarum ordinem digeſſit, ut ſumma Imis & ima ſummis citra confuſionem intermixta & analogiâ quadam ſimilia ſint; Unde Extrema Totius Opificii,
ſecreto quodam nexu, per media inſenſibilia ſtrictiſſimè inter ſe cohærent, ac ſponte omnia in ſupremi moderatoris Obſequium.   Et inferioris Naturæ Com-
modum conſentiunt, Solo nutu Ejus qui colligavit, ſolvi ſe paſſura. Rectè itaque *Hermes id quod inferius eſt, ſimile eſſe Ei quod eſt ſuperius*, affirmavit. §. 4. Qui
ſummum jus Univerſi in Naturam transfert aliam à Divinâ Naturâ, Deum negat: neque enim aliud in creatum Naturæ Numen, aut in producendis aut in con-
ſervandis Expanſæ hujus Machinæ Individuis, agnoſci fas eſt, præter Spiritum illum Divini Opificis, qui primis aquis incubuit & conſulta in Chao rerum ſemina
de potentia in Actum eduxit, eductâ per conſtantem alterationis Rotam verſans componendo & reſolvendo hæc inferiora Geometricè tractat.

Autor Enchiridii Phyſicæ Reſtitutæ. Can. 1. ſeq.

Figure 1. "Mundus Elementaris." *Musaeum hermeticum reformatum et amplificatum* (1678).

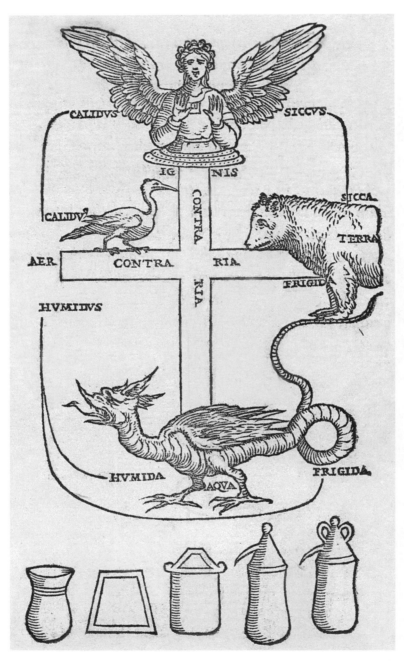

Figure 2. The four elements symbolized. Petrus Bonus, *Pretiosa margarita novella* (1546).

EX SVLPHVRE ET ARGENTO VIVO,
vt natura, sic ars producit me-
talla.

HOMAS AQVINAS ob singularem pieta-
tem & deuotionem *Sanctis* adnumeratus in
doctrinis & scientijs tam admirabilis toti
Christiano orbi apparuit, vt nomen *Angeli-*
ci doctoris adsciuerit; tanquam supra huma-
ni ingenij vim & captum ad spiritualem naturam ascenderet: Qui sanctitulus si cui hominum conue-
niat, illi imprimis inuidendus non erit. Tanta enim ille o-
pera quæstionibus subtilissimis & in diuinis & humanis

Thomas
Angelicus
doctor.

refer-

Figure 3. "Like Nature, Art makes metals out of sulphur and mercury." Michael Maier,
Symbola aureæ mensæ (1617).

In Chymicis verfanti Natura, Ratio, Experientia & lectio,
sint Dux, fcipio, perspicilia & lampas.

EPIGRAMMA XLII.

DUx Natura tibi, túque arte pedissequus illi
Esto lubens, erras, ni comes ipsa viæ est.
Det ratio scipionis opem, Experientia firmet
Lumina, quò possit cernere posta procul.
Lectio sit lampas tenebris dilucida, rerum
Verborúmque strues providus ut caveas.   Z   CAS-

Figure 4. Alchemist following Nature. Michael Maier, *Atalanta fugiens* (1617).

CREMERI CVIVSDAM ABBATIS WEST-
monasteriensis Angli Testamentum, hactenus nondum publi-
catum, nunc in diuersarum nationum gratiam editi, & figuris
cupro affabre incisis ornati operâ & studio
MICHAELIS MAIERI Phil. & Med. D. Com. P. &c.

FRANCOFVRTI
Ex Chalcographia Pauli Iacobi, impensis LVGÆ IENNIS.
Anno M.DC.XVIII.

Figure 5. Library and Laboratory. Michael Maier, *Tripus aureus* (1618).

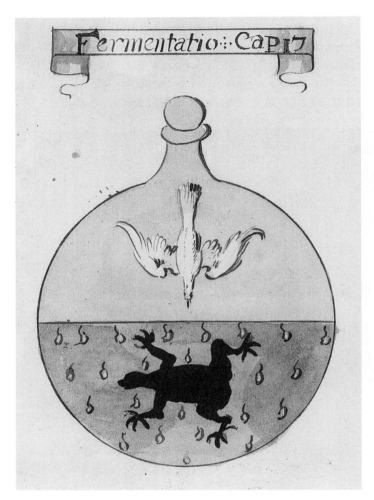

Figure 6. Fermentatio within the alchemical egg. University of Glasgow Library, MS Ferguson 253.

Figure 7. Conjunctio. Rosarium philosophorum. University of Glasgow Library,
MS Ferguson 74, f. 42ᵛ.

Figure 8. Winged Hermaphrodite. University of Glasgow Library, MS Ferguson 4, f. 97ᵛ.

Figure 9. Alchemical Master and Disciple. Elias Ashmole, *Theatrum Chemicum Britannicum* (1652).

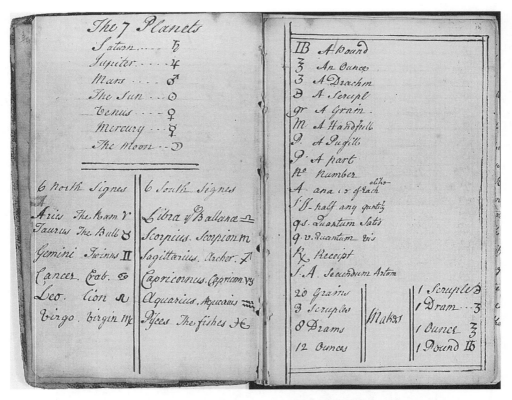

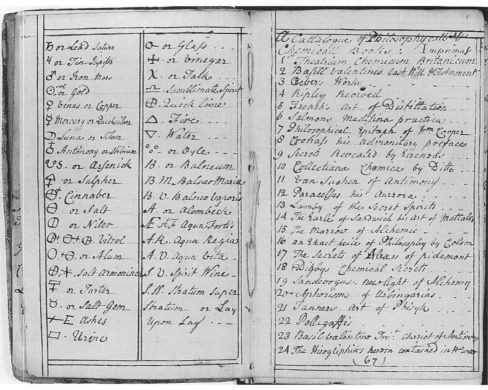

Figure 10. Alchemical signs and symbols with "A Cattalogue of Philosophycall &
Chemicall Books," University of Glasgow Library, MS Ferguson 155.

Figure 11. Resurrected Christ, *Rosarium philosophorum*. University of Glasgow Library, MS Ferguson 74, f. 191ᵛ.

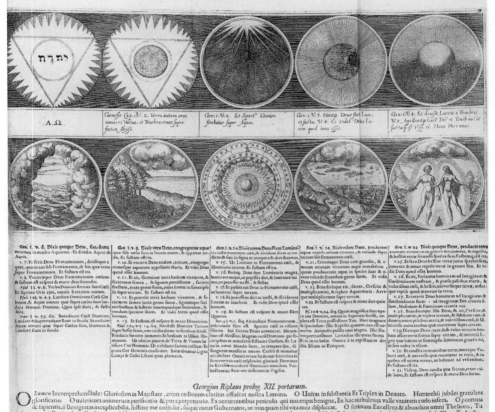

Figure 12. Alchemical Creation Design. *Musaeum hermeticum reformatum et amplificatum* (1678).

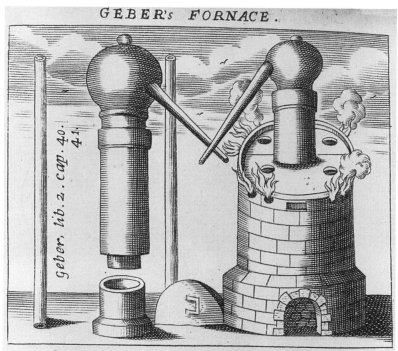

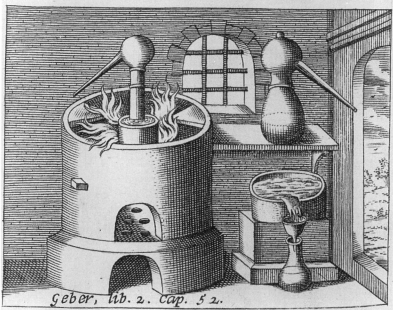

Figure 13. Geber's furnaces. William Salmon, *Medicina Practica, or Practical Physick* (London, 1692).

Figure 13. (*Continued*)

Figure 14. Tympanum. Nicolas Flamel, *Exposition of the Hieroglyphicall Figures* (1624).

Introduction

Writing nearly seventy years ago about the then-emerging academic interest in alchemy stimulated by Marcellin Berthelot's translation and editing of ancient Graeco-Egyptian texts, Arthur John Hopkins drew attention to certain problems in the study of alchemy that remain largely unresolved today: "A comprehensive explanation [is] still lacking," Hopkins noted, "such a theory as would coordinate the whole and make clear to the modern mind what was the purpose and underlying conception of the alchemist."[1] Subsequent years have witnessed growing interest, research, and scholarly activity devoted to alchemy, hermeticism, and related fields, none more than at the present time with its steady flow of new editions of primary texts, new critical books and articles, and the appearance of new journals and specialized conferences and colloquia devoted to these subjects. Furthermore, a visit to virtually any bookshop reveals that there continues to be a large – and steadily increasing – popular and semi-popular market for these diverse materials.

Two related characteristics mark the academic, research-oriented side of this burgeoning enterprise: its interdisciplinary nature and its tendency to reassess and reinterpret, often radically, the authors, works, and ideas that are its focus, often with the result of discovering a high level of alchemical and hermetic interest where previously it had not been suspected or at least readily admitted. This is seen, for example, in the continuing reevaluation of the role of alchemy in the scientific thought of Robert Boyle and Isaac Newton, which has demonstrated conclusively that, much more than an early or casual interest, alchemy was at the heart of the thought and method of each of these pioneers of modern science.[2] That such major reappraisals are occurring among historians of science is particularly telling since earlier generations had often refused to consider alchemy as a worthy subject of study because it seemed to represent all that was contrary to the modern, progressive, "rationalistic" spirit of modern science.

But the revolution in attitude toward the study of alchemy extends far beyond the history of science. Scholars representing many other fields and disciplines – literature, philosophy, history, art history, the history of medicine, religion, and psychology – are discovering that alchemy, as it is now broadly understood, contains vital points of contact

---

[1] *Alchemy: Child of Greek Philosophy* (Morningside Heights, NY: Columbia University Press, 1934), 3–4. Hopkins was referring to Berthelot's *Collection des anciens alchimistes grecs*, 3 vols. (Paris: Georges Steinheil, 1887–88).

[2] See Lawrence Principe, *The Aspiring Adept: Robert Boyle and his Alchemical Quest* (Princeton: Princeton University Press, 1998); and Betty Jo Teeter Dobbs, *The Foundations of Newton's Alchemy or "The Hunting of the Greene Lyon"* (Cambridge: Cambridge University Press, 1975), and *The Janus faces of genius: The role of alchemy in Newton's Thought* (Cambridge: Cambridge University Press, 1991).

with their own disciplines. Students of literature have become aware of the vast number of images and allusions drawn from alchemy that appear in literary works of the Middle Ages, Renaissance, and beyond. Students of philosophy and religion have found significant links between alchemy and Gnosticism,[3] Neoplatonism, and Rosicrucianism, just as art historians have discovered that artists from Bosch and Brueghel to the Surrealists have derived ideas and visual cues from alchemy. The extraordinarily rich visual and iconographic tradition reflected in alchemical manuscripts and early printed books, including emblem books, is providing a storehouse of interesting materials for study. Finally, for the historian of medicine, the emergence of interest in iatrochemistry – to cite only one example – and the related seventeenth-century controversy between followers of Galen and Paracelsus, has demonstrated how close is the relationship between alchemy and medical theory and practice. While not all of these interdisciplinary connections are discoveries of the late twentieth century – Jung's *Psychologie und Alchemie* was first published in 1944 – nonetheless, the cumulative effect of such links, both quantitatively and qualitatively, is such that alchemy has now emerged as the subject of interdisciplinary study *par excellence*.[4]

During the sixteenth and seventeenth centuries, the reading and study of expensive and often inaccessible alchemical treatises written over a long period of time and by authors of many different nations and languages was greatly facilitated through publication of anthologies which gathered together large numbers of such tracts for study and comparison. These were the successors to similar collections of materials in manuscript. Among the popular printed collections are *De Alchemia* published at Nuremberg by Petreium in 1541, which includes selections by Roger Bacon and Richard of England along with those of Geber, Hermes, and Hortulanus. The *Veræ Alchemiæ Artisque Metallicæ* of Guglielmo Gratarolo (Basel, 1561) added tracts by Arnald of Villanova, Raymond Lull, Albertus Magnus, John of Rupescissa and many others. Early in the seventeenth century, Lazarus Zetzner, a printer of Strasburg, produced the monumental *Theatrum Chemicum*; the most comprehensive anthology yet published, it included four volumes in the first edition, added a fifth in 1622, and a sixth in the edition of 1659–61. More localized was Elias Ashmole's popular anthology of English alchemical poetry, the *Theatrum Chemicum Britannicum* (1652); and in 1678 the famous *Musaeum Hermeticum reformatum et amplificatum*, containing

---

[3] For a recent, succinct account of similarities and – more important – differences between Hermetism and Gnosticism, see Roelof van den Broek, "Gnosticism and Hermetism in Antiquity: Two Roads to Salvation," in *Gnosis and Hermeticism from Antiquity to Modern Times*, ed. Roelof van den Broek and Wouter J. Hanegraaff (Albany: State University of New York Press, 1998), 1–20.

[4] The following references are highly selective, intended only as representative of studies of alchemy's interdisciplinary connections, and should be supplemented with additional citations from the headnotes to individual selections and the Bibliography, which incorporates a wide range of works for further reading. For literary connections, see Lyndy Abraham, *Marvell and Alchemy* (Aldershot, Hants.: Scolar Press, 1990), and my *Darke Hieroglyphicks: Alchemy in English Literature from Chaucer to the Restoration* (Lexington, KY: University Press of Kentucky, 1996); in art history, representative titles would include Jacques van Lennep, *Art & Alchimie* (Brussels: Éditions Meddens, 1971) and Laurinda S. Dixon, *Alchemical Imagery in Bosch's Garden of Delights* (Ann Arbor, MI: UMI Research Press, 1980); and in emblem studies, Alison Adams and Stanton J. Linden, eds., *Emblems and Alchemy*, Glasgow Emblem Studies, vol. 3 (Glasgow: University of Glasgow, 1998); for iatrochemical controversy and the influence of Paracelsus, see Allen G. Debus, *The Chemical Philosophy: Paracelsian Science and Medicine in the Sixteenth and Seventeenth Centuries*, 2 vols. (New York: Science History Publications,1977); and *The English Paracelsians* (New York: Franklin Watts, 1966). For a useful, comprehensive introduction, see Allison Coudert, *Alchemy: The Philosopher's Stone* (London: Wildwood House, 1980).

twenty-one treatises, was reissued in Frankfurt as an expansion of a nine-treatise first edition that had appeared in 1625.[5]

The results of these ambitious publication ventures, combined with the printing of single treatises and collected editions of individual authors, and the still-flourishing manuscript tradition, were more than sufficient to sustain interest in and knowledge of alchemy and assure preservation and dissemination of many authors and treatises that might otherwise have been lost. Renaissance readers who possessed one of these anthologies could expect authoritative texts of a large number of the choicest "flowers" of alchemical writing. Authors included would likely represent nearly the entire history of alchemical writing as it was then conceived: from the legendary Hermes Trismegistus, contemporary of Moses, down to those of the present and recent past; the originating cultures from which these treatises derived would have included the ancient Graeco-Egyptian era (roughly the first seven centuries AD), the Islamic period extending from the mid-seventh to the thirteenth century, followed by the Latin culture of medieval and Renaissance Europe.[6] In several instances, as with Ashmole's *Theatrum Chemicum Britannicum*, the texts were accompanied by extensive prefatory material, annotations, illustrations and indices. In short, whatever the purposes and intentions of our early modern reader, careful study of one of these miniature alchemical libraries would, at a minimum, have provided a solid, wide-ranging introduction to the art.

With a similar aim and method, albeit a more modest scale, *The Alchemy Reader: From Hermes Trismegistus to Isaac Newton* is an anthology of primary source readings – about thirty in all – dating from ancient times to the early eighteenth century. Included are works from Classical antiquity, the Graeco-Egyptian and Islamic periods, and the European Middle Ages and Renaissance. (Roughly one half of the selections were written during the sixteenth and seventeenth centuries or were then edited or translated from earlier manuscripts or printed editions.) This book offers an introduction to alchemy through the words of some of the art's most notable authorities, and because the number of works from which to make selections is enormous, few readers will perhaps be satisfied with all of the readings. Invariably, questions of inclusion (or exclusion) will arise that even the ablest defence may not justify. For example, the brief selections from Plato and Aristotle are included, not because they deal with alchemy per se – although many spurious alchemical treatises came to be fathered upon both philosophers – but because they set forth important background ideas (e.g., on prime matter, the transformation of the elements, and the formation of metals) that were long-lived and exerted considerable influence on subsequent alchemical theory.

Definitions and origins

While our knowledge of many aspects of alchemy has greatly advanced in the past fifty years, we still lack the "comprehensive explanation," the totalizing theory that would

---

[5] The 1678 collection (sometimes dated 1677) was edited and translated by A. E. Waite as *The Hermetic Museum, Restored and Enlarged*, 2 vols. (London: James Elliott and Co., 1893).

[6] In matters of dates and periodization, I am following those found in the still useful introductory work by John Read, *Prelude to Chemistry* (London: G. Bell and Sons, 1936).

"coordinate the whole and make clear to the modern mind what was the purpose and underlying conception of the alchemist," that A. J. Hopkins sought early in the twentieth century.[7] In fact, current scholarly concern is much more with the variety and diversity of conceptions of alchemy, the multiplicity of its definitions, the theoretical and practical malleability that makes alchemy useful and attractive to a broad interdisciplinary audience, and its origins in several ancient cultures. If Hopkins's search for a "unitary" explanation has not been entirely abandoned, it is now much more common to see alchemy as pluralistic rather than singular, as "alchemies" rather than "alchemy."[8] This will also be my approach in the balance of this introduction, where brief discussion of background topics will, it is hoped, provide the uninitiated reader with a core of useful information with which to engage the texts and an awareness of the complexities inherent in the materials and various approaches to them. In particular, readers are encouraged to pursue the further readings cited in the notes to this Introduction, the headnotes to individual selections, and in the bibliography. Background topics of special importance at the outset include basic definitions, types, and emphases of alchemy, brief consideration of places of origin, certain of its dominant principles and theories, and characterization of its written and pictorial traditions.

The Mirrour of Alchimy, a widely disseminated treatise long attributed to Roger Bacon, presents a useful instance of the problematical nature of defining alchemy. Chapter One "Of the Definitions of Alchimy" reads in its entirety:

> In many ancient Bookes there are found many definitions of this Art, the intentions whereof we must consider in this Chapter. For *Hermes* saith of this Science: *Alchimy* is a Corporal Science simply composed of one and by one, naturally conjoyning things more precious, by knowledge and effect, and converting them by a naturall commixtion into a better kind. A certain other saith: *Alchimy* is a Science, teaching how to transforme any kind of mettall into another: and that by a proper medicine, as it appeareth by many Philosophers Bookes. *Alchimy* therfore is a science teaching how to make and compound a certain medicine, which is called *Elixir*, the which when it is cast upon mettals or imperfect bodies, doth fully perfect them in the verie projection.[9]

For the author of this tract and his authorities, alchemy is both "art" and "science" and involves the conversion of inferior metals into those of a "better kind" through the operation of a "proper medicine" or *Elixir*. No less important is the *method* by which this process is acquired: knowledge of alchemy – largely dependent on tradition and authority, despite frequent protestations to the contrary – is obtained through study of "Philosophers Bookes," which were inevitably – again despite protestations – hermetic in their insistence

---

[7] See note 1.

[8] See, for example, Robert M. Schuler, "Some Spiritual Alchemies of Seventeenth-Century England," *Journal of the History of Ideas* 41 (April–June 1980): 293–318.

[9] Quoted from my edition of *The Mirror of Alchimy Composed by the Thrice-Famous and Learned Fryer, Roger Bachon* (New York and London: Garland Publishing, 1992), 3. This treatise bears the title of the small but influential collection of tracts in which it appears in both manuscript and printed versions. The collection was first printed in English in 1597, a version based directly on a French edition of 1557, which was, in turn, derived from the Latin edition printed in the aforementioned Latin collection, *De Alchemia* (Nuremberg, 1541).

on concealing, rather than revealing, plain truths. The author of this tract thus sets forth the primary meaning of *exoteric* alchemy as the "Corporal Science" concerned with the "perfecting" or physical transmutation of "mettals or imperfect bodies." Behind this definition is alchemy's centuries-old association with metallurgy, goldsmithery, glass-making, and the dyeing and tinting of metals.

For a definition that sees alchemy in very different terms, I turn to one that appeared less than ten years after publication of the English version of the *Mirror* (1597). Thomas Tymme, writing in *The Practise of Chymicall, and Hermetical Physicke* (1605), his translation of a work by Joseph Quersitanus, states:

> For *Halchymie* tradeth not alone with transmutation of metals (as ignorant vulgars thinke: which error hath made them distaste that noble Science) but shee hath also a chyrurgical hand in the anatomizing of every mesenteriall veine of whole nature: Gods created handmaid, to conceive and bring forth his Creatures.[10]

For Tymme, "Divine *Halchymie*" has powerful theological, philosophical, and epistemological resonances, which distinguish it from exoteric alchemy's preoccupation with metallic transmutation. Drawing on familiar tropes, Tymme describes God's creation of the world and its end, the Last Judgment ("that great & generall refining day"), as alchemical processes. For mankind in the present, it is a means of gaining knowledge and understanding of nature, visible creation, and God; in these *esoteric* aspects it deserves to be regarded as "Gods created handmaid." Although these two passages represent sharply opposing conceptions of alchemy, in point of fact, their differences were often muted even within the same author, treatise, or era: alchemy could at once display both exoteric and esoteric tendencies as the process for perfecting base metals was applied to the sinfully corrupt soul and psyche of man.

In discussing the origins of alchemy, historians generally review the various claims to primacy of Egypt, China, and India, examining the documents for evidence of exoteric or esoteric interests or of closely related bodies of knowledge. I will do little more than summarize some of this evidence and refer the reader to writings of the specialists. In discussing alchemical interests in ancient Egypt, John Read, for example, points to the early existence of highly developed craft traditions that relied on some knowledge of chemistry, such as metallurgy, gold-smithing (as early as 3000 BC), glass-making, and dyeing and tinting. For Read, linguistic evidence also suggests that the word "alchemy" itself may have had Egyptian origins: "Egypt, or Khem, the country of dark soil, the Hebrew 'Land of Ham', has often been pictured as the motherland of chemistry; so that later this 'art of the dark country' became known to Islam as *al Khem*, and through Islam to the Western world as *alchemy*." Also pointing toward alchemy's Egyptian origin is the centrality of Hermes Trismegistus (the "thrice-great") in its written tradition; the Greek counterpart of the Egyptian moon god Thoth (also identified with Athothis

---

[10] From Tymme's dedication to Sir Charles Blunt, Earle of Devonshire, of Joseph Quersitanus, *The Practise of Chymicall, and Hermetical Physicke . . . Translated by Thomas Timme, Minister* (London, 1605). His defence concludes: "This [alchemical] Phylosophy . . . is not of that kind which tendeth to vanity and deceit, but rather to profit and to edification, inducing first the knowledge of God, & secondly the way to find out true medicine in his creatures."

or Imhotep), Hermes, the Roman Mercury, has an extremely rich and diverse role in alchemical theory and practice.[11] The best known of the works attributed to this legendary
founder and patron saint of alchemy is the *Emerald Table* (*Tabula Smaragdina*) included in
this collection. As the result of these ancient connections and traditions, the way was prepared for new alchemical interests that flourished in the Graeco-Egyptian culture of the
Alexandrian age (fourth century BC to the seventh century AD), to which I will turn
shortly.

The standard work on ancient Chinese alchemy, as with perhaps all aspects of early
Chinese science, has been written by Joseph Needham, who begins his study with explanation of its three, Taoist-inspired primary emphases: (1) the search for "macrobiotic" plants,
i.e., those that, when specially prepared, can extend human life beyond the normal limits
of old age, even to immortality; (2) the discovery of chemical and metallurgical processes
both for making *imitation* gold, often with the intention to deceive ("aurifiction"), and
for artificial production – from other substances – of what the alchemists regarded as *real*
gold, as good as, if not better than, gold from the mines ("aurifaction"); and (3) the search
for mineral, i.e., non-organic, elixirs and curatives. Needham concludes that in China,
"Taoism, medicine and alchemy were always intimately connected, not only theoretically
but in practising individuals time after time."[12]

Chinese alchemy has been termed "older . . . than that of any other part of the world,"
and one of its texts, the *Chou I Tshan Thung Chhi* (Book of the Kinship of the Three) of
142 AD, is regarded as the "first book on alchemy in Chinese (and, indeed, in any other)
history."[13] That it was practiced before the Christian era is evidenced by a number of dat-
able texts and the fact that an injunction prohibiting counterfeiting gold and threatening
offenders with dire punishment was issued in 144 BC.[14] While Chinese alchemy shares a
number of characteristics with Western alchemy – its basis in a theory of the elements, correspondences between macrocosm and microcosm, its aurifictive and aurifactive aims, and
its insistence on the moral purity of the practitioner – there are also important differences.
The theory of elements in which it is grounded includes five elements, rather than the four
familiar in the West: wood, fire, earth, metal and water. Through the powerful influence of
Taoism, Chinese alchemy's mystical tendencies emphasizing spiritual perfection, the desire
for longevity, and the hope for immortality came to overshadow the search for the key to
metallic transmutation. Closely related is a final important feature of Chinese alchemical
theory: its doctrine of two opposing principles, the *Yin* and the *Yang*, which is thought
to have originated about the sixth century BC: "*Yin* was feminine, negative, heavy and
earthy; while *Yang* was masculine, positive, light, and fiery. *Yang* donates and *Yin* receives, . . .
By their interaction, the two contraries were held to give rise to the five elements constituting the material of the world."[15] *Yang* was associated with the sun, *Yin* with the moon.

---

[11] *Prelude to Chemistry*, 4–5. For fuller treatment, see Jack Lindsay, *The Origins of Alchemy in Graeco-Roman Egypt* (London: Frederick Muller, 1970), chap. 2.

[12] Joseph Needham, *Science and Civilisation in China*, vol. 5 *Chemistry and Chemical Technology*, Pt. 2 *Spagyrical Discovery and Invention: Magisteries of Gold and Immortality* (Cambridge: Cambridge University Press, 1974), 14–15. For a brief account, see E. J. Holmyard, *Alchemy* (Harmondsworth, Middlesex: Penguin, 1957), 31–40.

[13] Needham, *Science and Civilisation in China*, vol. 2, *History of Scientific Thought*, 241, 441.

[14] See especially Needham's discussion of Ko Hung's book *Pao Phu Tzu* (c. 320 BC), in *Science and Civilisation in China*, 5,2: 62–71; also Holmyard, *Alchemy*, 31.

[15] Read, *Prelude to Chemistry*, 20.

In their sexual and planetary differentiations as well as qualitative meanings, these principles have close counterparts in the sulphur-mercury theory of Western alchemy.

An important link between Chinese alchemy and that practiced in ancient India is suggested by the fact that the term for the Hindu medical tradition, *ayurveda*, means the "science of longevity." The concept of health implied therein is holistic, including psychological and spiritual as well as physical well being. Although his focus is primarily on medieval, tantric alchemy, David Gordon White has provided a larger historical outline of Indian alchemy (*rasayana*, or the science of rejuvenation) comprised of an early period (third to tenth centuries AD), in which gold-making was predominant; the period of tantric alchemy (tenth to thirteenth centuries), when emphasis was placed on "production of an elixir of immortal life with which to realize the supreme goals of bodily immortality, supernatural powers and a state of being identical to that of the supreme god Siva"; followed by a period of iatrochemical emphasis (the fourteenth through the twentieth centuries), in which mercurial and mineral formulations were prepared for medicinal use.[16] Thus, the exoteric and esoteric emphases previously seen in the cultures of Egypt and China were present in India as well; indeed, early Indian alchemical interest appears to have arisen out of exchanges with China and its Taoist tradition, which flourished between the third and eighth centuries AD. Within Indian tantric alchemy alone, lasting into the fourteenth century, there is emphasis on both transmutation and spiritual perfectibility and immortality: "on the bodily transformation of the living practitioner into a perfected immortal, a Siddha, Vidyādhara, or a 'second Siva.'"[17] But in addition to its esoteric strains, tantric alchemy also included teachings regarding metals that closely parallel several important principles of Western alchemy: the idea that metals were living substances, that natural gold was the end result of long "gestation" within earth's womb; and, adopting the metaphor of human and divine sexual differentiation and conjunction, that sulphur and mercury were the "reproductive fluids" from which metals arose.[18]

Greatly simplified, these are three views of alchemy's origin and early development. It should not be assumed, however, that its rise in either the East or the West occurred in a state of independence and isolation from the other, for just as alchemical knowledge was freely exchanged between China and India, it may also have passed between East and West by way of Egypt and Mesopotamia. John Read has stated that despite many uncertainties concerning the beginnings of alchemy, "there is no doubt that the incipient art was influenced during the Alexandrian age (4th century BC to 7th century AD) by the application of Greek philosophy to the technique of the Egyptian and other ancient cultures."[19]

Theory, rather than practice, is said to be the ancient Greeks' chief contribution to alchemy's development in the West. In addition to the theory of the *four elements* – earth, water, air, and fire – deriving from Empedocles, Plato, and Aristotle, and their *interconvertibility*,

---

[16] David Gordon White, "The Ocean of Mercury: An Eleventh-Century Alchemical Text," in *Religions of India in Practice*, ed. Donald S. Lopez, Jr. (Princeton: Princeton University Press, 1995), 281. See also White's *The Alchemical Body: Siddha Traditions in Medieval India* (Chicago: University of Chicago Press, 1996).

[17] White, *Alchemical Body*, 52–3, 62; White states, "The picture that emerges from this period is one of an ongoing exchange between India and China regarding matters alchemical, matters in which China, even if it appears always to have been ahead of India in innovations throughout this period, nonetheless looked to India for inspiration," 63.

[18] White, *Alchemical Body*, 189–93. [19] Read, *Prelude to Chemistry*, 8.

articulated most influentially in Plato's *Timaeus*, Hopkins posited several additional "psychic influences" that mark alchemy's Greek inheritance. From them, alchemy derived its *hylozoistic* conception of the universe, the idea that external nature is alive and sentient. It also relied on a close and harmonious relationship between *macrocosm* and *microcosm*, both the universe and the little world of man being directed by the same powers and principles. Additionally, the alchemists drew from the Greeks their belief in *astrological influences* as keys to success in transmutation.[20] In the larger scheme, this extraordinarily complex network of correspondences that characterized the alchemists' cosmology survived into the seventeenth century, as seen in the wonderfully detailed engravings of Robert Fludd's *Utriusque cosmi...historia* (1617, 1619), or the "Mundus Elementaris" diagram appearing in the *Musaeum hermeticum reformatum et amplificatum*, published in Frankfurt in 1678 (fig. 1).

Largely through the efforts of Arabian scholars and translators working between the seventh and tenth centuries when the power of Islam was at its height, much that was most important in Greek philosophical and scientific thought was preserved, translated, expanded, and transmitted to the Latin Middle Ages and then on to the Renaissance. Alchemy proved to be of great interest to Moslem scholars, and the Greek writings that they were instrumental in preserving provided the basis for many of their own subsequent advances. In addition to the genuine philosophical works of Plato and Aristotle, dozens – possibly hundreds – of spurious works, many of them alchemical, were attributed to them by later writers seeking prestige and notoriety resulting from association with these venerable ancients. Among the specifically alchemical writers of the pre-Christian era was Bolos Democritus, known also as Pseudo-Democritus or Bolos of Mendes, a Greek living in Egypt around 200 BC when Alexandria was enjoying its height as a center of learning. Works such as his *Physica et Mystica* were extremely popular in antiquity, rivalling those of Aristotle on topics related to natural history. Combining fact and much that was magical and supernatural, Bolos's works appear to be unsystematic collections based on earlier sources (including works of Democritus, the atomist of the fifth century BC), and also recall the recipes for making gems, purple dyes, silver and gold, of the artisanal traditions of Mesopotamia and Egypt. Bolos is set apart from these early craftsmen, however, because of his interest in transmutation: his belief that the nature of metals could be fundamentally altered and that these alterations were indicated by changes in the colors of the materials during the process.[21]

Both the change and the continuity of alchemical interests among the later Greeks is evidenced by writings that pass under the name of Zosimos of Panopolis (*ca.* 300 AD) and, later, Stephanos of Alexandria, who lived during the seventh century. Chief among Zosimos's works is a twenty-eight book encyclopedia addressed to his "spiritual sister," Theosebeia, which contains material that is both original and drawn eclectically from Platonic, Gnostic, and Judaic traditions.[22] Intent on setting forth alchemy's spiritual aspects,

---

[20] Hopkins, *Alchemy: Child of Greek Philosophy*, 28.

[21] On Bolos, see Charles C. Gillispie, ed., *Dictionary of Scientific Biography* (New York: Charles Scribner's Sons, 1970), s.v. "Bolos of Mendes," by Jerry Stannard, and also Lindsay, *The Origins of Alchemy in Graeco-Roman Egypt*, chaps. 5 and 6.

[22] On Zosimos, see *DSB*, s.v. "Zosimus of Panopolis," by M. Plessner, who notes that "it is not clear which texts can rightly be attributed to Zosimus. And the incomprehensibility of many of the writings makes textual criticism all the more difficult." See also Lindsay, *The Origins of Alchemy in Graeco-Roman Egypt*, chaps. 15 and 16, which include translated passages from Zosimos and commentary on them.

Zosimos's works often take the form of arcane allegorical visions or utilize highly cryptic symbols that appear to set forth instructions for the alchemical work, such as the famous Formula of the Crab.[23] In these respects, Zosimos employs the stylistic characteristics that, throughout its history, give alchemical discourse its easily recognizable stamp. Also representative of later tradition, as Plessner notes, is his expressed veneration for the great alchemical authorities of earlier times: Hermes, Agathodaemon, Zoroaster, Democritus, Ostanes, and Maria the Jewess; in fact, he alludes specifically to the *Corpus Hermeticum*, I and IV.[24]

Thus, during the more than four hundred years separating Bolos and Zosimos, important changes occurred in the way alchemy was conceived, practiced, and written about. During this time it appears to have been transformed from what was essentially a metallurgical craft to a secret and mysterious hermetic art. According to E. J. Holmyard,

> We now find [in the writings of Zosimos] a bewildering confusion of Egyptian magic, Greek philosophy, Gnosticism, Neo-platonism, Babylonian astrology, Christian theology, and pagan mythology, together with the enigmatical and allusive language that makes the interpretation of alchemical literature so difficult and so uncertain . . . In order to give some show of authority to their nebulous doctrines, alchemists busied themselves in composing treatises that they then attributed to any philosopher or celebrity of earlier times whom their whim led them to select. Thus works on alchemy were ascribed to Hermes, Plato, Moses, Miriam his sister, Theophrastus, Ostanes, Cleopatra, and Isis . . . Legends and myths were given alchemical interpretations: the golden fleece . . . was claimed to have been a manuscript on parchment, teaching the manner of making gold by alchemical art, and even the "Song of Solomon" was supposed to be an alchemical treatise couched in veiled language.[25]

This eclecticism of style and content typifies alchemical discourse throughout its history.

Hermes Trismegistus and the *Hermetica*

In this section of the introduction devoted to the origins and early development of alchemy, it remains to give brief attention to the figure of Hermes Trismegistus and the rise of the *Corpus Hermeticum*, the early collections of alchemical tracts attributed to him. The eclecticism that, for Holmyard, characterizes the writings of Zosimos and his milieu applies as well to Hermes Trismegistus (Hermes the Thrice-Great), the Graeco-Egyptian god – or priest, or divine man, according to which authority one reads – who is alchemy's founder and chief patron, authority, inspiration, and guide. Hermes Trismegistus was a product of broad cultural synthesis, evolving from the fusion of two complex divinities, the Egyptian Thoth and the Greek Hermes, who were perceived to have much in common: their association with the moon, with medicine and magic, and the realm of the dead, to which

---

[23] See Read, *Prelude to Chemistry*, 40, where the Formula of the Crab is reproduced.
[24] See the excellent study by Garth Fowden, *The Egyptian Hermes: A Historical Approach to the Late Pagan Mind* (Cambridge: Cambridge University Press, 1986), 8.
[25] Holmyard, *Alchemy*, 25–6.

they escorted the souls of the departed.[26] But in the Graeco-Egyptian (and later Roman) world of the first few centuries AD, Hermes Trismegistus burst forth from this familiar mythological model and assumed powers that were both greater and darker. In the Greek magical papyri, in Fowden's words, we see

> the new syncretistic Hermes as a cosmic power, creator of heaven and earth and almighty world-ruler. Presiding over fate and justice, he is also lord of the night, and of death and its mysterious aftermath . . . He knows 'all that is hidden under the heavenly vault, and beneath the earth', and is accordingly much revered as a sender of oracles.[27]

Symptomatic of the complexity of this composite divinity, as may be seen in the *Asclepius*, is the eventual appearance of a second, younger Hermes, grandson to the original Egyptian Hermes Thoth; he was the son of Agathos Daimon and the father of Tat. Within the somewhat bifurcated culture of Alexandrian Egypt, the older figure represented an earlier, distinctly Egyptian divinity and authorship; the later Hermes Trismegistus, without losing his "native" aspects, embodied a more humanized dimension associated with the Greek side of Egyptian culture. It was this younger Hermes who, in some quarters, was believed to have translated the sacred works of his grandfather into Greek. To add further to the confusion, controversy also arose as to whether Hermes Trismegistus originally was of a divine or human nature, when he lived, and whether he had prophesied the coming of Christianity.[28]

As one might expect of so ancient, omniscient, and ambiguous a figure, writings attributed to Hermes Trismegistus were numerous and diverse. In his treatise on the *Mysteries of Egypt* (c. 300 AD), the Neoplatonist Iamblichus reports, for example, that "Hermes has put everything together in his twenty thousand books (as Seleucus listed them) or thirty-six thousand five hundred and fifty-five (as Manetho tells it)."[29] The actual number is, of course, far less; according to the latest editor and translator of the *Hermetica*, some two dozen very early works attributed to Hermes or his immediate circle have survived.[30] It is common practice to classify these works into two groups: first, the "technical" *Hermetica*, consisting of writings on magic (much of it on papyri), the occult properties of stones, astrology and astrological medicine, and alchemy, which generally "describe techniques

---

[26] On the complex nature of the Egyptian Thoth, see Fowden, *The Egyptian Hermes*, esp. 18–31, who notes that "so important were the moon's phases in determining the rhythms of Egyptian national life, that Thoth came to be regarded as the origin both of cosmic order and of religious and civil institutions. He presided over almost every aspect of the temple cults, law and the civil year, and in particular over the sacred rituals, texts and formulae, and the magic arts that were so closely related . . . By extension he came to be regarded as the lord of knowledge, language and all science – even as Understanding or Reason personified" (22).

[27] *The Egyptian Hermes*, 25.

[28] See *The Egyptian Hermes*, 22–31, and Frances Yates's controversial classic, *Giordano Bruno and the Hermetic Tradition* (Chicago: University of Chicago Press, 1964), chap. 1. On the conception of the younger Hermes as translator, into Greek, of the original sacred hieroglyphics of his grandfather, Thoth, see also Brian P. Copenhaver, trans. and ed., *Hermetica: The Greek "Corpus Hermeticum" and the Latin "Asclepius" in a New English Translation* (Cambridge: Cambridge University Press, 1992), xv–xvi. All subsequent references to and quotations from the *Hermetica* are from this edition.

[29] Quoted in Copenhaver, *Hermetica*, xvi.   [30] Copenhaver, *Hermetica*, xvi.

rather than to reflect on their theoretical implications."[31] This diverse group of treatises is thought to date roughly from between the first centuries BC and AD. The second category of attributions, the "philosophical" or "theoretical" *Hermetica*, include the seventeen tracts that comprise the *Corpus Hermeticum*, as well as the *Asclepius* (in a Latin translation that appears to date from the fourth century), the Hermetic fragments that found their way into the *Anthology* of Stobaeus (fifth century), several codices from the recently discovered Nag Hammadi library of Gnostic texts, and other miscellaneous works. Current scholarship assigns the composition of the philosophical *Hermetica* to the period from the late first to the late third centuries, and there is strong evidence to suggest that, from early times, these texts circulated as collections to a far greater extent than the technical *Hermetica*. In what sense are these texts "philosophical" or "theoretical" in nature? Brian Copenhaver notes that they are "not much concerned with astrology, very little with magic and not at all with alchemy":

> They deal instead with theological or, in some loose sense, philosophical issues: they reveal to man knowledge of the origins, nature and moral properties of divine, human and material being so that man can use this knowledge to save himself... [They are] a blend of theology, cosmogony, anthropogony, ethics, soteriology and eschatology.[32]

Among the best known of the surviving works attributed to Hermes Trismegistus – but which apparently dates from before the medieval period – is the cryptic *Emerald Table of Hermes* (*Tabula Smaragdina*), a series of axioms that purport to reveal the secret of the preparation of the philosopher's stone. Interpretation of this mysterious and oft-quoted tablet came to be a major preoccupation for alchemists through the ages and was vital in perpetuating the legend of Hermes Trismegistus, since the original *Emerald Table*, supposedly inscribed in Phoenician characters, was believed to have been discovered in Hermes' tomb by Alexander the Great, or, alternately, this sacred scripture of alchemy was thought to have been taken from the hands of the dead Hermes in a cave near Hebron years after the Flood. Thus fanciful legend and a vast number of works believed to be authentic – along with Marsilio Ficino's Latin translation of the *Corpus Hermeticum* in 1471 – helped assure the popularity of Hermes Trismegistus even after these writings were correctly dated by Isaac Casaubon in 1614.[33]

Although even before the seventeenth century the figure of Hermes Trismegistus was fraught with uncertainties and ambiguity, these qualities, while undeniable, seem most often to have stimulated respect and reverence rather than hostility and skepticism. Essential to this theological and philosophical appeal was his assumed position in an unbroken line of writers of "wisdom" literature that extended backward many centuries before the birth of Christ. Ficino, only one of the expositors of this tradition, found in Hermes an embodiment of religious and moral authority that placed him at or near the beginning of the so-called *prisci theologi* or ancient theologians:

---

[31] Fowden, *Egyptian Hermes*, 89.

[32] Copenhaver, *Hermetica*, xxxii. See also the Introduction to Fowden's *Egyptian Hermes*.

[33] On Casaubon, his corrected dating of the *Hermetica* – from remote antiquity to the second and third centuries AD – and its consequences, see Yates's *Giordano Bruno and the Hermetic Tradition*.

[Hermes Trismegistus] is called the first author of theology: he was succeeded by Orpheus, who came second amongst ancient theologians: Aglaophemus, who had been initiated into the sacred teaching of Orpheus, was succeeded in theology by Pythagoras, whose disciple was Philolaus, the teacher of our Divine Plato. Hence there is one ancient theology (*prisca theologia*) . . . taking its origin in Mercurius and culminating in the Divine Plato.[34]

As a result of the conquest of Alexandria (642) and other centers of Greek learning, Islam came into possession of the corpus of Greek philosophical and scientific knowledge. In the case of alchemy, Greek writings were to provide the basis for subsequent Moslem advances; and Arabian scholars, such as Khalid, Jabir ibn Hayyan, Avicenna, and "Geber," enhanced the knowledge of alchemy in the West through preserving, translating, and transmitting this Greek heritage. Thus the way was prepared for the keen interest in alchemy shown by such medieval thinkers as Roger Bacon and Albertus Magnus and the host of alchemical authors and experimenters who were to follow.[35]

Alchemical principles and theories

At the beginning of this introduction, several definitions of alchemy were posited (e.g., alchemy as *science*, as *art*, as *alchemies* in the plural), and certain of its general types were noted (e.g., *exoteric* and *esoteric*). As preliminaries to the readings themselves, it is useful to consider a few of alchemy's recurring principles, assumptions, and theories, ones that, while not appearing in identical terms or with perfect consistency, are important concerns of alchemical authors from earliest times.

Art vs. Nature
Against the background of a simplified world in which all things exist either in their "natural" God-created state, or as a result of human artifice and ingenuity, the alchemists granted considerable – although not exclusive – power to Art over Nature. In the great Renaissance debate on the relative importance of these two forces, as seen for example in the famous "gillyvor" passage in *The Winter's Tale*, 4.1, they would have disapproved of Perdita's refusal to plant this variety of flower in her garden because their variegated "streaks" result from human artifice (in the form of hybridization) rather than from the purer, plainer, "natural" powers of God and "great creating Nature." Not wishing to appear to limit the powers of God, however, the alchemists might well have gone on to agree with Polixenes that the very means by which man "improves" Nature result from the operations of God and Nature: as he says, "Nature makes the mean." Some four hundred years before

[34] From Ficino's *Argumentum* preceding his translation of the *Pimander*, quoted in Yates, *Giordano Bruno*, 14; Yates (p. 15) notes that in the *Theologica Platonica*, Ficino places Zoroaster as the first *priscus theologus*, Hermes as the second.
[35] For historical sketches of the development of alchemy in the Middle Ages and Renaissance, see the previously cited works by Read and Holmyard; also F. Sherwood Taylor, *The Alchemists: Founders of Modern Chemistry* (New York: Henry Schuman, 1949).

Shakespeare wrote this scene, Roger Bacon had taken up the issue (he was not the first), and the opening sentence of his *Excellent Discourse of the Admirable Force and Efficacie of Art and Nature* is:

> Some there are that aske whether of these twaine bee of greatest force and efficacie, Nature or Art, whereto I make aunswere and say, that although Nature be mightie and marvailous, yet Art using Nature for an instrument, is more powerfull then naturall vertue, as it is to bee seene in many things.[36]

Early in the seventeenth century, one of the founders of the new experimental science, Francis Bacon, defined Art as "nature with man to help," stating that Art has the power to "change, transmute, or fundamentally alter nature."[37] On this principle both the old and the new science could readily agree because, for the alchemists, making "real" gold (aurifaction) through the transmutation of base metals rested on the premise that it is possible to change fundamentally one form into another. On the other hand, to deny that this basic change can occur, as Avicenna does in *De Congelatione et Conglutinatione* ("As to the claims of the alchemists, it must be clearly understood that it is not in their power to bring about any true change of species"), is to undercut the very foundation of alchemy. Aurifaction is merely aurifiction.

The natural production of metals

Well into the seventeenth century, explanations of the natural origin of metals were largely Aristotelian, as set forth in his *Meteorology*. They were based on the theory of the four elements (derived from Empedocles and Plato), the idea of a single, underlying prime matter; and vapors and exhalations – the moist and the dry – as the "parent principles" of all things that were quarried and mined. In contrast to Robert Boyle's modern conception of chemical elements as primary and discrete "nonreducible" substances, the four elements were regarded as different "forms" or "appearances" of an underlying matter or *prima materia*, from which all visible, material objects are derived, each composed of a different combination of hotness, dryness, coldness, and moistness.

Extending the anthropomorphic image of sexually differentiated metallic parents is the organic metaphor of the growth and maturing of metals within the womb of Mother Earth. Elias Ashmole, the seventeenth-century antiquary and champion of alchemy, notes that "If *Mineralls* as well as *Plants*, take Food and Nourishment, wax and grow in bignesse, all is clear, I hope, and void of doubt."[38] And in his *New Light of Alchymie*, Michael Sendivogius discusses at length the idea that metals grow from "seeds." In the view of both authors, metals and minerals are living beings, possessing not only bodies but souls and spirits, as well. Duration of maturation and the purity of the proximate materials are crucial factors in this "ripening" process and result in a hierarchically-arranged "scale of metals" with gold and silver occupying the two highest positions. This is evidence that they have been

---

[36] From the text included in *The Mirror of Alchimy*, ed.Stanton J. Linden, 49.

[37] In book 2 of the *De Augmentis*, in *The Works of Francis Bacon*, ed. James Spedding, Robert L. Ellis, and Douglas D. Heath, 14 vols. (1872; reprint, New York: Garret Press, Inc., 1968), 4:295.

[38] Elias Ashmole, *The Way to Bliss* (London, 1658), 130.

ripening for the longest period of time: Nature, as Aristotle influentially put it, always strives for perfection or "follows the best course possible."[39]

Primarily through the agency of the Arabian scholar Jabir ibn Hayyan (late eighth, early ninth centuries?), the Sulphur-Mercury theory (represented primarily by Geber in this collection) evolved from the idea of fundamental opposition implicit in the Aristotelian view: "Sulphur" is identified with fire and possesses the qualities of hotness and dryness; "Mercury," identified with water, possesses coldness and moistness. These two "principles," which are not to be confused with common sulphur and mercury or quicksilver, interact in the form of subterranean exhalations or vapors (the former "male," the latter "female"), and if the conjunction occurs under proper conditions – the degree of heat within the earth is especially important – metals are formed.

Finally, it is important to note that in the eclectically Platonic and Aristotelian world-view of the alchemists, all sublunary substances are in a state of transformation and flux, as the result of the imposition of different forms upon prime matter: a kind of natural state of alchemical change. This idea is set forth memorably in Plato's *Timaeus*, where transformation is implicit in the four elements theory because of the "convertibility" of the elements that comprise all substances: earth can be changed to water if its essential "dryness" is replaced by "wetness" and "coldness" remains constant. Similarly air could become fire if "dryness" came to replace "wetness." The ease of this conversion is suggested by the diagram of the four elements from Petrus Bonus's *Pretiosa margarita novella* (Venice, 1546), which includes, along the bottom edge, primitive representations of alchemical vessels and, above, uses symbol to enhance visualization of the four elements, the qualities of which they are composed, and their relationship (fig. 2). Metals, too, could be changed through artificially recombining or altering the proportion of the elements that comprise them, as George Ripley notes in his *Compound of Alchymy* (1471):

> But first of these elements make thou rotacion,
> And into water thine earth turne first of all,
> Then of thy water make ayre by levigacion,
> And ayre make fier, then Maister I will thee call
> Of all our secrets great and small.[40]

The imitation of Nature

Closely related to this conception of the formation of metals is the idea that to be successful the methods of alchemical art must *imitate* those of Nature, what Roger Bacon calls, "Art using Nature for an instrument." The advantage of alchemy's imitative methods for producing silver and gold over those of Nature chiefly involve duration of time: what takes Nature ages to accomplish within the earth, can be greatly shortened by the efforts of a knowledgeable alchemist. Ashmole, again, speaks precisely to this point in *The Way to Bliss*:

---

[39] Aristotle, *On the Heavens*, Bk. 2, 288a, in *The Complete Works of Aristotle*, ed. Jonathan Barnes, Rev. Oxford trans., Bollingen Ser. LXXI, 2. 2 vols. (Princeton: Princeton University Press, 1984), 1:475.

[40] *George Ripley's Compound of Alchymy (1591)*, ed. Stanton J. Linden (Aldershot, Hants.: Ashgate, 2001), 31. All subsequent references to this poem are to this edition.

As *Nature* in her work below used two hot *Workmen* so will I; and because we cannot tarry her leisure, and long time she taketh to that purpose, we will match and countervail her little *Heats* with proportions answerable and meet for our time, that we may do that in fourty dayes which she doth in as many years.[41]

This idea is represented graphically in figure 3, an engraving from Michael Maier's *Symbola aureæ Mensæ* showing an alchemist with his furnace atop a mountain, replicating the slow but "natural" production of sulphur and mercury taking place in the earth's bowels. The position of serious alchemical experimenters and writers, as opposed to the charlatans, on the relationship between Art and Nature is especially subtle and wide-ranging. Far from elevating the claims of Art far above those of Nature, there is general agreement that Nature's methods must provide the *model* for alchemical theory and practice. This is the theme of Michael Sendivogius's brilliant satire, *Dialogue between Mercury, the Alchymist and Nature* and a host of other treatises. The tradition of the humble alchemist often appears in the graphic arts and emblems as well: such is Maier's Emblema XLII (*De secretis Naturæ*) from his emblem book, *Atalanta fugiens* (1617), with its image of the bespectacled alchemist, staff and lantern in hand, carefully following in the footsteps of the goddess Nature (fig. 4). In Maier's engraving of the library and laboratory from his *Tripus aureus* (1618), we again see the close proximity of the philosophical and the practical sides of alchemy (fig. 5): three learned men hold consultation on the left side of the picture field, while on the right a technician minds the furnace.

The alchemical process

It is easier to describe aspects of the alchemical worldview that serve to explain transmutation or to show why its very existence is plausible according to these assumptions, than it is to try to understand what the alchemists believed was actually occurring within their alembics. Several obvious factors account for these difficulties: the remoteness of this worldview and alchemy from the knowledge and experience of the modern reader, our unfamiliarity with the alchemists' writings, and, above all, the deliberate obscurity of these works. For these reasons and the highly subjective nature of the alchemical experience itself – no two accounts are ever exactly alike – it is perhaps best to allow the authors represented in this collection to speak for themselves. Nonetheless, some very general guidelines (inevitably reflecting our own subjectivity and uncertainty), may be useful.

Besides the previously discussed theories of the *prima materia*, the four elements, and their interconvertibility, the alchemists envisioned a universe that was sentient and filled with life, reflecting the permeation of the spirit of God throughout its vastness. In the *Emerald Table*, Hermes had declared that "That which is above is like to that which is below, and that which is below is like to that which is above." And early in the seventeenth century Michael Sendivogius, accommodating this idea to Christianity, asserted in the *New Light of Alchymy* that "Nature is but one, true, plain, perfect, and entire in its own being, which

---

[41] *The Way to Bliss*, 134. Ashmole regards the "heat of heaven" and the particular "feed of the *Earth*," apparently brimstone or sulphur, as the subterranean "hot workmen"; "*Quicksilver* is the *Mother* of all the *Metalls*" (126).

God made from the beginning, *placing his spirit in it*." Thus macrocosm and microcosm were thought to be linked by indissoluble ties, and these animistic and hylozoistic doctrines provided the basis for astrology and natural magic, as well as alchemy. Like the magus, the alchemist saw himself as one who, although operating within the traditional worldview, was able to alter and manipulate the normal course of Nature through highly specialized knowledge and experience. He believed he could shorten the natural process of goldmaking within the earth by bringing base metals to perfection through secret formulas and recipes, just as the magus believed it possible to accomplish unusual feats through the help of familiar spirits invoked by occult powers. In each case Art was decidedly an "improver" of Nature.

The Philosopher's Stone (or "Medicine" or "Elixir," the names for it are legion!) was the means by which alchemists strove to effect this "improvement," whether it be cleansing base metals of their "leprosies" and bringing them to a state of golden perfection; healing the human body of its diseases and extending longevity; or giving spiritual and psychological relief to the operator's own sin-ridden mind and soul. At times, all three goals are simultaneously present in the same treatise: as the secrets of transmuting base metals are cryptically unfolded, the discourse's allegorical and moral levels impart instructions for the practitioner's spiritual regeneration and salvation; or, more commonly, the evolving "stone" becomes the symbol for, or direct reflection of, stages in the subject's inner purification. Regardless of which intention was uppermost, the final aim of alchemy was, then, to attain the secret to the making of this "treasure of treasures."

Thus, for mystically minded adepts, the purely chemical operations and reactions occurring within their womb- or egg-shaped vessels symbolized deeper spiritual meanings. Imperfect substances used as the proximate ingredients of the stone might be thought to undergo death and corruption in the initial stages of the alchemical process. But following the blackness and death of the *putrefactio* (and continuing the analogy with Christ's death, resurrection, and man's salvation), these base materials could appear to be "reborn" in the form of perfect, pure, and incorruptible gold, giving new meaning and authority to the oft-cited biblical verse, "Verily, verily, I say unto you, except a corn of wheat fall into the ground and die, it abideth alone; but if it die, it bringeth forth much fruit" (John 12:24). As noted earlier, this vein of alchemical allegorizing goes back to a time even earlier than the writings of Zosimos; it is not peculiar to Christianity.[42]

Color symbolism – particularly the primary sequence from black (putrefaction), to white (an intermediate stage associated with silver), to red (the ultimate stage, symbolizing attainment of the philosopher's stone or transmutation to gold) – also becomes a vital feature of discourse on making the Stone. For many writers, there are additional intermediate stages marked by specific colors, such as "yellowing" or Citrination, or the *cauda pavonis*, the

---

[42] See, for example, the selection from the *Dialogue of Cleopatra and the Philosophers*, probably dating from the second century AD. Its translator, F. Sherwood Taylor (*The Alchemists: Founders of Modern Chemistry* [London: William Heinemann, 1951], 57–9) notes that, "The changes in the chemicals contained in the alchemical vessels made a deep impression on the minds of those who saw them. The bright metal became a black formless mass, a stinking corruption; then another process brought this dead mass back to the state of metal again, and, so it seemed to them, perhaps because they wished it so, a more glorious and excellent metal. The process was, in fact, a symbol of what the age was seeking, what was found alike in Christianity and the mystery-religions – death and resurrection" (56–7). See also Betty Jo Teeter Dobbs, *Alchemical Death & Resurrection: The Significance of Alchemy in the Age of Newton* (Washington, DC: Smithsonian Institution Libraries, 1990).

peacock's tail, a dazzling display of varied colors. Moreover, many of the fanciful names for alchemical principles, substances and stages are accompanied by adjectives of color: white doves; black toads, crows, and vultures; green dragons and lions; red lions and red men with white wives (see fig. 6).

Quantitatively, perhaps more space in alchemical writing is devoted to the various stages in the production of the philosopher's stone than to any other topic. Unfortunately, there is nothing approaching uniformity and consistency in the names assigned to these stages, or to the nature of the processes described, their order, or even their number; for this reason, discussions of processes included in this collection, such as in Geber's *Sum of Perfection* or Paracelsus, should be regarded as somewhat arbitrary. To cite only one example, Sir George Ripley, one of the most famous alchemists of late medieval England, organizes his *Compound of Alchymy* (completed 1471; first published 1591), according to twelve stages or "gates," which must be opened if the reader of the text is to gain entrance to the "castle" of alchemical knowledge: *Calcination, Dissolution, Separation, Conjunction, Putrefaction, Congelation, Cibation, Sublimation, Firmentation, Exaltation, Multiplication, and Projection.*[43] Fortunately Ripley and other writers for whom the number of stages is sometimes smaller, often stipulate definitions for the steps they discuss, as in the following selected examples:

Calcination   Commonly defined as the reduction of a substance to an ashy powder or calx through intense heat, Calcination is said by Ripley to be "the purgation of our stone, / Restoring also of his naturall heate, / Of radicall humidities it looseth none." He then proceeds to describe the method and purpose of this initial stage in twenty-two stanzas of rhyme royal verse.

Conjunction   A favorite stage for graphic illustration (see fig. 7, from the *Rosarium Philosophorum*) and much discussed by Carl Jung and, indeed, by nearly all alchemical authors, Conjunction is the union of the two opposing, sexually differentiated *principles*, Sulphur and Mercury (not the common varieties), variously referred to as male and female, king and queen, the red man and the white wife, brother and sister, and many other forms. Based upon the anthropomorphic notion of the generation of metals earlier discussed, the "chemical wedding" was necessary to produce the philosopher's stone, often represented as the hermaphroditic offspring of this union (see fig. 8).

Putrefaction   Deriving from the conception of an alchemical death and resurrection through analogy with John 12:24, Putrefaction implied that the "seeds" of metals – like the "corn of wheat" – must also die if they are to be reborn as more perfect forms. The opening of Ripley's fifth "Gate" (Of Putrifaction), reveals how seriously alchemists regarded this biblical prototype: "For bodies els may not be altred naturally, / Sith Christ doth witnes, without the graine of wheate / Dye in the ground, encrease maist thou none get;" he continues with his definition:

---

[43] See my edition of *George Ripley's Compound of Alchymy*. For useful discussion of most of these stages, see Read, *Prelude to Chemistry*, esp. 136–42.

And Putrifaction may thus defined bee
After Philosophers sayings, to be of bodies the sleying;
And in our Compound a division of things three,
The killed bodies into corruption foorth leading,
And after unto regeneration them abling,
For things being in the earth, without doubt
Be engendred of rotation of the heavens about.

Sublimation   This distillation process, in name derived from the "elevation" or "exaltation" of the materials circulating in the still, includes, in Read's words, "the deposition of crystals in the cool upper part of a vessel containing heated solid material in its lower part. . . when repeated many times it was supposed to furnish the 'quintessence' of the material concerned."[44] For Ripley, its purposes are three: to make the body spiritual; to make the spirit corporal and "consubstantial" and "fixed" with the body; and to cleanse the "filthie originall."

Multiplication   As the process for preparing the philosopher's stone neared completion, it was believed that the potency of the powder (the "stone" was often described as a reddish powder) could be greatly augmented so that the size of the resulting transmutation in the final Projection would increase geometrically – and, remarkably, the amount of the powder would not be diminished. Ripley defines Multiplication thus: "*Augmentation* it is of the Elixer indeede, / In goodnes and quantitie both for white and red, / Multiplication is therefore as they doe write, / That thing that doth augment medicines in each degree, / In colour, in odour, in vertue and also in quantitee." For him, the key to this augmentation is repeatedly "feeding" the Stone with Mercury, a stage known as Cibation.

Projection   In his satirical masterpiece *The Alchemist* (1610), Ben Jonson brings to life both the Multiplication and Projection stages through the words of the arch-charlatan, Subtle, to Sir Epicure Mammon, the greediest of the greedy. Mammon has asked impatiently when Projection will take place, and Subtle responds by telling his hermetic "Son" to be patient, that augmentation of the stone's potency can come about only through iteration of the familiar dual processes of *solve et coagula*, Solution and Coagulation. Once the Stone has reached full strength or "virtue" it will be ready for Projection, that is, casting the powder upon the base metals to effect transmutation. Jonson's remarkable gift for "transmuting" the pedestrian details of the alchemical process into high comedy and satire justifies quoting the passage at length. Subtle speaks:

I exalt our med'cine,
By hanging him *in balneo vaporoso*,
And giving him solution; then congeal him;
And then dissolve him, then again congeal him:
For look, how oft I iterate the work,
So many times I add unto his virtue.

---

[44] *Prelude to Chemistry*, 138.

As, if at first one ounce convert a hundred;
After his second loose, he'll turn a thousand;
His third solution, ten; his fourth, a hundred.
After his fifth, a thousand thousand ounces
Of any imperfect metal, into pure
Silver and gold, in all examinations,
As good as any of the natural mine.
Get you your stuff here against afternoon,
Your brass, your pewter, and your andirons.[45]

Alchemical themes and conventions

Apart from incidental experimental techniques and by-products that it has bequeathed to modern chemistry and medicine, alchemy's legacy to posterity, in terms of viable theories and innovations, is quite small: insufficient to dissociate it from a larger reputation of ignorance, folly, superstition and quackery. Inasmuch as alchemy has survived into the twenty-first century, it has done so on the basis of things less tangible: as a procession of personalities – real and legendary – that still commands interest and attention; as a seminal nurturing ground in which the scientific insights of Boyle, Newton and many before them were planted, took root and flourished; as a storehouse of literary and artistic themes, motifs, images and symbols that have inspired writers and artists from Chaucer, Erasmus, Bosch and Brueghel to Marcel Duchamp, Leonora Carrington, Umberto Eco, and J. K. Rowling. Above all – and perhaps because it has little that is concrete to show for itself – alchemy survives primarily on the strength of its own remarkable literary tradition, one that extends from before the time of Christ to the eighteenth century and is truly international in scope. Because today alchemy exists primarily in and through its literature and (somewhat less) its artistic tradition, this final section seeks to isolate for brief discussion a few of the enduring and readily identifiable characteristics of its highly original discourse.

Unlike the idiom of modern experimental science with its emphasis on clear and objective communication of ideas and information to a broad audience so that further collaborative investigation is possible, alchemical discourse is known above all for its obscurity, its deliberate attempts to both reveal and conceal, and – to this end – its extravagant use of abstraction, allegory and analogy, and idiosyncratic displays of bizarrely fanciful images, symbols, and riddles.[46] From the time of Zosimos, through the writings of the Rosicrucians in the seventeenth and eighteenth centuries, and beyond to the Society of the Golden Dawn, fanciful rhetoric, designed to *conceal* meaning as much as reveal it, has been a vital part of alchemical tradition and, as careful reading of Chaucer's *Canon's Yeoman's*

---

[45] This and the later quotation from *The Alchemist* are from vol. 5 of *Ben Jonson*, ed. C. H. Herford and Percy and Evelyn Simpson, 11 vols. (Oxford: Clarendon Press, 1925–52).

[46] Brian Vickers, for one, has written on the semantics of occult discourse, concluding that its habit of analogical thinking is a major distinguishing characteristic from scientific thought and writing in the Renaissance; see his "On the Function of Analogy in the Occult," in *Hermeticism and the Renaissance: Intellectual History and the Occult in Early Modern Europe*, ed. Ingrid Merkel and Allen G. Debus (Washington, DC: Folger Shakespeare Library, 1988), 265–92. On riddles in alchemy, see Coudert, *Alchemy: The Philosopher's Stone*, chap. 3.

Tale or Jonson's *Alchemist* shows, a major point of attack. Again, here is Jonson's Sir Epicure Mammon attempting to convince the skeptical Surly that the story of Jason and the golden fleece is really an allegory explaining the method of making the philosopher's stone:

> I have a peece of IASONS fleece, too,
> Which was no other, then a booke of *alchemie*,
> Writ in large sheepe-skin, a good fat ram-vellam.
> Such was PYTHAGORA'S thigh, PANDORA'S tub;
> And, all that fable of MEDEAS charmes,
> The manner of our worke: The Bulls, our fornace,
> Still breathing fire; our *argente-vive*, the Dragon:
> The Dragons teeth, *mercury* sublimate,
> That keepes the whitenesse, hardnesse, and the biting;
> And they are gather'd, into IASON'S helme,
> (Th'*alembeke*) and then sow'd in MARS his field,
> And, thence, sublim'd so often, till they are fix'd.
> Both this, th'*Hesperian* garden, CADMUS storie,
> JOVES shower, the boone of MIDAS, ARGUS eyes,
> BOCCACE his *Demogorgon*, thousands more,
> All abstract riddles of our *stone*.
> (*The Alchemist* 2.1.89–104)

While Sir Epicure's rhetoric threatens to inundate the surly Surly, his absurd mythologizing, greatly exaggerated for reasons of comedy and satire, nonetheless follows an alchemical tradition in which myth, fable, historical incidents, biblical characters and stories, and much else, were ransacked to attain a kind of discourse commensurate with expressing the nature of the action believed to be occurring within the alembic, or to conceal the truths of the Art in order to prevent discovery by the vulgar and ignorant. The same tendencies are present in alchemy's extremely rich pictorial tradition, as may be seen in the illustrations in Michael Maier's emblem book, *Atalanta fugiens*.

Several additional conventions of alchemical writing contribute to this aura of secrecy. In the first of the two quotations from Jonson's *Alchemist* cited above, Subtle addresses his comments on Multiplication and Projection to his "Son," Sir Epicure Mammon. In doing thus, Jonson is employing (and again parodying) an age-old convention of alchemical writing in which a master adept imparts his knowledge to an initiate "son," usually with the admonition that the "priceless gift" be used wisely to benefit mankind, that the son maintain exemplary moral character and behavior (since God will not impart his secrets to the profligate), and that these secrets be revealed to no one else. Thus, alchemical knowledge tended to be transmitted in a manner resembling that of a secret society, completely contrary to the ideals of modern scientific communication. In fact, a major point of attack on alchemy in the seventeenth century by those who followed in the footsteps of Francis Bacon and the Royal Society was the deliberate obscurity of its prose style: the tradition of *ignotum per ignocius*, explaining the unknown by the more unknown. In these attacks it was common to include other notorious examples of obscurity, such as the Renaissance fascination with Egyptian hieroglyphics, cabalistic learning, and the rhetorical excesses of the Rosicrucians and other philosophical enthusiasts.[47]

Finally, in a number of different eras and cultures, there was a major practical necessity for secrecy on the alchemist's part: the practice of alchemy was often under close surveillance by both Church and State, was at times banned, and many of its practitioners were subject to threats, imprisonment, torture, and even death. To judge from surviving accounts, life even as a popular and successful alchemist in the courts of princes was precarious, in that apparent success in transmutation could easily foster greater greed and impatience in the court, jealousy on the part of competing alchemists, and – not infrequently – the risk of being stolen away by rival princes to work for them. On the other hand, the perils of failure to perform transmutations at court were even greater and more predictable.[48]

In the pictorial arts, the seriousness with which transmission of arcane wisdom was regarded appears in Robert Vaughan's fine engraving of an alchemical initiation that Elias Ashmole included in his *Theatrum Chemicum Britannicum* (fig. 9). Here, beneath the Holy Spirit and two angels, the Master places a book of secrets in the hands of the initiate, with the words, "Take God's gift under the holy seal." The initiate responds: "I will preserve the alchemical secrets in secrecy." Above, the scroll surrounding the angel on the left states: "Thou hast loved justice and hatest wickedness, therefore the Lord thy God hath anointed thee with oil."[49]

It must be noted, however, that at times the alchemists were faulted for obscurity resulting from their extensive use of symbols that anticipate – are arguably the same as – modern scientific notation. As early as Zosimos's Formula of the Crab, they had employed individual symbols to denote the various metals, minerals, the elements, planets and con-stellations, processes and procedures (see fig. 10 for a late seventeenth-century example). Among the treatises included in *The Alchemy Reader*, typographic symbols refer chiefly to the seven primary metals and their corresponding planetary signs:

Symbol	Metal	Planetary Analogue
☉	Gold	*Sol*, Sun
☽	Silver	*Luna*, Moon
♃	Tin	Jupiter, Jove
☿	Mercury	Mercury
♀	Copper	Venus
♂	Iron	Mars
♄	Lead	Saturn

Another aspect of alchemical discourse that invites comparison with modern exper-imental science is its attitude toward and use of authority. Neither in its exoteric nor

---

[47] See chap. 9 of my *Darke Hierogliphicks*.

[48] Some of the most interesting of such adventures involve John Dee and Edward Kelley at the court of Rudolf II in Bohemia. For an excellent account of the occult milieu in Rudolf's court, see R. J. W. Evans, *Rudolf II and His World: A Study in Intellectual History, 1576–1612* (Oxford: Clarendon Press, 1973). For discussion of other aspects of the courtly practice of alchemy in the context of the life of Johann Joachim Becher (1635–82), see Pamela Smith, *The Business of Alchemy: Science and Culture in the Holy Roman Empire* (Princeton: Princeton University Press, 1994).

[49] From the illustration facing p. 13 of the *Theatrum Chemicum Britannicum*.

esoteric dimensions was alchemy a body of knowledge that matured and developed in a steady, programmatic way toward a premeditated end. Lacking opportunities for both significant controlled laboratory experiment and first-hand investigation and reporting on the part of the operator, the alchemists relied heavily on written authority. "Show me the right way," the Dreamer asks the old man, Agothodæmon, in Zosimos's *Lesson 2*, and such pleas are explicit or implicit in much alchemical writing that follows. Authorities – Hermes, Plato, Aristotle, Lull, Geber, Roger Bacon, George Ripley, Paracelsus – are invoked repeatedly, to the extent that some treatises are little more than collections of the words (or attributed words) of the revered figures of the past. And, as the vast amount of pseudonymous literature shows, much of the writing that was handed down was accepted uncritically. For example, so great a hold on the imagination did "authority" command that even well after Isaac Casaubon had demonstrated the true date of the composition of the *Corpus Hermeticum*, its mid-seventeenth-century editor could state: "This Book may justly challenge the first place for antiquity, from all the Books in the World, being written some hundreds of yeers before *Moses* his time, as I shall endevor to make good."[50]

Spiritual Alchemy: In his *Table Talk*, DCCCV, Martin Luther wrote the following:

> The science of alchymy I like very well, and indeed, 'tis the philosophy of the ancients. I like it not only for the profits it brings in melting metals, in decocting, preparing, extracting, and distilling herbs, roots; I like it also for the sake of the allegory and secret signification, which is exceedingly fine, touching the resurrection of the dead at the last day. For, as in a furnace the fire extracts and separates from a substance the other portions, and carries upward the spirit, the life, the sap, the strength, while the unclean matter, the dregs, remain at the bottom, like a dead and worthless carcass; even so God, at the day of judgment, will separate all things through fire, the righteous from the ungodly. The Christians and righteous shall ascend upwards into heaven, and there live everlastingly, but the wicked and the ungodly, as the dross and filth, shall remain in hell, and there be damned.[51]

While the allegorical mode has been employed in alchemical writings from earliest times, in the sixteenth and seventeenth centuries, Christian authors were especially interested in setting forth the sacred implications of the art by devising or reaffirming intricate systems of correspondence that existed (or were thought to exist) between chemical processes and interactions occurring within their alembics and spiritual transformations taking place within their own hearts and souls. In each case the desired end was purification and perfection: the attainment of the philosopher's stone or the moral and spiritual regeneration of a believer whose soul, through God's grace, has been fitted for salvation. Central to this analogical system is the idea of Christ as the philosopher's stone: the agent of healing, deliverer from sin and baseness, rewarder of merit, author of grace and salvation, and creator of new heavens and a new earth "in that great & generall refining day,"[52] as one

---

[50] John French, in his preface to *The Divine Pymander of Hermes Mercurius Trismegistus, In XVII. Books* (London, 1650).

[51] *The Table Talk of Martin Luther*, trans. William Hazlitt (London: G. Bell, 1902), 326.

[52] From the Epistle Dedicatory to Thomas Tymme's translation of Joseph Duchesne [Quersitanus], *The Practise of Chymicall and Hermeticall Physicke* (London, 1605). On spiritual alchemy, and particularly Christian aspects, see C. G. Jung, *Psychology and Alchemy*, trans. R. F. C. Hull, 2nd ed. (New York: Princeton University Press, 1953), esp. 345–431, and Coudert, *Alchemy: The Philosopher's Stone*, 80–107.

seventeenth-century minister referred to the Second Coming. The successive stages in the preparation of the philosopher's stone are likened to Christ's nativity, crucifixion, and resurrection (fig.11), and, by a curious extension of the analogy, the two major events in the world's past and future, the Creation (fig. 12) and the Last Judgment, are often described in terms of alchemical process. Following this identification of the philosopher's stone with Christ, the alchemical imagination quickly discovered many other ingenious links between biblical themes, characters, and events and the search for the alchemical opus.

Editorial principles

Texts and editions from which selections are drawn are various: generally, works of ancient writers appear in authoritative, previously published twentieth-century translations; with a few exceptions, selections by Islamic, medieval, and early modern authors are derived from sixteenth- and seventeenth-century editions and translations. The brief introduction to each selection provides bibliographical information on the source text and the nature of any modernization employed within that selection. As a general policy, I have chosen to alter the original texts as little as possible, preserving as much of their "antique flavor" as is consistent with modern requirements for clarity and readability. I have therefore normalized early typographical conventions, e.g., v = u, u = v, i = j, j = i, but retained other early spellings and conventions of punctuation when they do not seriously interfere with meaning. (Readers will quickly learn that earlier ages often ignored our rigid distinctions between "then" and "than.") I have preserved original uses of capital letters and italics except when their sheer number becomes distracting, but corrected obvious typographical errors and introduced emendations where context and sense dictate the need to do so. It should be recognized at the outset that, unlike chemistry, alchemical discourse is fraught with ambiguity and uncertainty, deliberate obscurity, and the desire to both reveal and conceal. If one were to attempt to "modernize" alchemical writing thoroughly and consistently, to make it readily accessible to all, it would be impossible to stop with spelling and punctuation; it would be necessary to decode and "demystify" *all* distinctive "alchemical" features and conventions (e.g., allegory, imagery, analogy, symbol, metaphor, obscure reference and allusion, and arcane iconography). In short, alchemy would cease to become alchemy. There are many reasons for not wanting to venture upon so enormous and futile a task!

The introduction, brief headnotes to individual selections, footnotes, bibliography and glossary are designed primarily to assist the informed general reader. For this reason, initiates in the study of alchemy may find aspects of the apparatus to be unnecessarily elementary. Conversely, less experienced readers should not expect that *any* amount of explanation will satisfactorily illuminate all of the dark passages. Most of the illustrations are clustered in the introduction because they are intended to help explain important topics that are treated there. However, because much alchemical writing is highly visual, it is hoped that readers will find the illustrations to be useful points of reference while reading the treatises themselves.

Part I Ancient texts

1 Hermes Trismegistus
The Emerald Table (Tabula Smaragdina)

Hermes Trismegistus, the "thrice great," demands place at the beginning of this collection, not for reasons of "actual" existence, scientific dating, and absolute chronology, but by virtue of the deeply rooted psychological appeal of myth, legend, and tradition. Long identified as the Greek counterpart of the Egyptian Thoth, the god of wisdom, Hermes was known throughout the ancient world both for his religious and philosophical wisdom and his seer–like understanding of the most obscure areas of human speculation and experience: astrology, magic, the secrets of plants and stones, and alchemy. Because he was also credited with giving laws and letters to the Egyptians, his triple greatness consisted of preeminence as priest, philosopher, and king. These roles, combined with notions of Hermes' extreme antiquity – his lifetime was variously calculated according to the times of Atlas, Prometheus, Orpheus, Noah and Moses – assured the eponymous founder of hermeticism a high place in the wisdom tradition that extended down to Plato.

As might be expected, an extraordinary number of writings were attributed to Hermes, including the "philosophical" or "theoretical" treatises that comprise the *Corpus Hermeticum* along with the Latin *Asclepius*. In addition, a vast number of "technical" hermetica – treatises and fragments on the practical aspects of astrology, alchemy, sympathetic magic, talismans, invocations, and the like – passed under his name, including the famously enigmatic *Emerald Table*[1] (or *Tabula Smaragdina*) printed below. In this brief tract the secrets of the preparation of the philosopher's stone were thought to be cryptically set forth on an emerald tablet. As shown by the many references to him in works included in this collection, the influence of Hermes or Mercurius was enormous and long-lasting, extending from the earliest alchemical writings down to the late seventeenth century. Sir Isaac Newton, for example, wrote a serious *Commentary* on the *Emerald Table*, which serves as the final selection in this anthology and should be consulted.

Publication of the late Frances Yates's *Giordano Bruno and the Hermetic Tradition* in 1964 has stimulated much controversy over the influence of Hermetic thought on Renaissance culture and the impact of the "correct" dating of the *Corpus Hermeticum* by Isaac Casaubon in 1614. Casaubon proved that the Hermetic writings were not those of an ancient Egyptian divinity or priest who lived in primordial times but were composed anonymously during the period of the Roman Empire and the first few centuries AD with their eclectic mix of Egyptian, Greek, Roman, and Christian thought, and philosophical diversity, including Platonism, Neoplatonism, Gnosticism and Stoicism. The English translation of the *Emerald*

---

[1] Steele and Singer note that for ancient Egyptians and Greeks, "emerald" might refer to any green substance, such as granite or jasper (488); "table" refers to a tablet.

Table that follows – from a twelfth-century Latin translation of an Arabic version – is by Robert Steele and Dorothea Waley Singer and appeared in the *Proceedings of the Royal Society of Medicine* [London] 21 (1928): 486; it is reprinted with kind permission of the *Journal of the Royal Society of Medicine*. Additional readings (see Bibliography for full citations): Frances Yates, *Giordano Bruno*, chaps. 1–3; Brian Copenhaver, trans., *Hermetica*, Introduction; Garth Fowden, *The Egyptian Hermes*, chap.1.

True it is, without falsehood, certain and most true. That which is above is like to that which is below, and that which is below is like to that which is above, to accomplish the miracles of one thing.

And as all things were by contemplation of one, so all things arose from this one thing by a single act of adaptation.[2]

The father thereof is the Sun, the mother the Moon.[3]

The wind carried it in its womb, the earth is the nurse thereof.

It is the father of all works of wonder throughout the whole world.

The power thereof is perfect.

If it be cast on to earth, it will separate the element of earth from that of fire, the subtle from the gross.

With great sagacity it doth ascend gently from earth to heaven.

Again it doth descend to earth, and uniteth in itself the force from things superior and things inferior.[4]

Thus thou wilt possess the glory of the brightness of the whole world,[5] and all obscurity will fly far from thee.

This thing is the strong fortitude of all strength, for it overcometh every subtle thing and doth penetrate every solid substance.

Thus was this world created.

Hence will there be marvellous adaptations achieved, of which the manner is this.

For this reason I am called Hermes Trismegistus, because I hold three parts of the wisdom of the whole world.

That which I had to say about the operation of Sol is completed.

[2] Paragraphs 1–2 appear to refer to the familiar correspondences between heaven and earth and macrocosm and microcosm, and the unity of creation as effected by a single – perhaps platonically conceived – creative force. Throughout, parallels between the creation of the world and the formulation of the philosopher's stone are suggested.

[3] The philosopher's stone results from the interaction of binary opposites, male and female, father and mother, sun and moon.

[4] Images of ascension and descent may suggest various laboratory processes, such as solution, separation, and distillation, necessary in producing the stone.

[5] I.e., the alchemical quintessence.

2 Plato (*c.* 427–347 BC)

From the *Timaeus*

Despite the fact that Plato authored no dialogues that dealt with alchemy as such, he is perhaps the one to whom more spurious alchemical works were attributed than any other ancient source except Hermes Trismegistus (see Singer, below). His name was also cited frequently by later writers as a revered alchemical authority, and it is quite possible that the dialogue form itself – so popular with alchemical authors – had its basis in the Platonic model. The reasons for this pseudonymous popularity are interesting and instructive. The names of Plato, Aristotle, Raymund Lull, Geber and others were frequently appropriated by lesser alchemical authors who sought to make their works appear important by attaching them to eminent authorities past or present. In the case of Plato, however, there were other more compelling reasons for the association with alchemy. Alchemy's existence and credibility depended heavily on "platonic" ideas and doctrines that were readily available – although not exclusively so – in the *Timaeus*, Plato's Creation account. Here, for example, are discussed such important topics as the world's creation following the pattern of a "living creature," complete with body and soul; the Four Elements theory (not original to Plato) and the elements' circle of interconvertibility; the world soul or *anima mundi*, and the relationship between form and matter, all of which were theoretically relevant. For the alchemists, descriptions of the making of the philosopher's stone frequently employed analogies with the Creation; the transformation of one element into another – the underlying matter or *prima materia* remaining constant – was the key to transmutation; and the notion of universal animism supported a host of theoretical and practical concerns. Thus Platonic ideas, combined with and expanded by those of the later Neoplatonists, were essential to the entire Hermetic edifice. The larger influence of the *Timaeus*, primarily through the Latin translation and commentary by Chalcidius in the fourth century AD, extended throughout the Middle Ages. It was, in fact, the only Platonic dialogue available in the West during this period.

The following selections are from the translation of the *Timaeus* by Benjamin Jowett, in *The Collected Dialogues of Plato*, ed. Edith Hamilton and Huntington Cairns, Bollingen Series LXXI (New York: Pantheon Books, 1961); Timaeus is the speaker throughout. On pseudonymous works assigned to Plato, see Dorothea Waley Singer, "Alchemical Texts Bearing the Name of Plato," *Ambix* 2, 3–4 (Dec. 1946): 115–28.

TIMAEUS: All men, Socrates, who have any degree of right feeling, at the beginning of every enterprise, whether small or great, always call upon God. And we, too, who are going to discourse of the nature of the universe, how created or how existing without creation, if we be not altogether out of our wits, must invoke the aid of gods and goddesses and pray that our words may be above all acceptable to them and in consequence to ourselves. Let this, then, be our invocation of the gods, to which I add an exhortation of myself to speak in such manner as will be most intelligible to you, and will most accord with my own intent.

[*Being and becoming*] First then, in my judgment, we must make a distinction and ask, What is that which always is and has no becoming, and what is that which is always becoming and never is? That which is apprehended by intelligence and reason is always in the same state, but that which is conceived by opinion with the help of sensation and without reason is always in a process of becoming and perishing and never really is. Now everything that becomes or is created must of necessity be created by some cause, for without a cause nothing can be created. The work of the creator, whenever he looks to the unchangeable and fashions the form and nature of his work after an unchangeable pattern, must necessarily be made fair and perfect, but when he looks to the created only and uses a created pattern, it is not fair or perfect. Was the heaven then or the world, whether called by this or by any other more appropriate name – assuming the name, I am asking a question which has to be asked at the beginning of an inquiry about anything – was the world, I say, always in existence and without beginning, or created, and had it a beginning? Created, I reply, being visible and tangible and having a body, and therefore sensible, and all sensible things are apprehended by opinion and sense, and are in a process of creation and created. Now that which is created must, as we affirm, of necessity be created by a cause. But the father and maker of all this universe is past finding out, and even if we found him, to tell of him to all men would be impossible. This question, however, we must ask about the world. Which of the patterns had the artificer in view when he made it – the pattern of the unchangeable or of that which is created? If the world be indeed fair and the artificer good, it is manifest that he must have looked to that which is eternal, but if what cannot be said without blasphemy is true, then to the created pattern. Everyone will see that he must have looked to the eternal, for the world is the fairest of creations and he is the best of causes. And having been created in this way, the world has been framed in the likeness of that which is apprehended by reason and mind and is unchangeable, and must therefore of necessity, if this is admitted, be a copy of something...

[*The Creator*] TIMAEUS: Let me tell you then why the creator made this world of generation. He was good, and the good can never have any jealousy of anything. And being free from jealousy, he desired that all things should be as like himself as they could be. This is in the truest sense the origin of creation and of the world, as we shall do well in believing on the testimony of wise men. God desired that all things should be good and nothing bad, so far as this was attainable. Wherefore also finding the whole visible sphere not at rest, but moving in an irregular and disorderly fashion, out of disorder he brought order, considering that this was in every way better than the other. Now the deeds of the best could never be or have been other than the fairest, and the creator, reflecting on the things which are by nature visible, found that no unintelligent creature taken as a whole could ever be fairer than the intelligent taken as a whole, and again that intelligence could not be present in anything which was devoid of soul. For which reason, when he was framing the universe, he put intelligence in soul, and soul in body, that he might be the creator of a work which was by nature fairest and best. On this wise, using the language of probability, we may say that the world came into being – a living creature truly endowed with soul and intelligence by the providence of God.[1]

This being supposed, let us proceed to the next stage. In the likeness of what animal did the creator make the world? It would be an unworthy thing to liken it to any nature which exists as a part only, for nothing can be beautiful which is like any imperfect thing. But let us suppose the world to be the very image of that whole of which all other animals both individually and in their tribes are portions. For the original of the universe contains in itself all intelligible beings, just as this world comprehends us and all other visible creatures. For the deity, intending to make this world like the fairest and most perfect of intelligible beings, framed one visible animal comprehending within itself all other animals of a kindred nature. Are we right in saying that there is one world, or that they are many and infinite? There must be one only if the created copy is to accord with the original. For that which includes all other intelligible creatures cannot have a second or companion; in that case there would be need of another living being which would include both, and of which they would be parts, and the likeness would be more truly said to resemble not them, but that other which included them. In order then that the world might be solitary, like the perfect animal, the creator made not two worlds or an infinite number of them, but there is and ever will be one only-begotten and created heaven. [27c–31b]

[*Four elements*] Now the creation took up the whole of each of the four elements, for the creator compounded the world out of all the fire and all the water and all the air and all the earth, leaving no part of any of them nor any power of them outside. His intention was, in the first place, that the animal should be as far as possible a perfect whole and of perfect parts, secondly, that it should be one, leaving no remnants out of which another such world might be created, and also that it should be free from old age and unaffected by disease. Considering that if heat and cold and other powerful forces surround composite bodies and attack them from without, they decompose them before their time, and by bringing diseases and old age upon them make them waste away – for this cause and on these grounds he made the world one whole, having every part entire, and being therefore perfect and not liable to old age and disease. And he gave to the world the figure which was suitable and also natural. Now to the animal which was to comprehend all animals, that figure would be suitable which comprehends within itself all other figures. Wherefore he made the world in the form of a globe, round as from a lathe, having its extremes in every direction equidistant from the center, the most perfect and the most like itself of all figures, for he considered that the like is infinitely fairer than the unlike. . . Of design he was created thus – his own waste providing his own food, and all that he did or suffered taking place in and by himself. For the creator conceived that a being which was self-sufficient would be far more excellent than one which lacked anything, and, as he had no need to take anything or defend himself against anyone, the creator did not think it necessary to bestow upon him hands, nor had he any need of feet, nor of the whole apparatus of walking. But the movement suited to his spherical form was assigned to him, being of all the seven that

---

[1] Throughout this section Plato introduces the idea of the world soul and the animistic, rational, and harmonious universe, doctrines vital to alchemical thought. In the next section, he describes the equally important Four Elements theory.

which is most appropriate to mind and intelligence, and he was made to move in the same manner and on the same spot, within his own limits revolving in a circle. All the other six motions were taken away from him, and he was made not to partake of their deviations.[2] And as this circular movement required no feet, the universe was created without legs and without feet.

[*Body and soul*] Such was the whole plan of the eternal God about the god that was to be; he made it smooth and even, having a surface in every direction equidistant from the center, a body entire and perfect, and formed out of perfect bodies. And in the center he put the soul, which he diffused throughout the body, making it also to be the exterior environment of it, and he made the universe a circle moving in a circle, one and solitary, yet by reason of its excellence able to converse with itself, and needing no other friendship or acquaintance. Having these purposes in view he created the world a blessed god.

Now God did not make the soul after the body, although we are speaking of them in this order, for when he put them together he would never have allowed that the elder should be ruled by the younger, but this is a random manner of speaking which we have, because somehow we ourselves too are very much under the dominion of chance. Whereas he made the soul in origin and excellence prior to and older than the body, to be the ruler and mistress, of whom the body was to be the subject. [32c–34c]

Now when the creator had framed the soul according to his will, he formed within her the corporeal universe, and brought the two together and united them center to center. The soul, interfused everywhere from the center to the circumference of heaven, of which also she is the external envelopment, herself turning in herself, began a divine beginning of never-ceasing and rational life enduring throughout all things. [36d–e]

[*Four elements and interconvertibility*] Thus far in what we have been saying, with small exceptions, the works of intelligence have been set forth, and now we must place by the side of them in our discourse the things which come into being through necessity – for the creation of this world is the combined work of necessity and mind. Mind, the ruling power, persuaded necessity to bring the greater part of created things to perfection, and thus and after this manner in the beginning, through necessity made subject to reason, this universe was created. But if a person will truly tell of the way in which the work was accomplished, he must include the variable cause as well, and explain its influence. Wherefore, we must return again and find another suitable beginning – as about the former matters, so also about these. To which end we must consider the nature of fire and water and air and earth, such as they were prior to the creation of the heaven, and what was happening to them in this previous state, for no one has as yet explained the manner of their generation, but we speak of fire and the rest of them, as though men knew their natures, and we maintain them to be the first principles and letters or elements of the whole, when they cannot reasonably be compared by a man of any sense even to syllables or first compounds...

In the first place, we see that what we just now called water, by condensation, I suppose, becomes stone and earth, and this same element, when melted and dispersed,

---

[2] In establishing the world's motion as being circular upon its own axis, Plato denies it the other six motions: upward and downward, backwards and forwards, and to the left and right.

passes into vapor and air.[3] Air, again, when inflamed, becomes fire, and, again, fire, when condensed and extinguished, passes once more into the form of air, and once more, air, when collected and condensed, produces cloud and mist – and from these, when still more compressed, comes flowing water, and from water comes earth and stones once more – and thus generation appears to be transmitted from one to the other in a circle. Thus, then, as the several elements never present themselves in the same form, how can anyone have the assurance to assert positively that any of them, whatever it may be, is one thing rather than another? No one can . . .

[*Matter and form*] Let me make another attempt to explain my meaning more clearly. Suppose a person to make all kinds of figures of gold and to be always remodeling each form into all the rest; somebody points to one of them and asks what it is. By far the safest and truest answer is, 'That is gold,' and not to call the triangle or any other figures which are formed in the gold 'these,' as though they had existence, since they are in process of change while he is making the assertion, but if the questioner be willing to take the safe and indefinite expression, 'such,' we should be satisfied. And the same argument applies to the universal nature which receives all bodies – that must be always called the same, for, inasmuch as she always receives all things, she never departs at all from her own nature and never, in any way or at any time, assumes a form like that of any of the things which enter into her; she is the natural recipient of all impressions, and is stirred and informed by them, and appears different from time to time by reason of them . . . Wherefore the mother and receptacle of all created and visible and in any way sensible things is not to be termed earth or air or fire or water, or any of their compounds, or any of the elements from which these are derived, but is an invisible and formless being which receives all things and in some mysterious way partakes of the intelligible, and is most incomprehensible. In saying this we shall not be far wrong; as far, however, as we can attain to a knowledge of her from the previous considerations, we may truly say that fire is that part of her nature which from time to time is inflamed, and water that which is moistened, and that the mother substance becomes earth and air, in so far as she receives the impressions of them. [47e–51b]

[*Gold*] Of all the kinds termed fusile, that which is the densest and is formed out of the finest and most uniform parts is that most precious possession called gold, which is hardened by filtration through rock; this is unique in kind, and has both a glittering and a yellow color. A shoot of gold, which is so dense as to be very hard, and takes a black color, is termed adamant. There is also another kind which has parts nearly like gold, and of which there are several species; it is denser than gold, and it contains a small and fine portion of earth and is therefore harder, yet also lighter because of the great interstices which it has within itself, and this substance, which is one of the bright and denser kinds of water, when solidified is called copper. [59b–c]

---

[3] In setting forth the interconvertibility of the elements and primacy of change in the natural order of things, Plato provides the prototype for alchemical transmutation. From earliest times onward, alchemical authors describe this rotation of the elements as a circle or wheel in which various forms are impressed upon one basic, unchanging matter, which Plato here calls the "mother and receptacle of all created and visible . . . things."

3 Aristotle (384–322 BC)

From the *Meteorology*

Like Plato, Aristotle exerted a long and profound influence on alchemical thought through both his genuine works and the many pseudonymous writings attributed to him. Among the latter, the *Secreta Secretorum* purported to be a treatise written by Aristotle to his pupil Alexander the Great, but was in fact compiled from Syriac sources in the eighth century, then translated into Arabic, then into Latin in the thirteenth century by Philip of Paris, and from Latin into the modern languages of western Europe. The work's popularity – its diverse topics included the importance of religion, the proper appearance of a king, the principles of wise governing, the means to good health, astronomy, and alchemy – was such that Elias Ashmole included a version of its alchemical content in the *Theatrum Chemicum Britannicum* of 1652, entitled "John Lydgate Monke of St. Edmunds Bury, In his Translation of the second Epistle that King Alexander sent to his Master Aristotle."

Among the genuine writings, Aristotle's *Meteorology*, despite its title, included important material on the "natural" subterranean formation of metals and minerals, and since alchemists believed that their Art imitated Nature, this treatise also became an established text on the artificial production of metals and related matters. In the following selection, Aristotle begins familiarly with the four elements, their "principles" (coldness, moistness, hotness, and dryness), and interconvertibility. He then proceeds to his theory of interacting vapors and exhalations within the bowels of the earth, which was to lead eventually to the development of the sulphur-mercury theory, the most widely accepted account of the generation of metals and minerals until the rise of the phlogiston theory late in the seventeenth century.

The following selections are from the translation of the *Meteorology* by E. W. Webster, in *The Complete Works of Aristotle*, Revised Oxford Translation, ed. Jonathan Barnes, Bollingen Series 71.2, vol. 1 (Princeton: Princeton University Press, 1984), and are reprinted with permission of the Princeton University Press.

[*The elements*] We have already laid down that there is one principle which makes up the nature of the bodies that move in a circle, and besides this four bodies[1] owing their

---

[1] These "four bodies" are the elements: earth, air, water and fire. The "bodies that move in a circle" are almost certainly the planets; however, it is difficult to determine the precise meaning of this sentence.

existence to the four principles,[2] the motion of these latter bodies being of two kinds: either from the centre or to the centre. These four bodies are fire, air, water, earth. Fire occupies the highest place among them all, earth the lowest, and two elements correspond to these in their relation to one another, air being nearest to fire, water to earth. The whole world surrounding the earth,[3] then, the affections of which are our subject, is made up of these bodies. This world necessarily has a certain continuity with the upper motions;[4] consequently all its power is derived from them. (For the originating principle of all motion must be deemed the first cause. Besides, that element is eternal and its motion has no limit in space, but is always complete; whereas all these other bodies have separate regions which limit one another.) So we must treat fire and earth and the elements like them as the material causes of the events in this world (meaning by material what is subject and is affected), but must assign causality in the sense of the originating principle of motion to the power of the eternally moving bodies... Fire, air, water, earth, we assert, come-to-be from one another, and each of them exists potentially in each, as all things do that can be resolved into a common and ultimate substrate.[5] [Bk. 1, 339a 11–339b 2]

So at the centre and round it [the earth-centred world] we get earth and water, the heaviest and coldest elements, by themselves; round them and contiguous with them, air and what we commonly call fire. It is not really fire, for fire is an excess of heat and a sort of ebullition; but in reality, of what we call air, the part surrounding the earth is moist and warm, because it contains both vapour and a dry exhalation from the earth. But the next part, above that, is warm and dry. For vapour is naturally moist and cold, exhalation warm and dry; and vapour is potentially like water, exhalation potentially like fire. [Bk. 1, 340b 19–28]

[*The origin of metals*] We recognize two kinds of exhalation, one moist, the other dry. The former is called vapour: for the other there is no general name but we must call it a sort of smoke, applying to the whole of it a word that is proper to one of its forms. The moist cannot exist without the dry nor the dry without the moist: whenever we speak of either we mean that it predominates. Now when the sun in its circular course approaches, it draws up by its heat the moist evaporation: when it recedes the cold makes the vapour that had been raised condense back into water which falls and is distributed over the earth. (This explains why there is more rain in winter and more by night than by day: though the fact is not recognized because rain by night is more apt to escape observation than by day.) But there is a great quantity of fire and heat in the earth, and the sun not only draws up the moisture that lies on the surface of it, but warms and dries the earth itself. Consequently, since there are two kinds of exhalation, as we have said, one like vapour, the other like smoke, both of them are necessarily generated. That in which moisture predominates is the source of rain, as we explained before, while the dry one is the source and substance of all winds. [Bk. 2, 359b 29–360a 13]

Some account has now been given of the effects of the exhalation above the surface of the earth; we must go on to describe its operations below, when it is shut up in the parts of the earth.

---

[2] The four principles which comprise the elements: hot, dry, cold, and moist.
[3] The microcosm.   [4] The higher reaches of the celestial world, primarily god, the first cause.
[5] Aristotle supports the Platonic notions of the interconvertibility of the elements and the *prima materia*.

Its own twofold nature gives rise here to two varieties of bodies, just as it does in the upper region. We maintain that there are two exhalations, one vaporous the other smoky, and there correspond two kinds of bodies that originate in the earth, things quarried and things mined. The heat of the dry exhalation is the cause of all things quarried. Such are the kinds of stones that cannot be melted, and realgar, and ochre, and ruddle, and sulphur, and the other things of that kind, most things quarried being either coloured lye or, like cinnabar, a stone compounded of it. The vaporous exhalation is the cause of all things mined – things which are either fusible or malleable such as iron, copper, gold. All these originate from the imprisonment of the vaporous exhalation in the earth, and especially in stones. Their dryness compresses it, and it congeals just as dew or hoar-frost does when it has been separated off, though in the present case the metals are generated before that separation occurs. Hence, they are water in a sense, and in a sense not. Their matter was that which might have become water, but it can no longer do so; nor are they, like savours, due to a qualitative change in actual water. Copper and gold are not formed like that, but in every case the evaporation congealed before water was formed. Hence, they all (except gold) are affected by fire, and they possess an admixture of earth; for they still contain the dry exhalation.

This is the general theory of all these bodies, but we must take up each kind of them and discuss it separately. [Bk. 3, 378a 14–378b 6]

We have explained that the causes of the elements are four, and that their combinations determine the number of the elements to be four.

Two of the causes, the hot and the cold, are active; two, the dry and the moist, passive.[6] We can satisfy ourselves of this by looking at instances. In every case heat and cold determine, conjoin, and change things of the same kind and things of different kinds, moistening, drying, hardening, and softening them. Things dry and moist, on the other hand, both in isolation and when present together in the same body are the subjects of that determination and of the other affections enumerated. The account we give when we define their natures shows this too. Hot and cold we describe as active, for combining is a sort of activity; moist and dry are passive, for it is in virtue of its being acted upon in a certain way that a thing is said to be easy to determine or difficult to determine. So it is clear that some are active and some passive. [Bk. 4, 378b 10–25]

We must now describe the next kinds of processes which the qualities already mentioned set up in actually existing natural objects as matter.

Of these concoction is due to heat; its species are ripening, boiling, broiling... Concoction is a process in which the natural and proper heat of an object perfects the corresponding passive qualities, which are the proper matter of any given object. For when concoction has taken place we say that a thing has been perfected and has come to be itself. It is the proper heat of a thing that sets up this perfecting, though external influences may contribute in some degree to its fulfilment... In some cases of concoction the end of the process is the nature of the thing – nature, that is, in the sense of the form and essence. [Bk. 4, 379b 10–26]

---

[6] In this paragraph, Aristotle's views on the opposing principles that result in the formation of metals anticipate the later sulphur-mercury theory.

Homogeneous bodies differ to touch by these affections and differences, as we have said. They also differ in respect of their smell, taste, and colour.

By homogeneous bodies I mean, for instance, the stuffs that are mined – gold, copper, silver, tin, iron, stone, and everything else of this kind and the bodies that are extracted from them . . . [Bk. 4, 388a 10–15]

4 Pseudo-Democritus (first or second century AD)

From *The Treatise of Democritus On Things Natural and Mystical*

Robert Steele, its translator, asserts that *On Things Natural and Mystical* is the "earliest known chemical treatise" (88); however, its date of composition and authorship remain highly uncertain. He attributes this work to followers of Democritus of Abdera (*ca.* 460–357 BC), the Greek philosopher best known for his atomistic theories, stating that it dates "certainly not later than the first centuries" AD. Matters of authorship and time of composition are complicated by the fact that pseudo-Democritean writings proliferated in the ancient world, as in the case of the Egyptian Bolos of Mendes (or Bolos the Democritean) who seems to have flourished *ca.* 200 BC and is known to have collected chemical and metallurgical recipes of the sort included in the present treatise. However, during this time, Democritus's reputation was not only that of a philosopher and scientist; in Pliny's *Natural History* (bk. 30:1), for example, he is deplored as a pupil of Ostanes and popularizer of magic: "Democritus especially instilled into men's minds the sweets of magic" (Loeb edn., 8:285). Thus, attribution of *On Things Natural and Mystical* to him is at least plausible and may even be correct. In any case, the variety of recipes and formulae included is great, as is the range of experimental procedures described. One finds glimmerings of "proto-scientific" methodology – as in statements of objectives, technical vocabulary, close attention to the appearances of substances, and concern with practical (if sometimes deceptive) outcomes – along with frequent and enthusiastic rhapsodies on the power and glory of Nature. As in the later Leyden and Stockholm Papyri, one is reminded of the close links between early alchemy and chemistry and the crafts tradition from which they evolved. The following text is a nearly complete version of the translation by Robert B. Steele that appeared in *Chemical News*, 61 (1890): 88–125; a number of Steele's notes have been incorporated in the annotations.

FRAGMENT OF ANCIENT INTRODUCTION

"Nature rejoices with Nature; Nature conquers Nature; Nature restrains Nature."

We (his disciples) greatly wondered at how briefly he had bound up the whole science. I come into Egypt, bearing the treatises of nature, that thou mayest cast off confused and superfluous matter.

1. *Copper is Whitened with Mercury-Amalgam or Arsenic, and is then Coloured Golden by Electrum or Powdered Gold.*

Taking mercury, thrust it into the body of magnesia,[1] or into the body of Italian antimony, or of unfired sulphur, or of *silver spume*,[2] or of quick lime, or to alum from Melos, or to arsenic, or as thou knowest, and throw in *white earth of Venus*, and thou shalt have clear *Venus*; then throw in yellow *Luna*,[3] and thou shalt have gold, and it will be chrysocoral[4] reduced into a body.

Yellow arsenic also makes the same, and prepared sandarach,[5] and well bruised cinnabar, but quicksilver alone makes brass shining; for nature conquers nature.

2. *Sulphide of Silver is Treated with Sulphides of Lead or Antimony, and the Resulting Alloy is Coloured Golden.*

Treat silver marcasite, which is also called siderites, and do what is usual that it may be melted. It melts with *yellow* or white litharge, or in Italian antimony, and cleanse it with lead (not simply, say I, lest thou err, but with that from *Scissile*,[6] and our black litharge), or as thou knowest; and heat, and throw it made yellow to the material, and it becomes coloured; for nature rejoices with nature.

3. *Copper Pyrites is Roasted and Treated with Salt and Alloyed with Silver or Gold to Form Gold-Coloured Alloys.*

Treat pyrites till it becomes incombustible, casting off darkness, but treat with brine, or fresh urine, or sea water, or oxymel, or as thou knowest, until it becomes as an incombustible shaving of gold; and as it becomes so, mix with it unfired sulphur, or yellow alum, or Attic ochre, or what thou knowest, and add to luna for sol, and to sol for auriconchylium;[7] for nature conquers nature.

4. *Claudian Metal is Rendered Yellow by Sulphur or Arsenic, and Alloyed on Gold or Silver.*

Taking claudianum,[8] thou shalt make a marble, as of custom, until it becomes yellow. Thou shalt not render the stone yellow, I say, but that which is useful of the stone. Thou shalt yellow it with alum burnt with sulphur, or with arsenic, or sandarach, or lime, or that thou knowest, and if thou apply it to *luna* thou makest *sol*, but if to *sol* thou makest auriconchylium; for victorious nature restrains nature.

5. *Silver or Bronze are Treated with an Amalgam of Iron to Produce Gold or Electrum.*

Make cinnabar white by oil, or vinegar, or honey, or brine, or alum, then yellow by misy, or sory, or chalcanth,[9] or live sulphur, or that thou knowest, and add to *luna* and

---

[1] Any white body, steatite or soapstone (Steele 125). In later alchemical writing, magnesia has a broad range of meanings, including the quintessence or an ingredient of the philosopher's stone.

[2] Argentiferous litharge (Steele 125).   [3] Venus and Luna stand for copper and silver, respectively.

[4] "Gold solder" or chrysocolla, a name given to a specific mineral or minerals in ancient times (*OED*).

[5] Red arsenic sulphide, or realgar.   [6] Alum schist.

[7] Sol represents gold; auriconchylium is gold in powder, coquille d'or (Steele 125).

[8] Steele notes that claudianum "was a metal, named from its manufacturer. An alloy of tin and lead, with copper, zinc, &c." (125).

[9] Misy: a mixture of iron and copper sulphate; sory: basic sulphate of iron (Steele 125); chalcanth: copperas or ferrous sulphate.

it will be *sol* if thou colourest golden, or to bronze for electrum. Nature rejoices with nature.

6. *A Yellow Golden Varnish for Metals.*
Whiten, I say, *copper, cadmia,* or *zonytes,* as of custom, afterwards make it yellow. But you will yellow it with the bile of a calf, or terebinth,[10] or castor oil, or radish oil, or yolks of eggs, which can render it yellow, and add to *luna,* for it will be gold for gold; for nature conquers nature.

7. *The Treatment of Silver by Superficial Sulphidation to Render it Gold Coloured.*
Treat androdamas[11] with bitter wine, or sea water, or acid brine, which things can attack its nature, melt with Chalcidonian antimony, and treat it again with sea water, or brine, or acid brine; wash until the blackness of the antimony goes away, heat or roast it until it begins to grow yellow, and thou shalt treat with untouched *divine* water, and lay it on silver, and when thou addest live sulphur thou makest chrysosomium *into golden liquid*; for nature conquers nature. This is the stone called chrysites.[12]

8. *An Alloy of Copper and Lead is Formed, which is turned Yellow.*
Taking white earth from ceruse, I say, *or from the scoriæ of silver,* or of Italian antimony, or of magnesia, or even of white litharge, whiten it with sea water, or acid brine, or with water from the air under the dew, I say, and the sun, that it, when dissolved, may become white as ceruse. Heat then this in the furnace, and add to it the flowers of copper,[13] or scraped rust of copper, worked up by art, I say, or burnt bronze sufficiently corroded, or chalcites, or *cyanum*;[14] then it becomes compact and solid, but it becomes so easily. This is molybdochalium.[15] Test it therefore, whether it has cast off its blackness, but if not, blame not the bronze, but rather thyself, since thou hast not conducted the operation rightly; therefore thou shalt brighten it, and dissolve it, and add what is necessary to yellow it, and roast till it begins to grow yellow, and throw it into all bodies; for bronze colours every body where it is shining and yellow; for nature conquers nature.

9. *Copper and Silver are made Yellow by Sulphate of Iron; with a Process of Cementation.*[16]
Rub up sory and chalcanth with unfired sulphur; but sory is, as leprous cyanus, always found in misy, they call it green chalcanth. Roast it, therefore, in the middle of coals for three days, until it becomes a *red* drug, and throw it into Venus, or Luna made by us, and it will be Sol. Place this, cut up in sheets, in vinegar, and chalcanth, and misy, and alum, and sal cappadociæ,[17] and red nitre, or as thou knowest, for three, or five, or six days,

---

[10] The tree that serves as the source of turpentine or – most likely in this context – the resin itself.

[11] "Arsenical pyrites; from its silvery lustre used with silver" (Steele 125).

[12] "A mixture of silver and lead, which becomes yellow on heating" (Steele 125).

[13] "Small black scales of oxide of copper, which separate on cooling" (Steele 125).

[14] Chalcites is copper pyrites; cyanum is blue carbonate of copper or Azurite (Steele 125).

[15] An alloy of copper and lead.

[16] "The process by which one solid is made to penetrate and combine with another at high temperature without liquefaction taking place" (Abraham *DAI* 32).

[17] A variety of sal gemma or rock salt (Steele 125).

until it becomes a rust, and it tinges; for chalcanth makes sol a rust. Nature rejoices with nature.

10. *An Alloy of Gold is Heated by Superficial Cementation.*
Treat Macedonian chrysocolla, which is like the rust of bronze, by dissolving it in the urine of a young girl until it entirely changes; for the nature is hidden within. When, therefore, it is changed, dip it into castor oil, often heating it, and tinging it, afterwards roast with alum, first dissolving with misy or unfired sulphur; render it yellow, and colour the whole body of gold.

11. O! NATURES, Governors of natures! O! natures, how great, conquering natures with their changes! O! natures above Nature, delighting natures! Therefore these are great natures; no others are more excellent among tinctures than these natures; none are like, none are greater, all these take effect as solutions. You therefore, O! *wise men*, I plainly understand are not ignorant, but rather wonder, since ye know the power of nature, but the young men are much in error, and will not put faith in what is written, since they are ignorant of matter, not noticing that *physicians* where they wish to prepare a useful drug, do not set about making it inconsiderately, but first test it, whether it is warming, and how much cold, or humid, or other substance necessary, joined with it will make a medium temperament. They, on the other hand, boldly and inconsiderately desiring to prepare that valuable medicine and ending of all diseases, do not learn that they are running into danger. As they consider that we speak in fables and not mystically, they display no diligence in inquiring into the species of things. For example, if this is cleansing, but that unimportant; and if this is fitted to receive a colour, but that to prepare (for receiving it); *and if this tinges the surface, or if the tincture gives off an odour from the surface*, or vanishes from the interior of the metallic body; or if this resists fire, but that mixed with anything enables it to resist fire. For example, if salt cleanses the surface of *Jove*[18] it cleanses its interior parts; and if the exterior part contracts rust after the cleansing, the interior parts do so also; and if mercury whitens and cleanses the surface of *Venus*, it whitens also the interior; and if it leaves the exterior, it leaves the interior also. If the young men had been skilled in this kind of knowledge, applying their minds judiciously to the actions of substances, they would have suffered less loss; they know not the antipathies of nature, that one species may change ten, as a drop of oil stains much purple, and a little sulphur burns many things. Let these things be said, therefore, of *medicines*, and of the extent to which what is written may be relied on.

12. *A Gold Varnish for Silver.*
Let us deal with liquids in their turn. Taking Pontic rhubarb, rub it up in bitter Aminean wine[19] to the consistency of wax, and take a thin piece of *Luna* to make *Sol*, the pieces of which may be a full nail in breadth, *that thou mayest use the drug again and again*; place it in an empty vessel, which, luting on all sides, gently heat from beneath until the middle (of

---

[18] Jove represents tin, Venus copper.
[19] In ancient alchemical treatises, substances frequently bear the names of their places of origin, as in the references to rhubarb and wine in this passage and the crocus of Cilicia below.

the leaf) is reached. Then place the leaf in the remainder of the drug, and complete the action with the aforesaid wine, as long as the liquid appears thick. In this, throw at once the uncooled leaf, and allow it to absorb, then take it and place it in a crucible; and thou shalt find Sol.

But if the rhubarb be dried with age, mix it with equal parts of celandine, preparing it, as of custom, for celandine has a relationship to rhubarb. Nature rejoices with nature.

13. *Another Gold Varnish.*

Take crocus of Cilicia, and leave it with the crocus flower, and the aforesaid juice of the vine, and thou shalt have a liquor, as is accustomed to be done. Colour silver, cut into leaves, until it seems shining to thee. But if the leaf be bronze it will be better, but first cleanse the bronze, as customary. Then taking two parts of the herb aristolochia,[20] and double of crocus, and celandine, make it of the consistency of wax, and anointing the sheet, do as before, and wonder, since the crocus of Cilicia has the same effect as mercury, as also cassia with cinnamon. Nature conquers nature.

14. *Another Gold Varnish.*

Taking our lead made *shining* by Chian earth,[21] and *pyrites*, and alum, burn with chaff, and melt into pyrites; and rub up crocus and cnicum, and the flower œcumenicus with the sharpest vinegar, and make a liquid, as of custom, and dip the lead into it, and allow it to absorb it, and thou shalt find Sol but let the composition have a little unburnt sulphur; for nature conquers nature.

15. *This is the plan of Hepammenes, which he showed to the priests of Egypt, and it remains to the times of these philosophers, the matter of the Chrysopeia.*[22]

Nor should ye wonder if one thing performs a mystery of this kind. Do ye not see that many drugs can with difficulty, even in the progress of time, heal up *wounds produced by iron*, but human excrement succeeds in no long interval of time; *and many drugs employed for burns* produce often no good, and most in no way diminish the pain, but lime alone, when rightly prepared, drives out the ailment; and if various cures are tried for ophthalmia,[23] they generally increase it, but the plant buckthorn, used to all sickness of this kind, cures perfectly. Vain and unsuitable matter should therefore be despised, but things be used according to their natures. Now therefore learn from these also, that no one has ever been successful without the aforesaid natures. But if nothing can be done without these, why do we desire a forest of many things; what is our need of the concourse of many species for the work, when one surpasses all? Let us now see the composition of the species from which silver can be made.

THE BOOK OF SILVER

16. *The Surface of a Copper Alloy is Whitened by an Arsenical Compound.*

Fix quicksilver from arsenic, or sandarach, or that thou knowest, as of custom, and mix *Venus* with iron treated with sulphur, and it will be whitened; but whitened magnesia is also excellent, and *sublimed* arsenic, and calcined cadmia, unfired sandarach, whitened pyrites,

---

[20] A type of shrub, one species of which is the Common Birthwort.
[21] Earth obtained from the Aegean island of Chios, used as "an astringent and a cosmetic" (*OED*).
[22] Gold-making, the art of transmutation.   [23] Inflammation of the eye.

and ceruse roasted with sulphur. Thou dissolvest iron by throwing into magnesia, or the half of sulphur, or a little of loadstone, since that has affinity with iron. Nature rejoices with nature.

17. *A Composition for Amalgamating the Surface of Alloys.*
Taking the aforesaid vapour, heat it with castor or radish oil, mixing with a little alum; then taking tin, purge it with sulphur, as of custom, or *marchasite*, or what is known to thee, and throw it into the vapour, mixing the whole. Roast, covered with coals, and thou shalt see this medicine formed, like to white lead, which whitens all (metallic) bodies, but by anointing. Mix with it Chian earth, or Asterites, or Aphroselinum,[24] or that thou knowest, since Aphroselinum associated with mercury whitens all (metallic) bodies. Nature conquers nature.

18. *The Same Applied to Orichalium Alloy.*
Take white magnesia; thou shalt whiten it with brine and alum, in sea-water, or citron juice, or with the smoke of sulphur; for the fume of sulphur, when it is white, whitens all things. But others say that the fume of cobathia[25] whitens it. Mix with it, after whitening, equal parts of lye, that it may become white enough. Taking of whitish bronze, of orichalium, I say, 4 ounces, place it in a crucible, placing under it little by little 1 ounce of previously purged tin, agitating until the substances unite; it will be frangible. Throw on, therefore, the half of white medicine, and it will be the *chief*; for whitened magnesia does not render bodies fragile, or allow the blackness of bronze to come forth. Nature restrains nature...

24. *Another Tincture of Amalgamation.*
Take 1 ounce of arsenic, and half an ounce of nitre, and 2 ounces of the cortex of the tender little leaves of *Persea*,[26] and half (an ounce) of salt, and 1 ounce of mulberry juice, and equal parts of scissile, rub with vinegar, or urine, or of *unslaked lime of urine*, until a liquid is formed. Immerse in this *glowing leaves* of *Venus* growing black, and thou takest away the blackness. Nature conquers nature.

Thou hast all things which are required for gold and silver, nothing is left out, nothing is wanting, except the elevation of the vapour and of water.[27] But these I have omitted of purpose, seeing that I have dealt with them freely in my other writings. In this writing farewell.

[24] Asterites is arsenical pyrites (identical with androdamas); aphroselinum is selenite, sulphate of lime (Steele 125).
[25] Arsenical fumes of furnaces.
[26] "A sacred fruit-bearing tree of Egypt and Persia" (*OED*).   [27] Suggesting the process of distillation.

5 Anonymous (first or second century AD)
Dialogue of Cleopatra and the Philosophers

The Cleopatra of this early alchemical dialogue is not the famous Cleopatra VII (69–30 BC), last queen of the Ptolemy dynasty and lover of Mark Antony. Along with Mary Prophetess and Zosimos's Theosebia, this Cleopatra occupies a high place in alchemical lore as one of very few ancient female adepts who possessed the secret of the philosopher's stone. She thus became a revered authority widely cited in alchemical literature, and to her the invention of the alembic is sometimes attributed. The following *Dialogue of Cleopatra* is from the *Book of Komarios* (Komarios being the reputed teacher of Cleopatra), one of many surviving Greek alchemical manuscripts. The author of this *Dialogue* and others featuring Cleopatra probably lived in the first or second century AD and was perhaps part of the richly eclectic culture of Graeco-Roman Alexandria. He invests his work with elements from earlier Egyptian culture: for example, the legendary Ostanes, whom Pliny regards as the introducer of magic into Greece (*Natural History* 30:1), is presented as a participant in the dialogue. But pervasive allegory and symbolism are its most distinguishing features, lightly concealing the alchemical content beneath; as Ostanes says to Cleopatra, "In thee is concealed a strange and terrible mystery. Enlighten us, casting your light upon the elements." Cleopatra's response figures forth several highly visual motifs that were to become alchemical commonplaces: the analogy between the plant kingdom and the distillation process, or that between human birth and the formation of the philosopher's stone, or the death–resurrection motif, as applied to materials within the alchemical vas. In these respects, the Cleopatra *Dialogue* looks forward directly to the visions of Zosimos in the fourth century and more distantly to much of the alchemical imagery and rhetoric of the Renaissance. The text is taken from F. Sherwood Taylor's *The Alchemists: Founders of Modern Chemistry* (London: William Heinemann, 1951), 57–9, and is based on Berthelot's French translation in his *Collection des anciens alchimistes grecs.*

Then Cleopatra said to the philosophers. "Look at the nature of plants, whence they come. For some come down from the mountains and grow out of the earth, and some grow up from the valleys and some come from the plains. But look how they develop, for it is at certain seasons and days that you must gather them, and you take them from the islands of the sea, and from the most lofty place. And look at the air which ministers to them and the nourishment circling around them, that they perish not nor die. Look at the divine water which gives them drink and the air that governs them after they have been given a body in a single being."

Ostanes[1] and those with him answered Cleopatra. "In thee is concealed a strange and terrible mystery. Enlighten us, casting your light upon the elements. Tell us how the highest descends to the lowest and how the lowest rises to the highest, and how that which is in the midst approaches the highest and is united to it, and what is the element which accomplishes these things. And tell us how the blessed waters visit the corpses lying in Hades fettered and afflicted in darkness and how the medicine of Life reaches them and rouses them as if wakened by their possessors from sleep;[2] and how the new waters, both brought forth on the bier and coming after the light penetrate them at the beginning of their prostration and how a cloud supports them and how the cloud supporting the waters rises from the sea."

And the philosophers, considering what had been revealed to them, rejoyced.

Cleopatra said to them. "The waters, when they come, awake the bodies and the spirits which are imprisoned and weak. For they again undergo oppression and are enclosed in Hades, and yet in a little while they grow and rise up and put on divers glorious colors like the flowers in springtime and the spring itself rejoices and is glad at the beauty that they wear.[3]

For I tell this to you who are wise: when you take plants, elements, and stones from their places, they appear to you to be mature. But they are not mature until the fire has tested them. When they are clothed in the glory from the fire and shining color thereof, then rather will appear their hidden glory, their sought-for beauty, being transformed to the divine state of fusion. For they are nourished in the fire and the embryo grows little by little nourished in its mother's womb, and when the appointed month approaches is not restrained from issuing forth.[4] Such is the procedure of this worthy art. The waves and surges one after another in Hades wound them in the tomb where they lie. When the tomb is opened they issue from Hades as the babe from the womb."

[1] According to legend, Ostanes or Osthanes was one of the earliest Persian magi who also possessed alchemical wisdom; Pliny (*Natural History* 30:1) deplores the fact that magic, having originated in Persia with Zoroaster, was introduced by Ostanes into Greek culture. The philosopher Democritus was regarded as his pupil.

[2] The imagery of rising and falling in this passage reflects the vaporization and condensation of the liquids undergoing distillation. While purification of alchemical "spirit" continues, the corrupt "bodies" (*prima materia*) lie in dark imprisonment (Hades) at the bottom of the vas, awaiting rebirth.

[3] The imagery of death and resurrection in this passage signals reunification of the purified body and spirit of the metals and the rise of the philosopher's stone.

[4] Cleopatra's statement is a very early instance of use of the analogy between the the birth of a child and preparation of the philosopher's stone.

6 Anonymous (late third century AD)
From Leyden Papyrus X and the Stockholm Papyrus

The following selections represent the practical or "exoteric" side of alchemical writing with its exclusive concern for the physical and technical processes required to produce an object or substance or to improve that which is "natural" by means of artifice. Thus the recipes illustrate the close connections between early chemistry and metallurgy, dyeing, jewelry making, writing techniques, and various other crafts. The style is clear, simple, and methodical, vastly different from the highly imagistic allegories of the *Dialogue of Cleopatra and the Philosophers* and the *Visions* of Zosimos of Panopolis. If one ignores the persistent uncertainties about substances, measures, and durations of processes, it might be said that here are reasonable examples of technical writing – overlooking, of course, the rather common emphasis on fraud and deception.

Leyden Papyrus X and the Stockholm Papyrus, which bear the names of the cities in which they are deposited, are written in Greek – probably by the same writer – and date from the end of the third century AD. They are, in the words of Earle R. Caley, the translator, "by far the earliest original historical evidence that we have in our possession concerning the nature and the extent of ancient chemical knowledge" (1149). Leyden Papyrus X includes 111 recipes, often written in an "abbreviated, incomplete form such as workers, more or less familiar with the nature of the process, would use" (1150). In contrast to the metallurgical emphasis of the Leyden manuscript, the 154 recipes in the Stockholm Papyrus deal with a variety of other chemical arts, such as making dyes and imitations of precious stones.

For translation of the complete texts, notes, and additional commentary, see Earle Radcliffe Caley, "The Leyden Papyrus X: An English Translation with Brief Notes," *Journal of Chemical Education* 3,10 (Oct. 1926): 1149–66, and "The Stockholm Papyrus: An English Translation with Brief Notes," *Journal of Chemical Education* 4,8 (Aug. 1927): 979–1002. Reprinted with kind permission of the *Journal of Chemical Education*.

From Leyden Papyrus X

8. Manufacture of Asem.[1]
Take soft tin in small pieces, purified four times; take 4 parts of it and 3 parts of pure white copper and 1 part of asem. Melt, and after the casting, clean several times and make with

---

[1] An alloy intended to imitate gold or silver (Caley 1151).

it whatever you wish to. It will be asem of the first quality, which will deceive even the artisans.

15. The Coloration of Gold.
To color gold to render it fit for usage. Misy,[2] salt, and vinegar accruing from the purification of gold; mix it all and throw in the vessel (which contains it) the gold described in the preceding preparation; let it remain some time, (and then) having drawn (the gold) from the vessel, heat it upon the coals; then again throw it in the vessel which contains the above-mentioned preparation; do this several times until it becomes fit for use.

25. Gold Polish.
For treating gold, otherwise called, purifying gold and rendering it brilliant: Misy, 4 parts; alum, 4 parts; salt, 4 parts. Pulverize with water. And having coated the gold (with it), place it in an earthenware vessel deposited in a furnace and luted with clay, (and heat) until the above-named substances have become molten, then withdraw it and scour carefully.

34. A Procedure for Writing in Letters of Gold.
To write in letters of gold, take some mercury, pour it in a suitable vessel, and add to it some gold in leaves; when the gold appears dissolved in the mercury, agitate sharply; add a little gum, 1 grain for example, and, (after) letting stand, write in the letters of gold.

38. For Giving to Objects of Copper the Appearance of Gold.
And neither touch nor rubbing against the touchstone[3] will detect them, but they can serve especially for (the manufacture of) a ring of fine appearance. Here is the preparation for this. Gold and lead are ground to a fine powder like flour, 2 parts of lead for 1 of gold, then having mixed, they are incorporated with gum, and one coats the ring with this mixture; then it is heated. One repeats this several times until the object has taken the color. It is difficult to detect (the fraud), because rubbing gives the mark of a gold object, and the heat consumes the lead but not the gold.

43. Testing of Gold.
If you wish to test the purity of gold, remelt it and heat it: if it is pure it will keep its color after heating and remain like a piece of money. If it becomes white, it contains silver; if it becomes rougher and harder some copper and tin; if it blackens and softens, lead.

87. Doubling of Gold.
For augmenting the weight of gold. Melt (it) with a fourth part of cadmia, and it will become heavier and harder.

---

[2] A mixture of iron and copper sulphate.
[3] A touchstone is a black siliceous stone used to test the purity of gold and silver by the color of the streak produced on it by rubbing it with either metal.

95. The Preparation of Purple [dye].

Break into small pieces stone of Phrygia; put it to boiling, and having immersed the wool, leave it until it cools. Then throwing in the vessel a mina[4] of seaweed, put it to boiling and throw in it (again) a mina of seaweed. Let it boil and throw the wool into it, and letting cool, wash in sea water . . . [the stone of Phrygia is roasted before being broken] . . . until the purple coloration appears.

96. Dyeing with Purple (Two Methods).

Grind lime with water and let it stand over night. Having decanted, deposit the wool in the liquid for a day; take it out (and) dry it; having sprinkled the alkanet[5] with some vinegar, put it to boiling and throw the wool in it and it will come out dyed in purple . . . alkanet boiled with water and natron produces the purple color.

Then dry the wool, and dye it as follows: Boil the seaweed with water and when it has been exhausted, throw in the water an imperceptible quantity of copperas, in order to develop the purple, and then plunge the wool in it, and it will be dyed. If there is too much copperas, it becomes darker.

From the Stockholm Papyrus

1. Manufacture of Silver.

Plunge Cyprian copper, which is well worked and shingled[6] for use, into dyer's vinegar and alum and let soak for three days. Then for every mina of copper mix in 6 drachmas each of earth of Chios, salt of Cappadocia and lamellose alum, and cast. Cast skillfully, however, and it will prove to be regular silver. Place in it not more than 20 drachmas of good, unfalsified, proof silver, which the whole mixture retains and (this) will make it imperishable.

18. Manufacture of a Pearl.

Take and grind an easily pulverized stone such as window mica. Take gum tragacanth and let it soften for ten days in cow's milk. When it has become soft, dissolve it until it becomes as thick as glue. Melt Tyrian wax; add to this, in addition, the white of egg. The mercury should amount to 2 parts and the stone 3 parts, but all remaining substances 1 part apiece. Mix (the ground mica and the molten wax) and knead the mixture with mercury. Soften the paste in the gum solution and the contents of the hen's egg. Mix all of the liquids in this way with the paste. Then make the pearl that you intend to, according to a pattern. The paste very shortly turns to stone. Make deep round impressions and bore through it while it is moist. Let the pearl thus solidify and polish it highly. If managed properly it will excel the natural.

---

[4] A unit of weight used in ancient Egypt and Greece.
[5] Red dye produced from the root of the European plant, *Alkanna tinctoria*.
[6] To subject a mass of iron to "blows with a hammer so [as] to expel impurities" (*OED*).

101. Cold Dyeing of Purple Which Is Done in the True Way.

Keep this as a secret matter because the purple has an extremely beautiful luster. Take scum of woad[7] from the dyer, and a sufficient portion of foreign alkanet of about the same weight as the scum – the scum is very light – and triturate it in the mortar. Thus dissolve the alkanet by grinding in the scum and it will give off its essence. Then take the brilliant color prepared by the dyer – if from kermes[8] it is better, or else from kirmnos – heat, and put this liquor into half of the scum in the mortar. Then put the wool in and color it unmordanted[9] and you will find it beyond all description.

[7] A blue dye-stuff extracted from the European plant, *Isatis tinctoria*.
[8] A red dye produced from the dried bodies of a scale insect, *Kermes ilices*.
[9] I.e., without a substance used to fix the color in the wool.

7   Zosimos of Panopolis (*fl. c.* 300 AD)
Of Virtue, Lessons 1–3

Zosimos of Panopolis has a much stronger claim to historical reality than any of the other early alchemical writers introduced thus far. He is thought to have lived in the late third and early fourth centuries AD and, like the author of the *Dialogue of Cleopatra and the Philosophers*, to have been deeply influenced by the tangle of religious and philosophical elements that constituted the culture of Alexandria at that time. Garth Fowden speaks of him as "a man of strong spiritual urges and little conventional scholarship, who moved in an eclectic milieu compounded of Platonism and gnosticism together with Judaism and…the 'oriental' wisdom of Hermes and Zoroaster" (120). Although Zosimos and his "spiritual sister" Theosebia are assumed to have had practical experience in alchemical laboratories, they also believed that its primary goal was purificatory and contemplative, esoteric not exoteric. This is apparent in the broadly allusive *Visions*, where Zosimos's syncretic religious and intellectual environment is reflected in dense allegory, enigmatic expression, and obscure symbolism. In the selection that follows, the dream vision itself – with its motifs of transformation from body into spirit, torture and violence, death and regeneration, and cryptic humanoid figures – has made Zosimos a challenging subject for the Jungian analyst no less than for the student of alchemy or of the fantastic.

The following translation is from F. Sherwood Taylor, "The Visions of Zosimos," *Ambix* 1,1 (May 1937): 88–92, and is reprinted with the kind permission of *Ambix*. Additional readings: Garth Fowden, *The Egyptian Hermes* (Princeton: Princeton University Press, 1986), 120–26; for texts and psychoanalytic commentary, see C. G. Jung, *Alchemical Studies*, trans. R. F. C. Hull (Princeton: Princeton University Press, 1967), 57–108.

Lesson 1.

1. The composition of waters,[1] the movement, growth, removal, and restitution of corporeal nature, the separation of the spirit from the body, and the fixation of the spirit on the body are not due to foreign natures, but to one single nature reacting on itself, a single species, such as the hard bodies of metals and the moist juices of plants.

---

[1] More than mere physical element, the "waters" here introduced are the means of transmutation: the agent of both the "death" of the metals and their revivification, as figured forth in Zosimos's visions. For Jung, the *aqua divina* "transformed the *nigredo* into the *albedo* through the miraculous 'washing' (*ablutio*); it animated inert matter, [and] made the dead to rise again" (*Alchemical Studies*, 68).

And in this system, single and of many colours, is comprised a research, multiple and varied, subordinated to lunar influences and to the measure of time, which rule the end and the increase according to which the nature transforms itself.

2. Saying these things I went to sleep, and I saw a sacrificing priest standing before me at the top of an altar in the form of a bowl.[2] This altar had 15 steps leading up to it. Then the priest stood up and I heard a voice from above saying to me, 'I have accomplished the descent of the 15 steps of darkness and the ascent of the steps of light and it is he who sacrifices, that renews me, casting away the coarseness of the body; and being consecrated priest by necessity, I become a spirit.' And having heard the voice of him who stood on the bowl-shaped altar, I questioned him, wishing to find out who he was. He answered me in a weak voice, saying 'I am Ion, the priest of the sanctuary, and I have survived intolerable violence. For one came headlong in the morning, dismembering me with a sword, and tearing me asunder according to the rigour of harmony. And flaying my head with the sword which he held fast, he mingled my bones with my flesh and burned them in the fire of the treatment, until I learnt by the transformation of the body to become a spirit.'

And while yet he spoke these words to me, and I forced him to speak of it, his eyes became as blood and he vomited up all his flesh. And I saw him as a mutilated little image of a man, tearing himself with his own teeth and falling away.

And being afraid I awoke and thought 'Is this not the situation of the waters?' I believed that I had understood it well, and I fell asleep anew. And I saw the same altar in the form of a bowl and at the top the water bubbling, and many people in it endlessly. And there was no one outside the altar whom I could ask. I then went up towards the altar to view the spectacle. And I saw a little man, a barber, whitened by years, who said to me 'What are you looking at?' I answered him that I marvelled at the boiling of the water and the men, burnt yet living. And he answered me saying 'It is the place of the exercise called preserving (embalming). For those men who wish to obtain virtue come hither and become spirits, fleeing from the body.' Therefore I said to him 'Are you a spirit?' And he answered and said 'A spirit and a guardian of spirits.' And while he told us these things, and while the boiling increased and the people wailed, I saw a man of copper having in his hand a writing tablet of lead. And he spoke aloud, looking at the tablet, 'I counsel those under punishment to calm themselves, and each to take in his hand a leaden writing tablet and to write with their own hands. I counsel them to keep their faces upwards and their mouths open until your grapes be grown.' The act followed the word and the master of the house said to me, 'You have seen. You have stretched your neck on high and you have seen what is done.' And I said that I saw, and I said to myself, 'This man of copper you have seen is the sacrificing priest and the sacrifice, and he that vomited out his own flesh. And authority over this water and the men under punishment was given to him.'

And having had this vision I awoke again and I said to myself 'What is the occasion of this vision? Is not this the white and yellow water, boiling, divine (sulphurous)?' And I found that I understood it well. And I said that it was fair to speak and fair to listen, and fair to give and fair to receive, and fair to be poor and fair to be rich. For how does the nature learn to give and to receive? The copper man gives and the watery stone receives;

---

[2] I.e. the hermetic "egg" or vessel in which the violent torture of the ingredients of the philosopher's stone takes place, the transformation of the material into the spiritual, here personified in the priest Ion.

the metal gives and the plant receives; the stars give and the flowers receive; the sky gives and the earth receives; the thunderclaps give the fire that darts from them.

For all things are interwoven and separate afresh, and all things are mingled and all things combine, all things are mixed and all unmixed, all things are moistened and all things dried and all things flower and blossom in the altar shaped like a bowl. For each, it is by method, by measure and weight of the 4 elements, that the interlacing and dissociation of all is accomplished. No bond can be made without method. It is a natural method, breathing in and breathing out, keeping the arrangements of the method, increasing or decreasing them. When all things, in a word, come to harmony by division and union, without the methods being neglected in any way, the nature is transformed. For the nature being turned upon itself is transformed; and it is the nature and the bond of the virtue of the whole world.

And that I may not write many things to you, my friend, build a temple of one stone, like ceruse in appearance, like alabaster, like marble of Proconnesus,[3] having neither beginning nor end in its construction. Let it have within it a spring of pure water glittering like the sun. Notice on which side is the entry of the temple and, taking your sword in hand, so seek for the entry. For narrow is the place at which the temple opens. A serpent lies before the entry guarding the temple; seize him and sacrifice him. Skin him and, taking his flesh and bones, separate his parts; then reuniting the members with the bones at the entry of the temple, make of them a stepping stone, mount thereon, and enter. You will find there what you seek. For the priest, the man of copper, whom you see seated in the spring and gathering his colour, do not regard him as a man of copper; for he has changed the colour of his nature and become a man of silver. If you wish, after a little time you will have him as a man of gold.

Lesson 2.

1. Again I wished to ascend the seven steps and to look upon the seven punishments, and, as it happened, on only one of the days did I effect an ascent. Retracing my steps I then went up many times. And then on returning I could not find the way and fell into deep discouragement, not seeing how to get out, and fell asleep.

And I saw in my sleep a little man, a barber, clad in a red robe and royal dress, standing outside the place of the punishments, and he said to me 'Man, what are you doing?' And I said to him 'I stand here because, having missed every road, I find myself at a loss.' And he said to me 'Follow me.' And I went out and followed him. And being near to the place of the punishments, I saw the little barber who was leading me cast into the place of punishment, and all his body was consumed by fire.

2. On seeing this I fled and trembled with fear, and awoke and said to myself 'What is it that I have seen?' And again I reasoned, and perceiving that the little barber is the man of copper clothed in red raiment, I said 'I have understood well; this is the man of copper; one must first cast him into the place of punishment.' Again my soul desired to ascend the third step also. And again I went along the road, and as I came near to the punishment again I lost my way, losing sight of the path, wandering in despair. And again in the same

---

[3] The temple built of "one stone" symbolizes the philosopher's stone; Proconnesus is an island in the Sea of Marmora, famous for its marble quarry.

way I saw a white-haired old man of such whiteness as to dazzle the eyes. His name was Agathodæmon,[4] and the white old man turned and looked on me for a full hour. And I asked of him 'Show me the right way.' But he did not turn towards me, but hastened to follow the right route. And going and coming thence, he quickly gained the altar. As I went up to the altar, I saw the whitened old man and he was cast into the punishment. O gods of heavenly natures! Immediately he was embraced entirely by the flames. What a terrible story, my brother! For from the great strength of the punishment his eyes became full of blood. And I asked him, saying, 'Why do you lie there?' But he opened his mouth and said to me 'I am the man of lead and I am undergoing intolerable violence.' And so I awoke in great fear and I sought in me the reason of this fact. I reflected and said 'I clearly understand that thus one must cast out the lead, and indeed the vision is one of the combination of liquids.'

Lesson 3.

1. And again I saw the same divine and sacred bowl-shaped altar, and I saw a priest clothed in white celebrating those fearful mysteries, and I said "Who is this?' And, answering, he said to me 'This is the priest of the Sanctuary. He wishes to put blood into the bodies, to make clear the eyes, and to raise up the dead.'

And so, falling again, I fell asleep another little while, and while I mounted the fourth step I saw, coming from the East, one who had in his hand a sword. And I saw another behind him, bearing a round white shining object beautiful to behold, of which the name was the meridian of the Sun, and as I drew near to the place of punishments, he that bore the sword told me 'Cut off his head and sacrifice his meat and his muscles by parts, to the end that his flesh may first be boiled according to method and that he may then undergo the punishment.' And so, awaking again, I said 'Well do I understand that these things concern the liquids of the art of the metals.' And again he that bore the sword said 'You have fulfilled the seven steps beneath.' And the other said at the same time as the casting out of the lead by all liquids, 'The work is completed.'

---

[4] To Agathodæmon was attributed an alchemical commentary on an oracle by Orpheus addressed to Osiris (*HMES* 1:195). Jung identifies him with the transformative substance (*Alchemical Studies* 74n27).

8 Stephanos of Alexandria (first half of seventh century AD)

From *The Great and Sacred Art of the Making of Gold*

Stephanos of Alexandria was a philosopher and public lecturer who flourished in Constantinople under the Byzantine emperor Herakleios (610–41 AD). His subjects included Plato, Aristotle (upon whom there is extant a commentary bearing Stephanos' name), as well as mathematics, astronomy, and music. Although attribution of the *Great and Sacred Art of the Making of Gold* to Stephanos is at times disputed for stylistic reasons, it is accepted as authentic by the translator, F. Sherwood Taylor, on the grounds that its Neoplatonism and numerous scientific allusions would have been familiar to him. This work, known also as *De chrysopoeia*, the Greek word for gold-making, was much copied and widely cited by Byzantine alchemists. If its highly rhetorical, enthusiastic style jars with that of Stephanos' scientific works, this may result, according to Taylor, from the fact that "a declamatory and rhetorical style may have been thought appropriate to lectures upon a subject of arcane character" (116). Such stylistic excesses may also be explained by the fact that the *Great and Sacred Art* consists of nine *lectures*, undoubtedly presented orally to their original audiences. It should be noted that early Greek scientific and alchemical treatises – such as those of Pseudo-Democritus and Cleopatra included in this collection – frequently employ ornate rhetoric. Whatever the reasons, *Lecture I*, in particular, is an unadulterated example of the author's rhapsodizing on the glory, beauty, and power of Nature and God. While not wholly abandoning this mystical style, beginning with the *Second Lecture*, Stephanos turns to subjects that are, at times, more philosophical and even empirical: the nature of the originating monad and of harmony; or processes related to dyeing, medicine, and "the marvellous making of gold."

The following translation of selections from the Greek is by F. Sherwood Taylor and appeared as "The Alchemical Works of Stephanos of Alexandria. Part I," *Ambix* 1,1 (May 1937): 116–39. Reprinted with the kind permission of *Ambix*. Additional readings: C. A. Browne, "Rhetorical and Religious Aspects of Greek Alchemy," *Ambix* 2, 3–4 (Dec. 1946): 129–37.

Lecture 1, with the Help of God.
Having praised God the cause of all good things and the King of all, and his only begotten Son resplendent before the ages together with the Holy Spirit, and having earnestly intreated for ourselves the illumination of the knowledge of Him, we will begin to gather the fairest fruits of the work in hand, of this very treatise, and we trust to track down the

truth. Now from a true theory of nature[1] our problem must be set out. O nature superior to nature conquering the natures, O nature become superior to itself, well regulated, transcending and surpassing the natures, O nature one and the same yielding and fulfilling the All,[2] O union completed and separation united, O identical and nowise alien nature, supplying the All from itself, O matter immaterial holding matter fast, O nature conquering and rejoicing in nature, O heavenly nature making the spiritual existence to shine forth, O bodiless body, making bodies bodiless, O course of the moon illuminating the whole order of the universe, O most generic species and most specific genus, O nature truly superior to nature conquering the natures, tell what sort of nature thou art – that which with affection receives itself from itself again, verily that which yields sulphur without fire and has the fire-resisting power, the archetype of many names and name of many forms, the experienced nature and the unfolding, the many-coloured painted rainbow, that which discloses from itself the All, O nature itself and displaying its nature from no other nature, O like bringing to light from its like a thing of like nature, O sea becoming as the ocean drawing up as vapour its many-coloured pearls, O conjunction of the tetrasomia[3] adorned upon the surface, O inscription of the threefold triad and completion of the universal seal, body of magnesia by which the whole mystery is brought about, O golden-roofed stream of heaven, and silver-crested spirit sent forth from the sea, O thou that hast the silver-breasted garment and providest the liquid golden curls, O fair exercise of the wisest intellects, O wise all-creative power of men most holy, O sea inscrutable by uninitiated men, O ignorance seized on beforehand by vainglorious men, O smoky kindling of disdainful mankind, O uncovered light of pious men, O countenance contemplated by virtuous men, O sweetly breathing flower of practical philosophers, O perfect preparation of a single species, O work of wisdom, having a beauty composed of intellect, O thou that flashest such a beam, from a single being upon all, O moon drawing a light from the light of the sun, O single nature itself and no other nature, rejoicing and rejoiced over, mastering and mastered, saved and saviour, what have you in common with the multitude of material things, since one thing is natural and is a single nature conquering the All? Of what kind art thou, tell me, of what kind? To you who are of good understanding I dedicate this great gift, to you who are clothed with virtue, who are adorned with respect to theoretical practice and settled in practical theory. Of what kind, show us, thou who hast indicated beforehand that we should have such a gift. Of what nature, I shall tell and will not hide. I confess the grace of the giving of light from above, which is given to us by the lights of the father. Hear ye as intelligences like to the angels. Put away the material theory so that ye may be deemed worthy to see with your intellectual eyes the hidden mystery. For there is need of a single natural <thing> and of one nature conquering the all. Of such a kind, now clearly to be told you, that the nature rejoices in the nature and the nature masters the nature and the nature conquers the nature. For it rejoices on account of the nature being its own, and

---

[1] In a manner reminiscent of pseudo-Democritus, Stephanos rhapsodizes on "nature," which is Taylor's translation of the Greek *physis*: "*that combination of the four elements which characterises* [a body] *and gives rise to its properties*" (135n23). Here the immediate context is the properties of metals and their interaction.

[2] The conception of the unity of all things underlies much alchemical thought, the metals consisting of both body and soul and existing in both living and dead states.

[3] An alloy of the four base metals.

it masters it because it has kinship with it, and, superior to nature, it conquers the nature when the corporeal operation of the process shall fulfil the initiation into the mysteries. For when the incorruptible body shall be released from death, and when it shall transform the fulfilment which has become spiritual, then superior to nature it is as a marvellous spirit; then it masters the body moved (by it), then it rejoices as over its own habitation, then it conquers that which in disembodied fashion haunts the whole which is engendered of the whole, that is admirable above nature. Which I say to you is the comprehensive magnesia.[4] Who will not wonder at the coral of gold perfected from thee? From thee the whole mystery is fully brought to perfection, thou alone shalt have no fear of the knowledge of the same, on thee will be spread the radiant eastern cloud; thou shalt carry in thyself as a guest the multiform images of Aphrodite, the cupbearer again serving the fire-throwing bearer of coals (then carrying such a brightness from afar, in bridal fashion you veil the same, you receive the undefiled mystery of nature). I will show moreover also the lustre of thy nature, I will begin to indicate thy multiform images. For then he, who intelligently interweaves thee that hast fire within thee, rekindles the fiery thing. For looking on thy many-coloured visions I shall be powerless as I circle round its beauties. For thy radiant pearl blinds the sight of my eye. Thy phengites[5] rekindling astounds all my vision, thy shining radiance gladdens all my heart, O nature truly superior to nature, conquering the natures. Thou, the whole, art the one nature. The same by which the whole becomes the work. For by an odd number[6] thy all-cosmos is systematized. For then thou shalt understand in what respects thou shalt look ahead, then thou shalt discover in what things shall be thy ambit, then thou shalt stop the struggles of the place, then thou shalt disclose the kingly purple, which also thou shalt bring with thee by the help of thy maiden. Then will not be the recent labour but a couch canopied with gold, then not a multiform ability but an all-wise sagacity, then no deprivation of virtuous men is found, but a fruition of perfect men is displayed. For such is the measure of it found in the odd number.

Thus those full of virtue will discover thee; hear ye who are lovers of wisdom and know the mighty deeds of the all-ruling God. For he it is that furnishes all wisdom, unapproachable light of houses, light which illumines each man as he comes into the world. For we are nothing apart from his Supreme Divinity; altogether nothing is the gift which is sought, in respect of his blessedness. Approach, O lovers of virtue, to that immaterial desire. Learn how sweet is the light of God. Unworthy are the things which are now wondered at, in respect of that happy lot. Alone we are made friends with him by love, and we receive from him the wisdom springing forth as an abyss from the abyss, that we may be enabled by the grace of our Lord Jesus Christ to gush forth rivers of living water; so that wondering at such wisdom of the demiurge we may praise his great kindness towards us. Why should we marvel at the species Chrysocorallos?[7] We should wonder

---

[4] A commonly used but extremely obscure concept in Greek alchemy. Taylor notes that Stephanos appears to identify it with the "universal nature underlying the whole universe" (136n34). In later alchemical writing, it retains a broad range of meanings, including the quintessence or an ingredient of the philosopher's stone.

[5] "A transparent or translucent type of stone" (*OED*), perhaps here the moonstone.

[6] One, the odd number, was the source of All, according to the Pythagorean philosophy of Stephanos (see also the emphasis on harmony and proportion in the *Second Lecture*).

[7] "Gold solder," a name given to some mineral or minerals in ancient times (*OED*).

rather at the infinite Beauty. So also I will fulfil your desire, that you may be made worthy to love such a One <and> with hymnody to discourse of the more than good goodness of God.

Second Lecture of the same Stephanos with the Help of God.

The multitude of numbers compounded together has its existence from one atom and natural monad; this, which itself exerts a mutual condition, comprehends and rules over the infinite as emanating from itself. For the *monad* is so called from its *remaining* immutable and unmoved. For it displays a circular and spherical contemplation of numbers like to itself, I speak of a completion of the five numbers and of the six. For from these they come round again to themselves. And every side of a rectangle generated from the same length has kinship to its like that it may restore a perfect fulfilment. For the sixtieth part of every great quantity and of fractions, taking origin from it <the monad> and returning again to it, being contracted together, complete the natural monad. The symbol of every circular sphere is the centre, likewise of every triangle and plane and solid figure set out by lines; let this same be thought of.

Also of the musical learning, both the lowest strings and that next the first, whether of four strings or upon the third ratio, that which is before it must be the antecedent and that after it the consequent, by which we preserve the binding together of the proportions and of the whole scale of harmony as a result of such musical learning.

For they who pluck the strings say that Orpheus made melody with rhythmical sounds so that the symphony should re-echo the co-ordinated movement of the elements and the sounding melody should be harmoniously perfected. For from the one instrument the whole composition takes its origin, whence also the organization of the articulate body is ordered in the bones and joints and parts and nerves, and by the plectrum of the air, given forth in the fashion of a moving instrument, a voice is sent forth to the One which is joined to its essence and which conquers and organizes it by its own life: the very mode and blending of the air. For of two extreme qualities there is found one mediator and conciliator which preserves the qualities of both on account of its resemblance and close kinship to them. And also the movement of the pole being spherical and stable, the light of the hemisphere which is above the earth, arising from the line dividing the mundane and the diaphanous pole, also radiates forth the fires of the sunlight <derived> from that which supplies it to all things. For from it not only do the stars partake of the order of the light, but also the appearance of the moon, giving out rays derived from the light, displays its nightly allotted torchbearing. And you shall have all such things to speak of singly, as derived from one of them, and as the essence of the very first returned again; they preserve the things of the nature and fulfil the contemplation. But were there time enough to consider our discourse in the progress of a proem, (I would speak of) that which falls from the moon's waning, how it is found, how it is treated, and how it has an unburnt nature. O wisdom of teaching of such a preparation, displaying the work, O moon clad in white and vehemently shining abroad whiteness, let us learn what is the lunar radiance that we may not miss what is doubtful. For the same is the whitening snow, the brilliant eye of whiteness, the bridal procession-robe of the management of the process, the stainless chiton, the mind-constructed beauty of fair form, the whitest composition of the perfection, the coagulated milk of fulfilment, the Moon-froth of the sea of dawn;

the magnesia of Lydia, the Italian stibnite, the pyrites of Achæa, that of Albania,[8] the many-named matter of the good work, that which lulls the All to sleep, that which bears the One which is the All, that which fulfils the wondrous work...Speak, tell to us the secrets of the work [of 'the marvellous making of gold']. 'After the cleaning of the copper', and how is one to clean the copper yet bearing all its *ios*?[9] How? I will tell you the accurate meaning of the phrase – Aphrodite walking through a cloud. 'After the cleaning of the copper', that is a trituration[10] well managed, a consideration well taught beforehand; 'After the attenuation of the copper', that is a finer condition of trituration, he also speaks of the blackness placed upon it and following upon these for the purpose of the later whitening; then is the solid yellowing. For when it shall spurn the blackness of the wrinkled crust, it is transformed to whiteness; then the moon of shining light shall send forth the rays; then <one comes> to the later whitening, when you shall see the white compound. For when the full of the moon appears, then the full moon discloses its light. Then solid is the yellowing. What is this? Say. The whiteness perceived. And how do you render the white yellow? Ye wisest of men, over-pass the reasoning, this answer is a secret, a mystic speech and consideration. I will tell you the hidden mystery, whence it is proclaimed above you. 'After the cleaning of the copper and its later attenuation and the blackening for the later whitening, then is the solid yellowing.' When you see the whitening taking place within it, recognize the concealed yellowing, then know the whitening as being yellow; then also being white, it becomes yellow by the hidden yellowness, by possessing the depths of its heart, by having the corporeal possession of the whiteness of the silver and, unutterably, the pervading whiteness in it. 'Then is the solid yellowing.' What is this? That which has become white, it is the yellow. For the same white appears in the colour, but the yellow nature overrules it. 'Nothing is left remaining, nothing is left behind except the vapour and the raising of the water'. Consider the most ancient one.[11] Do you not see what the wise man has declared? Thus he speaks in riddles as completely as possible. Thus he declares, as a teacher demonstrates everything, saying 'nothing is left remaining, nothing is lacking, except the vapour and the raising of the water'. Having shown in this the preparation of the whole, rendering all in few words, that ye may not overwhelm the moving things with much matter, that ye may not think about saffron of Cilicia and the plant of anagallis, and the Pontic rhubarb[12] for themselves, and of other juices, gall of quadrupeds and certain beasts, of stones and of destructive minerals, things that are dissimilar to the perfection-making, single and one nature, that men wandering shall not be led away from the truth, in order that in a natural existence they shall not seek for a non-existent tendency. What else? The most eminent man and counsellor of all virtue turns them around and draws them to the view of truth, that you may not, as I said (take note of) material furnaces and apparatus of glasses, alembics, various flasks, kerotakides[13] and sublimates. And those who

---

[8] In ancient alchemical treatises, substances frequently bear the names of their places of origin; here, Stephanos appears to refer to agents used for "whitening," i.e., the production of silver, associated with the moon.

[9] The rust or encrustation that must be removed if the metal is to be clean.

[10] To reduce to fine particles or powder by rubbing, bruising, pounding, crushing, or grinding.

[11] Democritus is the "most ancient one" and the "wise man."

[12] Plants from which yellow dye, probably used in the tinting of metals, could be made.

[13] Or *kerotakis*, a reflux apparatus used for treating metals with vapors for the purpose of coloring them (Roberts, *Mirror*, 108); its invention was attributed to Mary the Jewess.

are occupied with such things in vain, the burden of weariness is declared by them. But see how the All is fulfilled in the phrase. 'Nothing is left remaining, nothing is lacking save the vapour and the raising of the water.' What kind of vapour? Say. What is the vapour and what is the work brought to perfection by it? Show us most clearly the way in which we may recognize the power of the word. And on this matter the philosopher says: 'the vapour is the work of the composition of the whole', that which shines brightly through the divine water, that which makes the trituration naturally, that which appears in the course of the method, and is apprehended intellectually. The vapour is the unfolding of the work, the level manifestation, the thread bought with silver, the air-displaying voyage, the Celtic nard, the Atlantic sea, the Britannic metal,[14] the ocean garlanding the world, the unmeasured abyss, the sphere-shaped universe, the heavenly body, that which encompasses and embraces the all, the despised species, the longed-for contemplation, the sought-for spectacle, the one whole and whole one, the holy whitening of the whole worthy work, the whole preparation, the one work of wisdom, the conclusion of the fulfilment, that which is triturated and well managed, the perfectly fulfilled. 'For nothing is left remaining except the vapour and the raising of the water.' Having been wisely led on the path with respect to the way of the vapour, I will pursue my speech upon the raising of the water. What then is this which has been brought in? What is this raising of the water? Tell us, O guide: fulfil the gifts of thy grace. Enlighten our dim-sighted eyes, make plain the articulate substance of your doctrine, what is this raising of the water? And he is not silent on this matter: he says, the unmixed beauty does not receive into itself matter. The immaterial being, it is a single composition, the good thing of a myriad names. For being of a single essence, it is reduced into itself. Around it, it extinguishes the single ray. He does not wholly put in the moistening juices. For he did not perceive the loss, the life of the liquids. For he rejects the flowings of the water. For how is one to see the motion of that which does not shake off these things? Nothing is able to be filled full of it, unless first the ambient waters are drained dry from it. It is therefore needful that it should be swimming on the water, if it be not itself watery; that it may not be taught, that it may not be able, <to vanish> from us, that it may remain moist in a moist being. But we remove from it the embrace of the waters that we may see the great comeliness of its beauty. How shall we push it back from the participation with the waters? How shall we separate it, that there may easily be a raising of the water? There is need of panoply and courage. Who is man enough for this? Who is able to dry up the overflowing stream of waters? Who is to be found for the contest? Who is ready for service? There is found a purgation of the matter, so that we may clearly see the beauty of the cloud. The same is the practical gentle coction by means of sulphur. For just as the washing with water is in the mind, so also is the purification of the All by sulphur. For washing with the divine (sulphurous) waters now and managing the process fairly, we purify it again by fire and sulphur, that the body of the moon (or silver) may be revealed, that they may see the cloud the gift of the sun. O unspoken mysteries of a wise God, O rich gifts to those who have loved the Lord, O depth of wealth and wisdom and gnosis of the mysteries. If the present things are such marvels and extraordinary, from what source are everlasting things which no mind is able to explain? If the material work

---

[14] Presumably tin (Taylor 139n66).

is displayed thus to us by some unspeakable discourse, from what source are thy undefiled good and unfading beauties, which no one is capable of perceiving? I hymn and adore and glorify thee, triad superior to being, more than good and more than god. Who can speak forth to hymn thy marvels, that they may be glorified? All thy works, O Lord, thou hast made in wisdom.

9 Anonymous (eighth or ninth century AD)

The Poem of the Philosopher Theophrastos Upon the Sacred Art

Stephanos of Alexandria exerted a powerful influence on the rhetorical practice of Greek writers of the seventh and eighth centuries, one that is visible in four alchemical poems often preserved together in manuscript under the names of Heliodoros, Theophrastos, Hierotheos and Archelaos. Close analysis of style and content has led to the conclusions that these poems are the work of one anonymous writer who lived after the time of Stephanos, and that all are versifications of passages from his *Great and Sacred Art of the Making of Gold*. The following poem ascribed to Theophrastos was probably written by a Byzantine sophist between the years 700 and 900 AD.

In the commentary accompanying his translation of the poem, C. A. Browne describes the radical change in the style of scientific (and alchemical) writing that occurs in the last centuries of the first millennium:

> The science of the early Alexandrians had so far degenerated in the days of the Byzantines that it was made a theme for rhetoricians while the ancient clarity and conciseness, which made the scientific writings of Hippocrates and Archimedes models of expression, had now given way to deliberate obscurity of thought and to empty jingling of an inflated style (212).

Despite rhetorical extravagance, culminating in the outburst of praise, "O work divine, well-pleasing and concise!," this poem attributed to Theophrastos is interesting not only for its approach to the mysteries of alchemy but for the light that it throws on the Sophists.

The following text of *The Poem of the Philosopher Theophrastos Upon the Sacred Art* is the translation of C. A. Browne, published in *Scientific Monthly* 11 (Sept. 1920): 193–214. Browne's translation is interspersed with much useful discussion of Byzantine alchemy.

We sophists,[1] and the rhetoricians too,
Are fortunate and lead a life most wise;
We know the nature of created things,
The kinds of elements, and understand
How, by close union each to each, they tend

---

[1] Quite independent of its alchemical focus, Theophrastos's poem provides interesting insights into the outlook and teachings of the Sophists in the late Byzantine era, with its confident assurance of "lead[ing] a life most wise" and understanding the "nature of created things," as well as association with rhetoric.

To one new form, most fair and wholly strange,
With brilliant splendor filled, its make-up such
That it bestoweth wealth and great reward.
But most of all we wish with one accord
All mortals to be taught and disciplined
And trained in wisdom of the sophist school,
That they may shape themselves to perfect men,
That they may know the bounds of Nature's realm,
(How all things thrive and mix and interweave)
And last that they may nothing speak except
What words the wise old masters used to say.
Those masters urge all mortals who are wise
To be instructed in the mystic lore
Of sacred rites, whose meaning they proclaim
By actions rather than by words of mouth.

We, who foretell just where the stars shall be
Who know their natures, heights and intervals,
Their occultations, when they rise and set,
Their measured bounds and what their orbs portend,
Do not misread their signs, though far away,
For when assisted by a knowing mind
Our sense of vision sees them as they are.
We know the truth of what is in the sky
Above and are not ignorant of what
Is there performed, for we perceive it all
And make it evident to mortal minds,
As their experience can testify.

Yet more than this, the causes we reveal
Of each affliction in the body's frame;
Experimentally our school explores
The science, art and ends of medicine,
With such success that our prognosis shows
What sicknesses are destined to appear
And what is best to cure or ward them off;
Its findings also lead us to foretell
An end of life from sickness far from home.

Not only has our wisdom known the ways
By which to check each illness and disease,
– Prodigious wonders even though they be –
But with exactness we describe the flowers,
(Their qualities, their mixtures and their kinds),
And taste of juice and substances of plants.
Each class of growing herbs has been portrayed
For our prognosis and with words exact,

We also know the hues and kinds of stones,
The places where the metals are produced
And all their properties both good and bad.
The many kinds of creatures in the sea
Are known to us and all their many forms;
We teach mankind their natures, good and bad,
How some to use and others to avoid.
Nor do we slight the race of gay-hued birds,
Those strange in form and those who kill their kind,
Those who by nature are of use to man,
And so contribute to the joy of life.
Each class and race of reptiles we describe,
And so all living things find place within
Our catalogue. Nor have we falsified
In anything, for every word is true.
All we have said or shown to mortal men
Is for their use and happiness in life.

How then can those vile critics censure us,
They who in secret learning are inept,
And who in sophic wisdom have no share?
How can they say we sophists speak untruths
With their own minds so pitifully maimed
They give no thought or care to things divine?
They ask how gold is ever to be made,
How that can change which has a nature fixed,[2]
Placed there of old by God the demiurge,
Who formed its substance never to be moved
From that position which from early time
Was its abode and destined resting place;
They say gold thus abides, nor suffers change,
For naught can be transmuted from the class
Or species where its origin took place.
They who speak thus but trifle with their minds
And nothing say that bears the stamp of truth.

But we will show the end of this our art,
An end most useful and most quickly learned,
For nothing strange it needs save that one stock
From which all things by Nature are produced.

From Time's four transformations learn the way
By which the work most skilfully completes

---

[2] Theophrastus here engages attackers of alchemy who argue that each metal and mineral has its own unique "matter," which cannot undergo change and transmutation. He counter-argues that, while matter remains constant, form constantly varies, as in the analogy with the changing seasons.

The transformations of sophistic art.
The winter, cold and moist, controls the frost;
By him the fleeting clouds are borne on high
To drench the earth and quicken seeds to life;
Three months elapse before his time expires.
Next Spring, a season moist and warm comes in;
By her the earth is made to bloom with flowers
Of every kind; her course is also run
When three more months their transformation bring.
Next Summer, warm and very dry, appears;
By her Earth's bosom is released from damp
And, warmed from chilliness, is made to bear;
Her period in three more months is run.
The Autumn quickly comes upon his way,
A season dry and cold in which alas
The beauty of the flowers is all destroyed;
His rapid course in three more months is passed.
Through these four transformations runs the sun;
He makes his circuit in the dozen months
Which form the year and sheds his light on all
Beneath the sky. The splendor of his beams
Fills all the earth with mild increasing warmth;
With rapid course he summons things to life
And makes with gentle heat all trees to bud.
From him the moon receives her gleaming light
And all the wandering stars, the planets seven,
And likewise those whose shining orbs are fixed.

So understand the work, how to refer
The four mutations to one simple form
And from the four to make the work complete,
Seven colored,[3] even as the planets seven,
Whence Nature gets her species, kinds and forms,
Whence Luna's metal takes a whitened hue
And whence proceeds the yellow principle
(That gives a second splendid purple tint)
Which brightening all bodies tinges them
The brilliant golden color of the sun.

The white, augmented thrice within a fire,
In three day's time is altogether changed
To lasting yellow and this yellow then
Will give its hue to every whitened form.

---

[3] The seven primary metals and their planetary associations (see Introduction). "Luna's metal" is silver; following this "whitening" stage (*albedo*) is the *citrination* or yellowing stage, leading to production of gold.

This power to tinge and shape produces gold
And thus a wondrous marvel is revealed.

Though not a stone, it yet is made a stone
From metal, having three hypostases,
For which the stone is prized and widely known;
Yet all the ignorant search everywhere
As though the prize were not close by at hand.
Deprived of honor yet the stone is found
To have within a sacred mystery,
A treasure hidden and yet free to all.

A dragon springs therefrom which, when exposed
In horse's excrement for twenty days,
Devours his tail till naught thereof remains.
This dragon, whom they Ouroboros call,[4]
Is white in looks and spotted in his skin,
And has a form and shape most strange to see.
When he was born he sprang from out the warm
And humid substance of united things.
The close embrace of male and female kind,
– A union which occurred within the sea –
Brought forth this dragon, as already said;
A monster scorching all the earth with fire,
With all his might and panoply displayed,
He swims and comes unto a place within
The currents of the Nile; his gleaming skin
And all the bands which girdle him around
Are bright as gold and shine with points of light.

This dragon seize and slay with skillful art
Within the sea, and wield with speed thy knife
With double edges hot and moist, and then,
His carcass having cleft in twain, lift out
The gall and bear away its blackened form,
All heavy with the weight of earthy bile;
Great clouds of steaming mist ascend therefrom
And these become on rising dense enough
To bear away the dragon from the sea
And lift him upward to a station warm,
The moisture of the air his lightened shape
And form sustaining; be most careful then

---

[4] One of alchemy's most ancient symbols, the tail-biting serpent has many significations: e.g., the All, the unity of matter, eternity, rejuvenation, the circular nature of the alchemical process with the interconvertibility of the elements; and – especially in this passage – Mercurius, the agent of transformation that both kills (or is killed) and restores.

All burning of his substance to avoid
And change its nature to a stream divine
With quenching draughts; then pour the mercury[5]
Into a gaping urn and when its stream
Of sacred fluid stops to flow, then wash
Away with care the blackened dross of earth.
Thus having brightened what the darkness hid
Within the dragon's entrails thou wilt bring
A mystery unspeakable to light;
For it will shine exceeding bright and clear,
And, being tinged a perfect white throughout,
Will be revealed with wondrous brilliancy,
Its blackness having all been changed to white;
For when the cloud-sent water flows thereon
It cleanses every dark and earthy stain.

    Thus he doth easily release himself
By drinking nectar, though completely dead;
He poureth out to mortals all his wealth
And by his help the Earth-born are sustained
Abundantly in life, when they have found
The wondrous mystery, which, being fixed
Will turn to silver, dazzling bright in kind,
A metal having naught of earthy taint,
So brilliant, clear and wonderfully white.
Then seize again this dragon changed to white
(A change divinely wrought, as I have said,
By means of albifaction twice performed)
And slaying him again with knife of fire
Draw all his blood which gushes blazing hot
And red as shining flame when it ignites.
Then dip the dragon's skin into the blood
Which issued from his belly's gory wound
(As thou wouldst dip a whitened robe in dye
Of murex purple);[6] so wilt thou obtain
A brilliant glory, shining as the sun,
Of goodly form and gladdening the heart
Of mortals who behold its excellence.

    They praise the gift with wise and joyous words
As one divinely sent and great in worth;
And thus they speak and voice their thankfulness.

[5] The identification of the dragon with mercury is here made explicit. Throughout this passage, the images of heat and moisture and changes in color from black to white (*albedo* or albification) evoke the physical processes of alchemy.

[6] Purple dye derived from the shellfish *murex*.

O work divine, well-pleasing and concise!
O beauty brilliant with an aspect clear!
O marriage and conjunction most renowned!
O husband in a single union joined!
O wife united by affection deep!
O offspring famous and with glory filled!
O progeny of splendor, light and worth!
O robe with gold and silver overlaid!
O double-folded mantle bright as snow!
O metal which with gleaming silver teems!
O clear refreshing river of the sea!
O water than the loosened earth more free!
O ether rising far above the earth!
O clouds transformed from blackness into white!
O brilliant colored glory of the heaven!
O light which shines to all beneath the sky!
O system and bright circuit of the stars!
O lunar light reflected from the sun!
O sun whose darting beams engender gold!
From these the work of every sage begins
To reap in practise some deserving end;
In thee appears the object of our search;
Thou shinest scattering thy wondrous light,
A treasure most desired, all filled with pearls;
And bringing gain and wealth to mortal men.

   Who, then, beholding the great universe
Which Thou hast wisely wrought, – a well-designed
Production, made with singleness of art,
And faith inspiring in its glorious works –
Entranced with wonder would not be amazed?
He would extoll the boundless providence
Of reason's God and praise the sympathy
Which He, in ways both wise and manifold,
To us declares. As Lord beneficent
He wishes all mankind a happy life
And wealth by their activities to gain.

   Then let us shape life's course with reverence
And cherish piety's clear beacon light,
Our pathways brightening with godly deeds,
Our neighbor loving and the foreign guest;
And day and night with supplicating prayers
Our adoration pay, as servants wise,
To God the Lord, all-seeing King of all,
Forgiveness asking for our trespasses

And that all kin from danger may be spared
And from temptations freed, as they arise;
And let us never undertake a work
Unless we give the praise therefor to God,
The Father, who begot the only Son,
The Son, the holy Word from God produced,
The Holy Ghost, proceeding too from Him,
Both now and always everymore. Amen

Part II Islamic and medieval texts

10 Khalid ibn Yazid (635–c. 704)

From *Secreta Alchymiæ*

The Islamic rise to political and military power beginning in the seventh century had important consequences for the study and practice of alchemy. With the conquest of Alexandria (642) and other centers of Greek learning, the Moslems came into possession of the bulk of Greek philosophy and science, including alchemy. Thus, the writings of the Greeks became the basis for Moslem advancements in the field, and Arabian scholars helped extend the knowledge of alchemy in the West through preserving, translating, and transmitting the Greek heritage.

Khalid (Khalid ibn Yazid) of Damascus was among the first of the Moslem scholars to take a serious interest in alchemy. Under his direction, Arabian translations of Greek and Coptic treatises were completed. He is also said to have personally studied alchemy under the tutelage of the Christian scholar Morienus – himself a pupil of Stephanos of Alexandria – and to have written alchemical poems (Holmyard 64). The *Secreta Alchymiæ* is a reasonably clear and comprehensive summary of topics and themes that were to become central in alchemical writing in the West, including certain of its primary processes, relations between the body and soul of metals, degrees of fire, laboratory equipment, and the preparation of both the white and the red stones.

The following selections from the *Secreta Alchymiæ* are taken from *Kalidis Persici, Secreta Alchymiæ. Written Originally in Hebrew, and Translated thence into Arabick, and out of Arabick into Latin: Now faithfully rendred into English, By William Salmon*, printed in Salmon's *Medicina Practica* (1692). Chapters are numbered as in Salmon's collection, in which the Kalid selection begins with ch. 22. Additional readings: E. J. Holmyard, *Alchemy* (Harmondsworth, Middlesex: Penguin, 1968), chap. 5, esp. 60–68.

Chap. 22: Of the Difficulties of this Art.

1. Thanks be given to God, the Creator of all things, who hath made us, renewed us, taught us, and given us knowledge and understanding; for except he should keep us, preserve us, and direct us, we should wander out of the right way, as having no Guide or Teacher: Nor can we know any thing in this World, unless he teach us, who is the begining of all things, and the Wisdom it self, his power and goodness, it is, with which he over-shadows his People.

2. He directs and instructs whom he pleases, and by his long–suffering, and tender Mercies, brings them back into the way of Righteousness. For he has sent his Angels [*or Spirit*]

into the dark places, and made plain the Ways, and with his loving kindness replenishes such as love him.

3. Know then my Brother, that this Magistery of our Secret Stone, and this Valuable Art, is a secret of the Secrets of God, which he has hidden with his own People; not revealing it to any, but to such, who as Sons faithfully have deserved it, who have known his Goodness, and Almightiness.[1]

4. If you would request any Earthly thing at the Hand of God, the Secret of this Magistery is more to be desired, than any thing else. For the Wise Men, who have perfected the knowledge thereof, have not been wholly plain, but speaking of it, have partly concealed it, and partly revealed it: And in this very thing, I have found the preceeding Philosophers to agree, in all their so much valued Books.

5. Know therefore, that *Musa*, my own Disciple, (more valuable to me than any other) having diligently studied their Books, and laboured much in the Work of this Magistery, was much perplexed, not knowing the Natures of things belonging thereto: Where-upon he humbly begged at my Hands, my Explanation thereof, and my Directions therein.

6. But I gave him no other Answer, Than that he should read over the Philosophers Books, and therein to seek that which he desired of me: Going his way, he read above an hundred Books, as he found, or could get them, the true Books of the Secret of the Great Philosophers: But by them he could not attain the knowledge of that Mistery which he desired, tho' continually studying it, for the space of a Year, for which reason, he was as one astonished, and much troubled in mind.

7. If then *Musa* my Scholar, (who has deserved to be accounted among the Philosophers) has thus failed in the knowledge of this Mistery; what may be supposed from the Ignorant and Unlearned, who understand not the Natures of things, nor apprehend whereof they consist?

8. Now when I saw this in my most dear and chosen Disciple, moved with Piety and Love to him, by the Will also and Appointment of God, I wrote this my Book near the time of my Death, in which, tho' I have pretermitted many things which the Philosophers before me have mentioned in their Books; yet have I handled some things which they have concealed, and could not be prevailed withal to reveal or discover.

9. Yea, I have explicated, and laid open certain things, which they hid under Aenigmatical and dark Expressions; and this my Book I have Named, *The Secrets of Alchymie*, for that I have revealed in it, whatsoever is necessary to the knowledge of this Learning, in a Language befiting the matter, and to your sence and understanding.

10. I have taught four Magisteries far greater and better than the other Philosophers have done, of which number, The one is a Mineral Elixir, another Animal: The other two are Mineral Elixirs; but not *the one Mineral*, whose Virtue is to wash, cleanse, or purifie those which they call the Bodies. And another is to make Gold of *Azot vive*;[2] whose Composition or Generation is according to the Natural Generation in the Mines, or in the Heart and Bowels of the Earth.

---

[1] Khalid's statement concerning God's deliberate, selective concealment and revelation of the mysteries of alchemy is his variation on one of the art's oldest conventions, one which accounts for the obscurity of alchemical discourse and illustration.

[2] Quicksilver or mercury (from the Arabic *azot*), the first matter or principle of all metals.

11. And these four Magisteries or Works, the Philosophers have discoursed of, in their Books of the Composition thereof, but they are wanting in many things, nor would they clearly shew the Operation of it in their Books: And when by chance any one found it out, yet could he not throughly understand it; than which nothing was more grievous to him.

12. I will therefore in this Work declare it, together with the way and manner how to make it, but if you read me, learn to understand Geometrical proportion, that so you may rightly frame your Fornaces, not exceeding the mean, either in greatness or smalness; with all you must understand the proportion of your Fire, and the form of the Vessel fit for your Work.

13. Also you must consider, what is the groundwork and begining of the Magistery; which is as the Seed and Womb to the Generation of Living Creatures, which are shaped in the Womb, and therein receive their Fabrick, Increase, and Nourishment. For if the *prima materia* of our Magistery is not conveniently managed, the Work will be spoiled, and you will not find that which you seek after, nor shall you bring your Work to perfection.

14. For where the cause of Generation is wanting, or the root of the matter, and heat it self, your labour will be lost, and the Work come to nothing. The same also will happen, if you mistake in the proportion or weight; for if that be not right, to wit, the proportion of the parts compounding, the matter compounded missing of its just temperature will be destroyed, and so you shall reap no fruit...

Chap. 23: Of the four principal Operations, Solution, Congelation, Albification and Rubification.

1. Beginning now to speak of the *Great Work*, which they call *Alchymie*, I shall open the matter without concealing ought, or keeping back any thing, save that which is not fit to be declared: We say then, that the great work contains four Operations, *viz.* to Dissolve, to Congeal, to make White, and to make Red.

2. There are four quantities partakers together; of which, two are partakers between themselves; so also have the other two a coherence between themselves. And either of these double quantities has another quantity partaker with them, which is greater than these two.

3. I understand by these quantities, the quantity of the Natures, and weight of the Medicines, which are in order dissolved and congealed, wherein neither addition, nor diminution have any place. But these two, *viz.* Solution and Congelation, are in one Operation, and make but one Work, and that before Composition; but after Composition those Operations be divers.

4. And this Solution and Congelation which we have spoken of, are the solution of the Body, and the congelation of the Spirit, which two, have indeed but one Operation, for the Spirits are not congealed, except the Bodies be dissolved; as also the Bodies are not dissolved, unless the Spirit be congealed. And when the Soul and the Body are joyned together, each of them works its Companion into its own likeness and property.

5. As for example: When Water is put to Earth, it strives to dissolve the Earth, by its virtue, property, and moisture, making it softer than it was before, bringing it to be like it self, for the Water was more thin than the Earth. And thus does the

Soul work in the Body, and after the same manner is the Water thickened with the Earth, and becomes like the Earth in thickness, for the Earth was more thick than the Water.

6. Know also, that between the solution of the Body, and the congelation of the Spirit, there is no distance of time, nor diversity of work, as though the one should be without the other; as there is no difference of time in the conjunction of the Earth and Water, that the one might be distinguished from the other by its operation. But they have both one instant, and one fact; and one and the same work performs both at once, before Composition.

7. I say, before Composition, lest he that should read my Book, and hear the terms of Solution and Congelation should suppose it to be the Composition which the Philosophers treat of, which would be a grand Error both in Work and Judgment: Because Composition in this Work is a Conjunction or Marriage of the congealed Spirit with the dissolved Body, which Conjunction is made upon the fire.[3]

8. For heat is its nourishment, and the Soul forsakes not the Body, neither is it otherwise knit unto it, than by the alteration of both from their own virtues and properties, after the Conversion of their Natures: and this is the solution and congelation which the Philosophers first speak of.

9. Which nevertheless they have absconded by their Ænigmatical Discourses, with dark and obscure Words, whereby they alienate and estrange the minds of their Followers, from understanding the Truth . . .

10. But 'tis true, that unless there be a compounding, the Stone can never be brought to light: There must be a separation of the parts of the Compound, which separation is in order also to a conjunction. I tell you again, that the Spirit will not dwell with the Body, nor enter into it, nor abide in it, until the Body be made subtil and thin as the Spirit is.

11. But when it is attenuated and made subtil, and has caste off its thickness and grossness, and put on that thinness; has forsaken its Corporeity, and become Spiritual; then shall it be conjoyned with the subtil Spirits, and imbibe them, so that both shall become one and the same thing, nor shall they for ever be severed, but become like water mixt with water, which no Man can separate.

Chap. 24: Of the latter two Operations, viz. Albification and Rubification.

1. Suppose that of two like quantities which are in solution and congelation, the larger is the Soul, the lesser is the Body: Add afterwards to the quantity which is the Soul, that quantity which is in the Body, and it shall participate with the first quantity in virtue only: Then working them as we have wrought them, you will have your desire, and understand *Euclid* his Line or Proportion.[4]

2. Then take this quantity, weigh it exactly, and add to it as much moisture as it will drink up, the weight of which we have not determined: Then work them as before,

---

[3] This is the famous "chemical wedding," much discussed by alchemists. Abraham notes that "the coagulation or coniunctio is the triumphant moment of chemical combination where such opposite states and qualities as sulphur and mercury, hot and cold, dry and moist, fixed and volatile, spirit and body, form and matter, active and receptive, and male and female are reconciled of their differences and united" (*DAI* 35).

[4] This apparently metaphoric reference reflects familiarity with Euclid's *Elementa geometriae* .

with the same Operations of a first imbibing and subliming it: This Operation is called Albification, and they name it *Yarit*, that is, Silver or White Lead.[5]

3. When you have made this Compound white, add to it so much of the Spirit, as will make half of the whole, and set it to working, till it grows red, and then it will be of the colour of *Al-sulfur [Cinnabar]* which is very red, and the Philosophers have likened it to Gold, whose effects lead to that which the Philosopher[6] said to his Scholar *Arda*.

4. We call the Clay when it is white *Yarit*, that is Silver: But when it is red, we name it *Temeynch*,[7] that is Gold: Whiteness is that which tinges Copper, and makes it *Yarit*: And it is redness which tinges *Yarit*, *i.e.* Silver, and makes it *Temeynch*, or Gold.

5. He therefore that is able to dissolve these Bodies, to subtilize them, and to make them white and red, as I have said; that is, to compound them by imbibing, and convert them to the same, shall without doubt perform the work, and attain to the perfection of the Magistery, of which I have spoken.

6. Now to perform these things, you must know the Vessels for this purpose: the one is an *Aludel*,[8] in which the parts are separated and cleansed; in them the matter of the Magistery is depurated, and made compleat and perfect.

7. Every one of these *Aludels* must have a Furnace fit for them, which must have a similitude and figure fit for the Work. *Mezleme* and some other Philosophers, have named all these things in their Books, shewing the manner and form thereof.

8. And herein the Philosophers agree together in their Writings; concealing the matter under Symbols, in many Books, but seting forth the necessary Instruments for the said four Operations. The Instruments are chiefly two in number, one is a Cucurbit with its Alembick the other is a well made *Aludel*, or sublimatory.

9. There are also four things necessary to these, *viz. Bodies, Souls, Spirits, Waters*; and of these four does the Mineral Work, and Magistery consist, all which are made plain in the Books of Philosophers . . .

Chap. 25: Of the Nature of Things appertaining to this Work: Of Decoction, and its Effects.

3. And Corruption is in conjunction with Generation, Generation is retained with Generation, and Generation conquereth with Generation.

4. Now for the performance of these things, the Philosophers have in their Books taught us how to decoct, and how decoction[9] is to be made in the matter of our Magistery: This is that which generates, and changes them from their Substances and Colours, into other Substances and Colours.

---

[5] Of *Yharit*, Ruland states: "The Matter of the Work when it has reached that White Colour which the Philosophers term their Silver" (*Lexicon, Supp.* 464).

[6] E.g. Aristotle.

[7] Ruland identifies *Temeynchum* as "The Gold of the Philosophers or their Magistery at the Red Stage" (*Lexicon, Supp.* 429)

[8] An aludel is a glass used in sublimation. A cucurbit is a "vessel shaped . . . like an inverted cone" (*Lexicon* 120). The best known of the alchemists' vessels was the alembic, which was "set over the retort to receive and collect vapours" (*Lexicon* 21).

[9] In the decoction stage, the changes Kalid describes result from the application of heat or fire to the materials in the vas.

5. If you err not in the begining you may happily attain the end: But you ought to consider the seed of the Earth whereon we live, how the heat of the Sun works in it, till the Seed is impregnated with its influences and Virtues, and made to spring, till it grows up to ripeness: This is the first change or transmutation.

6. After this, Men and other Creatures feed upon it; and Nature, by the heat that is innate in Man, changes it again, into Flesh, Blood, and Bones.

7. Now like to this is the Operation or Work of our Magistery, the Seed whereof, (as the Philosophers say) is such, that its progress and perfection consists in the fire, which is the cause of its Life and Death . . .

Chap. 26: Of Subtilization, Solution, Coagulation, and Commixtion of the Stone.

1. Now except you subtilize the Body till it becomes water, it will not corrupt and putrefie, nor can it congeal the Fugitive Souls when the fire touches them; for the fire is that which by its force and spirit congeals and unites them.

2. In like manner the Philosophers commanded to dissolve the Bodies, to the end that the heat might enter into their Bowels, or inward parts: So we return to dissolve these Bodies, and congeal them after their solution, with that thing which comes near to it, till all the things mixed together by an apt and fit commixtion, in proportional quantities, are firmly conjoyned together.

3. Wherefore we joyn Fire and Water, Earth and Air together, mixing the thick with the thin, and the thin with the thick, so as they may abide together, and their Natures may be changed the one into the other, and made like, and one thing in the compound which before were simple.

4. Because that part which generates or ferments, bestows its virtue upon the subtil and thin, which is the Air; for like cleaves to its like, and is a part of the Generation, from whence it receives power to move and ascend upwards.

5. Cold has power over the thick matter, because it has lost its heat, and the water is gone out of it; and the driness appears upon it. This moisture departs by ascending up; and the subtil part of the Air has mingled itself with it, for that it is like unto it, and of the same nature.

6. Now when the thick body has lost its heat and moisture, and that the cold and dryness has power over it; and that their parts have mixed themselves, by being first divided, and that there is no moisture left to joyn the parts divided, the parts withdraw themselves.

7. And then the part which is contrary to cold, by reason it has continued, and sent its heat and decoction to the cold parts of the Earth, having power over them, and exercising such dominion over the coldness which was hidden in the said thick Body; *that*, by virtue of its generative power, changes the thick cold Body, and makes it become subtil and hot, and then strives to dry it up again by its heat.

8. But afterwards, the subtil part, (which causes the *Natures* to ascend) when it has lost its Occidental heat, and waxes cold, then the *Natures* are changed, and become thick, and descend to the center, where the earthly Natures are joyned together, which were subtilized, and converted in their generation, and imbibed in them.

10. In like manner we see, that whatsoever is in the World is held or retained by or with its contrary, as heat with cold, and dryness with moisture: thus when each of them has besieged its Companion, the thin is mixed with the thick, and those things are made

one substance, *viz*. their hot and moist Soul, and their cold and dry Body, are united, and made one . . .

Chap. 27: The manner of Fixation of the Spirit, Decoction, Trituration, and Washing.

1. When the Body is mingled with moisture, and that the heat of the fire meets therewith, the moisture is converted into the Body, and dissolves it, and then the Spirit cannot go forth, because it is imbibed with the Fire.
2. The Spirits are fugitive, so long as the Bodies are mixed with them, and strive to resist the fire, its heat and flame, and therefore these parts can scarcely agree without a good and continual Operation, and a steadfast, permanent, and natural heat.
3. For the nature of the Soul is to ascend upwards where its Center is; and he that is not able to joyn two or more divers things together, whose Centers are divers, knows nothing of this Work.
4. But this must be done after the conversion of their Natures, and change of their Substances, and matter, from their natural Properties, which is difficult to find out.
5. Whoever therefore can convert or change the Soul into the Body, and the Body into the Soul, and therewith mingle the subtil and volatile Spirits, they shall be able to tinge any Body.
6. You must also understand that Decoction, Contrition, Cibation, Mundification, and Ablution,[10] with Sweet Water, are most necessary, to the Secret of our Magistery.
7. And if you bestow pains herein, you may cleanse it purely; for you must clear it from its blackness and darkness, which appear in the Operation.
8. And you must subtilize the Body to the highest point of Volatility and Subtility; and then mix therewith the Souls dissolved, and the Spirits cleansed, and so digest and decoct, to the perfection of the matter.

Chap. 28: Of the Fire fit for this Work.

1. You must not be unacquainted with the strength and proportion of the fire, for the perfection, or destruction of our Stone depends thereupon: For *Plato* said, *The fire gives profit to that which is perfect, but brings hurt and destruction to that which is Corrupt.*
2. So that when its quantity or proportion shall be fit and convenient, your Work will thrice prosper, and go on as it ought to do: but if it exceed the measure, it shall without measure corrupt and destroy it.
3. And for this cause it was requisite, that the Philosophers have instituted several proofs of the strength of their Fires; that they might prevent and hinder their burning, and the hurt of a violent heat.
4. In *Hermes* it is said, *I am afraid, Father, of the Enemy in my House:* To whom he made Answer: *Son, Take the Dog of Corascene, and the Bitch of* Armenia,[11] *and joyn them together; so shall you have a Dog of the colour of Heaven.*

---

[10] Contrition is the "act of pounding, bruising or pulverizing" (*DAI* 46); Cibation is the process of "feeding" the Stone, so that it "will grow in size, strength and sweetness" (*DAI* 40); Mundification and Ablution both involve washing and purifying the proximate materials of the Stone, effecting the transition from the *nigredo* to the *albedo*.

[11] Ruland notes that Hermetic philosophers have given the names, bitch and dog, respectively, to "their Mercury, or Feminine Seed of their Stone" and "their Sulphur, or to the Masculine Sperm of their Stone" (*Lexicon, Supp.* 358).

5. *Dip him once in the Water of the Sea; so will he become thy Friend, and defend thee from thine Enemy, and shall go along with thee, and help thee, and defend thee wheresoever thou goest, nor shall he ever forsake thee, but abide with thee for ever.*

6. Now *Hermes* meant by the Dog and Bitch, such Powers or Spirits as have power to preserve Bodies, from the hurt, strength, or force of the Fire...

Chap. 29: Of the Separation of the Elements.

1. Afterwards take this precious Stone, (which the Philosophers have named, yet hidden and concealed) put it into a *Cucurbit* with its *Alembick*, and divide its Natures, *viz.* the four Elements, the Earth, Water, Air, and Fire.

2. These are the Body and Soul, the Spirit and Tincture: when you have divided the Water from the Earth, and the Air from the Fire, keep each of them by themselves, and take that, which descends to the bottom of the Glass, being the Fæces, and wash it with a warm fire, till its blackness be gone, and its thickness be vanished.

3. Then make it very white, causing the superfluous moisture to fly away, for then it shall be changed and become a white Calx, wherein there is no cloudy darkness, nor uncleanness, nor contrariety.

4. Afterwards return it back to the first *Natures* which ascended from it, and purifie them likewise from uncleanness, blackness and contrariety.

5. And reiterate these Works upon them so often, till they be subtilized, purified, and made thin, which when you have done, render up thanks and acknowledgments to the most Gracious God.

6. Know then that this Work is but one, and it produceth one Stone, into which *Garib* shall not enter, i.e. any strange or foreign thing. The Philosopher works with this, and therefrom proceeds a Medicine which gives perfection.

7. Nothing must be mingled herewith, either in part or whole: And this Stone is to be found at all times, and in every place, and about every Man; the search whereof is yet difficult to him that seeks it, wheresoever he be.

8. This Stone is vile, black, and stinking; it costs nothing; it must be taken alone, it is somewhat heavy, and is called the Original of the World, because it rises up, like things that bud forth; this is the manifestation and appearance of it, to them that seek truly after it...

Chap. 30: Of the Commixtion of the Elements which were separated.

1. Now you must begin to commix the Elements, which is the compass of the whole Work; there can be no commixtion without a Marriage and putrefaction. The *Marriage* is to mingle the thin with the thick: and *Putrefaction* is to rost, grind, water or imbibe so long, till all be mixt together and become one, so that there be no diversity in them, nor separation, as in water mixed with water.

2. Then will the thick strive to retain the thin, and the Soul shall strive with the fire and endeavour to sustain it, then shall the Spirit suffer it self to be swallowed up by the Bodies, and be poured forth into them: which must needs be, because the dissolved body, when it is commixed with the Soul, is also commixed with every part thereof...

Chap. 33: The Way and Manner how to make the Stone both White and Red.

1. When you attempt to do this, take this our precious Stone, and put it into a Cucurbit, covering it with an Alembick, which close well with *Lutum sapientiæ*,[12] and set it in Horse-dung, and fixing a Receiver to it, distil the matter into the Receiver, till all the water is come over, and the moisture dryed up, and dryness prevail over it.

2. Then take it out dry, reserving the water that is distilled for a future occasion; take, I say, the dry body, that remained in the bottom of the Cucurbit, and grind it, and put it into a Vessel answerable in magnitude to the quantity of the Medicine.

3. Bury it in very hot Horse-dung as you can get, the Vessel being well luted with *Lutum sapientiæ*: And in this manner let it digest. But when you perceive the Dung to grow cold, get other fresh Dung which is very hot, and put your Vessel therein to digest as before.

4. Thus shall you do for the space of forty days, renewing your Dung so often as the occasion or reason of the Work shall require, and the Medicine shall dissolve of itself, and become a thick White water . . .

9. Then (as before) grind it, putting thereto of the afore reserved Water, the aforesaid quantity, and bury it in like manner in hot Horse-dung, digesting it 10 days longer, then taking it forth, and this do the fourth time also.

10. Which done, take it forth and grind it, and bury it in Horse-dung, till it be dissolved: Afterwards take it out, and reiterate it once more, for then the Birth will be perfect, and the Work ended . . .

13. Then take a Dram from these 250 Drams, and project it upon 250 Drams of Steel, or Copper, and it shall whiten it, and convert it into Silver, better than that of the Mine; which is the greatest and last Work of the White, which it performs.

14. *To convert the said Stone into Red.* And if you desire to convert this Magistry into *Sol*, or Gold, take of this Medicine thus perfected (at ¶ 10. above) the weight of one Dram, (after the manner of the former Example), and put it into a Vessel, and bury it in Horse-dung for forty days, till it be dissolved.

15. Then give it the Water of the dissolved Body to drink, first as much as amounts to half its weight, afterwards bury it in hot Horse-dung, digesting it till it is dissolved, as aforesaid.

16. Then proceed in this Golden Work, as before in the Silver, and you shall have fine Gold, even pure Gold. Keep (my Son) this most secret Book, containing the Secret of Secrets, reserving it from Ignorant and Profane Hands, so shall you obtain your desire. *Amen.*

---

[12] Lute (often called the "Lute of Wisdom") is the substance alchemists used to seal their vessels to prevent the escape of vapors or "spirit."

11 Jabir ibn Hayyan (eighth century)/ Pseudo–Geber (thirteenth century)

From *Of the Investigation or Search of Perfection*; *Of the Sum of Perfection*; and *His Book of Furnaces*

Beginning in the eighth century, Islamic alchemy was strongly influenced by writings that passed under the name of Jabir ibn Hayyan (*ca.* 721–*ca.* 800): "Geber" as he came later to be known in the Latin West. Like Khalid, Jabir was instrumental in preserving alchemy's Greek heritage and transmitting it to Islamic culture; he is also believed to have written texts in Arabic on a wide range of subjects: mathematics and geometry, magic squares, astrology, medicine, military science, as well as alchemy. Problems of attribution, however, are especially acute in the case of Jabir, and it is now accepted that many works once regarded as his were actually fathered upon him by writers of the Isma'ilite sect in the tenth century (Plessner, Jabir, *DSB*; Holmyard 72–3). It is also common practice to distinguish between this earlier, Greek-inspired Arabic body of writings, the *Corpus Jabirianum*, and the highly influential body of Latin writings that appeared falsely under the name of "Geber" in the thirteenth and fourteenth centuries. This latter group includes such well-known works as the *Summa perfectionis magisterii, Liber de investigatione perfectionis, Liber de inventione veritatis, Liber fornacum*, and the *Testamentum Geberi*. Selections presented in this collection are drawn from the Latin writings and treat topics for which "Geber" achieved fame among medieval and Renaissance alchemists: the sulphur-mercury theory; the major processes in the preparation of the Stone (sublimation, descension, distillation, calcination, solution, coagulation, fixation, and ceration); furnaces and the "degrees" of fire; and other types of laboratory equipment. *Of the Sum of Perfection* is thus a concise and clearly written summary of alchemical theory and practice. The question remains as to whether it is a translation of an original Arabic treatise or one composed in Latin and ascribed to Jabir/Geber to stimulate interest. Scholarly opinion favors the latter.

Selections are from *The Works of Geber, The Most Famous Arabian Prince and Philosopher*, Faithfully Englished by R[ichard] R[ussell] a Lover of Chymistry (London: Printed for N. E. by Thomas James, 1678). I have somewhat modernized the text by drastically reducing the use of italics and capitalization. Additional readings: M. Plessner, "Jabir ibn Hayyan," in *Dictionary of Scientific Biography*; E. J. Holmyard, *Alchemy*, 68–82, 134–41.

From *Of the Investigation or Search of Perfection* (final chapter)

Chap. 11: Of the Properties of the Greater Elixir.

We have now sufficiently determined the preparation and subtiliation of perfect bodies, that every discreet Operator may be enabled to attain his intention. Therefore let him attend to the properties and ways of action of the composition of the Greater Elixir: For we endeavour to make one substance, yet compounded and composed of many; so permanently fixed, that being put upon the fire, the fire cannot injure; and that it may be mixed with metals in flux, and flow with them, and enter with that which in them is of an ingressible substance; and be permixed with that, which in them is of a permixable substance; and be consolidated with that, which in them is of a consolidate substance; and be fixed with that, which in them is of a fixable substance; and not be burned by those things which burn not Gold and Silver; and take away consolidations and weights with due ignition.

Yet you must not think all this can be effected by preparation at once, in a very short time, as a few dayes and hours; but in respect of other Modern Physicians, and also in respect of the operation of Nature, the verity of the Work is sooner terminated this way. Whence the *Philosopher* saith,[1] *It is a Medicine requiring a long space of time*. Wherefore I tell you, you must patiently sustain labour, because the work will be long; and indeed festination is from the Devils part: Therefore let him that hath not patience desist from the Work, for credulity will hinder him making overmuch haste. And every natural action hath its determinate measure and time, in which it is terminated, *viz.* in a greater or lesser space. For this Work three things are necessary, namely, patience, length of time, and aptness of instruments; of which we speak to the Artificer, in the *Sum of the Perfection of our Magistery*, in divers chapters, wherein he may find them, if he be sufficiently skilled in our Works. In which, by manifest and open proof we conclude, that our *Stone* is no other than a *Fœtent* (or fruitful) *Spirit and Living Water*, which we have named *dry water*, by natural proportion cleansed, and united with such union, that they can never be absent each from other. To which two must also be added a third, for abbreviating the Work; that is a perfect body attentuated.

From *Of the Sum of Perfection: The First Book*

The Preface, Touching the Way of Describing this Art, and of those that are fit Disciples.

Our whole Science of Chymistry, which, with a divers compilation, out of the books of the Ancients, we have abbreviated in our volumes; we here reduce into one *Sum*. And what in other books written by us is diminished, that we have sufficiently made up, in writing of this our book, and supplied the defect of them very briefly. And what was absconded by us in one part, that we have made manifest in the same part, in this our volume; that the compleatment of so excellent and noble a part of Philosophy, may be apparent to the wise.

Therefore, most dear *Son*, know that in this Work the whole operation of our Art is sufficiently contained in general heads, with an universal discourse, without any diminution. And he, who shall operate according to this book, he shall (through God) with joy find,

---

[1] Probably from one of the many supposititious works attributed to Aristotle throughout the Middle Ages. The term "philosopher" was commonly accorded to serious, respectable, and authoritative alchemists, as opposed to charlatans; see references to Euclid and Altudenus in Bacon's *Radix Mundi*.

that he is come to the true end of this Art. But you must also know, that he, who in himself knows not natural principles, is very remote from our Art; because he hath not a true root, whereon to found his intention. And he, who knows his natural principles, and all causes of minerals, yet hath not acquired the true end and proficiency of this Art; hath a more easie access to the principles of this Art, than he who is ignorant in his intention of the method of his Work, and is but a little remote from the entrance of Art. But he who knows the principles of all things, and the causes of minerals, and the way of generation; which consists, according to the intention of Nature, is indeed but a very little short of the compleatment of the Work; without which our Science cannot be perfect: because Art cannot imitate Nature in all Works, but imitates her as exactly as it can. Therefore most dear *Son*, we discover a secret to you, *viz.* that Artificers erre in this, namely that they desire to imitate Nature in all differences of the properties of action, wherefore labour studiously in our volumes, and endeavour to ponder them very often in your mind, that you may acquire the true intention of our words; because in them you may find whereon to establish your own mind, and by them know how to escape errors, and in what you may be able to imitate Nature in the artifice of your Work.

The first part of this First Book, treating of the impediments which hinder the Artists from attaining to the true end of this Art.

Chap. 1: The Division of Impediments.
The impediments incident to this Work are generally two, *viz.* natural impotency, and defect of necessary expence, or occupations and labours. Yet we say, natural impotency is manifold; *viz.* partly from the organs of the Artist, and partly from his soul. From the organ of the Artificer, it is also manifold; for either the organ is weak, or wholly corrupted. And it is manifold from the impotencies of the soul; either because the soul is perverted in the organ (having nothing of rectitude, or Reason in it self) as the soul of a mad infatuate man; or because it is fantastical, unduly susceptive of the contrary of forms, and suddenly extensive from one thing knowable, to its opposite, and from one will to its opposite likewise.

Chap. 3: Of the Impediments from the part of the Artist's Soul.
... It now remains, that we briefly declare the impediments from the part of his soul, which mostly hinder the compleatment of this Work. Therefore, we say, he that hath not a natural ingenuity, and soul, searching and subtily scrutinizing natural principles, the fundamentals of Nature, and artifices which can follow Nature, in the properties of her action, cannot find the true radix of this most precious Science. As there are many who have a stiff neck, void of ingenuity in every perscrutation;[2] and who can scarcely understand common speech, and likewise with difficulty learn works vulgarly common. Besides these, we also find many who have a soul easily opinionating phantasie; but what they believe they have found true, is all phantastick, deviating from Reason, full of error, and remote from natural principles: because their brain, repleat with many fumosities, cannot receive the true intention of natural things. There are also, besides these, others who have a soul

---

[2] "A thorough searching or investigation" (*OED*).

movable, from opinion to opinions... And these are so changeable, that they can scarcely accomplish the least of that they intend... There are likewise others, who cannot see any truth in natural things, no more than beasts; as if they were witless, mad-men and children. There are others also who contemn the Science, and think it not to be; whom in like manner this Science contemns, and repels them from the end of this most precious Work. And there are some, who are slaves, loving money, who do affirm this to be an admirable Science, but are afraid to interposit the necessary charges. Therefore, although they approve it, and according to Reason seek the same, yet to the experience of the Work they attain not through covetousness of money: therefore, this our Science comes not to them. For how can he who is ignorant, or negligent in the search of Science, attain easily to it?

The Second Part of this First Book: in which are related the Reasons of Men denying this Art, which are afterward confuted.

Chap. 1: The true Reasons of Men simply denying this Art.
There are divers who deny and annihilate this Art. Some simply, others only supposing it to be. For some, simply affirming this Art not to be, sophistically strengthen their argument, thus: they say, there are distinct species and diversities of things, because the proportions, in commixtion of elements each with other, are divers and distinct. For an ass is divers in species from a man; because, in his composition, he had a more divers proportion of elements. So also it is in all other diversities of things, therefore in minerals. Wherefore the proportion of things mixable (by which is acquired the form and perfection of the thing) being unknown, how can we know both the mixture, and to form what is to be mixed? But we are ignorant of the true proportion of the elements of the Sol and Luna, therefore we must be ignorant how to form them.

In like manner, they also otherwise argue, condemning our Magistery. For say they, although you should know the proportion of elements, yet the way of mixing them together you know not; because Nature procreates these in caverns, in mines, and in hidden places; therefore, seeing you know not the way (or method) of their mixtion, you are also ignorant how to make them. In like sort, they argue: although you should duly know this, yet in the action of mixtion you understand not how to equalize the agent heat, by mediation of which the thing is so perfected...

Further, they bring you Reason and experience: this Science (say they) hath been so long sought by wise men, that if it were possible to attain to it any way, they would a thousand times, before now, have been masters of it. Likewise also, seeing Philosophers seem to treat of it in their volumes, yet in them we find no truth: 'tis manifest and probable enough by this, that this Science is not. So likewise, many princes and kings of this world, having infinite treasure, and abundance of Philosophers, have desired to attain to this Science, yet could never reach to the fruit of this most precious Art. This is a sufficient argument, that the Art is frivolous in its probation...

So also [the detractors of alchemy continue]... seeing metals differ in themselves, can you transform one into another, according to its species, or of such a species make such a species?[3] This seems to us sufficiently absurd, and remote from the verity of natural

---

[3] This is essentially the basis of Avicenna's rejection of transmutation in *De Congelatione et Conglutinatione Lapidum.*

principles. For, Nature perfects metals in a thousand years; but how can you, in your artifice of transmutation, live a thousand years, seeing you are scarcely able to extend your life to an hundred? Yet if to this, it be thus answered, What Nature cannot perfect in a very long space of time, that we compleat in a short space by our artifice; for Art can in many things supply the defect of Nature ... [Further, in regard to astrological influences] how then will you supply the defect in your Work, being ignorant of the diversity of sites of the stars, according to the motion of them? And admit you did know the certain site of one or more stars, by which perfection is given to metals, yet you could not perfect your *Work* according to your Intent ...

The Third Part of this First Book: Of Natural Principles, and their Effect.

Chap. 2: Of the Natural Principles of Metals, according to the Opinion of Modern Philosophers, and of the Author.

But others say otherwise, that Argentvive in its nature was not the principle, but altered, and converted into its Earth, and Sulphur likewise altered and changed into Earth. Whence they say, that in the intention of Nature, the principle was other than a fœtent spirit, and fugitive spirit. And the reason that moved them hereunto was this, *viz.* because, in the Silver mines, or in the mines of other metals, they found not any thing that is Argentvive in its nature, or any thing that is Sulphur likewise; but they found each of them separated in its proper mine, in its own nature. And they also affirm this for another reason, *viz.* because there is no transition (as they say) from contrary to contrary, unless by a middle disposition. Therefore, seeing it so is, they are compelled to confess and believe that there is no transition (or passing) from the softness of Argentvive, to the hardness of any metal, unless by a disposition which is between the hardness and softness of them. But in the mines they find not any thing, in which this middle disposition may be salved; therefore they are compelled hence to believe, that Argentvive and Sulphur, in their nature, are not the principles according to the intention of Nature: but another thing, which follows from the alteration of their essences, in the root of Nature, into an earthy substance. And this is the way, by which each of them is turned into an earthy nature; and from these two earthy natures, a most thin fume is resolved, by heat multiplied in the bowels of the Earth; and this duplicate fume is the immediate matter of metals.

This fume, when it shall be decocted by the temperate heat of the mine, is converted into the nature of a certain Earth; therefore it receives a certain fixation, which afterward the water (flowing through the bowels of the minera,[4] and spongiosity of the Earth) dissolves, and is uniformly united to it, with a natural and firm union. Therefore, so opining, they thus said, that the water flowing through the passages of the Earth, finds a substance dissolvible from the substance of the Earth in the bowels thereof, and dissolves the same, and is uniformly with it united, until the substance also of the Earth in the mines is dissolved, and the flowing dissolving water and it become one with natural union. And to such a mixtion come all the elements, according to a due natural proportion, and are mixed through their least parts, until they make an uniform mixtion. And this mixtion, by successive decoction in the mine, is thickned, hardned, and made a metal.

---

[4] "The matrix in which a metal or a precious stone was supposed to grow" (*OED*).

And indeed, these men, although they be nigh the truth, yet they do not conjecture the very truth.

Chap. 4: Of Sulphur.

Therefore we say, that Sulphur is a fatness of the Earth,[5] by temperate decoction in the mine of the Earth thickned, until it be hardned and made dry; and when it is hardned, it is called Sulphur. Indeed Sulphur hath an homogeneal and most strong composition, and is of an uniform substance in its natural parts, because it is homogeneal. Therefore, its oyl is not taken from it, as from other things having oyl by Distillation. Wherefore they, who strive to calcine it, not losing any thing of the substance of that with which it should be cured, do labour in vain; because it cannot be calcined, unless by great industry, and with loss of much of the substance thereof...

   Also, he who in preparation knows how to commix, and unite [Sulphur] amicably with bodies, knows one of the greatest secrets of Nature, and one way of perfection: for there are many ways to one effect, and one intent. And whatsoever body is calcined with it, undoubtedly receives weight; yea, Copper from it assumes the effigies of Sol.[6] Also Mercury is associated with it, and by Sublimation becomes Usifar (or Cinnabar). Lastly, all bodies, except Sol and Jupiter, are easily calcined with it; but Sol most difficultly... Yet let no man think that Sulphur can by it selfe compleat the Work of alchimy...

Chap. 5: Of Arsenick.

It now remains that we at present speak of Arsenick. We say it is of a subtile matter, and like to Sulphur; therefore it needs not be otherwise defined than Sulphur. But it is diversified from Sulphur in this, *viz.* because it is easily a tincture of whiteness, but of redness most difficultly; and Sulphur, of whiteness most difficultly: but of redness easily. Of Sulphur and Arsenick there is a twofold kind, *viz.* citrine and red, which are profitable to this Art; but the many other kinds not so. Arsenick is fixed as Sulphur; but the Sublimation of either is best from the calx of metals. Yet Sulphur and Arsenick are not the perfective matter of this Work: for they are not compleat to perfection; yet they may be an help to perfection in the case.

Chap. 6: Of Argentvive, or Mercury.

Argentvive, which also is called Mercury by the Ancients, is a viscous water in the bowels of the Earth, by most temperate heat united, in a total union through its least parts, with the substance of white subtile Earth, until the humid be contempered by the dry, and the dry by the humid, equally. Therefore it easily runs upon a plain superficies, by reason of its watery humidity; but it adheres not, although it hath a viscous humidity, by reason of the dryness of that which contemperates it, and permits it not to adhere. It is also (as some say) the matter of metals with Sulphur. And it easily adheres to three minerals, *viz.* to Saturn, and Jupiter, and Sol, but to Luna more difficultly. To Venus more difficultly than to Luna; but to Mars in no wise, unless by artifice.[7] Therefore hence you may collect a very great

---

[5] "Fatness" is commonly applied to sulphur and suggests an oily layer or deposit in the earth (*OED* 3.b), as well as fertility.

[6] I.e., copper assumes the appearance of gold.

[7] See the listing of metals with their planetary correspondences in the Introduction.

secret. For it is amicable and pleasing to metals, and the medium of conjoyning tinctures; and nothing is submerged in Argentvive unless it be Sol. Yet Jupiter and Saturn, Luna and Venus, are dissolved by it, and mixed; and without it, none of the metals can be gilded. It is fixed, and it is a tincture of redness of most exuberant refection, and fulgid splendor; and then it recedes not from the commixtion, until it is in its own nature. Yet it is not our Medicine in its nature; but it can sometimes likewise help in the case.

Chap. 8: Of Sol, or Gold.

We have already given you, in a general chapter the sum of the intention of metals; and here we now intend to make a special declaration of each one. And first of Gold. We say, Gold is a metallick body, citrine, ponderous, mute, fulgid, equally digested in the bowels of the Earth, and very long washed with mineral water; under the hammer extensible, fusible, and sustaining the tryal of the cupel,[8] and cement. According to this definition, you may conclude that nothing is true Gold, unless it hath all the causes and differencies of the definition of Gold. Yet, whatsoever metal is radically citrine, and brings to equality, and cleanseth, it makes Gold of every kind of metals. Therefore, we consider by the work of Nature, and discern, that Copper may be changed into Gold by artifice...

Also Gold is of metals the most precious, and it is the tincture of redness; because it tingeth and transforms every body. It is calcined and dissolved without profit, and is a Medicine rejoycing, and conserving the body in youth... [Subsequent chapters treat Luna or Silver, Saturn or Lead, Jupiter or Tin, Venus or Copper, and Mars or Iron.]

The Fourth Part of this First Book, touching the Artificial Principles of this Art.

Chap. 3: What Sublimation is, and of the Degrees of Fire in it to be observed.

Wherefore we say, *Sublimation* is the elevation of a dry thing by fire, with adherency to its vessel. But Sublimation is diversly made, according to the diversity of spirits to be sublimed. For the Sublimation of some is made with strong ignition, of others with moderate, and of some with a remiss heat of fire.[9] Therefore, when Arsnick or Sulphur are to be sublimed, their Sublimation must necessarily be made by remiss fire: because they having their most subtile parts uniformly conjoyned with the gross, their whole substance would ascend without any purification; yea, blackned and combust. Therefore, that the Artificer may separate the unclean earthy substance, he hath a necessity to find out the dispositions of two kinds, viz. the proportion of the fire, and Mundification[10] with commixtion of the feces: because commixtion with the feces, comprehends the gross parts, and holds them depressed in the bottom of the Sublimatory, not suffering them to ascend.

Whence also it is necessary, that the Artificer should apply to his Sublimation a threefold degree of fire: one proportionate in such wise, that by it may ascend only the altered, and more clean, and more lucid; until by this he manifestly see, that they are cleansed from their earthy feculency. The other degree is that what is of the pure essence of them remaining in the feces, may be sublimed with greater force of fire, *viz.* with ignition of the bottom of

---

[8] The process of assaying precious metals in a cupel, the "small flat circular porous vessel, with a shallow depression in the middle, made of pounded bone-ash pressed into shape by a mould" (*OED*).

[9] Moderate or mild heat (*OED* 4.b).

[10] Washing and purifying the proximate ingredients of the Stone.

the vessel, and of the feces therein, which may be seen with the eye. The third degree of fire is that unto the Sublimate without the feces, a most weak fire be administred, so that scarcely any thing of it may ascend, but that only which is the most subtile part thereof, and which in our Work is of no value; because it is a thing, by mediation of which, Adustion[11] is made in Sulphurs.

Therefore, the whole intention of Sublimation is that the earthiness of the Sublimate being removed by a due administration of fire, and likwise the most subtile and fumous part of it, which brings Adustion, with corruption, being cast away, to us may be left that part which consists in equality, which makes simple fusion upon the fire, and without any Adustion flying from the fire, without inflamation thereof. That what is most subtile is Adustive, is proved by most evident arguments. For fire converts to its own nature every of those things which is of affinity to it; because it is of affinity to every adustible thing, and to the subtile adustible, it is of greater affinity; and yet more of affinity to what is more subtile: therefore also most of affinity to what is most subtile. Likewise, the same is proved by experience, because Sulphur or Arsenick not sublimed, is most swiftly inflamed; but of the two, Sulphur more easily. Yet either, being sublimed, is not directly inflamed, but flies away, and is extenuated without inflamation; yet with a precedent fusion. By these therefore it is manifest that our discourse is most true.

Chap. 7: Of what Matter, and in what Form the Vessel Aludel (or Sublimatory) is to be made.

But the intention of the vessel Aludel is, that it be made of thick glass; for other matter is not sufficient, unless it be thick; and of like substance with glass. Because glass only, and its like (wanting pores) is able to retain spirits from flight, and that they be not exterminated by the fire; but no other matter is fit: because through the pores of them the spirits are gradually diminished, and vanish. Nor are metals serviceable in this case, because spirits (by reason of their amity and convenience) penetrate them, and are united therewith; wherefore, passing through them they vanish, as is manifestly proved, by what are determined by us. And it is found necessarily, and by experience, that this we have said is true. Therefore we are not by any thing excused, from taking glass in the composition of the Aludel.

Chap. 8: Of the Sublimation of Mercury and Argentvive.

Now we will determine the whole intention of Sublimation of Argentvive. This work is compleated, when its terrestreity is highly purified, and its aquosity wholly removed. For we are excused from the labour of removing its Adustion, because it hath none. Therefore we say that the ingenuity of seperating its superfluous Earth, is to mix it with things wherewith it hath not affinity, and often to reiterate the Sublimation of it from them. Of this kind, is talc, and the calx of egg-shells, and of white marble. Likewise also glass most subtily beaten, and every kind of salt prepared. For by these it is cleansed, and by other things, having affinity with it (unless they be bodies of perfection) it is rather corrupted; because all such things have a sulphureity, which, ascending with it in Sublimation, corrupt it. And this you find true by experience, because, when you sublime it from Tin or Lead, you find it (after Sublimation) infected with blackness. Therefore its Sublimation is better

---

[11] The state of being burned or scorched; parched dryness (*OED*).

made by those things which agree not with it; but it would be better, by things, with which it doth agree, if they had not sulphureity. Wherefore, this Sublimation is better made from calx than from all other things; because that agrees little with it, and hath not sulphureity.

But the way of removing its superfluous aquosity, is, that when it is mixed with calxes, from which it is to be sublimed, it be well ground and commixed with them by *Imbibition*,[12] until nothing of it appear, and afterward the wateriness of Imbibition removed by a most gentle heat of fire; which receding, the aquosity of Argentvive recedes with it. Yet the fire must be so very gentle, as that by it the whole substance of Argentvive ascend not. Therefore from the manifold reiteration of Imbibition, with *Contrition* and gentle *Assation*,[13] its greater aquosity is abolished; the residue of which is removed by repeating the Sublimation often. And when you see it most white, excelling snow in its whiteness, and to adhere (as it were dead) to the sides of the vessel; then again reiterate its Sublimation, without the feces; because part of it adheres fixed with the feces, and can never by any kind of ingenuity be separated from them. Or afterward, fix part of it; as shall expressly be taught you in the following: and when you have fixed it, then reiterate Sublimation of the part remaining, that it may be likewise fixed.

Being fixed, reserve it; but first prove it upon fire. If it flow well, then you have administred sufficient Sublimation, but if not, add to it some small part of Argentvive sublimed, and reiterate the Sublimation . . . till your end be answered; for if it hath a lucid and most white colour, and be porous, than you have well sublimed it, if not, not. Therefore in the preparation of it made by Sublimation be not negligent; because such as its *Mundation* (or cleansing) shall be, such will be its perfection, in *Projection* of it upon any of the imperfect bodies, and upon its own body unprepared. Yet here note, that some have by it formed Iron, others Lead; some Copper, and others Tin. Which happened to them, through negligence of preparation; sometimes of it alone, sometimes of Sulphur, or of its compeer, mixt with it. But if you shall by Subliming directly cleanse and perfect this subject, it will be a firm and perfect tincture of whiteness, the like of which is not.

Chap. 12: Of Descension, and the way of Purifying by Pastills.

The intentions of Sublimation, with all their causes, being already declared, it remains, that we now shew the way of *Descension*, with its causes, and determinate and compleat order likewise. For there was a threefold cause of its invention. One, that when any matter is included in that vessel, which is called a *Chymical Descensory*,[14] after its fusion it may descend through the hole thereof, and by its descent we be assured that it hath admitted fluxing. Another cause, that weak bodies may by it be preserved from combustion, after *Reduction* from their calxes. For when we attempt to reduce weak bodies from their calxes, we cannot reduce all their whole substance at one time. Therefore, if that part which is first reduced into body, should expect the reduction of the whole, a great quantity of it would vanish by the fire. Wherefore it was necessarily devised, that one part, so soon as reduced, might be taken from the fire. And this is done by a Descensory. The third cause

---

[12] Soaking or saturation with liquid, specifically "the return of distilled liquid to the residue or 'earth' at the bottom of the alembic, followed by further distillation" (*DAI* 105).

[13] Assation is removing the water through roasting or baking the substance.

[14] A vessel or retort used for distillation "by descent," employed especially in extracting oil (see chap. 13).

of the invention of it, was the *Depuration* of bodies from every thing extraneous. For the body descends in flux clean, and leaves every thing that is extraneous in the concavity thereof.

Chap. 13: Of Distillation and its Causes, and of Three kinds of the same, *viz.* by Alembeck, by a Descensory, and by Filter.

Therefore, following our purpose, 'tis convenient we should speak of *Distillation*, with its causes. Distillation is an elevation of aqueous vapours in their vessel. And Distillation is diversified. For some Distillations are by fire, and some without fire. Those made by fire are of two kinds; one, which is by elevation into the Alembeck; and the other by Chymical Descensory, by mediation of which the oyl of vegetables is extracted.

The cause why Distillation was invented, and the general cause of the invention of every Distillation, is the *Purification* of liquid matter from its turbulent feces, and conservation of it from *Putrefaction*. For we see a thing distilled (by what kind soever of Distillation) to be rendred more pure, and to be better preserved from Putrefaction. But the special cause of that Distillation, which is made by ascent into the Alembeck, is the desire of acquiring water pure without Earth. The experience of which is, that we see water so distilled, to have no feculency. The cause of the invention of pure water, was the *Imbibition* of spirits, and of clean Medicines. As for example, when we need Imbibition, we must have pure water, which leaves no feces after its resolution; by which feculency, our Medicines and cleansed spirits might be infected and corrupted. But the cause of that invention, which is made by descent, was the extraction of oyl pure in its nature; because by ascent, oyl cannot be had in its combustible nature. And such an inquisition also was, that the colour which is permixed with its substance, might be had; for this may be helpful in the case. But Distillation which is made by filter is performed without fire; and the cause of its invention was clearness of the water only.

Now we will shew you the methods of Distillations, with their causes. Therefore of that which is made by ascent, there is a twofold way or method. For one is performed in an earthen pan full of ashes; but the other with water in its vessel, with hay or wool, orderly so disposed, that the Cucurbit, or Distillatory Alembeck, may not be broken before the Work be brought to perfection. That which is made by ashes, is performed with a greater, stronger, and more acute fire; but what is made by water, with a mild and equal fire. For water admits not the acuity of ignition, as ashes doth...

The disposition of that which is made by ashes, is, that a strong earthen-pan be taken and fitted to the furnace, like to the aforesaid furnace of Sublimation, with the same distance from the sides of the furnace, and with like ventholes; upon the bottom of which pan sifted ashes must be put to the thickness of one finger, and upon the ashes the vessel of Distillation set, and covered round about with the same, almost as high as to the neck of the Alembeck. This being done, put in the matter, which you intend shall be Distilled. Lastly cover the vessel with its Alembeck, the neck of which must inclose the neck of the inferior Cucurbit, even up to the curved channel of the Alembeck, lest what is to be Distilled should flie away; and lute the Alembeck firmly with its Cucurbit, and give fire to it, until it begin to Distill. But the Alembeck and its Cucurbit, must be both of glass. And the Fire must be increased according to the exigency of the Distillation, until it be found, by urging the fire, that all which should be Distilled is Distilled off...

Chap. 14: Of Calcination, as well of Bodies as of Spirits, with its Causes and Methods.

After the narration of Distillation, we proceed to discourse of *Calcination*. Calcination is the Pulverization of a thing by fire, through privation of the humidity consolidating the parts. The cause of the invention of it is, that the adustive, corrupting and defiling sulphureity, may be abolished by fire. Yet it is diversified, according to the diversity of things to be calcined. For bodies are calcined, and spirits are calcined; yea, other things also extraneous from the nature of these; yet with a diverse intention. And seeing there are imperfect bodies of two kinds; *viz.* hard, as Venus and Mars, and soft, as Jupiter and Saturn; all which are calcined: there was a necessity of calcining them with a divers intention, *viz.* general and special. They are all calcined with one general intention; which is, that their corrupting and defiling sulphureity may be abolished by fire. For so every adustive sulphureity, which could not be removed without Calcination, is burnt away from every thing whatsoever . . .

Likewise, the common intention in it is *Depuration* of the earthiness: for it is found, that bodies are cleansed by reiterated Calcination and Reduction; as we shall shew in the following . . .

But the cause of the invention of the Calcination of spirits, is, that they may the better be fixed, and be the more easily dissolved into water. Because every kind of things calcined is more fixed than the not calcined, and of easier solution; and because the parts of the Calcinate more subtiliated by fire, are more easily mixed with waters, and turned into water. And this you will find so to be, if you be experienced. The Calcination of other things is subservient to the exigency of the preparation of spirits and bodies; of which preparation we shall speak more at large in the following. But any of these things, or such as these, is not of perfection.

. . . Therefore the first Calcination by fire only is thus prepared: you must have a vessel of Iron or Earth, formed after the similitude of a Porringer, the structure of which must be very firm, and fitted to the furnace of Calcination, in such wise, that under it the coals may be cast in and blowed. These being thus ordered, you must cast in Lead or Tin into your vessel, which must be firmly set upon a trivet of iron, or on three stone-columes, and likewise surely fastned to the walls of its furnace, with three or four stones set in stiff between the furnace-sides and the vessel, that it may not be stirred . . . Therefore in that furnace kindle fire under your vessel of Sublimation, sufficient for fusion of the body to be calcined. And when the body shall, by heat of fire, contract a black skin upon it, gather that off from it by a slice,[15] or other fit instrument of Iron or stone, that will not permit it self to be burnt to the infection of the calx. This drawing off, or taking off the skin, must so long be continued, as until the whole body be converted to powder. If it be Saturn, a greater fire must be administred, until the calx be changed into a colour most yellow or red. If it be Jupiter, it must likewise be exposed and continued in the fire, until the calx be changed into compleat whiteness . . .

But the form of the furnace of this Calcination, is the same with the form of the furnace of Distillation, only that this must have one great hole left in the crown of it,

---

[15] A "flattish utensil (sometimes perforated) used for various purposes in cookery" (*OED*).

whence it may free it self from fumosities. And the site of things to be calcined, must be in the midst of the furnace, that the fire may have free access to them round about. But the vessel must be of earth, made in the form of a Porringer or deep dish.

The way of Calcination of spirits, is, that to them approaching to Fixation be administred fire, gradually, and very leisurely increased, that they fly not, until they be able to sustain the greatest fire. Their vessel must be round, every way closed, and their furnace the same with this lastly mentioned. With a like furnace, and like vessel, every thing is likewise calcined...

Chap. 15: Of Solution, and its Cause.

Now we intend to speak of *Solution*. Solution is the reduction of a dry thing into water. Therefore, we say, that every perfection of Solution is compleated with subtile waters, and especially the acute, and sharp, and saline waters, having no feces; as is distilled vinegar, sowre grapes, pears of very great sharpness, pomegranets, and the like of these distilled.

The cause of the invention of this was the Subtiliation[16] of those things, which neither have fusion nor ingress; by which was lost the great utility of fixed spirits, and of those things which are of their nature. For every thing which is dissolved must necessarily have the nature of salt, or of allom, or of their like. And the nature of them is, that they give like fusion... And since they in their own nature, agree with bodies, and each with other, fusion being acquired, they must by that necessarily penetrate bodies, and penetrating transmute the same. But they neither penetrate, nor transmute, without our Magistery, which is this, *viz.* that after Solution and Coagulation of the body, to it be administred some one of the spirits purified, not fixed; and that so often sublimed from it, as until it remain with it, and give to it a more swift fusion, and conserve the same in fusion from Vitrification. For the nature of spirits is, not to be vitrified, and to preserve the mixture from Vitrification, as long as they are in it. Therefore the spirit, which more retains the nature of spirits, more defends from Vitrification...

But the way of Solution is twofold, *viz.* by hot dung, and by boyling or hot water. Of both which there is one intention, and one effect. The way of Dissolving by dung, is, that the Calcinate be put into a glass vessel, and upon the same poured of distilled vinegar, or the like, double its weight, and the mouth of the vessel well closed, that nothing may respire; and then this matter, with its vessels, set in hot dung to be dissolved, and the Solution afterwards by filter separated...

The way of Dissolving by boyling water, is more swift, and it is thus: the Calcinate must in like manner be put into its vessel, with vinegar poured on it as before, and the orifice well closed, that nothing expire; then the vessel must be set, buryed in straw, into a pan full of water, and in the way of Distillation by water, we before appointed; and afterward fire kindled under it, until the water boyl for an hour. This being done, the Solution must be filtred, and kept apart. But the not dissolved, again calcined, and again in the same manner dissolved; until by repeating the labour, the whole be dissolved.

---

[16] "The action of making a thing 'subtile', thin, or fine; rarefaction; purification by separating the fine parts from the coarse" (*OED*).

Chap. 16: Of Coagulation, and its Causes, and of diverse ways of coagulating Mercury; and of dissolved Medicines.

Coagulation is the reduction of a thing liquid, to a solid substance, by privation of the humidity. But there is a twofold cause of its invention; one is, the *Induration*, or hardning of Argentvive; the other cause of invention is the freeing of Medicines dissolved, from the wateriness with them admixed. Therefore it is diversified, according to the multiplicity of things to be coagulated. For Argentvive needs one Coagulation, but dissolved Medicines another. Yet there is a twofold Coagulation of Argentvive. One, by washing away its whole innate humidity from it: the other, by *Inspissation* (or thickning) of its humidity, until it be hardned . . .

Thus we have shewed you the properties of the Medicine, by which you may attain to it; and this we have determined in a very proper speech. Therefore studiously exercise your self thereabout, and you will find it. But that you may not blame us, as if we had not sufficiently spoken thereof, we say, that this Medicine is extracted from metallick bodies themselves, with their Sulphur, or Arsnick prepared: likewise from Sulphur alone, or Arsnick prepared; and it may be extracted from bodies only. But from Argentvive alone it is more easily, and more nearly, and more perfectly found; because Nature more amicably embraceth its proper Nature, and in it more rejoyceth, than in an extraneous Nature. And in it is facility of extraction of the substance thereof, seeing it already hath a substance subtile in act. But the ways of acquiring this Medicine are by Sublimation, as is by us sufficiently declared.

Chap. 17: Of Fixation, and its Causes, and of the diverse ways of fixing Bodies and Spirits.

Fixation is the convenient disposing a fugitive thing, to abide and sustain the fire. The cause of the invention of this Fixation, is, that every Tincture, and every Alteration, may be perpetuated in the thing altered, and not changed. But it also is diversified according to the diversity of things to be fixed; which are certain bodies diminished from perfection, as Saturn, Jupiter, Mars, and Venus: and according to the diversity of spirits also, which are Sulphur and Arsnick in one degree, and Argentvive in another; but Marchasite, Magnesia, Tutia, and the like of these, in the third.

Therefore these bodies diminished from perfection, are fixed by their Calcination; because thereby they are freed from their volatile and corrupting sulphureity. And this we have sufficiently declared in the chapter of Calcination. But Sulphur and Arsnick are fixed two ways, *viz.* by reiteration of their Sublimation in the vessel Aludel, until they remain fixed. Therefore, according to this, the intention of hastening the Fixation of them, is, that the invention of repeating a manifold Sublimation in a short time, be observed therein; which reiteration is made by two Aludels, with their two heads or covers, in the following order, that you may never cease from the work of Sublimation, until you have fixed them. Therefore, so soon as they have ascended in one vessel, put them into the other; and so do continually, never suffering them long to abide adhering to the sides of either vessel; but constantly keep them in the elevation of fire, until the elevation of them ceaseth. For, the sooner you can multiply the manifold repetitions of Sublimation, the more swiftly and better will you abbreviate the time of Fixation. For this cause, there was a second way of Fixion found out, which is by precipitating of it sublimed into heat, that it may constantly abide therein, until it be fixed. And this is done by a long glass vessel, the bottom of which (made of Earth, not of glass, because that would crack) must be artificially connexed with good luting; and the ascending matter, when it adheres to the sides of the vessel, with a spatula of Iron or Stone, thrust down to the heat of the bottom, and this Precipitation repeated, till the whole be fixed...

Chap. 18: Of Ceration, and its Cause.

Ceration is the mollification of an hard thing, not fusible unto liquefaction. Hence it is manifest, that the cause of the invention of this was, that the matter which had not ingress into the body for alteration, by reason of privation of its liquefaction, might be mollified so as to flow, and have ingress; therefore some thought Ceration was to be made with liquid oyls and waters: but that is erroneous, and wholly remote from the principles of this Natural Magistery, and reproved by the manifest Works of Nature. For we find not in those metallick bodies, that Nature hath posited an humidity soon terminable; but rather long durable, for the necessity of their fusion and mollification; because, if she had insited in them an humidity soon terminable, it would necessarily follow that the bodies must be totally deprived of it in one only ignition. Whence also it would follow, that every body could neither be hammered nor melted, after one ignition.

Wherefore, imitating the Works of Nature as much as we can, we must necessarily follow her way in cerating. She cerates in the radix of fusible things, with an humidity, which is above all humidities, able to sustain the heat of fire: therefore it is necessarily expedient for us also, to cerate with like humidity...

The way of Ceration by them is, that the Sublimation of them be so often multiplied upon the thing to be cerated, until remaining with their humidity in it, they give good fusion. Yet this cannot be effected, before the perfect cleansing of them from every corrupting thing. But it seems better to me, that the oyls of these should be first fixed, by Oyl of Tartar, and every Ceration, competent and necessary for this Art, be made with them.

The end of the First Book of Geber of the Sum of Perfection, or of the Perfect Magistery.

From *His Book of Furnaces*

The Preface:

...We have writ this *Book of Furnaces* (see fig. 13), in which we shall deliver the manual practice, in preparations both of *Spirits* and of *Bodies*; that Artificers may the better attain to the compleatment of the Work...We intend first to treat of all the *wayes of operating*; as namely, what the *Furnace* is, with its *Instruments*, which hath respect to every thing to be prepared, even unto compleatment of the Work, with the *Regimen of Fire* appropriate to it; and what *Vessels* are fit for the purpose, that the Artist may with them compleat his Operation. Secondly, we will shew what things are to be prepared; that he may be able, of things simple or commixt, to generate *Sol*, or *Luna*, with splendour. Thirdly, we will declare those things, which may be perfected with alternatives, and which are naturally altered with total compleatment...

Chap. 1: Of the Calcinatory Furnace.

Let the *Calcinatory Furnace* be made square, in length four foot, and three foot in breadth, and let the thickness of the walls be half a foot; after this manner: *Luna, Venus, Mars,* or other things to be calcined, must be put into dishes or pans of most strong clay, such as of which Crucibles are made, that they may persist in the asperity of Fire, even to the total combustion of the thing to be calcined. Calcination is the Treasure of a Thing; be not you weary of Calcination; but study what we have said in our volumes. For imperfect bodies are cleansed by Calcination, and by reduction of the Calcinate into a solid body or mass. Then is our Medicine projected upon them, and cause give to you of Joy.

12 Avicenna (c. 980–1037)

De Congelatione et Conglutinatione Lapidum

In addition to his achievements in medicine and philosophy, the Persian-born Avicenna ("Prince of Physicians," "Aristotle of the Arabians") is well known for his studies in mathematics, physics, music, and alchemy. Like Jabir, Avicenna accepted the sulphur–mercury theory of the origin of metals in the earth, yet expressed total disbelief in the possibility that the essences of metals could be changed through alchemical transmutation. As we have seen, skepticism about transmutation was not widely shared by other Moslem authorities; nonetheless, Avicenna's position came to be extremely influential, largely as the result of a bibliographical accident. About 1200 the Englishman William of Sareshel translated into Latin a meteorological passage from Avicenna's work, the *Kitâb al-Shifâ'* (the *Book of the Remedy*) and placed it at the end of an earlier translation of Aristotle's *Meteorology*, where it came to be regarded as the "missing" conclusion to the fourth book. Entitled *De Congelatione et Conglutinatione Lapidum* or *De Mineralibus*, this short section was quickly accepted as a genuine Aristotelian work: thus, Avicenna's skeptical attack was launched albeit under the cover of Aristotle's name. The work's authorship remained in question until 1927, when E. J. Holmyard and D. C. Mandeville demonstrated conclusively that *De Congelatione* was, in fact, "partly a direct translation and partly a *résumé*" (8) of Avicenna's book. The attack on belief in the possibility of alchemical transmutation occupies the last five paragraphs of the selection, beginning with "As to the claims of the alchemists"; earlier topics of interest include Avicenna's views on the properties and formation of metals, the sulphur-mercury theory, the primacy of mercury, and alchemy as an art of imitation.

The following text is reproduced from *Âvicennæ de Congelatione et Conglutinatione Lapidum being sections of the Kitâb al-Shifâ'*, trans. E. J. Holmyard and D. C. Mandeville (Paris: Paul Geuthner, 1927), 33–42. Additional readings: *The Summa Perfectionis of Pseudo-Geber*, ed. and trans. William R. Newman (Leiden: E. J. Brill, 1991), 2–5; E. J. Holmyard, *Alchemy*, 92–7.

On Stones and Mountains

In short, it is in the nature of water, as you know, to become transformed into earth through a predominating earthy virtue; you know, too, that it is in the nature of earth to become transformed into water through a predominating aqueous virtue. In this connection, there is a substance used by those folk who have lost their way amid their artful contrivances which, when they are so minded, they call *Virgin's Milk*;[1] it is compounded of two waters which coagulate into a hard solid.

The Formation of Minerals

The time has now arrived for us to give an account of the properties of mineral substances. We say, therefore, that mineral bodies may be roughly divided into four groups, *viz.* stones, fusible substances, sulphurs and salts. This is for the following reason: some of the mineral bodies are weak in substance and feeble in composition and union, while others are strong in substance. Of the latter, some are malleable and some are not malleable. Of [the former, *i.e.*] those which are feeble in substance, some have the nature of salt and are easily dissolved by moisture, such as alum, vitriol, sal-ammoniac and *qalqand*,[2] while others are oily in nature and are not easily dissolved by moisture alone, such as sulphur and arsenic [sulphides].

Mercury is included in the second group, inasmuch as it is the essential constituent element of malleable bodies or at least is similar to it.

All malleable bodies are fusible, though sometimes only indirectly, whereas most non-malleable substances cannot be fused in the orthodox way or even softened except with difficulty.

The material of malleable bodies is an aqueous substance united so firmly with an earthy substance that the two cannot be separated from one another. This aqueous substance has been congealed by cold after heat has acted upon it and matured it. Included in the group [of malleable bodies], however, are some which are still quick[3] and have not congealed on account of their oily nature; for this reason, too, they are malleable.

As regards the stony kinds of naturally-occurring mineral substances, the material of which they are made is also aqueous, but they have not been congealed by cold alone. Their congelation has, on the contrary, been brought about by dryness which has converted the aquosity into terrestreity. They do not contain a quick, oily humidity and so are non-malleable; and because their solidification has been caused mainly by dryness, the majority of them are infusible unless they are subjected to some physical process which facilitates fusion.

Alum and sal-ammoniac belong to the family of salts, though sal-ammoniac possesses a fieriness in excess of its earthiness, and may therefore be completely sublimed. It consists of water combined with a hot smoke, very tenuous and excessively fiery, and has been coagulated by dryness.

In the case of the sulphurs, their aquosity has suffered a vigorous leavening with earthiness and aeriness under the leavening action of heat, so far as to become oily in nature; subsequently it has been solidified by cold.

The vitriols are composed of a salty principle, a sulphureous principle and stone, and contain the virtue of some of the fusible bodies [metals]. Those of them which resemble *qalqand* and *qalqatâr*[4] are formed from crude vitriols by partial solution, the salty constituent alone dissolving, together with whatever sulphureity there may be. Coagulation follows,

---

[1] Among several definitions cited in the *DAI*, Abraham terms Virgin's Milk "the transforming mercurial waters, the white mercury of the philosophers" (211).
[2] Green vitriol, $FeSO_4 \cdot 7H_2O$ (translator's note).   [3] "Alive," as in quicksilver.
[4] "Yellow vitriol in which are shining golden eyes" (translator's note).

after a virtue has been acquired from a metallic ore. Those that acquire the virtue of iron become red or yellow, *e.g. qalqatâr*, while those which acquire the virtue of copper become green. It is for this reason that they are so easily prepared by means of this art.

Mercury seems to be water with which a very tenuous and sulphureous earth has become so intimately mixed that no surface can be separated from it without something of that dryness covering it. Consequently it does not cling to the hand or confine itself closely to the shape of the vessel which contains it, but remains in no particular shape unless it is subdued. Its whiteness is derived from the purity of that aquosity, from the whiteness of the subtle earthiness which it contains, and from the admixture of aeriness with it.

A property of mercury is that it is solidified by the vapours of sulphureous substances; it is therefore quickly solidified by lead or by sulphur vapour. It seems, moreover, that mercury, or something resembling it, is the essential constituent element of all the fusible bodies, for all of them are converted into mercury on fusion. Most of them, however, fuse only at a very high temperature, so that their mercury appears red. In the case of lead, an onlooker does not doubt that this is mercury, since it melts at a lower temperature, but if during the fusion it is heated to the high temperature [mentioned above], its colour becomes the same as that of the other fusible bodies, i.e. fiery-red.

It is for this reason, *viz.* that it is of their substance, that mercury so easily clings to all these bodies. But these bodies differ in their composition from it by reason of variation in the mercury itself – or whatever it is that plays the same part – and also through variation in what is mixed with it and causes its solidification.

If the mercury be pure, and if it be commingled with and solidified by the virtue of a white sulphur which neither induces combustion nor is impure, but on the contrary is more excellent than that prepared by the adepts, then the product is silver. If the sulphur besides being pure is even better than that just described, and whiter, and if in addition it possesses a tinctorial, fiery, subtle and non-combustive virtue – in short, if it is superior to that which the adepts can prepare – it will solidify the mercury into gold.

Then again, if the mercury is of good substance, but the sulphur which solidifies it is impure, possessing on the contrary a property of combustibility, the product will be copper. If the mercury is corrupt, unclean, lacking in cohesion and earthy, and the sulphur is also impure, the product will be iron. As for tin, it is probable that its mercury is good, but that its sulphur is corrupt; and that the commingling [of the two] is not firm, but has taken place, so to speak, layer by layer, for which reason the metal shrieks.[5] Lead, it seems likely, is formed from an impure, heavy, clayey mercury and an impure, fetid and feeble sulphur, for which reason its solidification has not been thorough.

There is little doubt that, by alchemy, the adepts can contrive solidifications in which the qualities of the solidifications of mercury by the sulphurs are perceptible to the senses, though the alchemical qualities are not identical in principle or in perfection with the natural ones, but merely bear a resemblance and relationship to them. Hence the belief arises that their natural formation takes place in this way or in some similar way, though alchemy falls short of nature in this respect and, in spite of great effort, cannot overtake her.

---

[5] "A reference to the well-known *cry of tin*" (translator's note).

Alchemy as an art of imitation only

As to the claims of the alchemists,[6] it must be clearly understood that it is not in their power to bring about any true change of species. They can, however, produce excellent imitations, dyeing the red [metal] white so that it closely resembles silver, or dyeing it yellow so that it closely resembles gold. They can, too, dye the white [metal] with any colour they desire, until it bears a close resemblance to gold or copper; and they can free the leads from most of their defects and impurities. Yet in these [dyed metals] the essential nature remains unchanged; they are merely so dominated by induced qualities that errors may be made concerning them, just as it happens that men are deceived by salt, *qalqand*, sal-ammoniac, *etc.*

I do not deny that such a degree of accuracy may be reached as to deceive even the shrewdest, but the possibility of eliminating or imparting the specific difference has never been clear to me. On the contrary, I regard it as impossible, since there is no way of splitting up one combination into another. Those properties which are perceived by the senses are probably not the differences which separate the metals into species, but rather accidents or consequences, the specific differences being unknown. And if a thing is unknown, how is it possible for anyone to endeavour to produce it or to destroy it?

As for the removal or imparting of the dyes or such accidental properties as odours and densities, these are things which one ought not to persist in denying merely because of lack of knowledge concerning them, for there is no proof whatever of their impossibility.

It is likely that the proportion of the elements which enter into the composition of the essential substance of each of the metals enumerated is different from that of any other. If this is so, one metal cannot be converted into another unless the compound is broken up and converted into the composition of that into which its transformation is desired. This, however, cannot be effected by fusion, which maintains the union and merely causes the introduction of some foreign substance or virtue.

There is much I could have said upon this subject if I had so desired, but there is little profit in it nor is there any necessity for it here.

---

[6] Here begins the passage made famous in the Middle Ages because of its attribution to Aristotle and inclusion in *Meteorology*, bk. 4, where it was widely accepted as genuine. In fact, it is a translation (*ca.* 1200) by Alfred of Sareshel of the meteorological section of Avicenna's *Kitâb al-Shifâ'*. The passage's notoriety stems from its abrupt rejection of metallic transmutation and contention that alchemists perform only aurifiction, not aurifaction; Nature is decidedly superior to Art.

13 Albertus Magnus (1193? or 1206?–1280)

From the *Libellus de Alchimia*

Although answers to many questions about the life, writings, travels, places of residence – even the birth date – of Albertus Magnus are uncertain, his preeminence in medieval Latin European culture is beyond dispute. In the words of Lynn Thorndike, Albertus was "the most prolific of its writers, the most influential of its teachers, the dean of its scholars, the one learned man of the twelfth and thirteenth centuries to be called 'the Great'" (*HMES* 2:521). Born in Swabia in Germany, Albertus achieved distinction as a member of the Dominican order and holder of high ecclesiastical offices, such as the bishopric of Ratisbon, 1260–62. His greatest fame, however, resulted from studies in most of the known fields of learning, which, following the plan of his master Aristotle, included physics, psychology, celestial phenomena, geography, botany, zoology, minerals, medicine, and optics, as well as theology. Only in the last of these was he exceeded by his pupil, Thomas Aquinas.

Albertus's writings on the "occult" arts of alchemy, astrology, and magic are often regarded as spurious, and it is difficult to separate the genuine from the false. The *Libellus de Alchimia*, from which the following selections are taken, is as likely to be authentic as any of the alchemical attributions and provides an excellent overview of the art in the early medieval period. It is also remarkable for its avoidance of the obscure rhetoric that plagues so much medieval and early modern alchemical writing. For these reasons, the brief tract enjoyed wide circulation in manuscript.

Selections, including the later "Additions," are from the *Libellus de Alchimia, Ascribed to Albertus Magnus*, ed. and trans. by Sister Virginia Heines, S.C.N. (Berkeley and Los Angeles: University of California Press, 1958), and are reprinted with the kind permission of the University of California Press. Additional readings: J. R. Partington, "Albertus Magnus on Alchemy," *Ambix* 1,1 (May 1937): 3–20; Pearl Kibre, "Alchemical Writings Ascribed to Albertus Magnus," *Speculum* 17,4 (Oct. 1942): 499–518.

1. On Various Errors.

Now, in this little work of mine, I shall describe for you, briefly and simply, how you should undertake the practice of such a great art. I shall first point out, however, all the deviations, errors, and stumbling blocks of this art, into which many and, [indeed], nearly all [are inclined to] fall.

For I have seen some who, with great diligence, were performing certain sublimations and were incapable of carrying them out, because they failed to grasp the fundamentals.

I have seen others making a good beginning, but who, because of excessive drinking and other follies, were unable to carry on the work. I have seen others who made a good decoction, distillation, or sublimation, but because of the excessive length of the work, they left it uncompleted.

I have seen others who possessed the true art and who performed their operations with skill and diligence, but who lost spirits in sublimations because of porous vessels, and for this reason doubted, and cultivated the art no further.

I have seen still others who, desiring to pursue the art, but incapable of waiting the required time, performed too rapid sublimations, distillations, and solutions, because of which they found the spirits contaminated and decomposed, and the aqueous solutions and distillates turbid; and therefore they too lost faith.

I have seen many who were carrying forward the work with diligence and yet at length failed because they did not have the necessary means of support. Hence the verse:

When the work is in danger, mortal need increases:
You may know many things, [yet] without money, you
will be nought.

Hence this art is of no value to paupers, because one must have enough for expenses for at least two years. Thus, if one should happen to err in one's work or prolong it, one need not be reduced to penury, as I have seen occur many times.

I have seen some who made pure and good sublimations as many as five times, but then were unable to make any more and became deceitful; they whitened Copper, adding five or six parts of Silver, and thus cheated both themselves and others.

I have seen others who sublimed spirits and fixed them wishing with them to color Copper and Tin, and when they made no impression or penetration, they became doubtful [about the art].

I have seen also those who fixed spirits, covering them with a penetrating oil, until they made a penetration into the bodies, adding yet another part of Silver, and thus they whitened Copper – which is similar to Silver in malleation and testing and in whiteness – which withstood even a second and a third testing, and yet had not been perfected, for the Copper had not been calcined nor purged of its impurity. Hence Aristotle says: "I do not believe metals can be transmuted unless they are reduced to prime matter, that is, reduced to a calx by roasting in the fire, then [transmutation] is possible."[1]

Yet I saw other wise men who finished sublimations and fixations of powders and spirits, prepared solutions and distillations from the powders, then coagulated them and calcined the metals, whitened the bodies to white, and reddened the bodies to red, after which they reduced them to a solid mass and colored them to produce Gold and Silver, which were better than the natural in every testing and malleation.

Since seeing so many who have erred, I resolved that I would write of the true and tested works and of the better [ones] of all Philosophers, among whom I have labored and have had experience; nothing else shall I write beyond what I have seen with my own eyes.

---

[1] Like many of his contemporaries, Albertus misattributed to Aristotle the famous passage from Avicenna's *De Congelatione et Conglutinatione* in which alchemical transmutation appears to have been rejected. The passage had been appended to the fourth book of Aristotle's *Meteorology*.

2. How do Metals Arise?

Alchemy is an art invented by [the] Alchemist: the name is derived from the Greek *archymo*, which in Latin is *massa*. Through this art, corrupted metals in minerals are restored and the imperfect made perfect.

It should be noted that metals differ from one another only in their accidental form, not in their essential form; therefore the stripping of accidents in metals is possible. Hence, it is also possible, through this art, to bring about a new body, since all species of metals are produced in the earth from a commixture of sulphur and quicksilver[2] or because of foetid earth. Just as a boy in the body of his mother contracts infirmity from a diseased womb by reason of the accident of location and of infection, though the sperm is healthy, yet, the boy becomes a leper and unclean because of the corruption of the womb. Thus it is in metals which are corrupted, either because of contaminated sulphur or foetid earth; thus there is the following difference among all the metals, by which they differ from one another.

When pure red sulphur comes into contact with quicksilver in the earth, gold is made in a short or long time, either through the persistence [of the contact] or through decoction of the nature subservient to them. When pure and white sulphur comes into contact with quicksilver in pure earth, then silver is made, which differs from gold in this, that sulphur in gold will be red, whereas in silver it will be white. When, on the other hand, red sulphur, corrupt and burning, comes into contact with quicksilver in the earth, then copper is made, and it does not differ from gold except in this, that in gold it was not corrupt, but here [in copper] it is corrupt. When white sulphur, corrupt and burning, comes into contact with quicksilver in the earth, tin is made, [as is indicated from the fact that] it crackles between the teeth[3] and quickly liquefies, which happens because the quicksilver was not well mixed with the sulphur. When white sulphur, corrupt and burning, comes into contact with quicksilver in foetid earth, iron is made. When sulphur, black and corrupt, comes into contact with quicksilver, lead is made. Aristotle says of this that lead is leprous gold.

Now sufficient has been said about the origin of metals and how they differ from one another in accidental but not in essential form. It remains now to examine the proofs of the philosophers and authorities, to see how they demonstrate that this is the true art, so that we may be able to contend with those who maintain that it is not true.

3. The Proof that the Alchemical Art is True.

Some persons, and they are many, wish to contradict us, especially those who neither know anything about the art nor are acquainted with the nature of metals, and who are ignorant of the intrinsic and extrinsic properties of metals, understanding very little about their dimensions and densities. To these, when they set against us the words of Aristotle, who says, "let the masters of Alchemy know that the species of things cannot be changed,"[4] we must answer that he said this about those who believe in and wish to effect

---

[2] Albertus follows the popular sulphur-mercury theory of the origin of metals identified chiefly with Geber. These were not the common, ordinary sulphur and mercury but "principles of causation" related to the subterranean smoky and vaporous exhalations posited in Aristotle's *Meteorology*. The alchemists held that the philosopher's stone resulted from the conjoining of philosophical (or "sophic") sulphur and mercury.

[3] Cf. Avicenna's reference to the "shrieking" of tin in *De Congelatione*.

[4] Again, the reference is to Avicenna's *De Congelatione*.

the transmutation of metals that are still corrupt, but this, without doubt cannot be done. Let us, therefore, listen to the words of Aristotle which say the following: "It is true that experiment destroys the form of the species, and especially in metals, and this is the case when some metal is calcined and hence is reduced to ashes and calx, which can be ground, washed, and softened with acid water until made white and natural: and thus these bodies through calcinations and various medicines may lose the brown corrupt vapor, and acquire an airy, vivifying vapor, and the whitened calx will be reduced to a solid mass, which can be colored white or red." For this reason, Hermes says that spirits cannot enter bodies unless they are purified, and then they enter only through the instrumentality of water. Aristotle says: "I do not believe that metals can be transmuted unless they are reduced to prime matter, that is, purified of their own corruption by roasting in the fire."

To those still dissenting and unbelieving, I wish to make myself clearer because we know whereof we speak and have seen what we are asserting: we see different species receive different forms at different times; thus it is evident that by decoction, and persistent contact, what is red in *arsenicum* will become black and then will become white by sublimation; this is always the case.

If, by chance, someone should say that such species can easily be transmuted from color to color, but that in metals it is impossible, I will reply by citing the evident cause through various indications and proofs, and will thoroughly destroy their error.

For we see that azure, which is called *transmarinum*, is produced from silver; since, as is more easily seen, when it is perfected in nature losing all corruption, the accidental is destroyed rather than the essential. We see, furthermore, that copper receives a yellow color from calamine stone,[5] and yet neither the copper nor the calamine stone is perfect, since fire acts on both.

We see that litharge is made from tin, but tin through too much decoction turns a golden color; however, it is possible to convert it to a species of silver, since it is of this nature.

We see iron converted to quicksilver, although this may seem impossible to some; why it is possible I have already stated above; namely, that all metals are made from quicksilver and sulphur; wherefore, since quicksilver is the origin of all metals, it is possible also for iron to be reconverted to quicksilver. Do you not perceive, for example, that water solidifies in the winter time through excess cold, and becomes ice, and that ice melts by the heat of the sun and returns to water as before? Thus from quicksilver, wherever it is in the earth, and from sulphur, if this also is present, a union of these two comes about and through a very mild decoction over a long period of time, in which they are combined and hardened to a mineral stone, from which the metal may be extracted.

Likewise, we see that cerussa is made from lead, minium from cerussa, and lead from minium.[6]

Behold, now, it has already been sufficiently proved how species are changed from color to color even to the third or fourth form. From this it must not be doubted at all, that corrupted metals can become pure by their own medicines.

Since the foundation for this art has now been laid, let us see what we shall build upon. For if we build upon hay or wood or straw, fire will consume all. Therefore, let us

[5] Ores of zinc (Heines's note).   [6] For details of these preparations, see sections 27–29 (Heines).

procure stones, which are neither destroyed by fire nor by decay; then we will be free from all anxiety.

From what we have said concerning the difficulties of the art – its principle, and, finally, concerning its proof – it is evident that we have established that it is the true art. Now it remains to be seen how to proceed, and at what time and in what place.

First, at the outset, certain precepts are to be laid down.

The first precept is that the worker in this art must be silent and secretive and reveal his secret to no one, knowing full well that if many know, the secret in no way will be kept, and that when it is divulged, it will be repeated with error. Thus it will be lost, and the work will remain imperfect.

The second precept is that he should have a place and a special house, hidden from men, in which there are two or three rooms in which are carried on the processes for sublimating and for making solutions and distillations, as I will show later.

The third one is that he should observe the time in which the work must be done and the hours for sublimations and solutions; because sublimations are of little value in the winter; but solutions and calcinations may be made at any time: All these things, however, I will show clearly in [the discussion of] these operations.

The fourth is that the worker in this art should be careful, and assiduous in his efforts, and not grow weary, but persevere to the end. For, if he begins and does not persevere, he will lose both materials and time.

Fifth, it should be done according to the usage of the art: first in collecting [supplies], second in sublimations, third in fixations, fourth in calcinations, fifth in solutions, sixth in distillations, seventh in coagulations, and so on in order. If he should wish to color besides subliming, and to both coagulate and distill, he will lose his powders, because when they will have been volatilized he will have nothing left of them whatever, but they will be very quickly dispersed. Or, if he wishes to color with fixed powders which are neither dissolved nor distilled, they will neither penetrate nor mix with the bodies [to be colored].

The sixth is that all vessels in which medicines may be put, either waters or oils, whether over the fire or not, should be of glass or glazed. For, if acid waters are placed in a copper vessel, they will turn green; if placed in an iron or lead one, they will be blackened and corrupted; if placed in earthenware, the walls will be penetrated and all will be lost.

The seventh is that one should be on one's guard before all else against [associating oneself] with princes or potentates in any [of these] operations, because of two dangers: If you have committed yourself, they will ask you from time to time, "Master, how are you succeeding? When will we see some good results?" and, not being able to wait for the end of the work, they will say that, it is nothing, it is trifling, and the like, and then you will experience the greatest dissatisfaction. And if you are not successful, you will suffer continued humiliation because of it. If, however, you do succeed, they will try to detain you permanently, and will not permit you to go away, and thus you will be ensnared by your own words and caught by your own discourses.

The eighth precept is that no one should begin operations without plenty of funds, so that he can obtain everything necessary and useful for this art: for if he should undertake them and lack funds for expenses then he will lose the material and everything.

4. The Kind and Number of Furnaces that are Necessary.

Now it must be seen how furnaces are made as well as the number and kind needed.

Regarding which it should be observed that the quantity of the work at hand should determine the number of furnaces to be made. For if you have sufficient supplies and want to undertake a great amount of work then you should construct many of them. If, on the other hand, there is a scarcity, construct the furnaces according to the amount of powders and medicines you have.

I desire to set forth a plan of furnaces as well as the number, which will be suitable to the rich workers as well as to the poor ones.

First, the philosopher's furnace must be described. Build it near a wall, where the wind can approach: so that the furnace is about an arm's distance from the wall, in this fashion. Dig a pit in the earth to the depth of the elbow, about two spans wide or a little more, and spread all over with the clay of the master [potter]: above this [pit], erect a circular wall lined with the same clay.

5. On the Quality and Quantity of Furnaces.

Take common clay and to four parts add a fifth part of potter's clay and grind well, and add a little sand, grind again (some prudently add manure or salt water in which manure will have been dissolved); after doing this make a wall, as mentioned before, above the pit, two feet high or a little less, one span thick, and permit to dry. Then have a disc made of potter's clay, which can sustain strong fire, everywhere perforated with fifty or sixty holes, according to the size of the disc [with the perforations] made like a finger, the upper part narrow and the lower wider so that ashes can easily descend. Below, in the earth, make a canal through earth and wall before the disc has been put in place; this should be narrow at the pit end, while outside, at the wall, it should be wider, about one span in width, so that the wind may enter. This canal should be lined with clay; then the disc should be placed on top, in such a way that the wider openings of the perforations are on the underside. Next a wall is built upon the first wall and the disc, to the thickness of one span, but the wall should be above the disc to about the distance of one arm. The furnace should have a hole in the middle above the disc where the coals will be laid. At the top there should be a hole through which calcining vessels may be placed: this hole is to be covered over afterwards with a tight cover. The furnace may also have beneath four or five small holes about three digits wide.

This is the general plan of the furnace.

Note also that a clay tripod should be placed above the disc, upon which are to be placed the calcining vessels, and under which the coals.

6. How many, what kind, and of what use are the Sublimation Ovens?

Now sublimation ovens must be considered, of which there should be at least two or four, and made throughout with disc, canal, and perforations like the philosopher's oven, but smaller in size: moreover, they should be in one place for convenience [of supervision].

10. The Four Spirits of Metals which Color.

Note that the four spirits of metals are mercury, sulphur, auripigmentum or arsenicum, and sal ammoniac. These four spirits color metals white and red, that is, in Gold and

Silver: yet not of themselves, unless they are first prepared by different medicines for this, and are not volatile, and when placed in the fire burn brilliantly. These spirits fashion Silver from Iron and Tin, or Gold from Copper and Lead.

Thus, as I shall say briefly, all metals may be transmuted into Gold and Silver, which are like all the natural metals, except that the iron of the Alchemist is not attracted by adamantine stone and the gold of the Alchemist does not stimulate the heart of man, nor cure leprosy, while a wound made from it may swell, which does not happen with natural gold. But it is evident that in all other operations, as malleation, testing, and color, it will last forever. From these four spirits the tincture is made, which in Arabic is called *elixir*, and in Latin, *fermentum*.

11. What is Elixir, and how many of the Metals are Transmuted through these Four Spirits?

Elixir is the Arabic name and *fermentum* is the Latin: because, just as bread is leavened and raised through good yeast, so the matter of metals may be transmuted through these four spirits into white and red, but especially through mercury, because it is the source and origin of all metals.

12. On the Genera of Medicines and their Names.

The following is a list of the other spirits and medicines and how they are named: sal commune [common salt], sal alkali, sal nitrum, sal borax, Roman alum, alum from Yemen, tartar, atramentum, green copper, calamine stone, copperas, tutia,[7] cinnabar, minium, cerussa, hen's eggs, eggshells, vinegar, urine, cadmia, marchasita, magnesia, and many other things of which we have no need in this book.

These substances do not color, but the spirits are serviceable, for they are quickly prepared and dissolved, and with their solutions they macerate the calx of the metals, and [cause] these bodies to take on rectifying vapors.

Their preparation, occurrence, and the manner of calcining and solution, we will show in order in the following chapters.

13. What is Mercury and what is its Origin?

Mercury is viscous fluid united in the interior of the earth with a white subtle earth, through the most moderate heat until there is equal union of the two. It rolls on a flat plane with ease and, despite its fluid nature, does not stick to it, and it may possess a viscous form because of its dryness, which tempers it, and prevents adherence [to a surface].

It is the matter of metals when combined with sulphur, that is, as a red stone from which quicksilver can be extracted; and it occurs in the mountains, especially in old drains, in great quantities.

By nature mercury is cold and moist and is the source of all metals, as has been said above. It is created with all metals, is mixed with iron, and without it no metal can be gilded.

---

[7] Atramentum is "a crude mixture of copper and iron sulphates." "Tuchia, which is frequently used in the transmutation of metals, is an artificial and not a natural mixture, for tuchia is made from the smoke which rises and is coagulated by adhering to hard bodies, when the brass is purified from the stones and tin which are in it" (*Liber de mineralibus* [VIII, viii, 102], quoted in Heines).

ADDITION.[8] Quicksilver and sulphur, sublimed with sal ammoniac is converted into a brilliant red powder, but when burned in the fire returns to a fluid and humid substance.

14. What is Sulphur, its Properties, and its Occurrence?

Sulphur, the fatness of the earth,[9] is condensed in minerals of the earth through temperate decoction, whereby it hardens and becomes thick; and when hardened it is called sulphur.

Sulphur has a very strong action, and is a uniform substance throughout; for this reason its oil cannot be separated from it by distillation, as from other substances having oil, but rather by means of acute waters, by boiling sulphur in them. It occurs in the earth, sometimes in the mountains and sometimes in the marshes. There are many varieties; namely white, red, green, yellow, or black: and besides it occurs in the dead form. It is living when extracted from fusible earth, and is effective against the itch. It is dead when it is poured into cylinders, as it is found among apothecaries.

ADDITION. Sulphur has a fiery nature, liquefies as gum and is entirely smoky.

30. What is Sublimation and in how many ways can it be done?

Sublimation is the volatilizing of a dry substance by fire, causing it to cling to the sides of the vessel. Sublimation in fact is diversified according to the diversity of the spirits of those things to be sublimated. One kind [is accomplished] by ignition, as with marchasita, magnesia or tuchia; another with moderate ignition as with mercury and arsenic; and still another with a low fire as with sulphur. Indeed, in one type of sublimation of mercury the separation of its earth will result and there will be a change in its fluidity. On the other hand, it is natural that superfluous earth very often is mixed with things with which it has no affinity, hence its sublimation has thus to be repeated more often. Examples of these are the calx of eggshells and of white marble, and finely ground glass, and every kind of prepared salt. From these latter, it [the earth] is cleansed, from others it is not, unless the bodies are [in a state of] perfection; however, they are rather more corrupt, because all such things have sulphureity which, ascending with it in sublimation, corrupts the work. Because of this, if you sublimate from tin or lead you will note that after the sublimation it is contaminated with blackness. Therefore, sublimation is better accomplished with those things with which it does not agree [in nature]. However, sublimation, in general, would be more readily accomplished with those things with which it [the substance to be sublimated] agrees [in nature] if it were not for the sulphureity [in any of the components] with which it does not agree [in nature]. A method of removing moisture is to mix and grind with calxes − with which the sublimation should be done − until the metal can no longer be detected, and then the moisture is removed by slow heating. As [the moisture] of [the mixture] recedes, the moisture of the mercury will recede with it, as I shall teach you in the following sublimations of spirits.

31. What is Calcination and in how many ways can it be done?

Calcination of any kind is the pulverizing of substances by fire to remove the moisture uniting the parts. Bodies diminished of their own perfection are calcined.

---

[8] The "ADDITIONS" included in the Heines edn. consist of materials "added to the original text at a date much later than the first recension of the text" (xxi).

[9] Cf. Geber, *Sum of Perfection*, bk. 1, pt. 3, chap. 4.

There are also different kinds of calcinations. Bodies are calcined so that the sulphureity corrupting and defiling them may be removed. In fact, each sulphureity may be burned from the substance with which it is combined, but which without calcination cannot be removed. Soft bodies are, indeed, particularly hardened by it, but they [also] take an impression more clearly and harden more readily. Spirits are calcined the better to fix them and bring them more quickly into solution. Every kind of calcined body is more fixed, and more easily sublimed than the uncalcined; hence, soft bodies can be easily calcined through fire; hard bodies need very strong fire [to be calcined], as I shall teach you at the end [of this book].

ADDITION. Silver may be calcined thus: take an ounce of purest Silver, or more if you wish, and from this make plates thin as the [finger] nails of the hand. Add a third part of common salt, from the preparation commonly prepared and calcined, and a fourth part of sublimated mercury, making a powder of said mercury and salt by grinding. Afterwards cement the plates together in the sublimatory, by placing first a layer of the powder, then a second layer of the sheets, and follow layer by layer; then sublime with a slow fire until all the moisture of the mixture evaporates. Close well the opening and increase the fire through the natural day; take care not to remove the vessel from the fire immediately, but let it cool [for] three hours. Do not open the vessel until it is cold, because the spirits will evaporate. When the vessel is cold, take out the sublimed mercury, clear as a crystal, and set [it] aside; then take out the silver that remains half-calcined with the common salt. If possible, crush the salt and the half-calcined Silver at once above the *porphyry*. If it cannot be ground, put it into a glass *cassola* and separate the whole salt with fervent waters, until you perceive no salty taste; dry the remaining calx in the bottom of a *paropsis*,[10] and calcine once again with new salt and mercury sublimed five or six times. Alternate the calcining and washing of the Silver calx until you detect no salty taste. Your calcined Silver will then be the whitest and cleanest [kind], like the rays of the stars, so that if you melt part of the said calx with borax, or with good sal nitrum or sal alkali, you will find your Silver converted to white gold.

32. What is Coagulation and why is it used?

Coagulation is the reduction of liquid substances to a solid mass by deprivation of their vapors. It was devised to harden mercury and purify medicinal solutions of moisture mixed in them. Mercury is coagulated by its frequent precipitation with violence to the dryness of the fire. The dryness of the fire removes the moisture. This is accomplished in a long narrow vessel.

33. What is Fixation and in how many ways are Bodies fixed?

Fixation is the appropriate tempering of a volatile substance in fire. It was devised so that every coloring, and every alteration is perpetuated in another and is not changed: for bodies, whose perfection has been diminished through calcination, are fixed when they are freed from corrupting and volatile sulphureity. Sulphur and arsenicum are fixed in two ways: one method is the repetition of their sublimation from one state to another, or until

---

[10] A *cassola* is "a kind of saucepan with a handle"; a *paropsis* is a "small dish" (Heines's notes).

they achieve stability. Spirits are also fixed in another way, either with the solutions of metals or with oil of tartar, as I shall say below.

ADDITION. Take sublimed mercury, an equal amount of sal ammoniac, and sublime seven times, or until melted, [then] let the stone remain at the bottom; crush it and expose to damp air so it will become a liquid. Soak metallic arsenicum in this water, dissolve in distilled vinegar, and distill seven times, or congeal, and dissolve, and a stone will result.

Metallic arsenicum is made by melting one part of arsenicum with two parts of white soap. Another [procedure] is given in Geber's [*Liber*] *Fornacum*: where you may read [it], if you wish.

Either sublime mercury, or sulphur, or prepared arsenicum, or several of these, at the same time, along with sal tartarum or saltpeter, or sal ammoniac. Do this many times until they remain fixed, then extract [them] with warm water.

34. What is Solution and in how many ways is it done?

Solution is the resolution of any calcined substance into water. It was devised so that the intrinsic qualities of substances might become extrinsic and vice versa, and so that they might be made suitable for distilling; thus they are freed from every contamination. Solution is achieved either by heat and moisture or by cold and moisture, as I shall teach in the following [chapters].

ADDITION. Some [substances] dissolve after being calcined with an equal weight of sulphur, with water or the juice of limes, in a closed crucible.

35. What is Distillation and how is it done?

Distillation is the rising of the vapors of a liquid in its own container. There are different methods: with and without fire, that with fire is of two kinds; one, through rising vapors, as with an alembic; the other through a descensory,[11] as with a pipe, and through fire superimposed on vessels.

The general purpose of distillation is [the] purification of a liquid from its dregs. We can see that the distillate is rendered purer [than the original liquid]. The special purpose of pure water is the imbibition of spirits and clean medicines, so that we can have a pure solution when we need one, for the dregs that can contaminate our medicines and purified spirits will have been removed. Distillation was invented to extract, through a descensory, an oil pure in its nature, whenever we cannot [evidently] have an oil combustible in its nature, as is true of petroleum. However, distillation, through filtration, is devised solely to obtain a clear liquid.

36. What is Ceration and how is it done?

Ceration is the softening of dry and nonfusible substances. It is clear that this process was invented to mollify a body with a view to change (or inceration) and thus permit penetration of other substances, for a body deprived of liquefaction permits no penetration. Some think that ceration should be done with liquids and liquid oils, but that is an error; for in no substance is the whole moisture found better than in sulphur and arsenicum. By this method [sulphur and arsenicum] their sublimation may be multiplied a great many

---

[11] "A vessel or retort used for distillation by descent" (*OED*).

times because of the softened substance, to the point where, finding moisture in them, they attain a good fusion; on the other hand, this cannot be accomplished without perfectly cleansing them of all corruption. But it seems better to me that their oils should first be fixed by oil of tartar and with these oils every ceration can suitably be made. Concerning these things this will suffice.

42. From what substances is Fire made?

Since the principle of sublimation of spirits has been presented, it remains now to investigate the substance of fire. I assert, therefore, that fire should be made of coals for two reasons: first, because it is less work to lay coals than wood; second, because wood gives much more smoke and, because of the smoke, the work cannot be observed well. Vessels are broken by the heat of the fire, as happens oftener when the clay is not good or they [the vessels] are not well baked. And when they break to pieces, white smoke at once appears, which may easily be seen over a fire that is made from coals; hence when the vessels smoke let them be taken from the fire at once or else the sublimation will be lost. Take care that this does not happen.

Note that the upper vessel, namely an aludel, should be glazed, but this is not necessary for the lower [one]. It is customary also to harden the medicine that cannot be sublimed, on a scutella.[12] This is not to be doubted, but it [the medicine] should be ground a second time and mixed with a little more of the dregs and it will be sublimed thoroughly.

44. The Revelation and Teaching of the Secrets of this Art begin here.

Now I have already taught you how to collect various flowers full of the fine fragrances, redolent with health and beauty, and the glory of this world: this is the flower of flowers, the rose of roses, and the lily of the valley. Rejoice therefore, O Youth, in thy adolescence and gather the flowers, since I have introduced you into the garden of Paradise; make from these a wreath for your head, that you may rejoice and enjoy the delights of this world.

I have disclosed to you the meaning, now I will help you to understand the secrets of this art, and what was hidden for such a long time, I shall now bring to light.

Previously, I taught you how to sublimate and to collect the flowers of these substances, therefore, now I shall teach you how to plant them so that they may bear much fruit, and their fruit may last forever. I shall teach you how to fix the powders sublimed, that they may remain in the fire, be combined and mixed with bodies, and [I shall show you that this may be done] in two ways.

45. The Fixation of Powders, so that they can mix with Bodies, is taught here.

Take as much [powders] of these as you wish, one pound or two without anything else, and place in the vessel of fixation, and shape off the opening with good clay, not glazed, of the glassmakers, one digit thick, and close the cracks with good clay, namely, clay of wisdom.[13] When this is done, put [it] upon a sublimation furnace, and apply fire for a whole day. Now if done in summer, the amount of heat is as of sublimed mercury after mid-day; however, if it is done in the morning, turn the upper layer underneath, alternate two times at least, then open and see in this way if the powder is fixed; place a little of it

---

[12] Flat dish or saucer (Latin).   [13] The well-known *lutum sapientiæ* used to seal vessels.

over the coals: if it smokes, it is not yet fixed, but if it does not smoke, then it is fixed, and this is the sign of every spirit. If, however, it is not fixed, return to the furnace, closing the vessel as before, and apply fire for five days or until at length you hear a sound in the vessel like falling stones, as very often happens, when it is dried up too much. (Another direction says that it may be tested over a burning plate to see if it melts or flows, or fails to give off smoke.)

A second way [to fix powders] is with the imbibition of oil of tartar. However, you can do it this way: take sublimed arsenicum or sulphur or auripigmentum, and crush over the stone with oil of tartar, until all becomes liquid. Then place in a glass phial in ashes, which have been sifted through a fine sieve, and place the vessel with the ashes over a distillation furnace, and apply the fire at first very slowly as [is done] in masticating, lest the vessel be broken. After heating the glass, increase the fire; then dry the medicine in an open vessel, if you wish, but it is better [to do it] in a closed one. Place above it an alembic which collects the water distilled from it, because [this distillate] is useful for many things. When the medicine is dry, the vessel has to be broken, since you cannot empty it otherwise, and you will find the powders hardened like stone. This has to be well ground as before with the distilled oil [of tartar]. Using the same procedure, again break the glass, remove, grind well, place in another ampulla, and set [it] in a warm dung pit for seven days, and then it will be dissolved into a liquid. Then place the vessel in warm ashes and heat with a slow fire, then you will have the spirits fixed; and the color will remain firm and lasting. And of this powder, add one part to fifty parts of calcined Iron or Copper, and this will be good for every malleation and testing.

51. How can Gold and Silver be Calcined?
The calcination of all metals must now be noted. First, take the calcination of Gold and Silver. Place the filings of either one you wish in vinegar for nine days. Then remove and, when dried, crush into dry powder; afterwards add water [and] sal ammoniac, crushing and drying six times. Then place over a stone, as I have taught for dissolving, and distill and put aside; and from this liquid take the powder for the solution.

Note this, however, that you should use liquids of Gold for making red solutions and [liquids] of Silver for white [ones].

14 Roger Bacon (*c.* 1219–*c.* 1292)
From the *Radix Mundi*

Roger Bacon opens his *Excellent Discourse of the Admirable Force and Efficacie of Art and Nature* by asserting that "Art using Nature for an instrument, is more powerfull then naturall vertue" (from *The Mirror of Alchimy*, ed. Stanton J. Linden, 49). Through viewing Art and Nature as complementary and potentially cooperative forces – rather than as sharply opposing ones – Bacon opened the way for envisioning a host of futuristic technological inventions: large ships and chariots that steered themselves, flying machines, underwater craft, and powerful optical instruments. Bacon's fertile scientific imagination, the products of which anticipate the "miracles" Francis Bacon foresaw in Salomon's House in the *New Atlantis* four centuries later, also resulted in unfounded accusations of witchcraft and black magic, charges that survived into the Renaissance through, to cite but one channel, his portrayal in Robert Greene's comedy *Friar Bacon and Friar Bungay* (composed *ca.* 1589).

The Franciscan friar's education and subsequent lectureships at Oxford and the University of Paris reveal keen interest and proficiency in scholarly languages, mathematics, and natural philosophy; and his principal writings, the *Opus Majus*, *Opus Minus*, and *Opus Tertium* (*ca.* 1267–68), range over these as well as Aristotelian philosophy, astrology, alchemy, and optics. Scientific experimentation and means of achieving educational reform are also frequent themes; however, the size and originality of Bacon's contributions to these subjects is still open to debate. Bacon's discussions of alchemy are scattered throughout his works, and the following excerpts from the *Radix Mundi* at times recall Aristotle's theories concerning the origin of metals and Geber's sulphur-mercury theory; they are notable for their clarity of expression and general avoidance of alchemical jargon.

The following selections from *Radix Mundi* are drawn from the version translated from the Latin and claused by William Salmon, and published in Salmon's *Medicina Practica: or, Practical Physick* (London, 1692). I have modernized the text primarily through reduction of capitalization and italics; for the most part, original spellings and punctuation have been retained, as have Salmon's original chapter and paragraph numbering. Additional readings: *DSB*, s.v. "Bacon, Roger," by A. C. Crombie and J. D. North; Lynn Thorndike, *HMES*, 2: 615–91.

Chap. 37: Of the Original of Metals, and Principles of the Mineral Work.
1. The bodies of all natural things being as well perfect as imperfect from the original of time, and compounded of a quaternity of elements or natures, *viz.* fire, air, earth, water, are conjoyned by God Almighty in a perfect unity.

2. In these four elements is hid the secret of Philosophers: the earth and water give corporeity and visibility; the fire and air, the spirit and invisible power, which cannot be seen or touched but in the other two.

3. When these four elements are conjoyned and made to exist in one, they become another thing; whence it is evident, that all things in nature are composed of the said elements, being altered and changed.

4. So saith *Rhasis*,[1] *Simple Generation, and Natural Transformation is the Operation of the Elements.*

5. But it is necessary, that the elements be of one kind, and not divers, to wit, Simple: For otherwise neither action nor passion could happen between them: So saith *Aristotle, There is no true Generation, but of things agreeing in Nature.* So that things be not made but according to their natures.

6. The elder or oak trees will not bring forth pears; nor can you gather grapes of thorns, or figs of thistles; things bring not forth, but only their like, or what agrees with them in nature, each tree its own fruit.

7. Our secret therefore is to be drawn only out of those things in which it is. You cannot extract it out of stones or salt, or other heterogene bodies: neither salt nor alum enters into our mystery. But as *Theophrastus* saith, *The Philosophers disguise with Salts and Alums, the Places of the Elements.*

8. If you prudently desire to make our Elixir, you must extract it from a mineral root: for as *Geber* saith, *You must obtain the perfection of the Matter from the Seeds thereof*.

9. Sulphur and mercury are the mineral roots and natural principles upon which nature her self acts and works in the mines and caverns of the earth, which are viscous water, and subtil spirit running through the pores, veins, and bowels of the mountains.

10. Of them is produced a vapour or cloud, which is the substance and body of metals united, ascending, and reverberating upon its own proper earth, (as *Geber* sheweth) even till by a temperate digestion through the space of a thousand years, the matter is fixed and converted into a mineral stone, of which metals are made.

11. In the same manner of Sol which is our sulphur, being reduced into mercury by mercury, which is the viscous water made thick, and mixt with its proper earth, by a temperate decoction and digestion, ariseth the vapour or cloud, agreeing in nature and substance with that in the bowels of the earth.

12. This afterwards is turned into most subtil water, which is called the soul, spirit, and tincture, as we shall hereafter shew.

13. When this water is returned into the earth, (out of which it was drawn) and every way spreads through or is mixed with it, as its proper womb, it becomes fixed. Thus the wise man does that by Art in a short time, which Nature cannot perform in less than the revolution of a thousand years.

14. Yet notwithstanding, it is not we that make the metal, but Nature herself that does it. Nor do or can we change one thing into another; but it is Nature that changes them; we are no more than meer servants in the work.

---

[1] Rasis or Rhazes (*c.* 850–*c.* 923) was Abu Bakr Muhammad ibn Zakariyya al-Razi, Arabic physician and prolific author of works on medicine, natural science and alchemy.

15. Therefore *Medus* in *Turba Philosophorum*,[2] saith, *Our stone naturally contains in it the whole tincture*. It is perfectly made in the mountains and body of the earth; yet of it self (without Art) it has no life or power whereby to move the elements.

16. Chuse then the natural minerals, to which, by the advice of *Aristotle*, add Art: For Nature generates metaline bodies of the vapours, clouds, or fumes, of sulphur and mercury, to which all the Philosophers agree. Know therefore the principles upon which Art works, to wit, the principles or beginnings of metals: for he that knows not these things shall never attain to the perfection of the work.

17. *Geber* saith, *He who has not in himself the knowledge of the Natural Principles, is far from attaining the perfection of the Art*: being ignorant of the mineral root upon which he should work.

18. *Geber* also farther saith *That our Art is only to be understood and Learned through the true wisdom and knowledge of natural things*: that is, with a wisdom searching into the roots and natural principles of the matter.

19. Yet saith he, my Son, I shew thee a secret, though thou knowest the principles, yet therein thou canst not follow Nature in all things. Herein some have erred, in essaying to follow Nature in all her properties and differences.

Chap. 38: Of Mercury, the Second Principle of the Work.

1. The second principle of our Stone is called Mercury, which some Philosophers call (as it is simple of it self) a Stone. One of them said, *This is a Stone, and no Stone, and that without which Nature never performs any thing; which enters into, or is swallowed up of other Bodies, and also swallows them up.*

2. This is simply argent vive, which contains the essential power, which explicates the tincture of our Elixir or Philosophers Stone.

3. Therefore saith *Rhasis, such a thing may be made of it which exceedeth the highest perfection of Nature.* For it is the root of metals, harmonises with them, and is the medium that explicates and conjoyns the tincture.

4. Wherefore our Stone is called Natural, or Mineral, Vegetable, and Animal, for it is generated in the mines, and is the mother or womb of all metals, and by projection converts into metals; it springs or grows like a vegetable: and abounds with life like an animal, by piercing with its tincture, like spirit and life, every where, and through all particles.

5. *Morien* saith,[3] *This Stone is no Stone that can Generate a living Creature.* Another saith, *It is cast out upon the Dunghill as a vile thing, and is hidden from the Eyes or understandings of Ignorant Men.*

---

[2] The "Conflict of Philosophers" or "Assembly of the Sages" was an influential collection of alchemical discourses probably dating from the tenth century; Arabic in origin, it includes primarily Latin retranslations of Arabic versions of Greek writings.

[3] Morienus is a shadowy figure of the seventh century: a Christian Greek who became a hermit of Jerusalem, he is thought to have been the disciple of Stephanos as well as the alchemical master of Khalid. The *Book of Morienus* was translated from Arabic into Latin by Robert of Chester in 1144, thus introducing knowledge of alchemy to the Latin West.

6. Also in *Libro Speculi Alchymiæ*,[4] it is said, *Our Stone is a thing rejected, but found in Dunghils* (i.e. in putrefaction, or the matter being putrefied) *containing in itself the four elements, over which it triumphs, and is certainly to be perfected by humane industry.*

Chap. 39: Of the Purification of the Metals and Mercury for our Work.

1. This is a great and certain truth, that the clean ought to be separated from the unclean, for nothing can give that which it has not. For the pure substance is of one simple essence, void of all heterogeneity, but that which is impure and unclean consists of heterogene parts, is not simple, but compounded (to wit of pure and impure) and apt to putrifie and corrupt.
2. Therefore let nothing enter into your composition which is alien or foreign to the matter (as all impurity is), for nothing goes to the composition of our Stone that proceedeth not from it, neither in part nor in whole.
4. The Citrine bodies (as *Sol*, &c.) you must purge by calcination or cementation; and it is then purged or purified if it be fine and florid.
5. The metal being well cleansed, beat it into thin plates or leaves (as is leaf gold) and reserve them for use.
6. The White Liquor (as mercury) contains two superfluities, which must necessarily be removed from it, *viz.* its foetid *earthiness*, which hinders its fusion, and its *humidity*, which causes its flying.
7. The earthiness is thus removed. Put it into a marble or wooden mortar, with its equal weight of pure fine and dry salt and a little vinegar. Grind all with the pestle till nothing of the matter appears, but the whole salt becomes very black. Wash this whole matter with pure water till the salt is dissolved; this filthy water decant, and put to the mercury again as much more salt and vinegar, grinding it as before, and washing it with fair water, which work so often repeat, till the water comes clear from it, and that the mercury remains pure bright and clear...
9. *Rhasis* saith, Those Bodies come nearest to perfection, which contain most *Argent Vive*: he farther saith, That the Philosophers hid nothing but weight and measure, to wit, the proportions of the ingredients, which is clear, for that none of them all agree one with another therein, which causeth great error.
10. Though the matters be well prepared and well mixed, without the proportions or quantities of the things be just, and according to the reason of the work, you will miss of the truth, or the end, and lose all your labour; you will not indeed bring anything to perfection.
11. And this is evident in the examination: when there is a transmutation of the body or that the body is changed, then let it be put into the Cineritium or Test,[5] and then it will be consumed or otherwise remain; according as the proportions are more or less than just; or just as they ought to be.

[4] Several alchemical *speculi* attributed to various authors (e.g. Arnald of Villanova and Nicolaus Comes) are found in manuscripts and early printed editions; and a *Speculum alchemiae*, long misattributed to Bacon himself, appears frequently in manuscript and in Latin, French, and English printed editions in the sixteenth century. (See *HMES* 3: 163–75, and the introduction to my edition of *The Mirror of Alchimy*, ix–xvi.)

[5] *Cineritium* appears to be synonymous with *test*, defined as, "The cupel used in treating gold or silver alloys or ore; now esp. the cupel, with the iron frame or basket which contains it, forming the movable hearth of a reverberatory furnace" (*OED* 1).

12. If they be right and just, according to the reason of that, your body will be incorruptible and remain firm, without any loss, through all essays and tryals; you can do nothing in this work without the true knowledge of this thing, whose foundation is natural matter, purity of substance, and right reason or proportion.

Chap. 40: Of the Conjunction of the Principles, in order to [achieve] this great Work.

1. *Euclid* the Philosopher,[6] and a man of great understanding, advises to work in nothing but in *Sol* and *Mercury*; which joyned together make the wonderful and admirable Philosophers Stone, as *Rhasis* saith: White and Red, both proceed from one Root; no other Bodies coming between them.

4. For being broken and made one, they have in themselves the whole tincture both of the agent and patient. Wherefore saith *Rhasis*, make a Marriage (that is a Conjunction) between the *Red Man* and his *White Wife*,[7] and you shall have the whole secret.

5. The same saith *Merlin*[8]: *If you Marry the White Woman to the Red Man, they will be Conjoyned and Imbrace one another, and become impregnated. By themselves they are Dissolved, and by themselves they bring forth what they have conceived, whereby the two are made but one Body.*

6. And truly our Dissolution is only the reducing the hard body into a liquid form, and into the nature of *Argent Vive*, that the saltness of the *sulphur* may be diminished.

8. And therefore in the *Speculum Alchymiæ* it is said, *The first work is the reducing the Body into Water, that is into Mercury*. And this the Philosophers called *Dissolution*, which is the foundation of the whole art.

10. Wherefore saith *Rhasis*, the work of making our Stone is, that the matter be put into its proper Vessel, and continually Decocted and Digested, until such time as it wholly Ascends, or sublimes to the top thereof.

11. This is declared in [the] *Speculum Philosophorum*. The *Philosophers Stone is converted from a vile thing, into a pretious Substance: for the Semen Solare, is cast into the Matrix of Mercury, by Copulation or Conjunction, whereby in process of time they be made one.*

14. And *Geber* saith, all ought to be made of Mercury only: for when *Sol* is reduced to its first Original or Matter, by Mercury, then Nature embraceth Nature.

Chap. 41: Of the Vessel, Lute, Closing, and Times of the Philosophick Work.

1. The vessel for our Stone is but one, in which the whole Magistery or Elixir is performed and perfected; this is a *Cucurbit*, whose bottom is round like an egg, or an urinal, smooth within, that it may ascend and descend the more easily, covered with a *Limbeck* round and smooth everywhere, and not very high, and whose bottom is round also like an egg.

2. Its largeness ought to be such that the Medicine or matter may not fill above a fourth part of it, made of strong double glass, clear and transparent, that you may see through

---

[6] Khalid's *Secreta Alchymiæ* places Euclid in an alchemical context (chap. 24). Bacon's reference also indicates that Euclid was regarded as an alchemical authority, and so he appears in a work by John Dastin (see *HMES* 3:96).

[7] Red Man and White Wife are common designations for the opposing "principles" of sulphur and mercury that are conjoined in the chemical wedding to produce the philosopher's stone.

[8] Ferguson (*Bibl. Chem.* 2: 90) cites several printings of an alchemical allegory attributed to "Merlin."

it, all the colours appertaining to, and appearing in the work; in which the spirit moving continually, cannot pass or flie away.

3. Let it also be so closed, that as nothing can go out of it, so nothing can enter into it: as *Lucas* saith,[9] *Lute the Vessel strongly with Lutum Sapientiæ, that nothing may get in or go out of it.*

4. For if the Flowers,[10] or matter subliming, should breathe out, or any strange air or matter enter in, your work will be spoiled and lost.

5. And though the Philosophers oftentimes say that the matter is to be put into the vessel and closed up fast, yet it is sufficient for the operator, once to put the said matter in, once to close it up, and so to keep it even to the very perfection and finishing of the work. If these things be often repeated, the work will be spoiled.

6. Therefore saith *Rhasis, keep your Vessel continually close, encompassed with Dew,* [which demonstrates what kind of Heat you are to use] *and so well Luted that none of the Flowers, or that which sublimes, may get out, or vanish in Vapor or Fume.*

8. Also another Philosopher in his *Breveloquium* saith, *as there are three things in a natural Egg, viz. the Shell, the White, and the Yolk, so likewise there are three things corresponding to the Philosophers Stone, the Glass Vessel, the White liquor, and the Citrine Body.*

9. And as of the yolk and white, with a little heat, a Bird is made (the shell being whole, until the coming forth or hatching of the chicken) so it is in the work of the Philosophers Stone. Of the citrine body and white liquor with a temperate or gentle heat is made the *Avis Hermetis*, or Philosophers Bird.[11]

Chap. 42: Of the Philosophers Fire, the kinds and Government thereof.

1. The Philosophers have described in their books a two fold fire, a *moist* and a *dry*.

2. The *moist fire* they called the warm *Horse Belly*, in the which, so long as the humidity remains, the heat is retained; but the humidity being consumed, the heat vanishes and ceases, which heat being small, seldom lasts above five or six days: but it may be conserved and renewed, by casting upon it many times urine mixt [with] salt.

5. *Altudenus* the Philosopher saith likewise, *you must hide your Medicine in Horse dung, which is the fire of the Philosophers,* for this dung is hot, moist, and dark, having a humidity in it self, and an excellent light [or whiteness].

8. The *dry fire* is the fire of the bodies themselves; and the inflammability of every thing able to be burned: now the government of these fires is thus:

9. The Medicine of the White ought to be put into the moist fire, until the completement of the whiteness shall appear in the vessel. For a gentle fire is the conservation of the humidity.

12. Therefore saith *Rhasis, Be very diligent and careful in the sublimation and liquefaction of the matter, that you increase not your fire too much, whereby the water may ascend to the highest part of the Vessel;* for then wanting a place of refrigeration, it will stick fast there, whereby the sulphur of the elements will not be perfected.

---

[9] Lucas speaks in dicta 12 and 67 of the *Turba Philosophorum*, ed. A. E. Waite, 37, 192.

[10] The pulverized or powdery form of a substance, produced by sublimation.

[11] "The Bird of Hermes symbolizes the mercurial vapours as they ascend in the alembic during distillation and sublimation, and descend as celestial rain or dew, washing the black earth ... [And] the name of the philosophical bird or chick born from the vessel of the philosopher's egg" (*DAI* 25).

14. And the gentle or temperate fire is that only which compleats the mixture, makes thick, and perfects the work.

18. The happy prosecution of the whole work consists in the exact temperament of the fire: therefore beware of too much heat, lest you come to *Solution* before the time, [*viz.* before the matter is ripe:] For that will bring you to despair of attaining the end of your hopes.

19. Wherefore saith he [i.e., Rhasis], *Beware of too much fire, for if it be kindled before the time, the matter will be Red before it comes to ripeness and perfection*, whereby it becomes like an Abort, or the unripe fruit of the womb; whereas it ought to be first white, then red, like as the fruits of a tree: a cherry is first white, then red, when it comes to its perfection.

Chap. 43: Of the Aenigmas of Philosophers, their Deceptions, and Precautions concerning the same.

1. You ought to put on courage, resolution and constancy, in attempting this great work, lest you err, and be deceived, sometimes following or doing one thing, and then another.

2. For the knowledge of this art consisteth not in the multiplicity, or great number of things, but in unity; our Stone is but One, the matter is One, and the vessel is One: the government is One. The whole Art and Work thereof is One, and begins in One manner, and in One manner is finished.

3. Notwithstanding the Philosophers have subtily delivered themselves, and clouded their instructions with aenigmatical and typical phrases and words, to the end that their art might not only be hidden and so continued, but also be had in the greater veneration.

4. Thus they advise to decoct, to commix, and to conjoyn; to sublime, to bake, to grind, and to congeal; to make equal, to putrefie, to make white, and to make red; of all which things, the order, management and way of working is all one, which is only to *Decoct*.

Chap. 44: Of the Various Signs Appearing in every Operation.

1. This then is the thing that the vessel with the Medicine be put into a moist fire; to wit, that the middle or one half of the vessel be in a moist fire (or *Balneo*, of equal heat with horse-dung) and the other half out of the fire, that you may daily look into it.

2. And in about the space of forty days, the superficies or upper part of the Medicine will appear black as melted pitch: and this is the sign that the citrine body is truly converted into mercury.

6. This blackness the Philosophers called the first *Conjunction*; for then the male and female are joyned together, and it is the sign of perfect mixtion.

10. This blackness is called among the Philosophers by many names, to wit, *the Fires, the Soul, a Cloud, the Ravens-Head, a Coal, Our Oyl, Aqua vitæ, the Tincture of Redness, the shadow of the Sun, Black Brass, Water of Sulphur*, and by many other names.

11. And this blackness is that which conjoyneth the body with the spirit.

16. In the first *Decoction* (which is called *Putrefaction*) our Stone is made all black, to wit, a black earth, by the drawing out of its humidity; and in that blackness, the whiteness is hidden.

17. And when the humidity is reverted upon the blackness again, and by a continued soft and gentle digestion is made fixed with its earth, then it becomes white.

18. In this whiteness, the redness is hidden; and when it is decocted and digested by augmentation (and continuance) of the fire, that earth is changed into redness, as we shall hereafter teach.

Chap. 45: Of the Eduction of the Whiteness out of the Blackness or Black Matter.

1. Now let us revolve to the black matter in its vessel, [not so much as once opened, but] continually closed: Let this vessel I say, stand continually in the moist fire, till such time as the white colour appears, like to a white moist salt.

2. The colour is called by the Philosophers *Arsenick* and *Sal Armoniack*; and some others call it, *The thing without which no profit is to be had in the work.*

3. But inward whiteness appearing in the work, then is there a perfect conjunction and copulation, of the bodies in this Stone, which is indissoluble; and then is fulfilled that saying of *Hermes, The thing which is above, is as that which is beneath; and that which is beneath, is as that which is above,* to perform the mystery of this matter.[12]

7. And many times it shall be changed from colour to colour, till such time as it comes to the fixed whiteness.

9. But value none of these colours, for they be not the true tincture; yea many times it becomes citrine and redish, and many times it is dryed, and becomes liquid again, before the whiteness will appear.

12. The cause of the appearance of such variety of colours in the operation of your Medicine is from the extention of the blackness; for as much as blackness and whiteness be the extream colours, all the other colours are but means between them.

13. Therefore as often as any degree or portion of blackness descends, so often another and another colour appears, until it comes to whiteness.

14. Now concerning the ascending and descending of the Medicine, *Hermes* saith, *It ascends from the Earth into Heaven, and again descends from Heaven to the Earth, whereby it may receive both the superiour strength, and the inferiour.*

15. Moreover this you are to observe, that if between the blackness and the whiteness, there should appear the red or citrine colour, you are not to look upon it or esteem it, for it is not fixt but will vanish away.

16. There cannot indeed be any perfect and fixt redness, without it be first white; wherefore saith *Rhasis, no Man can come from the first to the third, but by the second.*

17. From whence it is evident, that whiteness must always be first lookt for, [after the blackness, and before the redness] for as much as it is the complement of the whole work.

18. Then after this whiteness appears, it shall not be changed into any true or stable colour, but into the red: thus have we taught you to make the white; it remains now that we elucidate the red.

---

[12] From the opening of the *Emerald Table.*

Chap. 46: Of the Way and Manner how to educe the Red Tincture out of the White.

1. The matters then of the white and red among themselves, differ not in respect to their essence; but the red Elixir needs more subtilization and longer digestion, and a hotter fire in the course of the operation, than the white, because the end of the white work is the beginning of the red work and that which is compleat in the one, is to be begun in the other.

2. Therefore without you make the white Elixir first, [*viz.*] make the matter become first white, you can never come to the red Elixir, that which is indeed the true red: which how it is be performed we shall briefly shew.

3. The Medicine for the red ought to be put into our moist fire, until the white colour aforesaid appear, afterwards take out the vessel from the fire, and put it into another pot with sifted ashes made moist with water, to about half full, in which let it stand up to the middle thereof, making under the earthen pot a temperate dry fire, and that continually.

4. But the heat of this dry fire ought to be double at the least, to what it was before, or than the heat of the moist fire; by the help of this heat, the white Medicine receiveth the admirable tincture of the redness.

7. Decoct the red matter or Medicine; the more red it is, the more worth it is; and the more decocted it is, the more red it is. Therefore that which is more decocted is the more pretious and valuable.

8. Therefore you must burn it without fear in a dry fire, until such time as it is clothed with a most glorious red, or a pure vermillion colour.

12. As *Hermes* saith in *Turba, Between the Whiteness and the Redness, one Colour only appears, to wit, Citrine, but it changes from the less to the more.*

13. *Maria*[13] also saith, *When you have the true White, then follows* the false and Citrine Colour; *and at last the Perfect Redness itself.* This is the glory and the beauty of the whole world.

Chap. 48: Of the Augmentation or Multiplication of our Medicine by Fermentation.

1. Our Medicine is multiplied by Fermentation; and the ferment for the white is pure *Luna*; the Ferment for the Red, is pure fine *Sol.*

2. Now cast one part of the Medicine upon twenty parts of the ferment and all shall become Medicine, Elixir, or Tincture; put it on the fire in a glass vessel, and seal it so that no air go in or out; dissolve and subtilize it, as oft as you please, even as you did for making of the first Medicine.

3. And one part of this second Medicine shall have as much virtue and power, as ten parts of the former.

5. You must then conjoyn it, that it may generate its like; yet you must not joyn it with any other that it might convert it to the same, but only with that very same kind, of whose substance it was in the beginning.

---

[13] Maria Prophetissa (or Mary the Hebrew or the Jewess) is one of the earliest alchemical authorities, fancifully identified by some with Miriam, the sister of Moses. She is often cited (chiefly by Zosimos) and credited with the invention of the water bath (*balneum Mariae*) and other pieces of laboratory equipment.

12. Wherefore we command argent vive to be mixed with argent vive, until one clear water be made of two argent vives compounded together.

13. But you must not make the mixture of them, till each of them apart or separately be dissolved into water: and in the conjunction of them, put a little of the matter upon much of the body, *viz.* First upon four; and it shall become in a short time a fine pouder, whose tincture shall be white or red.

14. This pouder is the true and perfect Elixir or Tincture, and the Elixir or Tincture, is truly a simple pouder.

16. Keep entire the fume or vapour, and take heed that nothing thereof flie out from it; tarry by the vessel and behold the wonders, how it changes from colour to colour, in less space than an hours time, till such time as it comes to the signs of whiteness or redness.

18. This pouder is the compleat and perfect Elixir or Tincture; now you may separate or take it from the fire and let it cool.

19. And first, part of it projected upon 1000 parts of any metalline body transmutes it into fine gold or silver, according as your Elixir or Tincture is for the red or the white.

20. From what has been said, it is manifest and evident that if you do not congeal argent vive, making it to bear or endure the fire, and then conjoyning it with pure silver, you shall never attain to the whiteness.

21. And if you make not argent vive red, and so as it may endure the greatest fire, and then conjoyn it with pure fine gold, you shall never attain to the redness.

22. And by dissolution, *viz.* by fermentation, your Medicine, Elixir, or Tincture, may be multiplied infinitely.

Chap. 49: Of the Differences of the Medicine and Proportions used in Projection.

3. The third order is of such Medicines, which being cast upon imperfect bodies, not only perfectly tinge them, but also take away all their corruption and impurities, making them incorrupt and perfect . . .

4. Let therefore this your perfect Medicine, or Elixir, be cast upon a thousand or more parts, according to the number of times it has been dissolved, sublimed, and made subtil. If you put on too little, you must mend it by adding more; otherwise the virtue thereof will accomplish a perfect transmutation.

5. The Philosophers therefore made three proportions, divers manner of ways, but the best proportion is this: let one part be cast upon an hundred parts of *Mercury*, cleansed from all its impurities; and it will all become Medicine, or Elixir; and this is the second Medicine, which projected upon a thousand parts, converts it all into good *Sol* or *Luna*.

6. Cast one part of this second Medicine upon an hundred of *Mercury* prepared, and it will all become Medicine, and this is the Third Medicine, or Elixir of the third degree, which will project upon ten thousand parts of another body and transmute it wholly into fine *Sol* or *Luna*.

7. Again, every part of this third Medicine being cast upon an hundred parts of prepared *Mercury*, it will all become Medicine of the fourth degree, and it will transmute ten hundred thousand times its own quantity of another metal into fine *Sol* and *Luna*, according as your fermentation was made.

8. Now these second, third, and fourth Medicines may be so often dissolved, sublimed, and subtilizated, till they receive far greater virtues and powers, and may after the same manner be multiplyed infinitely.

9. According to *Rhasis*, the proportion is thus to be computed. First, multiply ten by ten, and its product is an hundred; again 100 by 10, and the product is 1000; and a 100[0] by 10, and the product will be 10000.

10. And this 10000 being multiplyed by 10, produces an 100000; and thus by consequence you may augment it, till it comes to a number almost infinite.

Chap. 50: Of Projection, and how it is to bee performed upon the Metals.

1. Now the projection is after this manner to be done: put the body or metal upon the fire in a crucible, and cast thereon the Elixir as aforesaid, moving, or stirring it well; and when it is melted, become liquid, and mixed with the body, or with the spirit, remove it from the fire, and you shall have fine gold or silver, according to what your Elixir was prepared from.

2. But here is to be noted, that by how much the more the metaline body is the easier to be melted, by so much the more shall the Medicine have power to enter into, and transmute it.

3. Therefore by so much as Mercury is more liquid than any other body, by so much the more, the Medicine has power in being cast upon it, to wit, Mercury, to transmute it into fine Sol or Luna.

4. And a greater quantity of it shall your Medicine transmute, give tincture to, and make perfect, than of any other mineral body.

5. The like is to be understood to be performed in the same manner upon other mineral bodies, according as they are easie or hard to be fused or melted.

Chap. 51: Of the Compleatment, or Perfection of the whole Work.

1. And because prolixity is not pleasant, but induceth errour and clouds the understanding, we shall now use much brevity and shew the completement of the whole work, the premises being well conceived.

2. It appears that our work is hidden in the body of the Magnesias, that is, in the body of sulphur, which is Sulphur of Sulphur; and in the body of mercury, which is Mercury of Mercury.

3. Therefore our Stone is from one thing only, as is aforesaid, and it is performed by one act or work, with decoction: and by one disposition, or operation, which is the changing of it first to black, then to white, thirdly, to red: and by one projection, by which the whole act and work is finished.

4. From henceforth, let all pseudo-chymists, and their followers, cease from their vain distillations, sublimations, conjunctions, calcinations, dissolutions, contritions, and such other like vanities.

5. Let them cease from their deceiving, prating, and pretending to any other gold, than our gold; or any other sulphur than our sulphur, or any other argent vive than ours; or any other Ablution or washing than what we have taught.

6. Which washing is made by means of the black colour, and is the cause of the white, and not a washing made with hands.

7. Let them not say, that there is any other Dissolution than ours, or other Congelation than that which is performed with an easie fire: or any other Egg than that which we have spoken of by similitude, and so called an Egg.

9. But hear now what *Rhasis* saith, *Look not upon the multitude, or diversity of Names, which are dark and obscure, they are chiefly given to the diversity of Colours appearing in the Work.*

10. Therefore whatever the names be, and how many soever, yet conceive the matter or thing to be but one, and the work to be but one only.

12. And with this it is that we tinge and colour every body, bringing them from their beginnings and smalness, to their compleat growth, and full perfection.

15. If you that are searchers into this science, understand these words and things which we have written, you are happy, yea, thrice happy; if you understood not what we have said, God himself has hidden the thing from you.

16. Therefore blame not the Philosophers but your selves; for if a just and faithful mind possessed your souls, God would doubtless reveal the verity to you.

17. And know, it is impossible for you to attain to this knowledge unless you become sanctified in mind, and purified in soul, so as to be united to God, and to become one Spirit with him.

18. When you shall appear thus before the Lord, he shall open to you the gates of his treasure, the like of which is not to be found in all the earth.

19. Behold, I shew unto you the fear of the Lord, and the love of him with unfeigned obedience: nothing shall be wanting to them that fear God, who are cloathed with the excellency of his holiness, to whom be rendred all praise, honour, and glory to the Ages of Ages, *Amen.*

15 Nicolas Flamel (1330?–1417?)

From *His Exposition of the Hieroglyphical Figures*

Flamel's most recent editor, Laurinda Dixon, notes that the *Exposition of the Hieroglyphical Figures* (first French edition, 1612) "was destined to inspire debate and conjecture not only in its own century, but for three hundred years thereafter" (Introduction, *Nicolas Flamel: His Exposition of the Hieroglyphicall Figures (1624)*, xiii). The controversy centers primarily on questions about Flamel's identity as alchemist and author: was he – along with his beloved wife and alchemical partner, Perrenelle – a real, fabulously successful medieval adept whose transmutations resulted in many charitable acts in Paris and Boulogne (as reported in the Introduction to the *Exposition*, precisely dated 1413), or was the "Flamel legend" a fiction created by the work's first publisher, P. Arnauld de la Chevalerie, in the early seventeenth century? Current scholarly opinion favors the latter view, while admitting the existence of a wealthy medieval Parisian named Nicolas Flamel, a scrivener by trade, whose tombstone is still to be seen along a stairway in Paris's Musée de Cluny. Indeed, no manuscript or printed text of the *Exposition* that dates from before the seventeenth century has been discovered.

Flamel's *Exposition* is an excellent example of the combining of visual and verbal mediums so characteristic of alchemical discourse before and after the invention of printing. Most of the work is, in fact, given over to explication of the painted figures that he commissioned for an arch in the churchyard of the *Innocents* in Paris (see Figure 14); these were no ordinary representations but imitations of the allegorical illustrations from the famous book of Abraham the Jew, that had served as Flamel's alchemical inspiration. As he tells us, his painted figures can be interpreted on two intersecting levels: as shadowings of Christian truths or, for those skilled in interpreting alchemical symbolism, as revealing "all the principall and necessary operations of the *Maistery*." For Flamel, or the clever pseudonymous author who assumed his identity, these lines of interpretation lead not only to alchemical success but to moral and spiritual regeneration.

The following excerpts are taken from Nicholas Flammel, *His Exposition of the Hieroglyphicall Figures . . . Faithfully, and . . . religiously done into English out of the French and Latine copies. By Eirenæus Orandus* (London, 1624). Additional reading: the introduction, text, and notes in the previously cited edition by Laurinda Dixon.

The Introduction.

Although that I *Nicholas Flammel*, Notary, and abiding in *Paris*, in this yeere one thousand three hundred fourescore and nineteene, and dwelling in my house in the street of Notaries, neere unto the Chappell of St. *James* of the *Bouchery*; although, I say, that I learned but a little Latine, because of the small meanes of my Parents, which nevertheless were by them that envie me the most, accounted honest people; yet by the grace of God, and the intercession of the blessed Saints in *Paradise* of both sexes, and principally of Saint *James* of *Gallicia*,[1] I have not wanted the understanding of the Bookes of the *Philosophers*, and in them learned their so hidden secrets. And for this cause, there shall never bee any moment of my life, when I remember this high good, wherein upon my knees (if the place will give me leave) or otherwise, in my heart with all my affection, I shall not render thanks to this most benigne God, which never suffereth the child of the Just to beg from doore to doore, and deceiveth not them which wholly trust in his blessing.

Whilest therefore, I *Nicholas Flammel, Notary*, after the decease of my Parents, got my living in our Art of Writing, by making *Inventories*, dressing accounts, and summing up the Expenses of *Tutors* and *Pupils*, there fell into my hands, for the sum of two Florens, a guilded Booke, very old and large; It was not of Paper, nor Parchment, as other Bookes bee, but was onely made of delicate Rindes (as it seemed unto me) of tender yong trees: The cover of it was of brasse, well bound, all engraven with letters, or strange figures; and for my part, I thinke they might well be *Greeke Characters*, or some such like ancient language: Sure I am, I could not read them, and I know well they were not notes nor letters of the *Latine* nor of the *Gaule*, for of them wee understand a little. As for that which was within it, the leaves of barke or rinde, were ingraven, and with admirable diligence written, with a point of *Iron*, in faire and neate Latine letters coloured. It contained thrice seven leaves, for so were they counted in the top of the leaves, and always every seventh leafe was without any writing, but in stead thereof, upon the first seventh leafe, there was painted a *Virgin*, and *Serpents* swallowing her up; In the second seventh, a *Crosse*, where a *Serpent* was crucified; and in the last seventh, there were painted *Desarts*, or *Wildernesses*, in the middest whereof ran many faire fountaines, from whence there issued out a number of *Serpents*, which ran up and downe here and there. Upon the first of the leaves, was written in great Capitall Letters of gold, ABRAHAM THE JEW, PRINCE, PRIEST, LEVITE, ASTROLOGER, AND PHILOSOPHER, TO THE NATION OF THE JEWES, BY THE WRATH OF GOD DISPERSED AMONG THE GAULES, SENDETH HEALTH. After this it was filled with great execrations and curses (with this word MARANATHA,[2] which was often repeated there) against every person that should cast his eyes upon it, if hee were not *Sacrificer* or *Scribe*.

Hee that sold mee this Booke, knew not what it was worth, no more than I when I bought it; I beleeve it had beene stolne or taken from the miserable *Jewes*; or found hid in some part of the ancient place of their abode. Within the Booke, in the second leafe, hee comforted his *Nation*, counceling them to flie vices, and above all, *Idolatry*, attending with sweete patience the coming of the *Messias*, which should vanquish all the Kings of the Earth, and should raigne with his people in glory eternally. Without doubt this had beene some very wise and understanding man. In the third leafe, and in all the other writings

---

[1] The apostle and martyr, whose relics are enshrined in the famous pilgrimage church of Santiago de Compostela in Galicia (Spain).

[2] Cf. "If any man love not the Lord Jesus Christ, let him be Anathema Maranatha" (2 Cor. 16:22). "An Aramaic phrase . . . often erroneously regarded as composing with the word that precedes it in the text a formula of imprecation, ANATHEMA MARANATHA . . . [thus] a terrible curse" (*OED*).

that followed, to helpe his *Captive nation* to pay their *tributes* unto the *Romane* Emperours, and to doe other things, which I will not speake of, he taught them in common words the *transmutation of Mettalls*; hee painted the *Vessels* by the sides, and hee advertised them of the *colours*, and of all the rest, saving of the *first Agent*,[3] of the which hee spake not a word, but onely (as he said) in the fourth and fifth leaves entire hee painted it, and figured it with very great cunning and workemanship; for although it was well and intelligibly figured and painted, yet no man could ever have beene able to understand it, without being well skilled in their *Cabala*,[4] which goeth by tradition, and without having well studied their bookes. The fourth and fifth leafe therefore, was without any writing, all full of faire figures *enlightened*,[5] or as it were *enlightened*, for the worke was very exquisite. First he painted a *yong man*, with wings at his anckles, having in his hand a *Caducæan* rodde,[6] writhen about with two *Serpents*, wherewith hee strooke upon a helmet which covered his head; he seemed to my small judgement, to be the God *Mercury* of the *Pagans*: against him there came running and flying with open wings, a great old man, who upon his head had an *houre-glasse* fastened, and in his hands a hooke (or sithe) like *Death*, with the which, in terrible and furious manner, hee would have cut off the feet of *Mercury*.[7] On the other side of the fourth leafe, hee painted a faire *flowre* on the top of a very high *mountaine*, which was sore shaken with the *North wind*; it had the foot *blew*, the flowres *white* and *red*, the leaves shining like fine *gold*: And round about it the *Dragons* and *Griffons* of the *North* made their nests and abode. On the fifth leafe there was a faire *Rose-tree* flowred in the middest of a sweet *Garden*, climbing up against a hollow *Oake*; at the foot wherof boyled a fountaine of most *white water*, which ranne head-long downe into the depths, notwithstanding it first passed among the hands of infinite people, which digged in the Earth seeking for it; but because they were blinde, none of them knew it, except here and there one which considered the *weight*.

    On the last side of the first leafe, there was a *King* with a great *Fauchion*, who made to be killed in his presence by some *Souldiers* a great multitude of little *Infants*, whose Mothers wept at the feet of the unpittifull *Souldiers*: the bloud of which *Infants* was afterwards by other Souldiers gathered up, and put in a great vessell, wherein the *Sunne* and the *Moone* came to bathe themselves. And because that this History did represent the more part of that of the *Innocents* slaine by *Herod*, and that in this Booke I learned the greatest part of the *Art*, this was one of the causes, why I placed in their *Churchyard* these *Hieroglyphick Symbols* of this secret science. And thus you see that which was in the first five leaves: I will not represent unto you that which was written in good and intelligible Latine in all the other written leaves, for God would punish me, because I should commit a greater wickednesse, then he who (as it is said) wished that all the men of the World had but one

[3] The book of Abraham the Jew included marginal diagrams of alchemical vessels and explained the sequence of colors, but did not reveal the first matter of the philosopher's stone.

[4] " 'Kabbalah' is the traditional and most commonly used term for the esoteric teachings of Judaism and for Jewish mysticism, especially the forms which it assumed in the Middle Ages from the 12th century onward. In its wider sense it signifies all the successive esoteric movements in Judaism that evolved from the end of the period of the Second Temple and became active factors in Jewish history" (Gershom Scholem, *Kabbalah* 3).

[5] I.e., "illuminated" or decorated with painted pictures or designs.

[6] The *caduceus* was Hermes' or Mercury's serpent-entwined rod, a common alchemical symbol for the resolution of opposing forces or elements.

[7] Thus the scythe-bearing Saturn (lead) attempts to "fix" Mercury by cutting off his feet.

head that hee might cut it off at one blow.[8] Having with me therefore this *faire Booke*, I did nothing else day nor night, but study upon it, understanding very well all the operations that it shewed, but not knowing with what matter I should beginne, which made me very heavy and sollitary, and caused me to fetch many a sigh. My wife *Perrenelle*, whom I loved as my selfe, and had lately married, was much astonished at this, comforting mee, and earnestly demanding, if shee could by any meanes deliver mee from this trouble: I could not possibly hold my tongue, but told her all, and shewed her this *faire Booke*, whereof at the same instant that shee saw it, shee became as much enamored as myselfe, taking extreame pleasure to behold the *faire cover, gravings, images, and portraicts*, whereof notwithstanding shee understood as little as I: yet it was a great comfort to mee to talke with her, and to entertaine my selfe, what wee should doe to have the interpretation of them. In the end I caused to bee painted within my *Lodging*, as naturally as I could, all the figures and portraicts of the *fourth* and *fifth* leafe, which I shewed to the greatest Clerkes in *Paris*, who understood thereof no more then my selfe; I told them they were found in a Booke that taught the *Phylosophers stone*, but the greatest part of them made a mocke both of me, and of that blessed *Stone*, excepting one called *Master Anselme*, which was a *Licentiate* in *Physick*, and studied hard in this *Science*: He had a great desire to have seene my Book, and there was nothing in the world, which he would not have done for a sight of it; but I always told him, that I had it not; onely I made him a large description of the *Method*. He told mee that the first portraict represented *Time*, which devoured all; and that according to the number of the *sixe* written leaves, there was required the space of *sixe* yeeres, to perfect the *stone*; and then he said, wee must turne the *glasse*, and seeth it no more. And when I told him that this was not painted, but onely to shew and teach the first *Agent*, (as was said in the Booke) hee answered me, that this decoction for *sixe* yeeres space, was, as it were a *second Agent*; and that certainely the *first Agent* was there painted, which was the *white and heavy water*, which without doubt was *Argent vive*, which they could not *fixe*, nor cut off his *feete*, that is to say, take away his *volatility*, save by that long decoction in the purest bloud of young Infants; for in that, this *Argent vive* being joined with *gold* and *silver*, was first turned with them into an *herb* like that which was there painted, and afterwards by corruption, into *Serpents*: which *Serpents* being then wholly dried, and decocted by fire, were reduced into powder of *gold*, which should be the *stone*. This was the cause, that during the space of *one and twenty yeeres*, I tried a thousand broulleryes,[9] yet never with *bloud*, for that was wicked and villanous: for I found in my Booke, that the *Phylosophers* called *Bloud*, the minerall spirit, which is in the *Mettals*, principally in the *Sunne, Moone*, and *Mercury*, to the assembling whereof, I alwayes tended; yet these interpretations for the most part were more subtile then true. Not seeing therefore in my workes the *signes*, at the time written in my Booke, I was alwayes to beginne againe. In the end having lost all hope of ever understanding those *figures*, for my last refuge, I made a vow to God, and St. *James* of *Gallicia*, to demand the interpretation of them, at some *Jewish Priest*, in some *Synagogue* of *Spaine*: whereupon with the consent of *Perrenelle*, carrying with me the *Extract* of the *Pictures*, having taken the *Pilgrims* habit and staff, in the same fashion as you may see me,

---

[8] Laurinda Dixon identifies this as Caligula's statement "Utinam populus Romanus unam cervicem haberet" (Suetonius, *Gaius Caesar*, 30), in her *Nicolas Flamel: His Exposition of the Hieroglyphicall Figures (1624)*, 88n21.

[9] Possibly mixtures or combinations of things, from French *brouiller*.

without this same *Arch* in the *Church-yard*, in the which I put these *hyeroglyphicall figures*, where I have also set against the wall, on the one and the other side, a *Procession*, in which are represented by order all the colours of the *stone*, so as they come & goe, with this writing in French.

> *Moult plaist a Dieu procession,*
> *S'elle est faicte en devotion*: that is,
> *Much pleaseth God procession,*
> *If't be done in devotion.*

Which is as it were the beginning of King *Hercules* his Book, which entreateth of the colours of the *stone*, entituled *Iris*, or the *Rainebow*, in these termes, *Operis processio multum naturæ placet*, that is *The procession of the worke is very pleasant unto Nature*: the which I have put there expressly for the great *Clerkes*, who shall understand the *Allusion*. In this same fashion, I say, I put my selfe upon my way; and so much I did, that I arrived at *Montjoy*,[10] and afterwards at *Saint James*, where with great devotion I accomplished my vow. This done, in *Leon* at my returne I met with a Merchant of *Boloyn*, which made me knowne to a *Physician*, a *Jew*, by Nation, and as then a *Christian*, dwelling in *Leon* aforesaid, who was very skilfull in sublime Sciences, called Master *Canches*. As soone as I had showen him the figures of my *Extraict*, hee being ravished with great astonishment and joy, demanded of me incontinently, if I could tell him any newes of the *Booke*, from whence they were drawne? I answered him in *Latine* (wherein hee asked me the question) that I hoped to have some good newes of the *Book*, if any body could decipher unto me the *Enigmaes*: All at that instant transported with great Ardor and joy, hee began to decipher unto mee the beginning: But to be short, hee wel content to learn newes where this Book should be, and I to heare him speake; and certainly he had heard much discourse of the Booke, but (as he said) as of a thing which was beleeved to be utterly lost, we resolved of our voyage, and from *Leon* we passed to *Oviedo*, and from thence to *Sanson*, where wee put our selves to Sea to come into *France*: Our voyage had beene fortunate enough, & all ready, since we were entred into this Kingdome, he had most truly interpreted unto mee the greatest part of my figures, where even unto the very points and prickes, he found great *misteries*, which seemed unto mee wonderfull, when arriving at *Orleans*, this learned man fell extreamely sicke, being afflicted with excessive vomitings, which remained still with him of those he had suffered at Sea, and he was in such a continuall feare of my forsaking him, that hee could imagine nothing like unto it. And although I was alwayes by his side, yet would he incessantly call for mee, but in summe hee dyed, at the end of the *seventh* day of his sicknesse, by reason whereof I was much grieved, yet as well as I could, I caused him to be buried in the *Church* of the *holy Crosse* at *Orleans*, where hee yet resteth; God have his soule, for hee dyed a good *Christian*: And surely, if I be not hindered by death, I will give unto that *Church* some *revenew*, to cause some *Masses* to bee said for his soule every day. He that would see the manner of my arrivall, and the joy of *Perenelle*, let him

---

[10] Dixon notes that "the place called 'Montjoy,' where Flamel stopped on his way to Spain, can be interpreted symbolically, as the word also refers to a pile of stones made by travelers to mark places of sanctuary along a pilgrimage route. 'Montjoy' can also serve as an alchemical allegory, for 'rocks' and 'mountains' often symbolized the furnaces and flasks in which ingredients were warmed and nurtured, and appear as such in numerous illustrated alchemical books" (*Nicolas Flamel* xxv).

looke upon us two, in this *City* of *Paris*, upon the doore of the *Chappell* of St *James* of the *Bouchery*, close by the one side of my *house*, where wee are both painted, my selfe giving thankes at the feet of *Saint James of Gallicia*, and *Perrenelle* at the feet of St *John*, whom shee had so often called upon. So it was, that by the grace of God, and the intercession of the happy and holy *Virgin*, and the blessed Saints, *James* and *John*, I knew all that I desired, that is to say, the first *Principles*, yet not their first *preparation*, which is a thing most difficult, above all the things in the world: But in the end I had that also, after long errours of *three yeeres*, or thereabouts, during which time, I did nothing but study and labour, so as you may see me without this *Arch*, where I have placed my *Processions* against the two Pillars of it, under the feet of St. *James* and St. *John*, praying alwayes to God, with my Beades in my hand, reading attentively within a Booke, and poysing the words of the *Philosophers*: and afterwards trying and prooving the diverse operations, which I imagined to my selfe, by their onely words. Finally, I found that which I desired, which I also soone knew by the strong *sent* and *odour* thereof. Having this, I easily accomplished the *Mastery*, for knowing the *preparation* of the first *Agents*, and after following my Booke according to the *letter* I could not have missed it, though I would. Then the first time that I made *projection*, was upon *Mercurie*, whereof I turned halfe a pound, or thereabouts, into pure *Silver*, better than that of the *Mine*, as I my selfe assayed, and made others assay many times. This was upon a Munday, the 17. of *January* about noone, in my house, *Perrenelle* only being present; in the yeere of the restoring of mankind, 1382. And afterwards, following alwayes my Booke, from word to word, I made *projection* of the *Red stone* upon the like quantity of *Mercurie*, in the presence likewise of *Perrenelle* onely, in the same house, the *five and twentieth day* of *Aprill* following, the same yeere, about five a *clocke* in the *Evening*; which I transmuted truly into almost as much pure *Gold*, better assuredly than common *Golde*, more soft, and more plyable. I may speake it with truth, I have made it three times, with the helpe of *Perrenelle*, who understood it as well as I, because she helped mee in my operations, and without doubt, if shee would have enterprised to have done it alone, shee had attained to the end and perfection thereof. I had indeed enough when I had once done it, but I found exceeding great pleasure and delight, in seeing and contemplating the *Admirable workes of Nature*, within the *Vessels*. To signifie unto thee then, how I have done it *three times*, thou shalt see in this *Arch*, if thou have any skil to know them, three *furnaces*, like unto them which serve for our *opperations*: I was afraid a long time, that *Perrenelle* could not hide the extreme joy of her felicitie, which I measured by mine owne, and lest shee should let fall some word amongst her kindred, of the great *treasures* which wee possessed: for extreme *joy* takes away the understanding, as well as great *heavinesse*; but the goodnesse of the most great God, had not onely filled mee with this blessing, to give mee a *wife* chaste and sage, for she was moreover not onely capeable of reason, but also to doe all that was reasonable, and more discreet and secret, than ordinarily other women are. Above all, shee was exceeding *devout*, and therefore seeing her selfe without hope of children, and now well stricken in yeeres, she began as I did, to thinke of God, and to give our selves to the workes of *mercy*. At that time when I wrote this *Commentarie*, in the yeere *one thousand foure hundred and thirteene*, in the end of the yeere, after the decease of my faithfull companion, which I shall lament all the dayes of my life: she and I had already founded, and endued with revenewes 14. *Hospitals* in this *Citie* of *Paris*, wee had new built from the ground *three Chappels*, we had inriched with great gifts and good rents, *seven Churches* with many reparations in their *Church-yards*, besides that which we have done at *Boloigne*, which is not much lesse than that which we have done heere. I will not speake of the good which both of us have done to particular poore folkes, principally to *widdowes* and poore *Orphans*, whose names if I should tel, and how I did it, besides that my reward should be given mee in this World, I should likewise doe displeasure to those good persons, whom I pray God blesse, which I would not doe for any thing in the World. Building therefore these *Churches, Churchyards,* and *Hospitals* in this *City,* I resolved my selfe, to cause to be painted in the *fourth Arch* of the Church-yard of the *Innocents* [see fig. 14], as you enter in by the great gate in St. *Dennis street,* and taking the way on the right hand, the most true and essentiall markes of the *Arte,* yet under *vailes,* and *Hieroglyphicall covertures,* in imitation of those which are in the gilded Booke of *Abraham* the *Jew,* which may represent *two things,* according to the capacity and understanding of them that behold them: First, the *mysteries* of our future and undoubted *Resurrection,* at the day of judgement, and comming of good *Jesus,* (whom may it please to have mercy upon us) a Historie which is well agreeing to a *Churchyard.* And secondly, they may signifie to them, which are skilled in Naturall *Philosophy,* all the principall and necessary operations of the *Maistery.* These *Hieroglyphicke figures* shall serve as two wayes to leade unto the heavenly life: the first and most open sence, teaching the sacred *Mysteries* of our salvation; (as I will shew hereafter) the other teaching every man that hath any small understanding in the *Stone,* the lineary way of the worke; which being perfected by any one, the change of evill into good, takes away from him the roote of all sinne (which is *covetousnesse*) making him liberall, gentle, pious, religious, and fearing God, how evill soever hee was before, for from thence forward, hee is continually ravished with the great grace and mercy which hee hath obtained from God, and with the profoundnesse of his Divine & admirable works. These are the reasons which have mooved mee to set these formes in this fashion, and in this place which is a *Churchyard,* to the end that if any man obtaine this inestimable good, to conquere this *rich golden Fleece,*[11] he may thinke with himselfe (as I did) not to keepe the *talent* of *God* digged in the *Earth,* buying Lands and Possessions, which are the vanities of this world: but rather to worke charitably towards his brethren, remembring himselfe that hee learned this *secret* amongst the *bones* of the *dead,* in whose number hee shall shortly be found; and that after this life, he must render an account, before a just and redoubtable *Judge,* which will censure even to an idle and vaine word. Let him therefore, which having well weighed my *words,* and well knowne and understood my *figures,* hath first gotten elsewhere the knowledge of the first *beginnings and Agents,* (for certainely in these *Figures* and *Commentaries,* he shall not finde any step or information thereof) perfect to the glory of God, the *Maistery* of *Hermes,* remembring himself of the *Church Catholike, Apostolike,* and *Romane*; and of all other *Churches, Churchyards,* and *Hospitals*; and above all, of the *Church* of the *Innocents* in this *Citie,* (in the *Churchyard* whereof hee shall have contemplated these true demonstrations) opening bounteously his purse, to them that are secretly poore, honest people desolate, weake women, widdowes, and forlorne orphanes. So be it.

Chap. 1: Of the Theologicall Interpretations, which may be given to these Hieroglyphickes, according to the sence of mee the Authour.

I have given to this *Churchyard,* a *Charnell-house,* which is right over against this fourth *Arch,* in the middest of the *Churchyard,* and against one of the Pillers of this *Charnell house,* I have

---

[11] Alchemical allegorists often resorted to myth, Jason's adventures in pursuit of the golden fleece being one of the popular means of figuring forth the search for the philosopher's stone.

made bee drawne with a coale, and grosely painted, *a man all blacke,*[12] which lookes straight
upon these *Hieroglyphickes,* about whom there is written in *French; Je voy merveille donc moult
Je m'esbahi: that is, I see a marveile, whereat I am much amazed:* This, as also three *plates* of
Iron and *Copper* gilt, on the *East, West,* and *South* of the *Arch,* where these *Hieroglyphickes*
are, in the middest of the *Church-yard,* representing the holy *Passion* and *Resurrection* of the
Sonne of *God;* this ought not to be otherwise interpreted, than according to the common
Theologicall sence, saving that this *black man,* may as well proclaime it a wonder to see
the admirable workes of God in the *transmutation* of *Mettals,* which is figured in these
Hieroglyphicks, which he so attentively lookes upon, as to see buried so many *bodies,* which
shall rise againe out of their Tombes at the feareful day of *judgement.* On the other part
I doe not thinke it needfull to interpret in a *Theological* sence, that *vessell* of *Earth* on the
right hand of these figures, within the which there is a *Pen* and *Inkhorne,* or rather a vessell
of *Philosophy,* if thou take away the *strings,* and joyne the *Penner*[13] to the *Inkhorne*: nor the
other two like it, which are on the two sides of the figures of *Saint Peter* and *Saint Paul,*
within one of the which, there is an N. which signifieth *Nicholas,* and within the other an
F. which signifieth *Flammell.* For these vessels signifie nothing else, but that in the like of
them, I have done the *Maistery* three times. Moreover, he that will also beleeve, that I have
put these vessels in forme of *Scutchions,* to represent this *Pen* and *Inkhorne,* and the capitall
letters of my *name,* let him beleeve it if he will, because both these interpretations are true.

Neither must you interpret in a Theological sence, that writing which followeth, in
these termes, NICHOLAS FLAMMEL, ET PERRENELLE SA FEMME, that is *Nicholas
Flammel, and Perrenelle his wife,* in as much as that signifieth nothing, but that I and my wife
have given that *Arche.*

As to the third, fourth, and fifth Tables following, by the sides whereof is written,
COMMENT LES INNOCENTS FURENT OCCIS PAR LE COMMANDEMENT
DU ROY HERODES, that is, *How the Innocents were killed by the commandement of King
Herod.*[14] The *theologicall* sence is well enough understood by the writing, we must onely
speake of the rest, which is above.

The two *Dragons* united together the one within the other, of colour *blacke* and *blew,*
in a field *sable,* that is to say, *blacke,* whereof the one hath the *wings* gilded and the other
hath none at all, are the *sinnes* which naturally are *enterchayned,* for the one hath his *originall*
and birth from another: Of them some may be easily *chased* away, as they *come* easily, for
they flie towards us every houre; and those which have no *wings,* can never be chased away,
such as is the *sinne* against the *holy Ghost.* The *gold* which is in the *wings,* signifieth that the
greatest part of sinnes commeth from the *unholy hunger* after *gold;* which makes so many
people diligently to hearken from whence they may have it: and the colour *black* and *blew,*
sheweth that these are the desires that come out of the *darke* pits of hell, which we ought
wholly to flye from. These two *Dragons* may also morally represent unto us the Legions of
evill spirits which are alwayes about us, and which will accuse us before the just Judge, at
the feareful day of judgement, which doe aske, nor seeke nothing else but to sift us.

The man and the woman which are next them, of an *orange colour,* upon a field *azure*
and *blew,* signifie that men and women ought not to have their hope in this World, for the

---

[12] Symbolizing the *nigredo* or *putrefactio* stage of the alchemical process, which initiates the cycle of death, purification,
and regeneration.
[13] A case for pens (*OED*).   [14] See Matt. 2.

orange colour intimates despaire, or the letting goe of hope, as here; and the colour *azure* and *blew*, upon the which they are painted, shewes us that we must thinke of heavenly things to come, and say as the roule of the man doth, HOMO VENIET AD JUDICIUM DEI, that is, *Man must come to the judgement of God*, or as that of the *woman*, VERE ILLA DIES TERRIBILIS ERIT, that is, *That day will be terrible indeed,* to the end that keeping our selves from the *Dragons*, which are *sinnes*, God may shew mercy unto us.

Next after this, in a field of *Synople*, that is *greene*, are painted two men and one woman rising againe, of the which one comes out of a *Sepulchre*, the other two out of the *Earth*, all three of colour exceeding *white* and *pure*, lifting their hands towards their eyes, & their eyes towards Heaven on high: Above these three bodies there are two *Angels* sounding musicall Instruments, as if they had called these dead to the day of judgement; for over these two *Angels* is the figure of our Lord *Jesus Christ*, holding the world in his hand, upon whose head an *Angell* setteth a Crowne, assisted by two others, which say in their roules, *O pater Omnipotens, O Jesu bone*, that is *O Father Almighty, O good Jesu*. On the right side of this *Saviour* is painted St *Paul*, clothed with *white & yellow*, with a Sword, at whose feete there is a man clothed in a gowne of *orange colour*, in which there appeared pleights or folds of *blacke* and *white*, (which picture resembleth mee to the life) and demandeth pardon of his sinnes, holding his hands joined together, from betweene which proceed these words written in a roule, DELE MALA QUÆ FECI, that is to say, *Blot out the evils that I have done:* On the other side on the left hand is *Saint Peter* with his Key, clothed in *reddish yellow*, holding his hand upon a woman clad in a gown of *orange colour*, which is on her knees, representing to the life *Perrenelle*, which holdeth her hands joyned together, having a rowle where is written, CHRISTE PRECOR ESTO PIUS, that is, *Christ I beseech thee be pittifull:* Behind whom there is an *Angell* on his knees, with a roule, that saith, SALVE DOMINE ANGELORUM, that is, *All haile thou Lord of Angels*. There is also another *Angel* on his knees, behinde my Image, on the same side that *S. Paul* is on, which likewise holdeth a roule, saying, O REX SEMPITERNE, that is *O King everlasting*. All this is so cleere, according to the explication of the *Resurrection* and future judgement, that it may easily be fitted thereto. So it seemes this *Arch* was not painted for any other purpose, but to represent this. And therefore we needed not stay any longer upon it, considering that the least and most ignorant, may well know how to give it this interpretation.

Next after the *three* that are rising againe, come two *Angels* more of an *Orange colour* upon a *blew field*, saying in their *rowles*, SURGITE MORTUI, VENITE AD JUDICIUM DOMINI MEI, that is, *Arise you dead, come to the Judgment of my Lord*. That also serves to the interpretation of the *Resurrection*: As also the last Figures following, which are, *A man red vermillion*, upon a field of *Violet colour*, who holdeth the foot of a winged *Lyon*, painted of *red vermillion* also, opening his throate, as it were to devoure the *man*: For one may say that this is the Figure of an unhappy sinner, who sleeping in a Lethargy of his corruption and vices, dieth without repentance and confession; who without doubt, in this terrible Day shall bee delivered to the *Devill*, heere painted in forme of a *red roaring Lyon*, which will swallow and devoure him.

Chap. 2: The interpretations Philosophicall, according to the Maistery of Hermes.

I desire with all my heart, that he who searcheth the secrets of the *Sages*, having in his Spirit passed over these *Idæa's* of the life and resurrection to come, should first make his profit of them: And in the second place, that hee bee more advised than before, that hee sound and search the depth of my *Figures, colours,* and *rowles*; principally of my *rowles*, because that in this *Art* they speake not vulgarly. Afterward let him aske of himselfe, why the Figure of Saint *Paul* is on the right hand, in the place where the custome is to paint S. *Peter*? And on the other side that of Saint *Peter*, in the place of the figure of Saint *Paul*? Why the Figure of Saint *Paul* is clothed in colours *white* and *yellow*, and that of S. *Peter* in *yellow* and *red*? Why also the *man* and the *woman* which are at the feet of these two *Saints*, praying to *God*, as if it were at the Day of *Judgement*, are apparrelled in divers colours, and not naked, or else nothing but bones, like them that are rising againe? Why in this Day of *Judgement* they have painted this *man* and this *woman* at the feet of the *Saints*? For they ought to have beene more low on *earth*, and not in *heaven*. Why also the two *Angels* in *Orange colour*, which say in their rowles, SURGITE MORTUI, VENITE AD JUDICIUM DOMINI MEI, that is, *Arise you dead, come unto the Judgment of my Lord*, are clad in this colour, and out of their place, for they ought to bee on high in heaven, with the two other which play upon the *Instruments*? Why they have a field *Violet* and *blew*? but principally why their roule, which speaks to the dead, ends in the open throate of the *red and flying Lyon*? I would then that after these, and many other questions which may justly bee made, opening wide the eyes of his spirit, he come to conclude, that all this, not having beene done without cause, there must bee represented under this *barke*, some great *secrets*, which hee ought to pray *God* to discover unto him. Having then brought his beliefe by degrees to this passe, I wish also that he would further beleeve, that these *figures* and *explications* are not made for them that have never seene the Bookes of the *Philosophers*, and who not knowing the *Mettallicke* principles, cannot bee named *Children* of this *Science*; for if they thinke to understand perfectly these *figures*, being ignorant of the *first Agent*, they will undoubtedly deceive themselves, and never bee able to know any thing at all. Let no man therefore blame me, if he doe not easily understand mee, for hee will be more blame-worthy than I, inasmuch as not being initiated into these sacred and secret interpretations of the *first Agent*, (which is the *key* opening the gates of all *Sciences*) he would notwithstanding, comprehend the most subtile conceptions of the *envious Philosophers*, which are not written but for them who already know these principles, which are never found in any booke, because they leave them unto *God*, who revealeth them to whom he please, or else causeth them to bee taught by the living voyce of a *Maister*, by *Cabalisticall* tradition, which happeneth very seldome. Now then, *my Sonne*, let mee so call thee, both because I am now come to a great age, and also for that, it may be, thou art otherwise a *child* of this *knowledge*, (*God* enable thee to learne, and after to worke to his glory) Hearken unto mee then attentively, but passe no further if thou bee ignorant of the foresaid Principles.

   This *Vessell* of *earth*, in this forme, is called by the *Philosophers*, their *triple Vessell*, for within it, there is in the middest a Stage, or a floore, and upon that a dish or a platter full of luke-warm ashes, within the which is set the *Philosophicall Egge*,[15] that is, a viall of glasse full of *confections* of *Art* (as of the *scumme* of the *red Sea*, and the *fat* of the *Mercuriall winde*:) which thou seest painted in forme of a *Penner and Inkehorne*. Now this Vessell of *earth* is

---

[15] Probably the most common term for the vessel in which the philosopher's stone is created, so called because of its shape and the gentle heat considered essential for the incubation and hatching of the "philosophical chick" or "poulet," i.e., the Stone.

open above, to put in the *dish* and the *viall,* under which by the open gate, is put in the *Philosophicall fire,* as thou knowest. So thou hast *three vessels;* and the *threefold vessell:* The envious have called an *Athanor,* a *sive, dung, Balneum Mariæ,* a *Furnace,* a *Sphære, the greene Lyon,* a *prison,* a *grave,* a *urinall,* a *phioll,* and *a Bolts-head:*[16] I my selfe in my *Summarie* or *Abridgement of Philosophy,*[17] which I composed foure yeeres and two moneths past, in the end thereof named it the *house* and *habitation* of the *Poulet,* and the *ashes* of the *Platter,* the *chaffe* of the *Poulet;* The common name is an *Oven,* which I should never have *found,* if *Abraham* the *Jew* had not painted it, together with the fire proportionable, wherein consists a great part of the secret. For it is as it were the *belly,* or the *wombe,* containing the true naturall heate to animate our *yong King:* If this *fire* be not measured *Clibanically,* saith *Calid* the *Persian, sonne of Jasichus;* If it be kindled with a sword, saith *Pithagoras:* If thou fire thy Vessell, saith *Morien,* and makest it feele the heate of the fire, it will give thee a box on the eare, and burne his *flowres* before they be risen from the depth of his *Marrow,* making them come out *red,* rather than *white,* and then thy worke is spoiled; as also if thou make too little fire, for then thou shalt never see the end, because of the coldnesse of the *natures,* which shall not have had motion sufficient to digest them together.

The heate then of thy *fire* in this vessell, shall be (as saith *Hermes* and *Rosinus*)[18] according to the *Winter;* or rather, as saith *Diomedes,*[19] according to the heate of a *Bird,* which beginnes to flie so softly from the signe of *Aries* to that of *Cancer:* for know that the Infant at the beginning is full of *cold flegme,* and of *milke,* and that too vehement *heate* is an enemy of the *cold* and *moisture* of our *Embrion,* and that the two enemies, that is to say, our two elements of *cold* and *heate* will never perfectly imbrace one another, but by little and little, having first long dwelt together, in the middest of the temperate heate of their *bath,* and being changed by long decoction, into *Sulphur incombustible.* Govern therefore sweetly with equality and proportion, thy proud and haughty natures, for feare lest if thou favour one more then another, they which naturally are enemies, doe grow angry against thee through *Jelousy,* and dry *Choller,* and make thee sigh for it a long time after. Besides this, thou must entertain them in this temperate heate perpetually, that is to say, night and day, until the time that *Winter,* the time of the *moisture* of the matters, be passed, because they make their peace, and joyne hands in being heated together, whereas should these natures finde themselves but one onely half houre without *fire,* they would become for ever irreconcileable. See therefore the reason why it is said in the Book of the *seventy precepts,*[20] *Looke that their heate continue indefatigably without ceasing, and that none of their dayes bee forgotten.* And *Rasis,* the *haste,* saith hee, *that brings with it too much fire, is alwaies followed by the Divell, and Errour. When the golden Bird,* saith *Diomedes, shall be come just to Cancer, and that from thence it shall runne toward Libra, then thou maist augment the fire a little: And in like manner, when this faire Bird, shall fly from Libra towards Capricorne, which is the desired Autumne, the time of harvest and of the fruits that are now ripe.*

---

[16] "A long-necked, round-bottomed flask used in the distillation process" (*DAI* 29).

[17] Dixon notes that Flamel's *Summarium philosophicum,* or *Le Sommaire philosophique,* was first printed in 1561 (94n59).

[18] Ferguson cites several titles attributed to Rosinus that were printed early in the seventeenth century; this obscure figure is variously thought to be "of the Arabian school" or a Pole or Hungarian (*Bibl. Chem.* 2:294–95). Here he advocates very moderate heat.

[19] An authority cited in *The True Book of the Learned Synesius, A Greek Abbot . . . Concerning the Philosopher's Stone* (London, 1672), in *Basil Valentine His Triumphant Chariot of Antimony,* ed. L. G. Kelly, 170.

[20] Variously attributed to Aristotle or to Geber (*HMES* 2:251).

[The next five chapters present alchemical interpretations of individual details of the arch diagram; the two chapters printed below, the last in Flamel's treatise, concern the figures of St. Peter and Perrenelle on the right-hand side of the illustration and the winged lion atop a man at the far right.]

Chap. 8: The figure of a man, like unto Saint Peter, cloathed in a robe Citrine red, holding a key in his right hand, and laying his left hand upon a woman, in an orange coloured robe, which is on her knees at his feete, holding a Rowle.
Looke upon this *woman* clothed in a robe of *orange colour*, which doth so naturally resemble *Perrenelle* as she was in her youth; Shee is painted in the fashion of a *suppliant* upon her knees, her hands joyned together, at the feete of a *man* which hath a *key* in his *right hand*, which heares her graciously, and afterwards stretcheth out his *left hand* upon her. Wouldest thou know that this meaneth? This is the *Stone*, which in this operation demandeth two things, of the *Mercury of the Sunne*, of the *Philosophers*, (painted under the forme of a *man*) that is to say *Multiplication*, and a more rich *Accoustrement*; which at this time it is needfull for her to obtaine, and therefore the man so laying his hand upon her shoulder accords & grants it unto her. But why have I made to bee painted a *woman*? I could as well have made to bee painted a *man*, as a *woman*, or an *Angell* rather (for the whole natures are now spirituall and corporall, masculine and foeminine:) But I have rather chosen to cause paint a *woman*, to the end that thou mayest judge, that shee demaunds rather this, than any other thing, because these are the most naturall and proper desires of a woman. To shew further unto thee, that shee demandeth *Multiplication*, I have made paint the *man*, unto whom shee addresseth her prayers in the forme of *Saint Peter*, holding a *key*, having power to open and to shut, to binde and to loose; because the envious *Philosophers* have never spoken of *Multiplication*, but under these common termes of *Art, APERI, CLAUDE, SOLVE, LIGA*, that is *Open, shut, binde, loose; opening* and *loosing*, they have called the making of the *Body* (which is alwayes *hard* and *fixt*) *soft fluid*, and running like water: To *shut* and to *bind*, is with them afterwards by a more strong decoction to *coagulate* it, and to bring it backe againe into the forme of a *body*.

It behoved mee then, in this place to represent a *man* with a *key*, to teach thee that thou must now *open* and *shut*, that is to say, *Multiply* the budding and encreasing natures: for look how often thou shalt dissolve and fixe, so often will these natures multiply, in *quantity, quality*, and *vertue* according to the multiplication of *ten*; comming from this number to an *hundred*, from an *hundred* to a *thousand*, from a *thousand* to *ten thousand*, from *ten thousand* to an *hundred thousand*, from an *hundred thousand* to a *million*, and from thence by the same operation to *Infinity*, as I have done three times, praised be God. And when thy *Elixir* is so brought unto *Infinity*, one *graine* thereof falling upon a quantity of molten mettall as deepe and vaste as the *Ocean*, it will teine it, and convert it into most perfect *mettall*, that is to say, into *silver* or *gold*, according as it shall have been *imbibed* and *fermented*, expelling & driving out farre from himself all the impure and strange matter, which was joyned with the mettall in the first *coagulation*: for this reason therefore have I made to bee painted a *Key* in the hand of the *man*, which is in the forme of *Saint Peter*, to signifie that the *stone* desireth to be *opened* and *shut* for *multiplication*; and likewise to shew thee with what *Mercury* thou oughtest to doe this, & when; I have given the man a garment *Citrine red*, and the *woman* one of *orange* colour. Let this suffice, lest I transgresse the silence of *Pythagoras*, to teach thee that the *woman*, that is, our *stone*, asketh to have the rich Accoustrements and *colour* of *Saint Peter*. Shee hath written in her Rowle, CHRISTE PRECOR ESTO PIUS, that is *Jesu Christ be pittifull unto mee*, as if shee said, *Lord be good unto mee, and suffer not that hee that shal be come thus farre, should spoile all with too much fire; It is true, that from henceforward I shal no more feare mine enemies, and that all fire shall be alike unto me, yet the vessell that containes me, is alwaies brittle and easie to be broken: for if they exalt the fire overmuch, it will cracke, and flying apieces, will carry mee, and sow mee unfortunately amongst the ashes.* Take heed therefore to thy fire in this place, and governe sweetly with patience, this admirable *quintessence*, for the fire must be augmented unto it, but not too much. And pray the soveraigne *Goodnesse*, that it will not suffer the evill spirits, which keepe the *Mines* and *Treasures*, to destroy thy worke, or to bewitch thy *sight*, when thou considerest these incomprehensible motions of this *Quintessence* within thy vessell.

Chap. 9: Upon a darke violet field, a man red purple, holding the foote of a Lyon red as vermillion, which hath wings, & it seemes would ravish and carry away the man.

The field *violet* and *darke*, tels us that the *stone* hath obtained by her full decoction, the faire *Garments*, that are wholy *Citrine and red*, which shee demanded of *Saint Peter*, who was cloathed therewith, and that her compleat and perfect *digestion* (signified by the entire *Citrinity*) hath made her leave her old robe of *orange colour*. The *vermilion red* colour of this *flying Lyon*, like the pure & cleere *skarlet* in graine, which is of the true *Granadored*,[21] demonstrates that it is now accomplished in all right and equality. And that shee is now like a *Lyon*, devouring every pure *mettallicke* nature, and changing it into her true substance, into true & pure *gold*, and more fine then that of the *best mines*. Also shee now carrieth this man out of this vale of miseries, that is to say, out of the discommodities of *poverty & infirmity*, and with her wings gloriously lifts him up, out of the dead and standing waters of *Ægypt* (which are the ordinary thoughts of mortall men), making him despise this life and the riches thereof, and causing him night and day to meditate on *God* and his *Saints*, to dwell in the *Emperiall Heaven*, and to drinke the sweet springs of the Fountains of *everlasting hope*. Praised be *God* eternally, which hath given us grace to see this most fair & all-perfect *purple* colour; this pleasant colour of the *wilde poppy* of the *Rocke*, this *Tyrian*, sparkling and flaming colour, which is incapable of *Alteration* or *change*, over which the *heaven* it selfe, nor his *Zodiacke* can have no more domination nor power, whose bright shining rayes, that dazle the eyes, seeme as though they did communicate unto a man some supercoelestiall thing, making him (when he beholds and knowes it) to be astonisht, to tremble, and to be afraid at the same time. *O Lord, give us grace to use it well, to the augmentation of the Faith, to the profit of our Soules, and to the encrease of the glory of this noble Realme. Amen.*

---

[21] Possibly an obsolete spelling of Granada, as associated with a kind of red dye from the Spanish city; more likely a form of *grenat*, "of a deep red color, like that of garnet" (*OED*).

16 Bernard, Earl of Trevisan
(*fl.* late fourteenth century)
A Treatise of the Philosopher's Stone

Anthologies of alchemical treatises by divers hands were popular and influential in England and on the Continent in the sixteenth and seventeenth centuries, and ranged in size from Lazarus Zetzner's voluminous *Theatrum Chemicum*, first published in Ursel in 1602 and frequently reissued in expanded editions, to the *Collectanea Chymica*, which the London printer William Cooper produced in 1684. It included ten essays by both long established alchemical authorities, Roger Bacon, George Ripley, and Bernard of Trevisan, author of this work, and more recent writers, such as John Baptist van Helmont and Francis Antonie, whose recipe for aurum potabile appears later in this collection. Bernard of Trevisan (the Earl of Trevisa in Italy, or Trevisanus) probably flourished during the last half of the fourteenth century, although he has also been placed in the fifteenth. An autobiographical passage in one of his works, *De Chemico Miraculo*, presents Trevisan as one whose life was passionately devoted to searching for the secret of transmutation – which proved unsuccessful until his final years. He is perhaps best known for his alchemical correspondence with Thomas of Bologna, father of the poet, Christine de Pisan (*ca.* 1363–*ca.* 1431). Trevisan's *Treatise of the Philosopher's Stone* presents an unusually clear and succinct summary of the process.

The following text is complete and taken from the *Collectanea Chymica: A Collection of Ten Several Treatises in Chymistry* (London: Printed for William Cooper, at the Pelican in Little Britain, 1684). Additional readings: Thorndike, *HMES*, 3: 611–27; Robert M. Schuler, ed., *Alchemical Poetry 1575–1700*, 446–63.

Considering the long Desires and Hopes of the Students in the Chymick Art, I will in the present Treatise briefly and openly declare this Art. First therefore the Subject of the Art is to be known; in the second place, the Foundation; in the third, the Progress; fourthly and lastly, the Extraction of the Elements: Which being known, every one may most easily attain the end of the Art.

The Subject of this admired Science is *Sol* and *Luna*, or rather Male and Female, the Male is hot and dry, the Female cold and moyst, and know for a certain that our Stone is not compounded of any other thing, although many Philosophers name several other things, of which they speak Sophistically.

Nevertheless by *Scotus, Hortulanus,* St. *Thomas,* and *Christopher Parisiensis,*[1] and very many others, many other things for an other Cause are sophistically reckoned up, that Ignorant Men may be deceived, because it is not fit for Fools to know our Secrets: And this is it, which I thought fit at this time to propound concerning the Subject of our Art.

The Foundation of this Art, is the Knowledge of the four Qualities, and that in the beginning of the work, Coldness and Moysture have the Dominion: For as *Scotus* saith, As the Sun dryeth up the abundance of *Water* in Fenny and Boggy Places, after the same manner our Sulphur when it is joyned with its Water or Mercury, doth by little and little consume and drink up the same by the help of the Fire, and that by the assistance of the only living God.

The Progress is nothing else than a certain contrary Action, for the Description of contrary things is one and the same, and if thou shalt have twice made this equality, thou shalt finish the whole Progress.

But now all skill consisteth in drawing forth the Elements, wherefore read over that which followeth so often, until thou canst conceive and understand it; and know that no one ever spoke so plainly as I in this Place, as thou wilt find by what followeth: Therefore give thanks to the great God, and be grateful to thy Friend who communicated to thee this Tractate: Live also according to God and reason, because Divine Wisdom will not enter into a wicked Soul, nor into a Body subjected to Sins.

The Extraction of the Elements is a certain Composition of Blackness, Whiteness, Yellowness, and Redness: And know that Natures ought to be drawn from their Root. But the Root is a certain Congregation of Elements, consisting in Sulphur and Mercury, which they call a confused Mass. But the Natures, which are drawn forth from the Root are Sulphur and Mercury, which when they are joyned together are separated, and purified, that they may be the better mingled afterwards, and united with the Body, out of which they are drawn. And after the Colours have passed, and that which is above, is made like that which is below, and that which is below like that above, then Miracles will from thence appear. Which being done, thou hast a Triangle in a Quadrangle, and a fifth thing which is contained in four.[2]

Now remaineth the Multiplication, in which this briefly is to be noted; That the *Elixir* ought to be nourished out of the same things, from which at first it had its Composition. No Philosopher before now hath so openly declared this, as I have here done; and that for two Causes, first because from the beginning to the end of the work a long time is required, although some Philosophers do say, the Stone may be made in one day, and others in one month: But know that they speak Enigmatically, and that their words ought not thus to be understood.

Nevertheless I say with *Scotus* that the Stone or perfect work may be made in one year. Secondly, because Man's Life is short, and he groweth Old before he comprehendeth and understandeth what is needful to be done in the Composition of the Stone. And therefore

---

[1] Scotus is Michael Scot, thirteenth-century scholar, magician, alchemist, and astrologer in the court of Frederick II, king of Germany and Holy Roman Emperor (1215–50). St. Thomas is Aquinas (1224–74), to whom several alchemical treatises were dubiously attributed; Christopher of Paris was a fifteenth-century alchemist and author of the *Elucidarius.*

[2] Here Trevisan sets forth three of alchemy's most notable arcana: color sequence; connections between microcosm and macrocosm and the purification process through reference to the *Emerald Table*; and the squaring of the circle.

I have here so openly explained all things, lest this, so noble a Science, should be lost and perish.

The Theory of the same Author

Use venerable Nature, for the Philosophers from their own Authority have imposed various Names on this Nature, by reason of divers Colours appearing in its Alteration. For when it appeareth under the form of Water, they have called it *Argent vive*, Permanent Water, Lead, Spirit, Spittle of *Lune*, Tinn, &c. And when it's made dry and becometh white, they have named it Silver, Magnesia, and white Sulphur. And when it groweth red, they call the same Gold and Ferment. But they do not vary in the thing it self, when that is always one thing only, and the same matter, and always of the same Nature, in which nothing entreth which is not drawn from it, and this which is next to it, and of its Nature. And this is most true, to wit, the Stone is one, and one Medicine, and it is a Water clear, and bright, permanent, pure and shining, of a Celestical Colour. And if Water did not enter into our Medicine, it could not purifie nor mend it self, and so thou couldst not obtain thy desire: But that which doth mend it is *Sol*, for the Water cannot be made better without it: For without Sol and his shadow a tinging Poyson[3] cannot be generated. Whoever therefore shall think that a Tincture can be made without these two Bodyes, to wit *Sol* and *Lune*, he proceedeth to the Practice like one that is blind. For Body doth not Act upon Body, nor Spirit upon Spirit: Neither doth Form receive an Impression from Form, nor Matter from Matter, when as like doth not Exercise either Action or Passion upon its like: For one is not more worthy than an other, wherefore there can be no Action betwixt them, when as like doth not bear Rule over like. But a Body doth receive Impression from a Spirit, as Matter doth from its Form, and a Spirit from its Body, because they are made and created by God, that they may Act and suffer each from other. For Matter would flow infinitely, if a Form did not retard and stop its Flux. Wherefore when the Body is a Form informing, it doth inform and retain the Spirit, that it afterwards cannot flow any more.

The Body therefore doth tinge the Spirit, and the Spirit doth penetrate the Body, whereas one Body cannot penetrate an other Body, but a subtil Spiritual congealed Substance doth penetrate and give Colour to the Body. And this is that Gummy and Oleaginous Stone, proportioned in its Natures, containing a Spiritual nature occultly in it self together with the Elements purifyed. Therefore the Philosophers Stone is to be wholly reduced into this Gumminess by the last Reiteration or Inceration of a certain gentle Flux, resolving all the Elements, that they flow like Wax. But when it is the Stone, it appeareth like Copper, whereas nothwithstanding it is a certain Spiritual Substance, penetrating and colouring or tinging all Metallick Bodys.

From hence thou mayst easily guess, that this doth not proceed from the crassitude and grossness of the Earth; but from a Spiritual Metallick Substance, which doth penetrate and enter. Wherefore it behoveth thee to resolve the Body into a subtil Metallick Spirit, and afterwards to congeal and fix, retain and increate it,[4] that it may flow before it

---

[3] This "tinging Poyson" is later identified as argent-vive; Sol is the sulphuric principle, which is said nonetheless to be present *within* argent-vive. Thus the opposing masculine and feminine qualities reside in the single, perfect (because interactive) matter of the stone, a fusion of body and spirit.

[4] Inceration means mixing the substances to the consistency of moist wax or "gumme."

tinge. For Gold doth Colour nothing besides it self, unless first its own Spirit be extracted out of its own Belly; and it be made Spiritual.

And know that our Mercurial Water is a living Water, and a burning Fire, mortifying and tearing in pieces Gold more than common Fire. And therefore by how much more it is better mixed, rubbed and ground with it, by so much more it destroyeth it, and the living fiery Water is more attenuated. But now when three are made one in the Form of a congealed Substance, then it hath in it a true Tincture, which can endure the Violence of the Fire. Therefore when the Body is so tinged, it can tinge another, and it hath in it self all Tincture and Virtue. And from hence all they who tinge with *Sol* and his Shadow, (viz.) with the Poyson,[5] that is *Argent vive*, do perfectly compleat our Stone, which we call the great and perfect Gumm. And know for certain that it is not necessary, that our Stone or Gumm lose its first Mercurial Nature in the Sublimation of its crude and first Spirit: for the Oyl and Gumm pertaining to this Stone are nothing else, then the Elements themselves Mercurialized, and made equal together, shut up and coagulated, resoluble and living, retained or bound in the viscosity of the Oyly Earth, and inseparably mixed. And we ought to know that that Gum or Oyl is first drawn out of the Bodys, which being added, it is reduced into a Spirit, until the superfluous humidity of the Water be turned into Air, drawing one Element out of another by digestion until the Form of Water be converted into the Nature of Oyl, and so our Stone in the end getteth the Name of Gumm and Sulphur.

But whosoever hath brought the Stone thus far, that it appear like a mixing Gumm, and suffereth it self to be mixed with all imperfect Bodies, he verily hath found a great Secret of Nature, because that is a perfect Stone, Gum and Sulphur.

This stone then is compounded of a Body and Spirit, or of a volatile and fixed Substance, and that is therefore done, because nothing in the World can be generated and brought to light without these two Substances, to wit, a Male and Female: From whence it appeareth, that although these two Substances are not of one and the same species, yet one Stone doth thence arise, and although they appear and are said to be two Substances, yet in truth it is but one, to wit, *Argent vive*. But of this *Argent vive* a certain part is fixed and digested, Masculine, hot, dry, and secretly informing: But the other which is the Female, is Volatile, crude, cold and moyst; and from these two Substances the whole may easily be known, and the whole Stone intirely understood. Wherefore if our Stone did only consist of one Substance, in it there could be no Action and passion of one thing towards the other; for one would neither touch nor come nigh or enter into the other: As a Stone and piece of Wood have no Operation on each other, since they do consist of a different matter, and hence they can by no means, no not in the least be mixed together, and there is the same reason for all things that differ in matter. Wherefore it is evident and certain that it should be necessary for the Agent and Patient to be of one and the same Genus; but of a different species, even as a man differeth from a Woman. For although they agree in one and the same Genus, yet nevertheless they have diverse Operations and Qualities, even as the Matter and Form. For the Matter suffereth, and the Form acteth assimilating the matter to it self, and according to this manner the Matter naturally thirsteth after a Form,

---

[5] On the inextricable linkage between sun and shadow, body and spirit that Trevisan elaborates upon in this section, see *DAI* 195–6.

as a Woman desireth an Husband, and a Vile thing a precious one, and an impure a pure one, so also *Argent vive* coveteth a Sulphur, as that which should make perfect which is imperfect: So also a Body freely desireth a Spirit, whereby it may at length arrive at its perfection. Therefore Learn thou the Natural Roots, and those that are better, with which thou oughtest to reduce thy Matter, whereby thou mayst perfect thy work. For this blessed Stone hath in it all things necessary to its perfection.

The Practick of the same Author

If we well consider the Words of *Morienus* that great Philosopher in *Alchimy*, who saith, Mix together Water, Earth, Air, and Fire in a due weight, without doubt thou wilt obtain all the Secrets of this Divine Science. And first, when he saith, put into the Water, or putrifie the Earth in Water, this signifieth nothing else, then the Extraction of Water out of Earth, and the pouring of Water upon the Earth, so long until the Earth putrifie and be cleansed, otherwise it would not bring forth its Fruit. Secondly when he saith, mix Water and Air, it's no more then if he should have said, mix Water now prepared with Air dissolved, or joyn and mix together dissolved Air with Water. Judge ye your selves: For you know that Air is warm and moyst, and ye have the saying of *Morienus* concerning the dissolution of Air, Earth, Fire and Water. Some when they speak of Dissolution, say that the Solution of the Fire is better, because whatsoever is dissolved in the Fire, that floweth in the Air. And Note that the Fire of the Philosophers is nothing else then the Air dissolved and congealed. This you may better comprehend from similitude, and suppose that first you have Air dissolved and congealed, to which add Fire. The Earth ought to be first prepared, and the Fire dissolved, before they are mixed.

For the Earth together with the Fire ought to be put into a fit Vessel, and after is to be introduced the inextinguishable Fire of Nature, which when it descendeth upon the Earth, devoureth the whole together with its Gumm, and converteth it into its own Nature. Wherefore if ye consider well the Sayings and Precepts of the Philosophers, and understand their Mystical Sence, ye shall come to all the Secrets of the Divine Chymick Art.

17 George Ripley (1415–1490)

The Epistle of George Ripley written to King Edward IV

George Ripley is the best known English alchemist and alchemical author of the late medieval period. Although a canon regular of the Augustinian priory at Bridlington in Yorkshire, he travelled extensively on the Continent in search of alchemical knowledge ("Great secrets...in farre countries I did learne," *Epistle*, st. 3) and supposedly laid the foundations for attainment of the philosopher's stone while studying in Italy. That Ripley was reputed to be successful is evident from the widely circulated account of his stay on the island of Rhodes where he was a guest of and a lavish contributor to the Knights of the Order of St John of Jerusalem.

A vast amount of Ripley material exists in manuscript, indicating that he was prolific and that his works were widely disseminated and highly regarded; in addition, his writings appeared in printed editions into the eighteenth century. Chief among his works is *The Compund of Alchymy*, a long alchemical poem written in rhyme royal and dedicated to King Edward IV. In it, Ripley purports to reveal the process for making the philosopher's stone through detailed discussion of each of its twelve stages or "gates." This work was first printed in 1591, 120 years after its composition, and also reprinted in Elias Ashmole's *Theatrum Chemicum Britannicum* (1652). Ripley's importance was recognized throughout the seventeenth century, as he is frequently cited by Robert Boyle and Isaac Newton, and the *Compound* received detailed commentary in Eirenaeus Philalethes' (i. e. George Starkey's) *Ripley Reviv'd* (1678). Ripley's dedicatory *Epistle...to King Edward the 4* summarizes many of the topics that receive fuller attention in the *Compound*, including theoretical and practical, as well as moral, religious, and political aspects of alchemy. The *Epistle* should be read in conjunction with Philalethes' commentary printed later in this collection. The text of Ripley's *Epistle* is taken from my edition of *George Ripley's Compound of Alchymy (1591)*.

1. O Honorable Lord, and most victorious Knight,[1]
With grace and vertue abundantly endewed,
The safegard of *England*, and maintainer of right;
That God you loveth, indeed he hath well shewed:

---

[1] In this *Epistle*, Ripley abandons rhyme royal used throughout the *Compound of Alchymy* and adopts an 8-line verse form rhyming ababbcbc. Edward IV (reigned 1461–70; 1471–83) was the first of the Yorkist kings and ruled throughout much of Ripley's later life (d. 1490).

Wherefore I trust this land shalbe renewed
With joy and riches, with charitie and peace,
So that olde ranckors new understrewed,
Tempestuous troubles, and wretchednes shall cease.

2. And therefore sith I see by tokens right evident,
That God you guideth, and how that you be vertuous,
Hating sinne, and all such as be insolent,
How that also manslaughter to you is odious,
Upon the judgement also that you be piteous:
Me seemeth ruthe it were but that you should live long;
For of your great fortune you are not presumptuous,
Nor vengeable of spirit to revenge you of each wrong.

3. These considered with others in your most noble State,
Like as God knoweth, and people doo witnes beare,
So entirely me mooveth, that I must algate
Record the same, and therein be no flatterer:
And not that only, but also to write here
Unto your Highnes, humbly to present
Great secrets, which in farre countries I did learne,[2]
And which by grace to me most unworthie are lent.

4. Once to your Lordship such things I did promise,
What time you did commaund to send unto me,
And sith that I wrote it in secret wise,
Unto your grace from the Universitie
Of *Lovaine*,[3] when God fortuned me by grace to see
Greater secrets and much more perfite,
Which onely to you I will disclosed to be,
That is the great Elixer both red and white.[4]

5. For like it you to trust that truly I have found,
The perfect way of most secret Alchymie,
Which I will never truly for marke nor for pound
Make common but to you, and that conditionally,
That to youre selfe you shall keepe it full secretly,
And only to use it as may be to Gods pleasure,
Else in time comming to God I should abye,[5]
For my discovering of his secret treasure.

---

[2] Probably in the 1460s and 1470s Ripley travelled for nine years in France, Germany and Italy, even as far as Rhodes, in search of alchemical knowledge.

[3] The University of Louvain (Belgium) was also included in Ripley's travels.

[4] I.e., the elixir that could transmute base metals into both gold and silver.

[5] Pay the penalty for (*OED*). The injunctions to secrecy and to lead a moral life are, of course, alchemical commonplaces. What is remarkable is that Ripley is exacting these vows of his monarch.

6. Therefore be you well advised and with good deliberation,
For of this secret shall know no other creature,
But onely you as I make faithfull protestation,
For all the time that herein life I shall endure,
Whereto I will your Lordship me ensure,
To my desire in this my oath for to agree,
Least I to me the wrath of God procure,
For such revealing of his great gift and privitie.

7. If God fortune you by me to win this treasure,
Serve him devowtly with more lawde and thanking,
Praying his Godhead in life that you may so endure,
His gifts of grace, and fortune to use to his pleasing,
Most especially intending over all thing,
To your power and cunning his precepts ten
So to observe, that into no danger your selfe you bring,
But that you in glory may see him hereafter, Amen.

8. And yet moreover I will your Lordship to pardon me,
For openly with pen I will it never it write,
But whensoever you list by practise you shall see,
By mouth also this precious secret, most of delight,
How may be made perfect Elixers both red and white,
Plaine unto your Lordship it shall declared be,
And if it please you, with easie expences and respite,
I will them worke by grace of the Trinitie.

9. But notwithstanding for perill that may befall,
If I dare not here plainely the knotte unbinde,
Yet in my writing I will not be so misticall,
But that by studie the true knowledge you may finde,
How that each thing is multiplied in his kinde,
And how the likenes of bodies metaline be transmutable
I will declare, that if you feele me in your minde,
My writing you shall finde true and no fained fable.

10. As Philosophers in the metheors doe write,[6]
The likenes of bodies metaline be not transmutable,
But after he added these wordes of more delight,
Without they be reduced to their beginning materiable,
Wherefore such bodies within nature be liquiable,

---

[6] Ripley is referring to an alchemical section of Avicenna's *Kitâb al-Shifâ'* that was translated into Latin about 1200 and inserted in the fourth book of Aristotle's *Meteorology*, where it was accepted as genuine and achieved great popularity as *De congelatione et conglutinatione lapidum* (see the text included in this collection). As Ripley notes in the next line, Avicenna's main contention is that alchemy cannot accomplish any fundamental transformation in the nature of the metals worked upon, only superficial changes in appearance.

Minerall and metaline may be mercurizate,[7]
Conceive you may this science is not opinionable,
But very true, by Raymond[8] and others determinate,

11. In the saide booke the Philosophers speake also,
Therein if it please your Highnes for to reade,
Of divers sulphures, and especially of two,
And of two mercuries joyned to them indeed,
Whereby he doth true understanders leade,
To the knowledge of the principle which is onely trew,
Both red, moist, pure, and white, as I have espied,
Which be neverthelesse found but of verie few.

12. And these two things be best, he addeth anone
For him that worketh the Alchymie to take:
Our golde and our silver therewith to make all one,
Wherefore I say who will our pearle and Ruby make,
The said principles looke he not forsake:
For at the beginning, if his principles be true,
And if so be by craft he can them also bake,
In th'end truly his worke he shall not rue.

13. But one great secret right needfull to be knowne,
That though the Philosophers speake plurally,
All is but one thing you may me well trowe,
In kinde which is our base principally,
Whereof doth spring both white and red naturally,
And yet the white must come first out of the red,
Which thing is not wrought manually,
But naturally, craft helping out of our lead.

14. For all the partes of our most precious stone,
As I can prove, be coessentiall and concrete,
Moreover there is no true principle but one,
Full long it was ere I therewith could meete,
Who can reduce him and knoweth his heate,
And onely kinde with kinde can well redresse,
Till filthie originall be clensed from his seate,
He likely is to finde our secrets more and lesse.

15. Therefore worke kinde onely with his owne kinde,
And so your Elements joyne that they not strive.
This poynt also for any beare in minde,
That passive natures you turne into active,

---

[7] Possible form of "mercurification," the action or process of obtaining the "mercury" of a metal; or "mercurify," to change a metallic mass into mercury (*OED*).
[8] Raymond Lull.

Of water, fire, and winde of earth make blive,
And of the quadrangle make a figure round,[9]
Then have thou the honie of our bee-hive,
One ounce well worth one thousand pound.

16. The principall secret of secrets all,
Is true proportion which may not be behinde,
Wherein I counsell thee be not superficiall,
The true conclusion if you thinke to finde,
Turne earth into water and water into winde,
Therefore make fire and beware of the flood
Of *Noah*, wherein many men are so blinde,
That by this science they get little good.[10]

17. I counsell you eate and drink temperately,
And beware well that Iposarcha[11] come not in place.
Neshe not your wombe by drinking immoderately,
Least you quench naturall heate in little space,
The colour will tell appearing in your face,
Drinke no more therefore than you may eate,
Walke up and downe after an easie pace,
Chafe not your bodie too sore to sweate.

18. With easie fire after moving when you sweate,
Warme your bodie and make it drie againe,
By rivers and fountaines walke after meate,
At morning time visit the high mountaine,
That Phisick so biddeth I read certaine,
So high the mountaines yet doe you not ascend,
But that you may downwardes your way have plaine,
And with your mantle from colde ye you defend.

19. Such labour is wholesome your sweat for to drie
With napkin, and after it see you take no colde,
For grosse humors be purged by sweate kindely,
Use Diacameron then confect with perfect golde,[12]
Hermidocles for watry humors good I holde,[13]

---

[9] This is Ripley's version of the famous "squaring of the circle," the alchemists' image for the transformation of the four conflicting elements into the quintessence, the completion of the alchemical opus itself.

[10] In st.16, Ripley expresses several common concerns of the alchemists: the importance of proper "proportion" among the ingredients placed in the alembic; the interchanging of the four elements; and caution about the "flood / Of *Noah*," which, Abraham notes, is a "symbol for the dissolution of the Stone's matter into the prima materia during the nigredo" (*DAI* 136).

[11] In sts. 17ff., Ripley turns to the subject of diseases and medicinal preparations formulated by alchemical processes. Iposarcha or hyposarca is a form of dropsy (*OED*); excessive drinking "neshes" or softens the "womb," i.e., belly.

[12] Diacameron, a medical preparation involving a mixture (confect) with gold, apparently appears only in Ripley (*OED*).

[13] Hermidocles is possibly the herb *hermodactyli*: "They are hot and dry, purge flegm, especially from the joints, therefore are good for gouts" (*The Complete Herbal by Nicholas Culpeper. A New Edition*, 314).

Use Ipericon perforat with milke of tithimall,[14]
And sperma Cæti[15] with red wine, and when you wax olde,
And Goats milke sod with wine nourisheth moysture radicall.

20. But a good Phisition who so intendeth to be,
Our lower Astronomie[16] needeth well to know,
And after that to learne well urine in a glasse to see,
And if it neede to be chafed the fire for to blow,
Then wittily it by divers wayes for to throw
After the cause to make a medicine blive,[17]
Truly telling the infirmities all on a row,
Who this can doe by his Phisick is like to thrive.

21. We have our heaven incorruptible of the quintessence,
Ornate with signes, Elements, and starres bright,
Which moysteth our earth by subtill influence,
And of it a secret sulphure hid from sight,
It fetcheth by vertue of his active might,
Like as the Bee fetcheth honey out of the flower,
Which thing could doe no other worldly wight.
Therefore to God be all glory and honour.

22. And like as yce to water doth relent,
Where it was congealed by violence of colde,
When Phœbus yet shineth with his heate influent,
Even so to water minerall reduced is our golde,
As witnesseth plainely, *Albert*, *Raymond*, and *Arnold*,
By heate and moysture and by craft occasionate,
Which congelation of the spirits, loe now I have tolde,
How our materialls together must be proportionate.

23. At the dyers craft you may learne this science,
Beholding with water how decoction they make
Upon the wad or madder[18] easily and with patience,
Till tinctures doe appeare which then the cloth doth take,
Therein so fixed that they will never forsake
The cloth, for washing after they joyned be,

---

[14] I.e., hypericon or hypericum; a drug prepared from *Hypericum perforatum*, a common species of St. John's-wort. *Tithimall* is a variant spelling of "tithymal," an old name of the Spurge species of plants, much used in herbal medicine (*OED*).

[15] Spermaceti is a fatty substance, derived from the head of a sperm-whale and purified, used in various medicinal preparations.

[16] Here and in sts. 21 and 29, Ripley describes the philosopher's stone as the microcosm or *astronomia inferior*, the making of which is a reinscribing of cosmic processes.

[17] Probably the obsolete form of "to remain" (*OED*, 1): the physician who masters the skills may produce a medicine that will remain or prove lasting.

[18] *Wad* or *woad* and *madder* are dye-stuffs. Thus sts. 23 and 24 affirm the ancient link between alchemy and the craft of dyeing.

Even so our tinctures with the water of our lake,
We draw by boyling with the ashes of *Hermes* tree.

24. Which tinctures when they by craft are made perfite,
So dyeth mettles with colours aye permanent,
After the qualitie of the medicine, red or white,
That never away with anie fire wilbe brent:
To this example if you take good tent,
Unto your purpose the rather you shall winne.
And let your fire be easie, and not too fervent,
Where nature did leave what time you did beginne.

25. First calcine, and after that putrifie,
Dissolve, distill, sublime, discend, and fixe,
With Aqua vitæ oft times both wash and drie,
And make a marriage the bodie and spirite betwixt,
Which thus together naturallie if you can mixe,
In loosing of the bodie the water congeald shalbe,
Then shall the bodie die utterlie of the flixe,[19]
Bleeding and changing his colours, as you shall see.

26. The third day againe to life he shall arise,
And devoure birds, and beasts of the wildernesse,
Crowes, popingaies, pies, peacocks, and mavois,
The Phœnix, with the Eagle, and the Griffin of fearfulnesse,
The greene Lion, with the red Dragon he shall distresse,
With the white Dragon, and the Antelop, Unicorne & Panther,
With other beasts and birds both more and lesse,
The Basiliske also, which almost each one doth feare.

27. In *bus* and *nibus*[20] he shall arise and descend,
Up to the Moone, and sith up to the Sunne,
Through the Ocean sea, which round is withouten end,
Onely shippen within a little glassen tunne;
When he is there come, then is the mastrie wonne:
About which journey, great goods you shall not spend,
And yet you shall be glad that ever it was begunne,
Patiently if you list to your worke attend.

28. For then both bodie and spirite with oyle and water,
Soule, and tincture, one thing both white and red,
After colours variable it containeth, whatsover men clatter;
Which also is called after he hath once been dead

---

[19] *Flixe* is an obsolete form of *flux*, here an abnormally large outpouring or discharge of "water" from the body
that brings about its death, to be followed by rebirth on the third day (see sts. 26 and 27).
[20] The context of heavenly ascent suggests that *nibus* may be an error for *nubilus* (cloudy) or *nimbus* (rain-cloud).

And is revived, our Markaside,[21] our Magnet, and our lead,
Our Sulphur, our Arsinike, and our true Calx vive,
Our Sunne, our Moone, our ferment and our bread,
Our toad, our Basiliske, our unknowen bodie, our man, our wife.

29. Our bodie thus naturally by craft when he is renovate
Of the first order, is medicine called in our Philosophie;
Which oftentimes againe must be spiritualizate,
The round wheele turning of our Astronomie,
And so to the Elixer of spirits you must come: for why
Till the sonne of the fixed by the sonne of the fixer be overgone,
Elixer of bodies, named it is onely,
And this found secret poynt, deceaveth manie one.

30. This naturall process by helpe of craft thus consummate,
Dissolveth Elixer spirituall in our unctuous humiditie,
Then in Balneo Mare together let them be circulate,
Like new honie or oyle, till perfectly they be thickned.
Then will that medicine heale all infirmitie,
And turne all mettals to Sunne and Moone perfectly,
Thus you shall make the great Elixer, and Aurum potabile,
By the grace and will of God, to whom be all honour and glorie.

Amen. quod George Ripley.

---

[21] I.e., marcasite or pyrites (*OED* cites *Compound* as earliest printed use). The following catalogue of names for the philosopher's stone is conventional.

Part III Renaissance and seventeenth-century texts

18 Paracelsus (1493–1541)

From *Of the Nature of Things* and *Paracelsus His Aurora*

Since the early sixteenth century, reactions to Theophrastus Philippus Aureolus Bombastus von Hohenheim or Paracelsus have often been as contentious and controversial as the subject himself. Both *enfant terrible* and revolutionary genius in his formulation of new medical theories and practical cures and procedures, the Swiss-born Paracelsus continued to provoke violent disagreement long after his death in 1541. In addition to medicine and surgery, he received early training in mining, metallurgy, and alchemy; his peripatetic education, like his later career, led him to many locations throughout Europe. Although Paracelsus practiced healing, lectured widely, and wrote voluminously on medical topics, his controversial views and disputatious manner made publication of his ideas rare until after his death. His major contribution to alchemy was its reorientation from gold-making and the pursuit of the philosopher's stone to the formulation and application of medicinal preparations from minerals and chemicals. This shift – combined with his outspoken anti-authoritarianism – necessarily brought him and his followers into conflict with the "official," academic medical establishment dominated by Galenic physicians and pharmacists who favored herbal medicines (see Allen G. Debus, *The English Paracelsians*). Paracelsus also wrote in German – not the preferred Latin – and his emphasis on practical experience, experiment, and folk medicine resulted in further alienation.

The following selections from two treatises, *Of the Nature of Things* and the *Aurora* (which may be the work of his editor and translator Gerard Dorn), introduce several key Paracelsian ideas, such as the "three-principles theory" (*tria prima*) of salt, sulphur, and mercury, the making of the homunculus, the generation of metals, the doctrine of signatures, and the role of magic and astrology in his practice of the "Spagyrical Art." These and other ideas were widely disseminated in single-text and collected editions and translations that began to appear about 1570, three decades after Paracelsus's death, thus assuring continued debate between supporters and detractors well beyond the seventeenth century. Today, questions concerning the influence of Paracelsus on medical reform are still topics of lively discussion.

Selections from *Of the Nature of Things*, with punctuation modernized, are from the text given in *A New Light of Alchymie... Written by Micheel Sandivogius [sic]... Also Nine Books of the Nature of Things, written by Paracelsus... Translated by J. F. M. D.* (London: printed by Richard Cotes, 1650). Selections from the *Aurora* are from *Paracelsus His Aurora, & Treasure of the Philosophers... Faithfully Englished. And Published by J. H. Oxon* (London: printed for Giles Calvert, 1569). Additional readings: *The Hermetic and Alchemical Writings of Paracelsus the Great*, trans. A. E. Waite, 2 vols.; *DSB*, s.v. "Paracelsus," by Walter Pagel, and Pagel's *Paracelsus: An Introduction to Philosophical Medicine in the Era of the Renaissance.* 2nd (rev.) edn.

Of the Nature of Things

From Book I: Of the generations of Naturall things.

The generation of all natural things is twofold: Naturall and without Art; and Artificiall, *viz.* by Alchymie. Although in generall it may bee said that all things are naturally generated of the Earth by means of putrefaction. For Putrefaction is the chiefe degree and first step to Generation. Now Putrefaction is occasioned by a moist heat. For a continuall moist heat causeth putrefaction, and changeth all naturall things from their first form and essence, as also their vertues and efficacy, into another thing. For as putrefaction in the stomach changeth and reduceth all meats into dung; so also putrefaction out of the stomach in a glasse, changeth all things from one form into another, from one essence into another, from one colour into another, from one smell into another, from one vertue into another, from one power into another, from one property into another, and generally from one quality into another. For it is evident and proved by daily experience that many good things which are wholsome and medicinable, become after putrefaction naught, unwholsome, and meer poison. So on the contrary, there are many bad, unwholsome, poisonous, and hurtfull things, which after their putrefaction become good, lose all their unwholsomnesse, and become wonderfull medicinable: because putrefaction produceth great matters, as of this wee have a most famous example in the holy Gospel, where Christ saith: Unless a grain of Wheat bee cast into the Earth, and be putrefied, it cannot bring forth fruit in a hundred fold.[1] Hence also we must know that many things are multiplyed in putrefaction so as to bring forth excellent fruit. For putrefaction is the change and death of all things, and destruction of the first essence of all Naturall things; whence there ariseth a regeneration, and new generation a thousand times better, &c...

And here wee must take notice of something that is greater and more then this: *viz.* if that living Chicke be in a vessell of glasse like a gourd,[2] and sealed up, burnt to powder, or ashes in the third degree of Fire, and afterward so closed in, be putrefied with the exactest putrefaction of Horse-dung, into a mucilaginous flegm, then that flegm may be brought to maturity and become a renewed and new made Chicke: to wit, if that flegm bee again inclosed in its former shell or receptacle. This is to revive the dead by regeneration and clarification, which indeed is a great and profound miracle of Nature...

Wee must also know that after this manner men may bee generated without naturall Father, or Mother, i.e., not of a Woman in a naturall way: but by the Art and industry of a skilfull Alchymist may a Man bee borne and grow, as afterwards shall bee shewed.

It is possible also that men may be born of beasts, according to naturall causes, but yet this cannot bee done without much impiety and heresie; to wit, if a man should couple

---

[1] See John 12:24.
[2] This familiar image of the birth of a chick from the egg figures forth the rise of the philosopher's stone within the philosopher's egg or alembic; it is a variation of the Bird of Hermes motif (see *DAI*, 23–26).

with a beast, and that beast should, as a woman doth, receive the Sperm of the man with desire and lust into her matrix, and conceive: then the sperm doth of necessity putrefie, and by the continual heat of the body, a man and not a beast is thence produced. For alwaies as the seed is that is sown, so also is the fruit that is brought forth; and unlesse it should be so, it would be contrary to the light of Nature, and to Philosophy . . .

In like manner also it is possible, and not contrary to Nature, that an irrationall bruit should bee produced by a woman and a man. Neither are wee to judge of, or censure the woman, as the man (in the former case); shee therefore is not to bee accounted impious or hereticall, as if shee acted contrary to Nature, but it is to be imputed to her imagination. For her imagination is alwaies the cause of it. And the imagination of a breeding woman is so powerful, that in conceiving the seed into her body, shee may change her infant divers wayes: because her inward starres are so strongly bent upon the infant that they beget an impression and influence upon it. Wherefore the infant in the Mothers wombe in its forming is put into the hand and will of its Mother, as clay in the hand of the Potter, who thence frames and makes what his will and pleasure is: so the Woman that is breeding forms the fruit in her body according to her imagination and her starres. Therefore it often falls out, that of the seed of a man, Cattle, and other horrid Monsters are begot, according as the imagination of the Mother is strongly directed upon the Embryo, &c. . .

But wee must by no means forget the generation of Artificiall men. For there is some truth in this thing, although it hath been a long time concealed, and there have been no small doubts and questions raised by some of the ancient Philosophers, whether it were possible for Nature or Art to beget a Man out[side] of the body of a Woman, and naturall matrix? To this I answer, that it is no way repugnant to the Art of Alchymy and Nature; yea it is very possible; but to effect it, we must proceed thus.

Let the Sperm of a man by it selfe be putrefied in a gourd glasse, sealed up, with the highest degree of putrefaction in Horse dung,[3] for the space of forty days, or so long untill it begin to bee alive, move, and stir, which may easily be seen. After this time it will bee something like a Man, yet transparent and without a body. Now after this, if it bee every day warily and prudently nourished and fed with the *Arcanum*[4] of Mans blood, and bee for the space of forty weeks kept in a constant, equall heat of Horse-dung, it will become a true and living infant, having all the members of an infant which is born of a woman, but it will bee far lesse. This wee call *Homunculus*, or Artificiall. And this is afterwards to be brought up with as great care and diligence as any other infant, untill it come to riper years of understanding. Now this is one of the greatest secrets that God ever made known to mortall, sinfull man. For this is a miracle and one of the great wonders of God, and secret above all secrets, and deservedly it ought to bee kept amongst the secrets until the last times when nothing shall be hid, but all things be made manifest . . .

Here it is necessary that we speak something of the generation of Metalls; but because we have wrote sufficiently of that in our book of the generation of Metals, wee shall very briefly treat of it here, only briefly adding what was omitted in that book. Know that all the seven Metalls are brought forth after this manner, out of a threefold matter, *viz.*

---

[3] A major source of the warm, moist, even heat that alchemical experiments required.

[4] Ruland's definition is apt: the arcanum is "the interior virtue of any substance which can achieve a thousand more wonders than the thing itself. The unrevealed principle, undying essence" (*Lexicon* 36).

Mercury, Sulphur, & Salt, yet in distinct and peculiar colours. For this reason *Hermes* did not speak amisse when he said, that of three substances are all the seven Metalls produced and compounded, as also the Tinctures and Philosophers Stone. Those 3 substances he calls the Spirit, Soul, and Body: but hee did not shew how this is to be understood, or what hee did mean by this, although haply hee might know the three Principles, but did not make mention of them. Wherefore we do not say that he was here in an error, but only was silent now, that those 3 distinct substances may be rightly understood, *viz.* Spirit, Soul, and Body, we must know, that they signifie nothing else but the three Principles, *i.e.* Mercury, Sulphur, Salt, of which all the seven Metalls are generated. For Mercury is the Spirit, Sulphur the Soule, and Salt the Body, but a Metall is the Soul betwixt the Spirit and the Body (as *Hermes* saith) which Soule indeed is Sulphur; and unites these two contraries, the Body and Spirit, and changeth them into one essence, &c.

Now this is not to bee understood so as that of every Mercury, every Sulphur, or of every Salt, the seven Metalls may be generated, or the Tincture, or the Philosophers Stone by the Art of Alchymie, or industry, with the help of Fire; but all the seven Metalls must be generated in the mountains by the *Archeius*[5] of the Earth. For the Alchymist shall sooner transmute Metalls, then generate or make them.

Yet neverthelesse living Mercury is the Mother of all the seven Metalls, and deservedly it may be called the Mother of the Metalls. For it is an open Metall, and as it contains all colours, which it manifests in the Fire, so also occultly it contains all Metalls in it selfe, but without Fire it cannot shew them, &c.

But generation and renovation of Metalls is made thus: As a man may return into the womb of his Mother, *i.e.* into the Earth, out of which hee was first made a man, and shall again bee raised at the last day: so also all Metalls may returne into living ☿ againe, and become ☿, and by Fire bee regenerated and purified, if for the space of forty weeks they bee kept in a continuall heat, as an infant is in his Mothers wombe. So that now there are brought forth not common Metalls, but Tinging Metalls. For if Silver bee regenerated (after the manner as wee have spoken) it will afterward tinge all other Metalls into Silver, so will Gold into Gold, and the like is to be understood of all the other Metalls.

Now forasmuch as *Hermes* said that the soule alone is that medium which joines the spirit to the body, it was not without cause hee said so. For seeing Sulphur is that soule, and doth like Fire ripen and digest all things; it can also bind the soule with the body, incorporating and uniting them together, so that from thence may bee produced a most excellent body. Now the common combustible Sulphur is not to bee taken for the soule of metalls, for the soule is another manner of thing then a combustible and corruptible body.

Wherefore it can bee destroyed by no Fire, seeing indeed it is all Fire itself: and indeed it is nothing else but the quintessence of Sulphur, which is extracted out of re-verberated Sulphur by the spirit of wine, being of a red colour and as transparent as a Rubie: and which indeed is a great and excellent *Arcanum*, for the transmuting of white metalls, and to coagulate living ☿ into fixt and true Gold. Esteeme this as an enriching treasure, and thou maist bee well contented with this onely secret in the Transmutation of Metalls. . . .

---

[5] "The immaterial principle supposed by the Paracelsians to produce and preside over the activities of the animal and vegetable economy; vital force" (*OED*).

Book 2: Of the growth, and increase of Natural things.

It is sufficiently manifest and knowne to every one, that all naturall things grow and are ripned through heat and moisture, which is sufficiently demonstrated by rain and the heat of the sun. For no man can deny that rain doth make the Earth fruitfull, and it is granted by all that all fruits are ripened by the sun.

Seeing therefore this is by divine ordination naturally possible, who can gain-say or not beleeve that a man is able, through the wise and skilfull Art of Alchymy, to make that which is barren, fruitfull, and that which is crude, to ripen, and all things to grow, and to be increased . . .

It is possible also that Gold, through industry and skill of an expert Alchymist, may bee so far exalted that it may grow in a glasse like a tree, with many wonderfull boughs and leaves, which indeed is pleasant to behold and most wonderful.

The process is this. Let Gold bee calcined with *Aqua Regis*,[6] till it becomes a kind of chalke, which put into a gourd glasse and poure upon it good new *Aqua Regis*, so that it may cover it foure fingers breadth, then again draw it off with the third degree of fire, untill no more ascend. The water that is distilled off, poure on againe, then distill it off againe. This doe so long untill thou seest the Gold to rise in the glasse and grow after the manner of a tree, having many boughes and leaves: and so there is made of Gold a wonderful and pleasant shrub, which the Alchymists call their Golden hearb and the Philosophers Tree. In like manner you may proceed with Silver and other Metalls, yet so that their calcination bee made after another manner, by another *Aqua fortis*,[7] which I leave to thine experience. If thou art skilled in Alchymie, thou shalt not erre in these things.

Book 4: Of the life of Naturall things.

No man can deny that Aire gives life to all things, bodies, and substances that are produced and generated of the Earth. Now you must know what, and what manner of thing the life of every thing in particular is; and it is nothing else then a spirituall essence, a thing that is invisible, impalpable, a spirit, and spirituall. Wherefore there is no corporeall thing which hath not a spirit lying hid in it, as also a life, which, as I said before, is nothing but a spirituall thing. For not only that hath life which moves and stirres, as Men, Animalls, Vermine of the earth, Birds in the Aire, Fish in the sea, but also all corporeall and substantiall things. For here wee must know that God in the beginning of the Creation of all things, created no body at all without its spirit, which it secretly contains in it.

For what is the body without a spirit? Nothing at all. Wherefore the spirit contains in it secretly the vertue and power of the thing, and not the body. For in the body there is death, and the body is the subject of death, neither is any else to be sought for in the body but death.

For that may severall wayes bee destroyed and corrupted, but the spirit cannot. For the living spirit remains for ever, and also is the subject of life: and preserves the body alive; but in the ruine of the body it is separated from it, and leaves behind it a dead body, and

---

[6] "A mixture of nitric and hydrochloric acids, so called because it can dissolve the 'noble' metals, gold and platinum" (*OED*).

[7] "The early scientific, and still the popular, name of the Nitric Acid of commerce (dilute HNO_3), a powerful solvent and corrosive" (*OED*).

returnes to its place from whence it came, *viz.* into the Chaos, and the Aire of the upper and lower Firmament. Hence it appears that there are divers spirits, as well as divers bodies.

For there are spirits Celestiall, Infernall, Humane, Metalline, Minerall, of Salts, of Gemmes, of Marcasites, of Arsenicks, of Potable things, of Rootes, of Juices, of Flesh, of Blood, of Bones, &c. Wherefore also know that the spirit is most truly the life and balsome[8] of all Corporeall things. But now wee will proceed to the species, and briefly describe to you in this place the life of every naturall thing in particular.

The life therefore of all men is nothing else but an Astrall balsome, a Balsamick impression, and a celestiall invisible Fire, an included Aire, and a tinging spirit of Salt. I cannot name it more plainly, although it bee set out by many names. And seeing wee have declared the best and chiefest, wee shall bee silent in these which are lesse materiall.

The life of Metalls is a secret fatnesse which they have received from Sulphur, which is manifest by their flowing, for every thing that flowes in the fire, flowes by reason of that secret fatnesse that is in it: unlesse that were in it, no Metall could flow, as wee see in Iron and Steel, which have lesse Sulphur and fatnesse then all the other Metalls, wherefore they are of a dryer Nature then all the rest . . .

Book 5: Of the Death, or ruine of all things.

The death of all naturall things is nothing else but an alteration and destruction of their powers and vertues, a predominancy of that which is evill and an overcoming of what is good, an abolishing of the former nature and generation of a new, and another nature. For you must know that there are many things that, whilst they are alive, have in them severall vertues, but when they are dead retaine little or nothing of their vertue, but become unsavory and unprofitable. So on the contrary many things, whilst they live, are bad, but after they are dead and corrupted, manifest a manifold power and vertue, and are very usefull. Wee could bring many examples to confirme this, but that doth not belong to our purpose. But that I may not seem to write according to mine own opinion only, but out of my experience, it will be necessary that I produce one example, with which I shall silence those Sophisters, who say that wee can receive nothing from dead things, neither must we seek or expect to find any thing in them. The reason is because they do esteem nothing of the preparations of Alchymists, by which many such like great secrets are found out. For looke upon Mercury, crude Sulphur, and crude Antimony, as they are taken out of their Mines, *i.e.* whilst they are living, and see what little vertue there is in them, how slowly they put forth their vertues; yea they do more hurt then good, and are rather poison then a Medicine. But if through the industry of a skilfull Alchymist they bee corrupted in their first substance, and wisely prepared (*viz.* if Mercury be coagulated, precipitated, sublimed, dissolved, and turned into an oyle; if Sulphur bee sublimed, calcined, reverberated, and turned into an oyle; also if Antimony bee sublimed, calcined, and reverberated and turned into oyle) you shall see how usefull they are, how much strength and vertue they have, and how quickly they put forth and shew their efficacy, which no man is able to speak enough in the commendation of, or to describe. For many are their vertues, yea more then

---

[8] Ruland states that "Balsam is a substance which preserves bodies from putrefaction. It is internal and external . . . It is also called a most tempered gluten of the nature of any body to which it belongs. Briefly, it is the liquor of an interior salt most carefully and naturally preserving its body from corruption" (*Lexicon* 69).

will ever bee found out by any man. Wherefore let every faithfull Alchymist and Physitian spend their whole lives in searching into these three: For they will abundantly recompense him for all his labour, study, and costs.

But to come to particulars, and to write particularly of the death and destruction of every naturall thing, and what the death of every thing is, and after what manner every thing is destroyed: you must know therefore in the first place, that the death of man is without doubt nothing else but an end of his daily work, the taking away of the Aire, the decaying of the Naturall balsome, the extinguishing of the naturall light, and the great separation of the three substances, *viz.* the body, soule, and spirit, and their return from whence they came. For because a naturall man is of the earth, the Earth also is his Mother, into which hee must return, and there must lose his natural earthly flesh, and so be regenerated at the last day in a new celestiall and purified flesh, as Christ said to *Nicodemus* when hee came to him by Night.[9] For thus must these words bee understood of regeneration.

The death and destruction of Metalls is the disjoining of their bodies and sulphureous fatnesse, which may bee done severall ways, as by calcination, reverberation, dissolution, cementation, and sublimation... [The balance of this chapter provides many examples of metallic death or mortification; its sequel, the sixth book, treats "*Of the Resurrection of Naturall things.*"]

Book 7: Of the Transmutation of Naturall things.

If wee write of the Transmutation of all Naturall things, it is fit and necessary that in the first place wee shew what Transmutation is. Secondly, what bee the degrees to it. Thirdly, by what Mediums, and how it is done.

Transmutation therefore is when a thing loseth its form and is so altered that it is altogether unlike to its former substance and form, but assumes another form, another essence, another colour, another vertue, another nature, or property, as if a Metall bee made glasse or stone: if a stone bee made a coale: if wood be made a coal: clay be made a stone or a brick: a skin bee made glew: cloth be made paper, and many such like things. All these are Transmutations of Naturall things.

After this, it is very necessary also to know the degrees to Transmutation,[10] and how many they be. And they are no more then seven. For although many doe reckon more, yet there are no more but seven which are principall, and the rest may bee reckoned betwixt the degrees, being comprehended under those seven: And they are these, Calcination, Sublimation, Solution, Putrefaction, Distillation, Coagulation, Tincture. If any one will climbe that Ladder, he shall come into a most wonderfull place, that hee shall see and have experience of many secrets in the Transmutation of Naturall things.

The first degree therefore is Calcination, under which also are comprehended Reverberation, and Cementation. For betwixt these there is but little difference as for Matter of Calcination: wherefore it is here the chiefest degree. For by Reverberation and Cementation, many corporeall things are calcined and brought into Ashes, and especially Metalls. Now what is calcined is not any further reverberated or cemented.

By Calcination therefore all Metalls, Mineralls, Stones, Glasse, &c. and all corporeall things are made a Coal and Ashes, and this is done by a naked strong Fire with blowing, by

---

[9] See John 3:1–21. [10] I.e., the steps or stages leading to transmutation.

which all tenacious, soft, and fat earth is hardened into a stone. Also all stones are brought into a Calx, as wee see in a Potters furnace of lime and bricks.

Sublimation is the second degree and one of the most principall for the Transmutation of many Naturall things: under which is contained Exaltation, Elevation, and Fixation; and it is not much unlike Distillation. For as in Distillation the water ascends from all flegmatick and watery things and is separated from its body; so in Sublimation, that which is spirituall is raised from what is corporeall, and is subtilized, volatile from fixed, and that in dry things, as are all Mineralls, and the pure is separated from the impure...

Let that which is sublimed be ground and mixed with its feces, and bee againe sublimed as before, which must bee done so long, till it will no longer sublime, but all will remaine together in the bottom and be fixed.

So there will bee afterward a stone, and oyle when and as oft as thou pleasest, *viz.* if thou puttest it into a cold place, or in the aire in a Glass. For there it will presently bee dissolved into an Oyle. And if thou puttest it againe into the fire, it will againe bee coagulated into a Stone of wonderfull and great vertue. Keep this as a great secret and mystery of Nature, neither discover it to Sophisters...

The third degree is Solution, under which are to bee understood Dissolution and Resolution, and this degree doth most commonly follow Sublimation and Distillation, *viz.* that the matter be resolved which remaines in the bottome. Now Solution is twofold: the one of Cold, the other of Heat; the one without Fire, the other in Fire.

A cold dissolution dissolves all Salts, all Corrosive things, & all calcined things. Whatsoever is of a Salt and Corrosive quality is by it dissolved into Oyle, Liquor, or Water. And this is in a moist, cold cellar or else in the Aire on a marble or in a glasse. For whatsoever is dissolved in the cold contains an Airy spirit of Salt, which oftentimes it gets, and assumes in Sublimation or Distillation. And whatsoever is dissolved in the cold, or in the Aire, may again by the heat of the Fire bee coagulated into powder or a stone...

Putrefaction is the fourth degree, under which is comprehended Digestion and Circulation. Now then Putrefaction is one of the principall degrees, which indeed might deservedly have been the first of all, but that it would be against the true order and mystery, which is here hid and known to few: For those degrees must, as hath been already said, so follow one the other, as links in a chain or steps in a ladder.

For if one of the linkes should bee taken away, the chain is discontinued and broken, and the prisoners would bee at liberty and runne away. So in a ladder, if one step bee taken away in the middle and bee put in the upper or lower part, the ladder would be broken and many would fall down headlong by it with the hazard of their bodies, and lives...

Now putrefaction is of such efficacy, that it abolisheth the old Nature and brings in a new one. All living things are killed in it, all dead things putrefied in it, and all dead things recover life in it.

Putrefaction takes from all Corrosive spirits, the sharpnesse of the Salt and makes them mild and sweet, changeth the colours, and separates the pure from the impure; it places the pure above and the impure beneath.

Distillation is the first degree to the Transmutation of all naturall things.[11] Under it are understood Ascension, Lavation, and Fixation.

---

[11] I.e., the fifth degree overall in Paracelsus's scheme.

By Distillation all Waters, Liquors, and Oyles are subtilized; out of all fat things Oyle is extracted, out of all Liquors, Water, and out of all Flegmaticke things Water and Oyle are separated.

Besides there are many things in Distillation fixed by Cohobation,[12] and especially if the things to bee fixed containe in them Water, as Vitriall doth, which if it bee fixed is called *Colcothar*...

Moreover, in Distillation many bitter, harsh, and sharp things become as sweet as Honey, Sugar, or Manna; and on the contrary, many sweet things, as Sugar, Honey, or Manna may bee made as harsh as Oyle of Vitriall or Vineger, or as bitter as Gall or Gentian, as Eager as a Corrosive...

Coagulation is the sixt degree: now there is a twofold Coagulation, the one by Cold, the other by Heat, i.e. one of the Aire, the other of the Fire: and each of these again is twofold, so that there are foure sorts of Coagulations, two of Cold, and two of Fire...the Coagulation of Fire, which alone is here to bee taken notice of, is made by an Artificiall and Graduall Fire of the Alchymists, and it is fixed and permanent. For whatsoever such a Fire doth coagulate, the same abides so.

The other Coagulation is done by the Aetnean and Minerall Fire in the Mountains, which indeed the Archeius of the Earth governs and graduates not unlike to the Alchymists, and whatsoever is coagulated by such a Fire is also fixed and constant; as you see in Mineralls and Metalls, which indeed at the beginning are a mucilaginous matter, and are coagulated into Metalls, Stones, Flints, Salts, and other bodies, by the Aetnean fire in the Mountaines, through the Archeius of Earth, and operator of Nature...

Tincture is the seventh and last degree, which concludes the whole worke of our mystery for Transmutation, making all imperfect things perfect and transmuting them into a most excellent essence, and into a most perfect soundnesse, and alters them into another colour.

Tincture therefore is a most excellent matter, wherewith all Minerall and Humane bodies are tinged and are changed into a better and more noble essence and into the highest perfection and purity.

For Tincture colours all things according to its own nature and colour.

Now there are many Tinctures and not only for Metalline but Humane bodies, because every thing which penetrates another matter, or tingeth it with another colour, or essence, so that it bee no more like the former, may bee called a Tincture...

For if a Tincture must tinge, it is necessary that the body or matter which is to bee tinged, bee opened and continue in flux, and unless this should bee so, the Tincture could not operate...

Now these are the Tinctures of Metalls, which it is necessary must bee turned into an Alcool[13] by the first degree of Calcination, then by the second degree of Sublimation, must get an easy and light flux. And lastly, by the degree of Putrefaction and Distillation are made a fixt and incombustible Tincture and of an unchangeable colour.

Now the Tinctures of Mens bodies are that they bee tinged into the highest perfection of health and all Diseases bee expelled from them, that their lost strength and colour bee

[12] Repeated distillation.
[13] An obsolete form of "alcohol." Here the meaning appears to be either a "fine impalpable powder produced by trituration, or especially by sublimation;" or "condensed spirit" (*OED* 2, 3b).

restored and renewed, and they are these, *viz.* Gold, Pearles, Antimony, Sulphur, Vitriall, and such like, whose preparation wee have diversly taught in other books…

Book 8: Of the Separation of Naturall things.

In the Creation of the world, the first separation began from the foure Elements, seeing the first matter of the world was one Chaos.

Of this Chaos God made the greater world, being divided into four distinct Elements, *viz.* Fire, Aire, Water, and Earth. Fire is the hot part, Aire the moist, Water the cold, and Earth the dry part of the greater world.

But that you may in brief understand the reason of our purpose in the 8th book, you must know that we doe not purpose to treat here of the Elements of all Naturall things, seeing wee have sufficiently discoursed of those Arcana in the *Archidoxis*[14] of the separation of Naturall things: whereby every one of them is apart and distinctly separated, and divided materially and substantially, *viz.* seeing that two, three, or foure, or more things are mixed into one body, and yet there is seen but one matter. Where it often falls out that the corporeall matter of that thing cannot bee known by any, or signified by any expresse name, untill there bee a separation made. Then sometimes two, three, four, five or more things come forth out of one matter, as is manifest by daily experience in the Art of Alchymie.

As for example, you have an *Electrum*,[15] which of it selfe is no Metall, but yet it hides all Metalls in one Metall. That if it be anatomized by the industry of Alchymie and separated: all the seven Metalls, *viz. Gold, Silver, Copper, Tinne, Lead, Iron,* and *Quicksilver* come out of it and that pure and perfect.

But that you may understand what Separation is, note that it is nothing else then the severing of one thing from another, whether of two, three, four, or more things mixed together: I say a separation of the three Principles, as of Mercury, Sulphur, and Salt, and the extraction of pure out of the impure: or the pure, excellent spirit and quintessence from a grosse and elementary body; and the preparation of two, three, four, or more out of one: or the dissolution and setting at liberty things that are bound and compact, which are of a contrary nature, acting one against the other untill they destroy one the other…

The first separation of which wee speake must begin from man, because hee is the Microcosme or little world, for whose sake the Macrocosme or greater world was made, *viz.* that hee might be the separator of it.

Now the separation of the Microcosme begins at his death. For in death the two bodies of Man are separated the one from the other, *viz.* his Celestial and Terrestial body, *i.e.* Sacramental and Elementary: one of which ascends on high like an Eagle; the other falls downward to the earth like lead…

After this separation is made, then after the death of the Man three substances, *viz. Body, Soule,* and *Spirit* are divided the one from the other, every one going to its own place, *viz.* its own fountaine, from whence it had its originall, *viz.* the body to the Earth, to the first matter of the Elements: the soul into the first matter of Sacraments, and lastly, the spirit into the first matter of the Airy Chaos…

---

[14] The *Archidoxis* is one of Paracelsus's major alchemical works; first published in Latin translation (from the German) in 1569, it became immediately popular on the Continent, and in England in the seventeenth century.

[15] I.e., an alloy of the seven metals.

Of the Separation of Vegetables (Book 8), Concerning Physicians.

All these Separations being made according to the Spagiricall Art, many notable and excellent medicines come from thence, which are to be used as well within as without the body.

But now seeing idlenesse is so much in request amongst Physitians, and all labour and study is turned only to insolency, truly I do not wonder that all such preparations are everywhere neglected, and coales sold at so low a price that if Smiths could be so easily without coales in forging and working their Metals, as Physitians are in preparing their Medicines, certainly Colliers would long since have been brought to extream want.

In the mean time I will give to Spagiricall Physitians[16] their due praise. For they are not given to idlenesse and sloth, nor goe in a proud habit or plush and velvet garments, often shewing their rings upon their fingers, or wearing swords with silver hilts by their sides, or fine and gay gloves upon their hands, but diligently follow their labours, sweating whole nights and dayes by their furnaces.

These doe not spend their time abroad for recreation but take delight in their laboratory. They wear Leather garments with a pouch and Apron wherewith they wipe their hands. They put their fingers amongst coales, into clay and dung, not into gold rings. Thy are sooty and black, like Smithes or Colliers, and doe not pride themselves with cleane and beautifull faces. They are not talkative when they come to the sick, neither doe they extoll their Medicines: seeing they well know that the Artificer must not commend his work, but the work the Artificer, and that the sick cannot be cured with fine words.

Therefore laying aside all these kinds of vanities, they delight to bee busied about the fire and to learn the degrees of the science of Alchymie . . .

[Conclusion of Book 8: On the "final separation" / Last Judgment].

And lastly in the end of all things shall bee the last separation, in the third generation, the great day when the Son of God shal come in majesty and glory, before whom shal be carried not swords, garlands, diadems, scepters, &c. and Kingly jewels with which Princes, Kings, Cesars, &c. doe pompously set forth themselves; but his Crosse, his crown of thorns, and nails thrust through his hands and feet, and spear with which his side was pierced, and the reed and spunge in which they gave him vineger to drinke, and the whips wherewith hee was scourged and beaten. He comes not accompanyed with troopes of Horse and beating of Drums, but foure Trumpets shall bee sounded by the Angells towards the foure parts of the world, killing all that are then alive with their horrible noise, in one moment, and then presently raising these again, together with them that are dead and buryed.

For the voice shall bee heard: *Arise yee dead, and come to judgment.* Then shal the twelve Apostles sit down, their seats being prepared in the clouds, and shal judge the twelve Tribes of *Israel.* In that place the holy Angels shall separate the bad from the good, the cursed from the blessed, the goats from the sheep. Then the cursed shall like stones and lead be thrown downward: but the blessed shall like eagles fly on high. Then from the tribunall of God shal go forth this voice to them that stand on his left hand: *Goe yee cursed into everlasting fire*

[16] Physicians who, like Paracelsus, employ the principles and materials of alchemy (e.g., metals and minerals) in effecting cures, rather than the herbal preparations of the Galenic school.

prepared for the Devill and his Angells from all eternity: For I was an hungry, and yee fed me not; thirsty, and you gave no drink; sick, in prison, and naked, and you visited me not, freed mee not, cloathed me not, and you shewed no pity towards me, therefore shalt you expect no pity from me. On the contrary, hee shall speak to them on his right hand: Come yee blessed, and chosen into my Fathers Kingdome, which hath been prepared for you, and his Angells from the foundation of the world. For I was hungry, and you gave me meat; thirsty, and you gave me drink; I was a stranger, and you took me in; naked, and you covered me; sick, and you visited me; in prison, and you came unto me. Therefore I will receive you into my Fathers Kingdom, where are provided many mansions for the Saints. You took pity on me, therefore will I take pity on you.[17]

All these being finished and dispatched, all Elementary things will returne to the first matter of the Elements and bee tormented to eternity and never bee consumed, &c. and on the contrary, all holy things shall return to the first matter of Sacraments: *i.e.* shall be purified, and in eternall joy glorifie God their Creator and worship him from age to age, from eternity to eternity, Amen.

Book 9: Of the Signature of Naturall things (Of Minerall Signes).

... But to returne to our purpose concerning Minerall signes, and especially concerning the Coruscation of Metalline veins, we must know that as Metalls which are yet in their first being send forth their Coruscation, i.e. Signes, so also the *Tincture of the Philosophers*, which changeth all imperfect Metalls into Silver and Gold (or White Metalls into Silver, and Red into Gold) puts forth its proper signs like unto Coruscation, if it be Astrally perfected and prepared. For as soon as a small quantity of it is cast upon a fluxil metall, so that they mix together in the fire, there ariseth a naturall Coruscation and brightnesse, like to that of fine Gold or Silver in a test, which then is a signe that that Gold or Silver is freed and purged without all manner of addition of other Metalls.

But how the Tincture of Philosophers is made Astrall, you must conceive it after this manner: First of all you must know that every Metall, as long as it lies hid in its first being, hath its certaine peculiar stars.

So Gold hath the stars of the Sun, Silver the stars of the Moon, Copper the stars of Venus, Iron the stars of Mars, Tinne the stars of Jupiter, Lead the stars of Saturne, Quicksilver the starres of Mercury.

But as soon as they come to their perfection and are coagulated into a fixt Metalline body, their stars fall off from them, and leave them as a dead body.

Hence it follows that all such bodies are afterwards dead and inefficacious, and that the unconquered star of Metalls doth overcome them all, and converts them into its nature and makes them all Astrall...

For which cause also our Gold and Silver, which is tinged and prepared with our tincture, is much more excellent and better for the preparation of Medicinall secrets then that which is naturall, which Nature generates in the Mines and afterwards is separated from other Metalls.

---

[17] Paracelsus's eschatological scene is drawn from Matt. 25:31–46.

The Aurora of the Philosophers

Chap. 1: Of the Original of the Philosophick Stone.

Adam was the first Inventor of Arts, because he had the knowledge of all things, as well after the fall as before the fall; from thence he presaged the worlds destruction by water; Hence also it came to pass that his Successors erected two tables of stone, in the which they ingraved all Natural Arts, and that in Hieroglyphical Characters, that so their Successors might also know this presage, that it might be heeded, and provision of care made in time of danger. Afterwards, *Noah* found one of the tables in *Armenia* under the Mount *Araroth*, when the deluge was over; In which [Table] were described the courses of the superiour Firmament, and of the inferiour Globe, and [also] of the Planets; then at length this Universal Notion of Knowledge was drawn into several particulars, and lessened in its Vigor and Power, in so much that by means of that separation, One became an Astronomer, another a Magus, another a Cabalist, and a fourth an Alchymist: *Abraham* that most great Astrologer and Arithmetitian conveyed [it] out of the Countrey of *Canaan* into *Aegypt*, whereupon the Egyptians arose to so great a head and dignity, that the wisdom [or science] of the same thing was derived from them to other Nations and Countreys. And for as much as the Patriarch *Jacob* painted [as twere] the sheep with various colours, it was done by a part or member of Magick;[18] for in the Theology of the Chaldeans, Hebrews, Persians and Egyptians, they proposed these arts (as the highest Philosophy) to be learned by their chiefest Nobles and Priests: So it was in *Moses* his time, wherein both the Priests and even the Physitians were chosen amongst the *Magi*; they indeed [*viz.* the Priests] for the Examination or Judging, of what related to soundness or health, especially in the knowledge of the Leprosie; *Moses* likewise was instructed in the Egyptian Schools at the Costs and Care of *Pharaohs* daughter, so that he excelled in all their Wisdom or Learning;[19] So was it with *Daniel*; he in his young dayes suckt in the Learning of the Chaldeans, so that he became a Cabalist, Witness his Divine foretellings, and expounding of those words, *Mene Mene Tekel Phares*:[20] These words are to be understood by the Prophetick and Cabalistick Art: The Tradition of this Cabalistical Art, was very familiar with Moses and the Prophets, and most of all in use; The Prophet *Elias* foretold many things by his Cabalistical Numbers.[21] Even so the Antient wise men, by this Natural and Mystical Art, learned to know God rightly, and abode and walked in his Laws and statutes very firmly; It likewise is evident in the Book of *Samuel*, that the Berelists did not follow the Devils part, but became (by Divine permission) partakers of Visions and true Apparitions, the which we shall treat more largely of in the book of Supercelestials. The gift thereof is granted by the Lord God to the Priests who walk in the divine precepts. It was a custom amongst the Persians, never to admit any one as King, unless a Sophist [or Wise man] exalted both in reality and name; and this is clear by the usual name of their Kings, for they were called Sophists. Such were those Wise men and Persian Magi that came from the East to seek out Christ Jesus, and are called natural Priests. Likewise the Egyptians having obtained this Magick and Philosophy from the Chaldeans

---

[18] An apparent reference to Jacob's use of sympathetic magic – placing white-streaked rods of wood where they will influence the conception of lambs – to outwit Laban and increase the size of his own flocks (Gen. 30:25–43).

[19] "And Moses was learned in all the wisdom of the Egyptians, and was mighty in words and in deeds" (Acts 7:22).

[20] See Dan. 5: esp. 25–28: "Thou art weighed in the balances, and art found wanting."

[21] See, for example, 1 Kings 17–18.

and Persians, would that their Priests should also learn the same wisdom, wherein they became so fruitfull and succesfull, that all the neighbouring Countreyes admired them. This was the cause why *Hermes* was truly stiled *Trismegistus* because he was both a King, a Priest, and a Prophet, a Magitian, and a Sophist of Natural things; such another also was *Zoroastes*.

Chap. 3: What was taught in the Schools of the Egyptians.

The Chaldeans, Persians and Egyptians had [all of them] the same knowledge of the secrets of nature and the same Religion, the names only being changed. The Chaldeans & Persians called their doctrine Sophia and Magick; and the Egyptians, because of the sacrifice, called their wisdom the Priest-hood. The Magick of the Persians, and Theology of the Egyptians were both of them heretofore taught in the Schools. Albeit there were many Schools and Learned men in *Arabia, Africa & Greece*, as *Albumazar, Abenzagel* [Abenragel?],[22] *Geber, Rasis* and *Avicenna* amongst the Arabians; *Machaon, Podalirius*,[23] *Pythagoras, Anaxagoras, Democritus, Plato, Aristotle* and *Rodianus* amongst the Grecians; but yet there were various opinions amongst themselves as to the Egyptian wisdom, wherein they differed, and disagreed from it. For this cause *Pythagoras* would not be called Sophist, because the Egyptian Priesthood and Wisdom was not at all perfectly taught as was fitting, although he received thence many Mysteries and Arcanums; and *Anaxagoras* [had received] most or exceeding many. This appears by the disputations which he made of *Sol* & the stone thereof, & which he left after his death, yet he was in many things contrary to the Egyptians; Wherefore even they would not be called Sophists nor Magi, but imitating *Pythagoras* in that thing they assumed the name of Philosophy; but yet they reaped no more then a few Glances like shadows, from the Magick of the Persians and Egyptians; but *Moses, Abraham, Solomon, Adam, Elias*, and the Magi that came from the East to Christ, were true Magi, and Divine Sophists, and Cabalists; which Art and Wisdom the Grecians knew very little of, or none at all; and therefore we shall leave that Philosophical Wisdom of the Grecians as a Speculation widely and largely distant, and separated from other true arts and sciences.

[In chapters here omitted, Paracelsus discusses several erroneous approaches to making the philosopher's stone, as well as the arcanums of arsenic, vitriol, and antimony.]

Chap. 16: Of the Universal Matter of the Stone of the Philosophers.

After the mortification of Vegetables[24] [they] by the concurrence of two Minerals, as Sulphur and Salt, are transmuted into a Mineral nature, so that at length they become perfect minerals; for in the Mineral holes and dens and wide fields of the earth, are found Vegetables which in long success of time, and by the continued heat of Sulphur, do put off the Vegetable nature, and put on a Mineral; And that doth chiefly happen, where the

---

[22] Albumazar (d. 886) was a famous astrologer of Baghdad, whose translated works were popular and influential well into the Renaissance. Abenragel was also an Arabian astrological authority (*HMES* 2:77).

[23] Machaon and Podalirius were sons of Asklepios and appear as good physicians and leaders in the *Iliad* 2: 731–32, and elsewhere.

[24] A kind of pulverisation "which disposes the mortified body towards a new generation, such as that of the seeds of vegetables" (*Lexicon, Supp.*).

appropriate nutriment is taken away from these Vegetables, whereby they are afterwards constrained to take their nourishment from the Sulphurs and Salts of the earth, so long, untill that which was afore a Vegetable, do pass into a perfect Mineral; And thus out of this Mineral condition a certain perfect Mettallick essence doth sometimes arise, and that by the progress of one degree into another; But to return to the stone of the Philosophers, the matter whereof (as some have mentioned) is a most difficult matter of all others to be found out, and abstruse for the understanding; Now the way and the most certain rule of the finding out of this as well as of all other things, what they contain, or are able to do, is a most diligent examination of their Root and Sperm, whereby knowledge is attained; for the accomplishment of which, the consideration of principles is very necessary; as also by what way, and medium nature doth at first go from imperfection to the end of perfection; For the consideration whereof, tis chiefly requisite, most certainly to know, that all things created by nature do consist of three principles, *viz.* of natural Sulphur, Mercury, and Salt,[25] mixt into one, [so] that in some things they are Volatile, in other things fixt: As often as a corporal Salt is throughly mixt with a spiritual Mercury and Animated Sulphur into one body, then doth nature begin to work in subterranean places, (which serves for its vessels,) by a separating fire, by which the gross and impure Sulphur is separated from the pure, and the Earth from the Salt, and the cloudiness from the Mercury, those purer parts being reserved, the which parts nature doth again decoct together into a pure Geogamick body. The which Operation is accounted [of] by the Magi, as a mixtion and conjunction by the Union of the three, *viz.* body, soul, and spirit. This Union being compleated, from thence doth result a pure Mercury, the which if it flows through the subterranean passages and Veins thereof, and meets with a Caheick Sulphur, the Mercury is Coagulated by this [Sulphur] according to the condition of the Sulphur. But notwithstanding, tis as yet volatile, and scarce decocted into a mettall for the space of an hundred years. Thence arose this so much common an opinion, that Mercury and Sulphur are the matter of mettals, the which is also evidenced by the Relation of the Miners. Yet common Mercury and common Sulphur are not the matter of mettals, but the Mercury and Sulphur of the Philosophers are incorporated and innate in perfect mettals, and in the forms of them, that they never fly from the fire, nor are depraved by the force of the corruption of the Elements. Verily by the dissolution of that same natural mixtion our Mercury is tamed or subjected, as all the Philosophers speak; Under [or from] this form of words, comes Mercury to be extracted out of perfect bodies, and [out of] the virtues [and puissance] of the earthly planets. The which *Hermes* affirms in these words, The ☉ and ☽ (saith he) are the roots of this art. The Son of *Hamuel* saith that the stone of the Philosophers is a Coagulated water, *viz.* in Sol and Lune; from whence tis evidently cleer, that the matter of the stone is nothing else but ☉ & ☽; this is also hereby confirmed, in that every like thing generates and brings forth its like; And we know that there are no more but two stones, white and red; there are also two matters of the stone, Sol and Lune coupled together in a proper Matrimony, both natural and artificial; And as we see, that either man or woman cannot generate without the seed of both; in like manner, our Man ☉ and his Woman ☽ cannot conceive, or frame ought for generation without both their Seeds and Spermes;

---

[25] These are the *tria prima*, or three famous principles of Paracelsus, later identified respectively with the soul, spirit, and body of metals.

Thence have the Philosophers gathered, that a third thing is necessary, *viz.* the Animated seed of both, of man and woman, without the which they have judged all their whole work to be vain and foolish: Now such a Sperm is [their] Mercury the which by a natural conjunction of both bodies of ☉ and ☽ receives their nature into itself in Union; and then at length and not before is the work fitted for congress, ingress and Generation by the manly and feminine virtue and power. On this account the Philosophers took occasion to say, that Mercury is composed of body, soul, and spirit, and that it hath assumed the nature & property of all the Elements. Therefore from a most powerfull ingenuity and discretion or understanding they have affirmed their stone to be animal, the which also they have called their *Adam*, who carryes his invisible *Eve* hidden in his own body, from that moment of time wherein they were united by the power of the most high God, the framer of all the creatures; for which cause it may deservedly be said, that the Mercury of Philosophers is nothing else but their most abstruse compounded Mercury, and not that common ☿: Therefore have they discretly told the wise, that there is in Mercury whatsoever the wise men seek. *Almadir* the Philosopher saith, we do extract our Mercury out of one perfect body, and two perfect natural conditions incorporated together; the which ☿ indeed doth thrust forth its perfection outwardly, whereby tis able to resist the fire, and that its intrinsecal imperfection may be defended by the extrinsecal perfections; By this place of the most witty Philosopher, is the Adamical matter[26] understood, the Limbus of the Microcosm, the homogeneal, Only matter of all the Philosophers, whose sayings also (which we have aforementioned) are meerly golden, and to be had in most high esteem, because they containe nothing superfluous, or invalid; Briefly therefore the matter of the Philosophers stone is nothing else but a fiery and perfect Mercury, extracted by Nature and Art, that is the artificially prepared and true Hermaphrodite *Adam*, and Microcosm, That most wise *Mercurius* the wisest of the Philosophers affirming the same, hath called the stone an Orphan:[27] Therefore our Mercury is that very same that contains in it self the perfections, forces and virtues of the Sun, and which runs through the Streets and houses of all the Planets, and in its regeneration hath acquired or gotten the virtue of things above and beneath; to the marriage also of which [things *viz.* above and below] it is compared, as is evident from the whiteness and redness wound or heaped up together therein.

17: Of the Preparation of the Matter of the Philosophers stone.

This is that which nature doth most chiefly require, *viz.* that its own Philosophick man be brought into a Mercurial substance, that it may spring forth into the Philosophick stone. Moreover you are to note, that those common preparations of *Geber, Albertus Magnus, Th. Aquinas, Rupescisca,*[28] *Polidorus*, and such like, are nothing else but some particular Solutions, Sublimations and Calcinations, not at all pertaining to our Universal [work] which [work] doth want only the most secret fire of the Philosophers; Therefore the fire and Azoth[29]

---

[26] The prime matter from which the universe and all within it was created.

[27] The Stone is an orphan because it is "born from the union and death of its parents, sulphur and argent vive" (*DAI* 139).

[28] John of Rupescissa was a controversial Catalonian Franciscan monk of the mid-fourteenth century, to whom many alchemical treatises were ascribed (see *HMES* 3:347–69).

[29] Azoth is quicksilver, the "universal medicine, to which all things are alike, uncovering every species of substance, and imparting an immense strength, and catholic central virtue" (*Lexicon*, 66).

may suffice thee; [And whereas] the Philosophers do make mention of some preparations, as of putrefaction, distillation, sublimation, calcination, coagulation, dealbation, rubification, ceration, fixation, &c. you are to understand, that in their Universal [work] Nature it self doth accomplish all the operations in the said matter, and not the workman, [and that] only in a Philosophical Vessel, and with a such like fire, not a common fire. The white and the red do proceed out of one root, without any medium. Tis dissolved by it self, coupled by it self, albifyes, and rubifyes; is made saffrony and black by it self, marries itself, and conceives in it self: Tis therefore to be decocted, to be baked, to be fused, it ascends, and descends. All which Operations, are indeed [but] one Operation made by the fire alone; But yet some of the Philosophers have by a most high-graduated essence of Wine, dissolved the body of Sol, have made it Volatile, so as to ascend by an Alembick, supposing that this is the Volatile, true Philosophick matter, whereas it is not; And although it be no contemptible Arcanum, to bring this perfect metalline body into a Volatile and spiritual Substance, yet notwithstanding they err in the Separation of the Elements; the which process of [those] Monks, *viz. Lully, Richard the Englishman,*[30] *Rupescisca,* and others, is erroneous; By which [process] they supposed to separate gold by this way into a subtile, spiritual, and elementary power, each one a part; [and] afterwards by circulation and rectification to couple them again into one, but in vain; for verily, although one Element may after a sort be separated from another, yet nevertheless every element, after this manner separated, may again be separated into another element, the which parts cannot at all (afterwards) either, by pellicanick[31] circulation or distillation, return into one again, but they always remain a certain volatile matter, an *Aurum Potabile* as they call it; The cause why they could never arrive to their intention, is this; because nature is not in the least willing to be thus distracted or separated, by humane disjunctions, as by terrene [things] glasses and instruments. She her self alone, knows her own operations, and the weights of the Elements, the separations, rectifications and copulations of which she accomplisheth, without the help of any Operator or Manual artifice; Only the matter is to be contained in the secret fire, and in its occult Vessel; The Separation therefore of the Elements is impossible [to be done] by man; which separation should it have some appearance, yet notwithstanding is not true, whatsoever is spoken thereof by *Raimond Lully,* and his English golden noble Work, which he is falsly supposed to have framed. For Nature it self hath in her self her proper Separater (which doth again conjoyn what it separates) without the help of man, and doth best know all [her Trade] and the proportion of every element, and not man; whatever such erroneous Scriblers do (in their frivolous and false receipts) boast of this their volatile Gold. This [then] is the opinion [or mind] of the Philosophers, that when they have put their matter into the more secret fire, it be all about cherished with its [own] moderate Philosophical heat, that [so] beginning to pass through corruption it may grow black; This operation they call putrefaction, and the blackness they name the head of the Crow: They call the ascension and descension thereof distillation, ascension and descension; they call the exsiccation, coagulation; and the dealbation,

---

[30] Raymond Lull (b. *c.* 1232–36, d. 1315) was an influential Spanish philosopher and theologian, mystic and missionary to whom many alchemical treatises were falsely attributed. Richard of England or Richardus Anglicus was a physician and alchemical author who probably lived during the twelfth century and is chiefly identified with the *Correctorium Alchymiae.*

[31] A pelican-shaped vessel used in distillation.

calcination:[32] And because it is fluid and soft in the heat, they have made mention of Ceration; when it hath ceased to ascend and remain liquid in the bottom, then they say fixation is present.

After this manner therefore, the Appellations and terms of the Philosophical operations are to be understood, and no otherwise.

18: Of the Instruments and Philosophical Vessel.

The Putatitious Philosophers have rashly understood [and imagined] the Occult and Secret Philosophical Vessel, and *Aristotle* the Alchymist[33] (not that Grecian Academical Philosopher) hath [conceited it] worser, in that he saith the matter is to be decocted in a threefold Vessel; but he hath worst of all [understood it] that says, *viz.* that the matter in its first separation, and first degree, requires a Mettalline Vessel; in the second degree of Coagulation and dealbation of its [own] earth, a glass Vessel; and in the third degree, for fixation, an earthen Vessel. Nevertheless the Philosophers do understand by this [Vessel] one Vessel only in all operations, even to the perfection of the Red Stone; seeing therefore, that our matter is our root for the white and the red; 'tis necessary that our Vessel ought to be on this wise, that the matter therein may be governed by the Celestial Bodies; for the invisible Celestial Influences and impressions of the Stars are exceeding necessary to the Work; otherwise 'twill be impossible for the invincible Oriental, Persian, Chaldean and Egyptian Stone to be accomplished; by which [Stone] *Anaxagoras* knew the vertues of the whole Firmament, and foretold of the great Stone that should descend [down] upon the earth out of Heaven, the which also happened after his death. Verily our Vessel is most chiefly known to the Cabalists, because it ought to be framed according to a truly Geometrical proportion and measure, and of [or by] a Certain [and assured] Quadrature of a Circle:[34] or thus, *that the Spirit and soul of our matter, may in this Vessel, elevate with themselves (answerable to the altitude of the heaven) the [things] separated from their own body.* If the Vessel be narrower or wider, higher or lower then is fit, and then the ruling and operating Spirit and Soul desires the heat of our Philosophical Secret Fire (which is indeed most acute) would stir up the matter too violently, and urge it to overmuch operation, that the Vessel would leap into a thousand pieces, to the hazard and danger of the body and life of the Operator: whereas contrariwise, if it be more wide or capacious then for the heat to operate upon the matter according to proportion, the work will also be frustrate and vain. And therefore our Philosophical Vessel is to be framed with the greatest diligence: But as for the matter of this our Vessel, they alone do understand it, that in the first Solution of our fixt and perfect matter, have adduced or brought this [matter] into its first Essence; and so much for this. The Operator must likewise most accurately note what it is, that the matter (in the first Solution) lets fall, and casts out from it self: The manner of describing the form of the Vessel is difficult; it must be such as nature it self requires [tis] to be sought for and searcht after,

---

[32] *Exsiccation* is "the action of drying what is moist; complete removal or absorption of moisture;" *dealbation* is "the action of whitening" (*OED*).

[33] During the Middle Ages many pseudonymous alchemical works attributed to Aristotle and Plato were in circulation; Paracelsus here refers to one such unknown author.

[34] "In the alchemical opus the square symbolizes the four elements . . . which are to be converted into the perfection of the circular quintessence, or the philosopher's stone which has the power to perfect all imperfections" (*DAI* 190). Paracelsus states that to function properly the alchemical vessel must be designed according to the same principles of harmony and proportion.

out of one and the other, that [so] it may (from the altitude of the Philosophick Heaven, elevated from the Philosophick Earth) be able to operate upon the fruit of its own earthly body. Verily it ought to have this Form, that a separation and purification of the Elements (when the Fire drives the One from the other) may be made, and that each [Element] may possess its own place in which it sticks; and the Sun and the other Planets may exercise their operations round about the Elemental Earth, and the course of them may not be hindred in their circuit, or be stir'd up with too swift a motion: Now according to all these things here spoken of, it must have a just proportion of Roundness and Height: But the Instruments for the first mundification of Mineral Bodies, are melting Vessels, Bellows, Tongs, Capel, Cupels, Tests, Cementatory Vessels,[35] Cineritiums, Cucurbits, Bocia's for *Aq[ua] fort[is]* and *Aq[ua] regia*, and also some things as are necessary for projection in the last Work.

---

[35] A *capel* is a large crucible; a *cementatory vessel* was used in the process "by which one solid is made to penetrate and combine with another at a high temperature so as to change the properties of one of them, without liquefaction taking place" (*OED*).

19 Francis Anthony (1550–1603)

Aurum-Potabile: or the Receit of Dr. Fr. Antonie

One of the best known alchemical medicines formulated by physicians and apothecaries of the Paracelsian persuasion was *aurum potabile*, i.e., potable (or drinkable) gold. Its underlying theory reasoned that since gold was the most perfect metal, medicines so derived would be unusually salutary, dispatching their virtues in the curing of all diseases. Thus solutions consisting of finely powdered gold dissolved in wine or vinegar came to be regarded as universal medicines. The London empiric and unlicensed physician Francis Anthony achieved great success and notoriety by dispensing medications based on the following chemical prescription; however, it also resulted in much professional difficulty for Anthony, including prosecution by the Royal College of Physicians, the conservative medical governing organization that continued to advocate ancient Galenic herbal cures.

Following is the complete text of *Aurum-Potabile: or the Receit of Dr. Fr. Antonie. Shewing, His Way and Method, how he made and prepared that most Excellent Medicine for the Body of Man*, in *Collectanea Chymica: a collection of Ten Several Treatises in Chymistry* (London, 1684), edited and printed by William Cooper. Additional readings: Allen G. Debus, *The English Paracelsians* (New York: Franklin Watts, 1966), 142–45; *DNB*, s.v. "Antony, Francis."

Take Block-tinn,[1] and burn it in an Iron Pan (making the Pan red-hot before you put it in) and keeping a continual Fire under it, and stirring it always till it be like unto Ashes, some will look red, it will be burning a day, or half a day at the least, it must be stirred with an Iron Cole-rake, a little one, the handle two Foot long.

G. H. M. made an Iron Pan a Foot and half long, and a Foot broad, the Brims two Inches deep, and made an Oven in a Chimney with Bars of Iron in the bottom, whereon he placed the Pan, and a place under to make Fire, and it will after this manner sooner be burned (*viz.* half a day) the Smoak will not hurt it.

This Ashes keep in a Glass close covered.
Take of these Ashes 4 ℥, and of the strongest red Wine Vineger 3 Pints; and put them in a Glass like an Urinal. The Ashes being put in first lute the Vessel, and let him stand in an hot Balneum[2] 10 days, which ended, take it forth, and set it to cool, and let it stand

---

[1] "Tin of second quality cast into blocks" (*OED* 1.b).   [2] *Balneum mariæ* or *bain-marie*, a water bath.

2 or 3 whole days that the Feces may sink unto the bottom, the glass must be shaken 6 or 7 times every day.

That which is clear let it run forth unfiltred by 2 or 3 Woolen-threds into a Glass Bason, and distil it in a Glasen Still, till the Liquor be stilled all forth; this distilled Water put upon 4 ounces of fresh Ashes, upon the Ashes from which the first Liquor was filtred, put also a Quart of strong red Wine Vinegar, lute the Glass as before, and put him into the Balneum, and there let him stand to digest 10 days, filter this, and distil it as aforesaid, thirdly pour on that Ashes one pint of the like Vineger, and put it in Balneum 10 days, filter it, and distil it as aforesaid, after the third Infusion throw away the Ashes.

Distil all the Infusions apart, till the Liquor be clean distilled forth.

Take this distilled Water as often as it is distilled, and pour it upon new Ashes, keeping the weight and order, their Infusions, Filtrings, and Destillations, reiterate 7 times.

And you shall have of this Water the *Menstruum*[3] sought for.

You must take heed that the Vineger be of red Wine, and very strong, otherwise your *Menstruum* will not perform your Expectation.

The Bishop gave Dr. *Anthony* 30 s. for a quart of *Menstruum*.

Take an ounce of pure refined Gold, (which costs 3 l. 13 s. 4 d.) cast into a Wedge and File it into small Dust, with a fine File, put this ounce of filed Gold into a Calcined Pot, and put to it so much white Salt as will near fill the Pot, and set it among Charcoals where it may stand continually hot 4 Hours, (if it stand too hot the Salt will melt) which 4 Hours ended take it forth, and let it stand to cool, then put it on a Painters Stone, and grind it very small with a Muller;[4] then put it into the Pot and Calcine it, and grind it again, till you have done it 4 or 5 times; if it look red and blew when you take it forth it is perfect good.

After this calcining, and grinding, put it into a Glass Bason, and put to it the Bason full of scalding hot Water, and stir it a good while, till the thick part is fully settled to the bottom, then pour away that Water, and put the like, stir it, and let it settle as before, and so do again, till the Water when it is settled have no taste of Salt, this will be doing two or three days.

Of this ounce of Gold, there will be hardly above 16 or 17 Grains brought into fine white Calx, but to separate it from the Gold, leave a little of the last fresh Water in the Bason, and stir it well together, the Calx will swim to the top, which softly pour from the Gold into another Bason, if all the white Calx go not forth, put a little more Water and stir it again, and pour it into the Bason to the other Calx, then let it settle, and pour away almost all the Water and Evaporate away all the rest over a heat till it be throughly dry, and so put it up into a Glass.

Then put the Gold which is not yet Calx to Salt as aforesaid, and Calcine it, and grind it four times again, and then wash it, and then take the Calx from it as before, and the Gold remains, calcine and wash, as before till it be all Calx.

---

[3] Abraham defines menstruum as "the mercurial solvent of the philosophers. It is the means by which the alchemists dissolve metals into the prima materia, and by which they ripen their matter into gold" (*DAI* 124). For Antonie, dissolved gold is the essence of this medicine.

[4] "A stone with a flat base or grinding surface, which is held in the hand and used, in conjunction with a grinding stone or slab, in grinding painters' colours, apothecaries' powders, etc." (*OED*).

Take an ounce of this Calx, and put it into an Urinal like Glass, containing about a pint, and put to it half a pint of the *Menstruum*. Set this Glass in a hot Balneum, six days (being close luted) and shake it often every day; when the six days are ended, let it stand two or three days, then pour away that which is clear, very gently, for fear of troubling the Feces; to these Feces put fresh *menstruum* but not fully so much as at the first, and so the third time, but not fully so much as at the second, then take the dry Feces which is the Calx, and keep it lest some Tincture remain in it.

These coloured Liquors put into a Glass Still, and distil them in a Balneum at the first, with a very gentle Fire, till all that which is clear be run forth, and that which remains be as thick as Hony, then take it forth, and set it to cool, then put the Glass into an Earthen Pot, and put Ashes about the Glass into the Pot, and fix the Pot into a little Furnace fast, and make a Fire under, so that the Glass may stand very warm till the Feces be black and very dry, (you may look with a Candle through the Glass Still, and see when it is risen with bunches and dry.) Then take away your Fire, and let the Glass be very cold, then take out the black Earth, this black Earth being taken forth, put it into a Glass Bason, and grind it with the bottom of another round Glass to Powder, then put it into an Urinal-like Glass containing about a pint, and to that put a little above half a pint of the Spirit of Wine, set this Glass in a cold place till it be red, which will be about ten days, shake it often every day, till within three days you pour it forth. Then pour away the clear Liquor gently, and that clear put into a Glass-Still (or other Glass till you have more), then put more Spirit of Wine to that Feces, and order it as before, and if that be much coloured put Spiritus Vini. to it the third time, as at the first, put all these coloured Liquors together, and distil them till the Feces (called the Tincture) be thick as a Syrrup.

Take an ounce of this Tincture, and put it into a pint of *Canary* Sack, and so when it is clear, you may drink of it, which will be about a day and a half.

The Preparation of the Vineger to make the Menstruum.

Glasses necessary get 3 or 4 Glasen Stills which will hold a gallon or two apiece, the Balneum 2 foot and a halfe square to hold many Glasses. Get about 6 gallons of the strongest red Wine Vinegar (Vineger of Claret or White-Wine are too weak) made of red Wine, Sack or Muscadine, and set as many Stills going at a time as your Balneum will hold, take a pint of that which runneth first, and put it away, as weak and not for this use, then Still out all the rest till the Still be dry, wash the Still with a little of the (flegm) first running, and then wipe him dry, then put in that which was distilled, and do as before, putting away the first pint, and so do five times, so of a gallon you shall have 3 Pints of the Spirit of Vineger, and of your 6 gallons, only two gallons and two Pints, and if your Spirit be yet too weak distill it oftner.

This keep in a Glass close stopped to make your *Menstruum* with; you may stop it with Cork, and Leather over it.

You must provide three strong green Glasses to make *Menstruum,* with little Mats round the bottoms, containing four Pints apiece.

To Lute them, fit a Wooden stoppel of dry Wood first boyled, and then dryed in an Oven, to the Mouth, then melt hard Wax to fill the Chinks, then paste a brown Paper next over that, then prepare luting of Clay, Horse-dung and Ashes, and stop over all that.

Glass Stills 2 or 3 to distil the first Infusions on the Earth, cover 3 or 4 Pints a piece of green Glass.

The Rule of all Stillings, you must paste brown Paper to the closing of the head of the Still, and also paste the Receiver and nose of the Still together so that no strength go forth.

Calcining Pots provide about a dozen, for many when they are put into a strong Fire will break, then must you let your Fire slack.

20 Michael Sendivogius (1566–1636 or 1646)

From *A New Light of Alchymie* and *A Dialogue between Mercury, the Alchymist and Nature*

Although many details of the life of Michael Sendivogius are obscure, there is no question as to his importance and influence on alchemical thought in the seventeenth century. Until recently, it was believed that the life of this Polish alchemist was closely entwined with that of the Scottish alchemist Alexander Seton, who was reputed to have performed successful transmutations at several European courts early in the seventeenth century. Late in 1603, at the court of Christian II, Elector of Saxony, Seton suffered a fate common to adepts who fell into the hands of avaricious monarchs; he was tortured and imprisoned for refusing to give Christian the secret of his transmuting powder. Thereupon Sendivogius entered the melodrama, helped the enfeebled Seton escape from Christian's prison, was rewarded with a portion of the remaining powder, and – following Seton's death in 1603 or 1604 – married his widow. Sendivogius then embarked on a career that was every bit as romantic and adventurous as that of Seton, eventually arriving in Prague at the court of Emperor Rudolf II, the "German Hermes." Alternately enjoying courtly triumph and suffering squalid imprisonment, Sendivogius at last declined into the living embodiment of the alchemist of literary satire, dying in poverty in Warsaw at the age of eighty. Such, at least, is the legend that Sendivogius was thought to have lived until late twentieth-century researchers vindicated his name from the seamier aspects of alchemical charlatanism and emphasized his noble background and education, his contributions to chemistry, and the honors received from royal patrons.

Sendivogius's reputation was firmly established through his writings, particularly the *Novum Lumen Chymicum*, his major work from which the following selections are taken. Its original Latin edition was published in Prague in 1604; other editions and translations into French, German, and English soon followed. Excerpts from this work are followed by Sendivogius's popular *Dialogue between Mercury, the Alchymist and Nature*, his comic masterpiece, which I have argued elsewhere appears to have been the direct source of Ben Jonson's masque, *Mercury Vindicated from the Alchemists at Court* (1616). Both texts are taken from *A New Light of Alchymie: Taken out of the fountaine of Nature, and Manuall Experience . . . Written by Micheel Sandivogius* [sic] *. . . All of which are faithfully translated out of the Latin into the English tongue. By J. F. M. D.* (London, 1650). Additional readings: Zbigniew Szydlo, *Water Which Does Not Wet Hands: The Alchemy of Michael Sendivogius* (Warsaw: Polish Academy of Sciences, 1994).

From *A New Light of Alchymie*

The First Treatise. Of Nature, what she is, and what her searchers ought to be.
Many wise and very learned men many ages since, yea (Hermes testifying the same) before the Floud wrote many things concerning the making the Philosophers Stone; and have bequeathed so many writings unto us, that unlesse Nature should daily worke things credible to us, scarce any one would beleeve it as a truth that there were any Nature at all: because in former ages there were not so many devisers of things, neither did our ancestors regard any thing besides Nature it selfe, and the possibility of Nature. And although they were contented with the plaine way alone of Nature, yet they found out those things, which we now imployed about divers things could not with all our wits conceive. This is because Nature, and the generation of things in the world is esteemed of us meane and plaine. And therefore we bend our wits not to things knowne and familiar, but to such things, which not at all, or very hardly can be done. Wherefore it happens that we are more dexterous in devising curious subtilties, and such which the Philosophers themselves did never thinke of, then to attain to the true processe of Nature, & the right meaning of Philosophers.[1] And such is the disposition of mens natures, as to neglect those things they know, and to be alwaies seeking after other things; such also and much more is that of mens wits and fancies, to which their nature is subjected. As for example, you see any Artificer, when he hath attained to the highest perfection of his Art, either searcheth into other Arts, or abuseth the same, which he already hath, or else leaves it off quite. So also is generous Nature alwaies active and doing to its very Iliad[2] utmost period, and afterward ceaseth. For there is given to Nature from the beginning a certaine kinde of grant or permission still to attaine to things better and better through her whole progresse, and to come to her full rest, towards which she tends with all her might, and rejoyceth in her end, as a pismire doth in her old age, at which time Nature makes her wings. Even so our wits have proceeded so farre, especially in the Phylosophicall Art, or praxis of the stone, that now we are almost come to the Iliad it selfe. For the Art of Chymistry hath now found out such subtilties, that scarce greater can be invented, and differ as much from the Art of the Ancient Philosophers as a Clock-smith doth from a plaine Black-smith. And although both worke upon Iron, yet neither understands the others labours, although both are masters of their Art. If Hermes himselfe, the father of Philosophers, should now be alive, and subtil-witted *Geber*, together with most profound *Raimundus Lullius*, they would not be accounted by our Chymists for Philosophers, but rather for Schollars: they would be ignorant of those so many distillations, so many circulations, so many calcinations, and so many other innumerable operations of Artists now adayes used, which men of this age devised, and found out of their writings. There is one only thing wanting to us, that is, to know that which they effected, *viz.* the Philosophers Stone or Physicall Tincture, we whilest we seeke that, finde out other things: and unlesse the procreation of man were so usuall as it is, and Nature did in that thing still observe her owne law and rules, we should scarce but not erre. But to returne to which I intended: I promised in this first treatise to explaine Nature, lest every idle fancy should turne us aside from the true and plaine way.

---

[1] Here and in his *Dialogue*, Sendivogius distinguishes sharply between the wise and noble alchemical "Philosopher" and the ignorant and unscrupulous "alchemist."

[2] I.e., a long series of trials or miseries.

Therefore I say Nature is but one, true, plaine, perfect, and entire in its owne being, which God made from the beginning, placing his spirit in it: but know that the bounds of Nature is God himselfe, who also is the originall of Nature. For it is certaine that every thing that is begun, ends no where but in that in which it begins. I say it is that only alone by which God workes all things: not that God cannot worke without it (for truely he himselfe made Nature, and is omnipotent) but so it pleaseth him to doe. All things proceed from this very Nature alone; neither is there any thing in the world without Nature. And although it happens sometimes that there be abortives, this is not Natures fault, but of the Artist or place. This Nature is divided into foure places, in which she workes all these things which appeare to us under shadowes; for truely things may be said rather to be shadowed out to us, then really to appeare. She is changed in male and female, and is likened to Mercury, because she joynes her selfe to various places; and according to the goodnesse or the badnesse of the place she brings forth things; although to us there seeme no bad places at all in the earth. Now for qualities there be only foure and these are in all things but agree not, for one alwaies exceeds another. Moreover, Nature is not visible although she acts visibly; for it is a volatile spirit which executes its office in bodies and is placed and seated in the will and minde of God. Nature in this place serves us for no other purpose but to understand her places, which are more sutable and of nearer affinity to her; that is, to understand how to joyne one thing to another according to Nature, that we mixe not wood and man together, or an oxe or any other living creature and metals together: but let every thing act upon its owne like: and then for certaine Nature shall performe her office. The place of Nature is no other then, as I said before, what is in the will of God.

The searchers of Nature ought to be such as Nature her selfe is: true, plaine, patient, constant, &c. and that which is chiefest of all, religious, fearing God, not injurious to their neighbour. Then let them diligently consider, whether their purpose be agreeable to Nature; whether it be possible, let them learne by cleare examples, *viz.* out of what things any thing may be made, how, and in what vessell Nature workes. For if thou wilt doe any thing plainly, as Nature her selfe doth doe it, follow Nature; but if thou wilt attempt to doe a thing better then Nature hath done it, consider well in what, and by what it is bettered, and let it alwaies be done in its owne like. As for example, if thou desirest to exalt a metall in vertue (which is our intention) further then Nature hath done, thou must take a metalline nature both in male and female, or else thou shalt effect nothing. For if thou dost purpose to make a metall out of hearbs, thou shalt labour in vaine, as also thou shalt not bring forth wood out of a dog, or any other beast.

The Second Treatise. Of the operation of Nature in our intention, and in Sperme.

I said even now that Nature was true, but one, every where seene, constant, and is knowne by the things which are brought forth, as woods, hearbs, and the like. I said also that the searcher of Nature must be true, simple hearted, patient, constant, giving his minde but to one thing alone, &c. Now we must begin to treat of the acting of Nature. As Nature is the will of God and God created her, or put her upon every imagination, so Nature made her selfe a seed, her will and pleasure in the Elements. She indeed is but one and yet brings forth divers things but workes nothing without a sperme:[3] Nature workes whatsoever the sperme pleaseth, for it is as it were an instrument of some Artificer. The sperme therefore of every thing is better and more advantagious to the Artificer, then Nature her selfe. For by Nature without seed, you shall doe as much as a Goldsmith shall without fire, gold, or silver, or a husbandman without corne or seed. If thou hast the sperme, Nature is presently at hand, whether it be to bad or good. She workes in sperme as God doth in the free will of man: and that is a great mysterie, because Nature obeyes the sperme, not by compulsion but voluntarily; even as God suffers all things which man wills, not by constraint, but out of his owne free pleasure: Therefore he gave man free will whether to bad or to good. The sperme therefore is the Elixir of every thing or Quint-essence, or the most perfect decoction, or digestion of a thing, or the Balsome of Sulphur, which is the same as the Radical moisture in metalls. There might truly be made a large discourse of this sperme; but we shall onely keep to that which makes for our purpose in the Chymicall Art. Four elements beget a sperme through the will and pleasure of God, and imagination of Nature: for as the sperme of man hath its center or vessell of its seede in the kidnies; so the foure Elements by their never ceasing motion (every one according to its quality) cast forth a sperme into the Center of the earth, where it is digested and by motion sent abroad. Now the Center of the earth is a certaine empty place, where nothing can rest. The foure Elements send forth their qualities into excentrall parts of the earth or into the circumference of the Center. As a man sends forth his seed into the entrance of the wombe of the woman, in which place nothing of the seed remaines, but after the wombe hath received a due proportion, casts out the rest; so also it comes to passe in the Center of the earth, that the magnetick vertue of the part of any place drawes to itselfe any thing that is convenient for its selfe, for the bringing forth of any thing; the residue is cast forth into stones and other excrements. For all things have their originall from this fountaine, neither hath any thing in the world any beginning but by this fountaine. As for example, let there be set a vessell of water upon a smooth even table, and be placed in the middle thereof, and round about let there be laid divers things and divers colours, also salt, and every one apart: then let the water be powred forth into the middle, and you shall see that water to runne abroad here and there, and when one streame is come to the red colour, it is made red by it, if to the salt, it takes from it the taste of the salt, and so of the rest. For the water doth not change the place, but the diversity of the place changeth the water. In like manner the seed or sperme being by the four Elements cast forth from the center into the circumference, passeth through divers places and according to the nature of the place, it makes things: if it comes to a pure place of earth and water, a pure thing is made. The seed and sperme of all things is but one, and yet it produceth divers things, as is evident by the following example. The seed of a man is a noble seed, and was created and ordained for the generation of man onely; yet nevertheless if a man doe abuse it, as is in his free will to doe, there is borne

---

[3] Like many alchemical authors, Sendivogius relies heavily on sexual metaphor to explain creation, although his is not the simple model of biological reproduction. The sperm or seeds here mentioned are produced by Nature, i.e., God's will, from the four elements, then "cast" into the center of the earth to undergo maturing and removal to other locations. In the process of creation, Nature operates entirely through sperm, using them as a kind of prime matter (or "Elixir" or "Quint-essence") which is variously shaped into different bodies depending on "the nature of the place."

an abortive. For if a man contrary to Gods most expresse command should couple with a cow or any other beast, the beast would presently conceive the seed of the man, because Nature is but one; and then there would not be borne a man, but a beast and an Abortive; because the seed did not find a place sutable to it self. By such an inhumane & detestable copulation of men with beasts there would be brought forth divers beasts, like unto men. For so it is, if the sperme goes into the center, there is made that which should be made there; but when it is come into any other place, and hath conceived, it changeth its forme no more. Now whilest the sperme is yet in the center, there may as easily be brought forth a tree as a metall from the sperme, and as soone an hearbe as a stone, and one more pretious then another, according to the purity of the place. But how the Elements beget a sperme is in the next place to be treated of, and it is done thus: the Elements are foure: two are heavy and two are light, two dry and two moist, but one which is most dry, and another which is most moist, are males, and females &c. Every one of these of it selfe is most apt to produce things like unto it selfe in its owne sphere, and so it pleased God it should be: These foure never are at rest but are alwaies acting one upon another; and every one by it selfe sendeth forth his owne thinness and subtlety, and they all meet in the center: now in the center is the Archeus,[4] the servant of Nature, which mixeth those spermes and sends them forth. And how that is done is to be seene more fully in the Epilogue of the 12 treatises.

The Third Treatise. Of the true first matter of Metalls.

... If thou hast eares or any sense, mark well what is here said, and thou shalt be safe, and out of the number not only of those who are ignorant of the place of the sperm, and endeavour to convert the whole corn into seed; but also of them all, who are employed in the fruitlesse dissolution of metalls, and are desirous to dissolve the whole of metalls, that afterwards by their mutuall commixtion they may make a new metall. But these men, if they considered the process of Nature, should see that the case is far otherwise; for there is no metall so pure, which hath not its impurities, yet one more or fewer then another. But thou, friendly Reader, shalt observe the first point of Nature, as is abovesaid, and thou hast enough: but take this caution along with thee; that thou dost not seek for this point in the metals of the vulgar, in which it is not.[5] For these metals, especially the gold of the vulgar, are dead, but ours are living, full of spirit, and these wholly must be taken: for know, that the life of metalls is fire whilst they are yet in their mines; and their death is the fire, *viz.* of melting. Now the first matter of metals is a certaine humidity mixed with warm aire, and it resembles fat water, sticking to every thing pure or impure, but in one place more abundantly then in another, by reason the earth is more open and porous in one place then in another, having also an attractive power. It comes forth into the light sometimes by itself, with some kind of covering, especially in such places where there was nothing that it could well stick to; it is known thus, because

---

[4] A cosmic force located at earth's center, the term apparently borrowed from Paracelsus. On this section of the treatise, see Paulo Alves Porto, "Michael Sendivogius on Nitre and the Preparation of the Philosophers' Stone," *Ambix* 48,1 (March 2001): 3–7.

[5] Alchemists invariably stress that the metals to be worked upon in preparing the opus are not the common, vulgar ones but rather, in Sendivogius's phrase, those that are "living, [and] full of spirit."

every thing is compounded of 3 principles: but in reference to the matter of metalls is but one, without any conjunction to any thing, excepting to its covering or shadow, *viz.* sulphur, &c.

The Fourth Treatise. How Metals are generated in the bowells of the earth.

Metalls are brought forth in this manner. After the foure Elements have sent forth their vertues into the center of the earth, the Archeus by way of distillation sends them up unto the superficies of the earth, by vertue of the heat of its perpetuall motion: for the earth is porous, and this wind, by distilling through the pores of the earth, is resolved into water, out of which all things are made. Therefore let the Sons of Wisdome know, that the sperm of metalls doth not differ from the sperm of all things, *viz.* the moist vapour: therefore in vain do Artists look after the reducing of metalls into their first matter, which is only a vapour. The Philosophers meant not such a first matter, but only the second matter, as *Bernardus Trevisanus*[6] learnedly discusseth it, though not so cleerly, because hee speaks of the four Elements, but yet hee did say as much, but he spake only to the Sons of Art. But I, that I might the more cleerly open the Theorie, would have all be admonished here to take heed how they give way to so many solutions, so many circulations, so many calcinations, and reiterations of the same; for in vain is that sought for in a hard thing, when as the thing is soft of itself and every where to be had. Let not the first, but the second matter only be sought after, *viz.* that, which as soon as it is conceived, cannot be changed into another form. But if thou inquirest how a metall may bee reduced into such a matter, in that I keep close to the intention of the Philosophers: this thing only above all the rest I desire, that the Sons of Art would understand the sense and not the letter of writings, and where Nature doth end, *viz.* in metallick bodies, which in our eyes seem to be perfect, there must Art begin. But to return to my purpose (for my intention is not here to speak of the stone only), let us now treate of the matter of metals. A little before I said, that all things were made of the liquid aire or the vapour, which the Elements by a perpetuall motion distill into the bowells of the earth; and then the Archeus of Nature takes and sublimes it through the pores, and according to its discretion distributes it to every place (as we have declared in the foregoing treatises) so from the variety of places proceeds the variety of things. There be some that suppose Saturne to have one kind of seed, and Gold another, and so all the rest of the metals. But these are foolish fancies; there is but one only seed, the same is found in Saturne which is in Gold, the same in Silver which is in Iron; but the place of the earth is divers, if thou understandest me aright, although in Silver Nature sooner hath done its work, then in Gold, and so of the rest. For when that vapour is sublimed from the center of the earth, it passeth through places either cold or hot: if therefore it passeth through places that are hot and pure, where the fatness of Sulphur sticks to the walls; I say that vapour which the Philosophers have called the Mercury of Philosophers[7] applyes it self to, and is joined to that fatnesse, which then it sublimes with

---

[6] Trevisanus (1406–1490) was an Italian alchemist who supposedly succeeded in making the philosopher's stone late in life; his works were popular in the sixteenth and seventeenth centuries. See his *Treatise of the Philosophers Stone* in this collection.

[7] Not the common mercury (Hg) but that which is specially prepared from the union of sulphur and argent-vive to be the agent of transmuting baser metals. In this section, however, Sendivogius describes how this "vapour," when transformed into a "fatnesse," becomes a principle ingredient in the subterranean formation of metals.

it self; and then becomes an unctuosity, and leaving the name of a Vapour, is called by the name of Fatnesse; which afterward coming by sublimation unto other places, which the fore-going vapour hath cleansed, where the earth is subtill, pure, and moist, fills the pores thereof, and is joined to it, and so it is made Gold; but if that fatnesse come to impure and cold places, it is made Lead; but if the earth bee cold and pure and mixed with sulphur, it is made Copper, &c. For by how much more a place is depurated, or clensed, by so much the more excellent it makes the metalls: for wee must know that that vapour goes out continually from the center to the superficies, and cleanseth those places through which it passeth. Thence it comes to passe, that now there may bee found Mines in those places where a thousand yeers agoe were none; for in its passage it alwaies subtilizeth that which is crude and impure, carrying it by degrees with it; and this is the reiteration and circulation of Nature; it is so long sublimed in producing new things, untill the place be very well purified; and by how much the more it is purified, by so much the nobler things it brings forth. Now in the winter when the air is cold, binding fast the earth, that unctuous vapour is congealed, which afterward when the spring returns, is mixed together with earth and water, and so becomes a Magnesia,[8] drawing to it self the Mercury of air, like unto it selfe, and gives life to all things through the concurrence of the beams of the Sun, Moon and Stars, and so it brings forth grass, flowers, and such like things. For Nature is not one moment of time idle. Now Metalls are thus made, the earth by long distillation is puriefied, then they are generated by the access or coming thither of the fatnesse: they are brought forth no other way, as is the foolish opinion of some that mis–interpret the writings of Philosophers.

The Tenth Treatise. Of the Supernaturall Generation of the Son of the Sun.
We have treated of things which Nature makes and which God hath made, that the Searchers of Art might the more easily understand the possibility of Nature. But to delay no longer, I will now enter upon the Manner and Art how to make the Philosophers stone. The Philosophers stone or tincture is nothing else but Gold digested to the highest degree: for vulgar Gold is like an herb without seed, when it is ripe it brings forth seed; so Gold when it is ripe yeelds seed or tincture. But, will some ask, why doth not Gold or any other Metall bring forth seed? The reason given is this, because it cannot bee ripe, by reason of the crudity of the air, it hath not sufficient heat, and it happens that in some places there is found pure Gold, which Nature would have perfected, but was hindred by the crude aire . . . but if at any time Nature be sweetly and wittily helped, then Art may perfect that which Nature could not. The same happens in Metalls: Gold may yeeld fruit and seed, in which it multiplyes it self by the industry of the skilfull Artificer, who knows how to exalt Nature, but if he will attempt to do it without Nature, he will be mistaken. For not only in this art, but also in every thing else, we can doe nothing but help Nature; and this by no other medium then fire or heat. But seeing this cannot be done, since in a congealed Metallick body there appear no spirits, it is necessary that the body be loosed

---

8 "Magnesia" possesses a wide range of meanings in alchemy, from one of the ingredients of the philosopher's stone (*OED*), to marcasite or a mixture of silver and mercury (*Lexicon*), to "the active, vitalistic alchemical agent Mercurius," or the quintessence itself (*DAI* 121). Sendivogius's context indicates that it is a life-giving natural force with attractive, possibly magnetic powers.

or dissolved, and the pores thereof opened, whereby Nature may work. But what that dissolution ought to be, here I would have the Reader take notice, that there is a twofold dissolution; although there be many other dissolutions, but to little purpose, there is onely one that is truely naturall, the other is violent, under which all the rest are comprehended. The naturall is this, that the pores of the body bee opened in our water, whereby the seed that is digested may bee sent forth, and put into its proper Matrix. Now our water is heavenly, not wetting the hands, not vulgar, but almost rain water:[9] The body is gold which yeelds seed; our Lune or Silver (not common Silver) is that which receives the seed of the gold: afterwards it is governed by our continual fire for seven months, and sometimes ten, untill our water consume three, and leave one; and that *in duplo*, or a double. Then it is nourished with the milk of the earth, or the fatnesse thereof, which is bred in the bowells of the earth and is governed or preserved from putrefaction by the salt of Nature. And thus the infant of the second generation is generated. Now let us passe from the Theorie to the Praxis.

The Eleventh Treatise. Of the Praxis, and making of the Stone, or Tincture by Art.

Through all these foregoing Chapters, our discourse of things hath been scattered by way of examples, that the Praxis might be the more easily understood, which must be done by imitating Nature after this manner.

Take of our earth, through eleven degrees, eleven graines of our Gold, and not of the vulgar one grain; of our Lune, not the vulgar, two graines: but be thou well advised, that thou takest not common Gold and Silver, for these are dead, take ours which are living: then put them into our fire, and let there be made of them a dry liquor; first of all the earth will be resolved into water, which is called the Mercury of Philosophers; and that water shall resolve those bodies of Gold and Silver, and shal consume them so that there shall remain but the tenth part with one part; and this shall be the radicall moisture of Metalls. Then take water of salt-nitre, which comes from our earth, in which there is a river of living water, if thou diggest the pit knee deep, therefore take water out of that, but take that which is cleer; upon this put that radicall moisture; and set it over the fire of putrefaction and generation, not on such a one as thou didst in the first operation. Govern all things with a great deale of discretion, untill colours appear like a Peacocks tail;[10] govern it by digesting it and be not weary, untill these colours be ended and there appear throughout the whole one green colour, and so of the rest; and when thou shalt see in the bottome ashes of a fiery colour and the water almost red, open the vessel, dip in a pen, and smeare some Iron with it; if it tinge, have in readinesse that water, which afterwards I shall speak of, and put in so much of that water as the cold aire was which went in; boil it again with the former fire, untill it tinge again. So far reached my experience, I can doe no more,

---

[9] Alchemists often refer to the universal solvent which opens the "pores" of metallic bodies, as the miraculous "water that does not wet the hands." Abraham notes that "the mercurial water is known as the water of life (aqua vitae) which first kills the metal or matter for the Stone, and then revives and regenerates it" (*DAI* 213).

[10] The multi-color or rainbow display known as the *cauda pavonis* signalled an intermediate stage in the alchemical opus, between the blackness (*nigredo*) and the whiteness (*albedo*), followed by redness (*rubedo*). Sendivogius also inserts green into the sequence.

I found out no more. Now that water must be the menstruum of the world, out of the sphere of the Moon, so often rectified, untill it can calcine Gold: I have been willing here to discover to thee all things; and if thou shalt understand my meaning sometimes and not the letter, I have revealed all things, especially in the first and second work.

Now it remains that we speak next of the fire. The first fire, or of the first operation, is a fire of one degree, continuall, which goes round the matter; the second is a naturall fire, which digests and fixeth the matter: I tell thee truly that I have opened to thee the governance or rules of the fire, if thou understandest Nature. The vessell remains yet to be spoken of. It must be the vessel of Nature, and two are sufficient; the vessel of the first work must be round; but in the second a glasse, a little lesse like unto a viall, or an egge. But in all these know that the fire of Nature is but one, and if it works variously, it is by reason of the difference of places. The vessell therefore of Nature is but one; but wee for brevities sake use a couple: the matter is one, but out of two substances. If therefore thou wilt give thy mind to make things, consider first things that are already made; if thou canst not reach or understand things presented to thy eyes, much lesse things that are to be made, and which thou desirest to make. For know that thou canst create nothing, for that is proper to God alone, but to make things that are not perceived, but lye hid in the shadow, to appear, and to take from them their vaile, is granted to an intelligent Philosopher by God through Nature . . . O wonderfull Nature, which knows how to produce wonderfull fruits out of Water in the earth, and from the Aire to give them life. All these are done, and the eyes of the vulgar doe not see them; but the eyes of the understanding and imagination perceive them, and that with a true sight. The eyes of the wise look upon Nature otherwise then the eyes of common men . . . [A]nd know that if thou dost not follow Nature all is in vain: and here I have spoken to thee through the help of God, what a father should speak to his son; Hee which hath ears let him heare, and he which hath his senses, let him set his mind upon what I say.

The Twelfth Treatise. Of the Stone, and its vertue.

In the foregoing Treatises it hath been sufficiently spoken concerning the production of Naturall things, concerning the Elements, the First matter, and Second matter, Bodies, Seeds, and concerning the Use and Vertue of them: I wrote also the Praxis of making the Philosophers Stone. Now I will discover so much of the vertue of it, as Nature hath granted to me and experience taught me. But to comprehend the argument of all these Treatises briefly and in few words that the Reader which fears God may understand my mind and meaning, the thing is this. If any man doubt of the truth of the Art, let him read the voluminous writings of ancient Philosophers, verified by reason and experience; whom wee may deservedly give credit to in their own Art: but if any will not give credit to them, then we know not how to dispute with them, as denying principles: for deaf and dumbe men cannot speak. What prerogative should all things in this world have before Metalls? Why should these alone by having seed without cause denied to them, be excluded from Gods universall blessing of multiplication, which holy writ affirms was put in, and bestowed on all created things presently after the world was made?[11] Now if they have Seed, who is so sottish to think that they cannot bee multiplyed in their Seed?

---

[11] See God's repeated injunction to "be fruitful and multiply" in Gen. 1.

The Art of Alchymie in its kind is true, Nature also is true, but the Artificer is seldome true: there is one Nature, one Art, but many Artificers. Now what things Nature makes out of the Elements, she generates them by the will of God out of the first matter, which God onely knowes: Nature makes and multiplies those things of the second matter, which the Philosophers know. Nothing is done in the world without the pleasure of God and Nature. Every Element is in its own sphere; but one cannot be without the other; one lives by vertue of the other, and yet being joined together they doe not agree; but Water is of more worth then all the Elements because it is the mother of all things; upon this swims the spirit of Fire. By reason of Fire, Water is the first matter, *viz.* by the striving together of Fire and Water, and so are generated Winds, and Vapours apt, and easy to bee congealed with the earth by the help of the crude aire, which from the beginning was separated from it . . .

A Dialogue between Mercury, the Alchymist and Nature

Upon a time there were assembled divers *Alchymists* together, and held a counsel how they should make & prepare the Philosophers stone, and they concluded that every one should declare his opinion with a vow. And that meeting was in the open aire, in a certaine meadow, on a faire cleer day. And many agreed that Mercury was the first matter thereof, others that Sulphur was, and others other things. But the chiefest opinion was of Mercury, and that especially because of the sayings of Philosophers, because they hold that Mercury is the first true matter of the Stone, also of Metalls: For Philosophers cry out and say, OUR MERCURY, &c. And so whilest they did contend amongst themselves for divers operations (every one gladly expecting a conclusion) there arose in the mean time a very great tempest, with stormes, showers of rain, and an unheard of wind, which dispersed that assembly into divers Provinces, every one apart without a conclusion. Yet every one of them fancied to himselfe what the conclusion of that dispute should have been. Every one therefore set upon his work as before, one in this thing, another in that thing seeking the Philosophers Stone, and this is done till this day without any giving over. Now one of them remembring the disputation that the Philosophers Stone is necessarily to be sought after in Mercury, said to himself: Although there was no conclusion made, yet I wil work in Mercury, and will make a conclusion my self in making the blessed Stone; for he was a man that was alwaies wont to talk to himselfe, as indeed all *Alchymists* usually doe. Hee therefore began to read the books of Philosophers, and fell upon a booke of *Alanus*,[12] which treats of Mercury; and so that Alchymist is made a Philosopher, but without any conclusion: And taking Mercury he began to work; hee put it into a glass and put fire to it, the Mercury as it is wont to do, vapoured away, the poor silly Alchymist not knowing the nature of it, beat his wife, saying: "No body could come hither besides thee, thou tookest the Mercury out of the glass." His wife crying excuseth her self and speaks softly to her husband: "Thou

---

[12] Probably Alanus de Insulis or Alain of Lille (1128–*c*.1202); Ferguson reports that "he entered the Cistercian order at Clairvaux, taught in Paris, and became Bishop of Auxerre" (*Bibl. Chem.* 1:14). Several alchemical tracts in verse were attributed to him, but see Thorndike, *HMES* 4:338–9.

wilt make a sir-reverence[13] of these." The Alchymist tooke Mercury again, and put it again into his vessell, and lest his wife should take it away, watched it. But the Mercury, as its manner is, vapoured away again. The Alchymist, remembering that the first matter of the Philosophers Stone must be volatile, rejoiced exceedingly, altogether perswading himselfe that he could not now be deceived, having the first matter. Hee began now to work upon Mercury boldly; he learned afterwards to sublime it and to calcine it divers ways, as with Salt, Sulphur, and Metalls, Mineralls, Bloud, Haire, Corrosive waters, Herbs, Urine, Vineger, but could find nothing for his purpose; he left nothing unassayed in the whole world, with which hee did not work upon good Mercury withall. But when he could doe no good at all with this, hee fell upon this saying, *that it is found in the dung-hill.* He began to worke upon Mercury with divers sorts of dung, together and asunder: and when hee was weary and full of thoughts he fell into a sleep. And in his sleep there appeared to him a vision: there came to him an old man who saluted him, and said: "Friend, Why art thou sad?" Hee answered, "I would willingly make the Philosophers Stone." Then said he, "Friend, Of what wilt thou make the Philosophers Stone?" *ALCHYMISTA.* "Of Mercury, Sir." *SENEX.* "Of what Mercury?" ALCH. "There is but one Mercury." SEN. "It is true, there is but one Mercury, but altered variously, according to the variety of places; one is purer then another." ALCH. "O Sir, I know how to purifie it very well with vinegar and salt, with nitre and vitriall." SEN. "I tell thee this is not the true purifying of it; neither is this, thus purifyed, the true Mercury: Wise men have another Mercury and another manner of purifying it," and so he vanished away. The Alchymist being raised from sleep thought with himselfe what vision this should be, as also what this Mercury of Philosophers should be: hee could bethinke himselfe of no other but the vulgar Mercury. But yet hee desired much that hee might have had a longer discourse with the old man: but yet hee worked continually, sometimes in the dung of living creatures, as boyes dung, and sometimes in his own. And every day hee went to the place where hee saw the vision, that he might speak with the old man again: sometimes hee counterfeited a sleep, and lay with his eyes shut expecting the old man. But when he would not come he thought he was afraid of him and would not beleeve that he was asleep; he swore therefore saying, "My good old Master be not afraid, for truly I am asleep; look upon my eyes, see if I be not": And the poor Alchymist after so many labours and the spending of all his goods, now at last fell mad, by alwaies thinking of the old man. And when hee was in that strong imagination, there appeared to him in his sleep a false vision, in the likeness of the old man, and said to him, "Doe not despaire, my friend, thy Mercury is good, and thy matter, but if it will not obey thee, conjure it, that it bee not volatile; Serpents are used to be conjured, and then why not Mercury?" and so the old man would leave him. But the Alchymist asked of him, saying, "Sir, expect," &c. And by reason of a noise this poore Alchymist was raised from sleep, yet not without great comfort. He took then a vessell full of Mercury, and began to conjure it divers wayes, as his dream taught him. And hee remembred the words of the old man, in that hee said, *Serpents are conjured*, and Mercury is painted with Serpents;[14] hee thought, so it must bee conjured as the Serpents. And taking a vessell with Mercury hee began to say, *Ux, Vx, Ostas, &c.* And where the name of the Serpent should be put, he

---

[13] In this context, probably human excrement (*OED*).

[14] I.e., the image of Mercury's serpent-entwined caduceus.

put the name of Mercury, saying: "And thou wicked beast Mercury," &c. At which words Mercury began to laugh and to speak unto him saying, "What wilt thou have, that thou thus troublest mee my Master Alchymist?" ALCH. "O ho, now thou callest me Master, when I touch thee to the quick, now I have found where thy bridle is, wait a little, and by and by thou shalt sing my song," and he began to speak to him, as it were angerly, "Art thou that Mercury of Philosophers?" MERC. (as if he were afraid answered) "I am Mercury, my Master." ALCH. "Why therefore wilt not thou obey mee? And why could not I fix thee?" MERC. "O my noble Master, I beseech thee pardon mee, wretch that I am, I did not know that thou wast so great a Philosopher." ALCH. "Didst not thou perceive this by my operations, seeing I proceeded so Philosophically with thee?" MERC. "So it is, my noble Master, although I would hide my selfe, yet I see I cannot from so honourable a Master as thou art." ALCH. "Now therefore dost thou know a Philosopher?" MERC. "Yea, my Master, I see that your worship is a most excellent Philosopher." ALCH. (being glad at his heart saith) "Truly now I have found what I sought for." (Again he spake to Mercury with a most terrible voice:) "Now go to, be now therefore obedient, or else it shall be the worse for thee." MERC. "Willingly, my Master, if I am able, for now I am very weake." ALCH. "Why dost thou now excuse thy selfe?" MERC. "I doe not, my Master, but I am faint and feeble." ALCH. "What hurts thee?" MERC. "The Alchymist hurts mee." ALCH. "What, dost thou still deride mee?" MERC. "O Master, no, I speak of the Alchymist, but thou art a Philosopher." ALCH. "O wel, well, that is true, but what hath the Alchymist done?" MERC. "O my Master, hee hath done many evill things to mee, for hee hath mixed mee, poor wretch as I am, with things contrary to mee: from whence I shall never bee able to recover my strength and I am almost dead, for I am tormented almost unto death." ALCH. "O thou deservest those things, for thou art disobedient." MERC. "I was never disobedient to any Philosopher, but it is naturall to mee to deride fools." ALCH. "And what dost thou think of mee?" MERC. "O Sir, you are a great man, a very great Philosopher, yea greater then *Hermes* himself." ALCH. "Truly so it is, I am a learned man, but I will not commend my selfe, but my Wife also said to mee, that I am a very learned Philosopher, she knew so much by me." MERC. "I am apt to beleeve thee, for Philosophers must be so, who by reason of too much wisdome and pains fall mad." ALCH. "Goe to then, tell me therefore what I shall doe with thee; how I shall make the Philosophers Stone of thee." MERC. "O my Master Philosopher, I know not, Thou art a Philosopher, I am a servant of the Philosophers, they make of me what they please, I obey them as much as I am able." ALCH. "Thou must tell mee how I must proceed with thee, and how I may make of thee the Philosophers Stone." MERC. "If thou knowest, thou shall make it, but if thou knowest not, thou shalt doe nothing, thou shalt know nothing by mee, if thou knowest not already my Master Philosopher." ALCH. "Thou speakest to mee as to some simple man, perhaps thou dost not know that I have worked with Princes, and was accounted a Philosopher with them." MERC. "I am apt to beleeve thee my Master, for I know all this very well, I am yet foul and unclean by reason of those mixtures that thou hast used." ALCH. "Therefore tell mee, art thou the Mercury of Philosophers?" MERC. "I am Mercury, but whether or no the Philosophers, that belongs to thee to know." ALCH. "Do but tell me if thou art the true Mercury, or if there be another." MERC. "I am Mercury, but there is another," and so he vanished away. The Alchymist cries out and speaks, but no body answers him. And bethinking himself saith: "Surely I am an excellent man, Mercury hath been pleased to talke with mee, surely hee loves mee," and then he began to sublime Mercury, distil, calcine, make Turbith[15] of him, precipitate, and dissolve him divers wayes, and with divers waters, but as hee laboured in vain before, so now also he hath spent his time and costs to no purpose. Wherefore at last hee begins to curse Mercury and revile Nature because shee made him. Now Nature when she heard these things called Mercury to her, and said to him: "What hast thou done to this man? Why doth he curse and revile me for thy sake? Why dost not thou doe what thou oughtest to doe?" But Mercury modestly excuseth himself. Yet Nature commands him to be obedient to the Sons of Wisdome that seek after him. Mercury promiseth that he will and saith: "Mother Nature, but who can satisfie fools?" Nature went away smiling: but Mercury being angry with the Alchymist goes also unto his own place. After a few days it came into the Alchymists mind, that he omitted something in his operations, and again hee hath recourse to Mercury, and now resolves to mix him with hogs dung; but Mercury being angry that he had falsely accused him before his mother Nature, saith to the Alchymist, "What wilt thou have of me, thou foole? Why hast thou thus accused mee?" ALCH. "Art thou he that I have longed to see?" MERC. "I am, but no man that is blind can see mee." ALCH. "I am not blind." MERC. "Thou art very blind, for thou canst not see thy selfe, how then canst thou see mee?" ALCH. "O now thou art proud, I speak civilly to thee, and thou contemnest mee: thou dost not know perhaps that I have worked with many Princes and was esteemed as a Philosopher amongst them." MERC. "Fools flock to Princes Courts, for there they are honoured and fare better then others. Wast thou also at the Court?" ALCH. "O thou art a devill, and not a good Mercury, if thou wilt speak thus to Philosophers: for before thou didst also seduce me thus." MERC. "Dost thou know Philosophers?" ALCH. "I my self am a Philosopher." MERC. "Behold our Philosopher" (smiling said: and began to talke further with him saying) "My Philosopher, tell mee therefore what thou seekest after, and what thou wilt have, what dost thou desire to make?" ALCH. "The Philosophers stone." MERC. "Out of what matter therefore wilt thou make it?" ALCH. "Of our Mercury." MERC. "O my Philosopher, now I wil leave you, for I am not yours." ALCH. "O thou art but a devill, and wilt seduce mee." MERC. "Truly my Philosopher thou art a devill to mee, not I to thee: for thou dost deale most sordidly with mee, after a devillish manner." ALCH. "O what doe I heare? This certainly is a devill indeed, for I do all things according to the writings of Philosophers and know very well how to work." MERC. "Thou knowest very well, for thou dost more then thou knowest, or readst of: for the Philosophers said that Nature is to be mixed with Natures; and they command nothing to bee done without Nature; but thou dost mix mee with almost all the sordid things that bee, as dung." ALCH. "I doe nothing besides Nature: but I sow seed into its own earth, as the Philosophers have said." MERC. "Thou sowest me in dung, and in time of harvest I do vanish away, and thou art wont to reap dung." ALCH. "Yet so the Philosophers have wrote, that in the dunghill their matter is to be sought for." MERC. "It is true what they have written; but thou understandest their letter and not their sense and meaning." ALCH. "Now happily I see that thou art Mercury; but thou wilt not obey mee." And he began to conjure him again, saying, *Ux Vx*. But Mercury laughing answered, "Thou shalt doe no good my friend." ALCH. "They do not

---

[15] A basic sulphate of mercury, "having emetic, cathartic, and sternutatory properties" (*OED*).

speak without ground, when they say thou art of a strange nature, inconstant and volatile."
MERC. "Dost thou say that I am inconstant, I resolve thee thus. I am constant unto a
constant Artificer; fixed to him that is of a fixed mind, but thou, and such as thou art, are
inconstant, running from one thing unto another, from one matter unto another." ALCH.
"Tell me therefore if thou art that Mercury, which the Philosophers wrote of, which they
said was, together with sulphur and salt, the principall of all things, or must I seek another?"
MERC. "Truly the fruit doth not fal far from the tree, but I seek not mine own praise,
I am the same as I was, but my years are differing. From the beginning I was young, so
long as I was alone, but now I am older, yet the same as I was before." ALCH. "Now
thou pleasest me because now thou art older: for I alwaies sought after such a one that
was more ripe and fixed, that I might so much the more easily accord with him." MERC.
"Thou dost in vain look after mee in my old age, who didst not know mee in my youth."
ALCH. "Did not I know thee, who have worked with thee divers wayes, as thou thy selfe
hast said? And yet I will not leave off till I have made the Philosophers Stone." MERC.
"O what a miserable case am I in? What shall I do? I must now be mixed again with dung
and be tormented. O wretch that I am! I beseech thee good Master Philosopher, doe not
mix me so much with hogs dung; for otherwise I shall be undone, for by reason of this
stink I am constrained to change my shape. And what wilt thou have mee doe more? Am
not I tormented sufficiently by thee? Doe not I obey thee? Doe not I mixe my self with
those things thou wilt have me? Am I not sublimed? Am I not precipitated? Am I not
made turbith? An Amalgama? A Past[e]? Now what canst thou desire more of me? My
body is so scourged, so spit upon, that the very stone would pity me:[16] By vertue of me
thou hast milk, flesh, bloud, butter, oyl, water, and which of all the metalls or minerals can
do that which I do alone? And is there no mercy to be had towards me? O what a wretch
am I!" ALCH. "O ho, it doth not hurt thee, thou art wicked, although thou turnest thy
self inside out, yet thou dost not change thy selfe, thou dost but frame to thy selfe a new
shape,[17] thou dost alwaies return into thy first forme again." MERC. "I doe as thou wilt
have me, if thou wilt have me be a body, I am a body: if thou will have me be dust, I am
dust, I know not how I should abase my self more, then when I am dust and a shadow."
ALCH. "Tell mee therefore what thou art in thy Center, and I will torment thee no more."
MERC. "Now I am constrained to tell from the very foundation. If thou wilt, thou maist
understand mee: thou seest my shape, and of this thou needest know further. But because
thou askest mee of the Center, my Center is the most fixed heart of all things, immortall
and penetrating: in that my Master rests, but I my selfe am the way and the passenger; I am
a stranger and yet live at home; I am most faithfull to all my companions; I leave not those
that doe accompany mee; I abide with them, I perish with them. I am an immortall body:
I die indeed when I am slaine, but I rise againe to judgement before a wise Judge." ALCH.
"Art thou therefore the Philosophers Stone?" MERC. "My Mother is such a one, of her
is born artificially one certain thing, but my brother who dwells in the fort, hath in his will
what the Philosophers desire." ALCH. "Art thou old?" MERC. "My Mother begat mee,
but I am older then my mother." ALCH. "What devill can understand thee, when thou

---

[16] Mercury's complaints about the pains inflicted upon him throughout the alchemical process are Sendivogius's version of the "torture of metals" motif common in alchemical writing.

[17] Mercury's reputation as a shape-shifter has its basis in the volatility of this metal, as does his teasing, mischievous, elusive character.

dost not answer to the purpose? thou alwaies speakest Riddles. Tell mee if thou art that fountain of which *Bernard* Lord *Trevisan* writ?" MERC. "I am not the fountaine but I am the water, the fountaine compasseth mee about." ALCH. "Is gold dissolved in thee, when thou art water?" MERC. "Whatsoever is with mee I love as a friend; and whatsoever is brought forth with mee, to that I give nourishment, and whatsoever is naked, I cover with my wings." ALCH. "I see it is to no purpose to speak to thee, I ask one thing and thou answerest another thing: if thou wilt not answer to my question, truly I will goe to work with thee again." MERC. "O master, I beseech thee be good to me, now I will willingly doe what I know." ALCH. "Tell me therefore if thou art afraid of the fire." MERC. "I am fire my selfe." ALCH. "And why then dost thou fly from the fire?" MERC. "My spirit, and the spirit of the fire love one another, and whither one goes, the other goes if it can." ALCH. "And whither dost thou goe, when thou ascendest with the fire?" MERC. "Know that every stranger bends towards his own countrey, and when he is returned from whence he came, hee is at rest and alwaies returnes wiser then he was when he came forth." ALCH. "Dost thou come back again sometimes?" MERC. "I doe, but in another forme." ALCH. "I do not understand what this is, nor any thing of the fire." MERC. "If any one knew the fire of my heart, hee hath seen that fire (a due heat) is my meat: and by how much the longer the spirit of my heart feeds upon fire, it will be so much the fatter, whose death is afterward the life of all things, whatsoever they bee in this Kingdome where I am." ALCH. "Art thou great?" MERC. "I am thus for example, of a thousand drops I shall be one, out of one I give many thousand drops: and as my body is in thy sight, if thou knowest how to sport with mee, thou maist divide me into as much as thou wilt, and I shall be one again: What then is my spirit (my heart) intrinsecally, which alwaies can bring forth many thousands out of the least part?" ALCH. "And how therefore must one deale with thee that thou maist be so?" MERC. "I am fire within, fire is my meat, but the life of the fire is aire, without aire the fire is extinguished; the fire prevails over the aire, wherefore I am not at rest, neither can the crude aire constringe[18] or bind mee: adde aire to aire, that both may be one and hold weight, join it to warm fire, and give it time." ALCH. "What shall bee after that?" MERC. "The superfluous shall be taken away, the residue thou shalt burn with fire, put it into water, boyl it, after it is boyled thou shalt give it to the sick by way of physick." ALCH. "Thou saist nothing to my questions. I see that thou wilt only delude mee with Riddles. Wife, bring hither the hogs dung, I will handle that Mercury some new wayes, untill hee tell mee how the Philosophers Stone is to bee made of him." Mercury hearing this begins to lament over the Alchymist, and goes unto his mother Nature: accuseth the ungratefull operator. Nature beleeves her son Mercury, who tells true, and being moved with anger comes to the Alchymist and calls him: "Ho thou, Where art thou?" ALCH. "Who is that, thus calls mee?" NAT. "What dost thou with my son, thou fool thou? Why dost thou thus injure him? Why dost thou torment him? who is willing to doe thee any good, if thou couldst understand so much." ALCH. "What devill reprehends me, so great a man, and Philosopher?" NAT. "O fool ful of pride, the dung of Philosophers, I know all Philosophers and wise men, and I love them for they love me and doe all things for me at my pleasure, and whither I cannot goe they help me. But you Alchymists, of whose order thou also art one, without my knowledge and consent, doe

---

[18] To "draw or squeeze together as by an encircling force," or constrict (*OED*).

all things contrary unto me; wherefore it falls out contrary to your expectation. You think that you deal with my sons rationally, but you perfect nothing; and if you will consider rightly, you do not handle them, but they handle you: for you can make nothing of them, neither know you how to do it, but they of you when they please, make fooles." ALCH. "It is not true: I also am a Philosopher and know well how to worke. I have been with more then one Prince and was esteemed a Philosopher amongst them; my wife also knows the same, and now also I have a manuscript, which was hid some hundreds of years in an old wall, now I certainly know I shall make the Philosophers Stone, as also within these few dayes it was revealed to mee in a dreame. O I am wont to have true dreams; Wife thou knowest it!" NAT. "Thou shalt doe as the rest of thy fellowes have done, who in the beginning know all things, and thinke they are very knowing, but in conclusion know nothing." ALCH. "Yet others have made it of thee (if thou art the true Nature.)" NAT. "It is true, but only they that knew me, and they are very few. But hee which knowes mee doth not torment my Sons; nor disturbe mee, but doth to mee what hee pleaseth, and increaseth my goods, and heals the bodies of my sons." ALCH. "Even so doe I." NAT. "Thou dost all things contrary to mee, and dost proceed with my Sonnes contrary to my will: when thou shouldst revive, thou killest; when fix, thou sublimest; when calcine, thou distillest; especially my most observant Sonne Mercury, whom thou tormentest with so many corrosive waters and so many poisonous things." ALCH. "Then I will proceed with him sweetly by digestion only." NAT. "It is well if thou knowest how to doe it, but if not, thou shalt not hurt him but thy selfe, and expose thy selfe to charges, for it is all one with him, as with a gem which is mixed with dung, that is alwaies good, and the dung doth not diminish it although it be cast upon it, for when it is washed, it is the same gemme as it was before." ALCH. "But I would willingly know how to make the Philosophers Stone." NAT. "Therefore doe not handle my Son in that fashion: for know, that I have many Sonnes and many Daughters, and I am ready at hand to them that seek mee, if they bee worthy of mee." ALCH. "Tell me therefore who that Mercury is?" NAT. "Know that I have but one such Sonne, and hee is one of seven,[19] and hee is the first; and hee is all things, who was but one; he is nothing, and his number is entire; in him are the foure Elements, and yet himselfe is no Element; he is a spirit, and yet hath a body; he is a man, and yet acts the part of a woman; hee is a child, and yet bears the armes of a man; hee is a beast, and yet hath the wings of a bird; hee is poison, yet cureth the leprosie; he is life, yet kills all things; hee is a King, yet another possesseth his Kingdome; hee flyeth from the fire, yet fire is made of him; he is water, yet wets not; hee is earth, yet hee is sowed; hee is aire, yet lives in water." ALCH. "Now I see that I know nothing but I dare not say so, for then I should lose my reputation, and my neighbors will lay out no more money upon mee, if they should know that I know that I know nothing: yet I will say that I doe certainly know, or else no body will give mee so much as bread: for many of them hope for much good from mee." NAT. "Although thou shouldst put them off a great while, yet what will become of thee at last? and especially if thy neighbours should demand their charges of thee again?" ALCH. "I will feed all of them with hope, as much as possibly I can." NAT. "And then what wilt thou doe at last?" ALCH. "I will try many ways privately: if either of them succeed, I will pay them; if not, I will goe into some other far Country

---

[19] I.e., the seven metals.

and doe the like there." NAT. "And what will become of thee afterward?" ALCH. "Ha, ha, ha, there bee many countryes, also many covetous men, to whom I will promise great store of Gold, and that in a short time, and so the time shall passe away, till at last either I, or they must die Kings, or Asses." NAT. "Such Philosophers deserve the halter: fie upon thee, make haste and be hanged and put an end to thy self and thy Philosophy; for by this meanes thou shalt neither deceive mee, thy neighbour, or thy self."

21 Robert Fludd (1574–1637)

From the *Mosaicall Philosophy*

A recent editor of Robert Fludd describes him as "the most prominent Renaissance Christian Neoplatonist alchemist of his time, and the greatest summarizer and synthesizer of that tradition of his age" (Huffman 13). To these accolades may be added his successful practice of medicine in London – which, despite sharp attacks on Aristotle and Galen, eventually resulted in Fludd's admission to the Royal College of Physicians – and his championing of the Rosicrucians. He was attacked by such giants of the New Philosophy as Kepler, Mersenne, and Gassendi; however, William Harvey and William Gilbert were influential friends. Fludd published extensively but appears to have attracted greatest interest on the Continent; he is best known today for his extraordinarily detailed study of interrelationships between the macrocosm and microcosm, the *Utriusque cosmi maioris scilicet et minoris, metaphysica, physica atque technica historia*, which directly reflects his religious and philosophical views and, accompanied by its exquisitely detailed engravings, first issued from the de Bry press in Oppenheim in 1617.

A sense of the range of Fludd's thought (with its frequent links to Paracelsus and the Neoplatonists) may be gained from his *Mosaicall Philosophy*, first published posthumously in Latin in 1638. Here may be noted, for example, his beliefs in the indebtedness of pagan philosophy to the writings of Moses; the Holy Spirit as the origin of all creation, which has its basis in the three "mosaic" principles of light, darkness, and a complex entity known as the "waters"; the world soul or *anima mundi*; man as microcosm; the doctrine of sympathies and antipathies; and the "magnetical" operation of the notorious cure known as the Weapon Salve.

Selections from Fludd's *Mosaicall Philosophy Grounded upon the Essentiall Truth or Eternall Sapience* are taken from the first English edition, published in London by Humphrey Mosely in 1659. Additional readings: Allen G. Debus, *The English Paracelsians*, 105–36 and *DSB*, s.v. "Fludd, Robert"; William H. Huffman, ed., *Robert Fludd: Essential Readings* (London: Aquarian Press, 1992).

From Bk. 2, Sec. 1, Chap. 3.

Lastly, I will conclude and finish this Chapter, with the miraculous and supernaturall effects it [i.e., the true Sophia or Wisdom] produceth, and the admirable acts which it bringeth to passe, beyond the capacity of mans imagination; for that the man which is partaker of this divine Agent, and can firmly unite it unto his own spirit, may do wonders: . . . [Scriptural passages follow, cited in Latin and English.] To conclude, *Moses, Joshua, Gideon, Samuel,*

Daniel, Elias, Elisha, with the other prophets; *Judas Maccabeus*, Christ and his Apostles, which were all the observant disciples unto the true wisdom, did by her secret art and operation, bring to passe all those miracles, which are mentioned in the holy Testament, both New and Old, as each man may find to be true, if he will be pleased to make a due enquiry into that holy story. But all this is most aptly expressed by the Prophet Daniel, in these words: *He is the revealer of things that are profound and hidden, and understandeth the things which lurk in darknesse, for light dwelleth with him* [Daniel 2:22]. All which being so, it is most apparent, that there is no art or science, whether it be abstruse and mysticall, or manifestly known, be it speculative or practicall, but had his root and beginning from this true wisdom, without the act and vertue whereof, no true and essentiall learning and knowledge can be gotten in this world, but all will prove bastardly or spuriously begotten, having their foundation not upon Christ, the true ground, firm rock, and stable cornerstone, on which all verity is erected, forasmuch as onely in him is the plenitude of divinity; but placing the basis or foundation of their knowledge upon the prestigious sands of imagination; namely, after the inventions or traditions of men, and according unto the elements of this world, from whence they gather the fruits of their worldly or human wisdom, that is quite opposite in effect unto the true wisdom; namely, the eternall one, which hath his root and originall from God, and not from man . . .

From Bk. 3, Sec. 1: Touching the essentiall Principles of the Mosaicall Philosophy. The Argument of this third Book.

In this present Book, the Author teacheth in a generality, the true and essentiall principles of the divine Philosophy; and in particular he expresseth, how various and differing the Ethnick Philosophers[1] have been in their opinions concerning the beginnings of all things; where he proveth, that the wisest amongst those Pagan Naturalists, did steal and derive their main grounds or principles, from the true and sacred Philosopher Moses, whose Philosophy was originally delineated by the finger of God, forasmuch as the fiery characters thereof, were stamped out or engraven in the dark Hyle,[2] by the eternall Wisdom, or divine Word. And sheweth, that although the foresaid pagan philosophers, did usurp the Mosaicall principles unto themselves, and, the better to maske their theft, did assigne unto them new Titles; yet because they were not able to dive into the centrall understanding of them, nor conceive or apprehend rightly, the mystery of the everlasting Word, they erected upon their principles or foundations but a vain and worldly wisdom, carved out, not from the essential Rock of truth, nor relying on Christ, the onely corner-stone, but framed after a human invention, and shaped out according unto the elements of this world; much like a Castle of straw or stubble, which though it be planted on a Rock, yet is subject to mutation, and is easily shaken, and tottered at every blast of winde. In conclusion, here our Author doth set down what the true Mosaicall principles are, namely, Darknesse, Water, and Light: Then, that all plenitude and vacuity in the world, doth consist in the presence or absence of the formall principle, which is Light. And lastly, he sheweth how the two apparent active properties, namely Cold and Heat, do issue from the two fore-said fountaines of

---

[1] I.e., the pagan or heathen philosophers, such as the pre-Socratics, Plato, and Aristotle, as opposed to those who were Jewish or Christian.

[2] Uncreated chaos; the first matter of the universe.

Darknesse and Light, as the two passive natures, Moysture and Drought, to challenge their originall from the said active . . .

From Bk. 3, Sec. 1, Chap. 1: Wherein is set down the uncertainty of the ancient Grecian and Arabian Philosophers, in their opinions, touching the principles or beginnings of all things.

Now the main errour of these [pre-Socratic] philosophers in their judgments concerning the [first metaphysical] principles, was, that they did not mark or consider, that the divine puissance or sacred word, was more ancient, and of a greater Antiquity, then were any of their foresaid principles; the which, if by a riper contemplation they had understood they would have confessed, being instructed and directed by reasons produced from the eternal unity, or essential point and beginning of all things, that the divine light, or sacred emanation (which Scriptures entitle by the name of the holy Spirit of wisdom) was the actuall beginning of all things, as nevertheless before it, there was another property in one and the same sacred essence, which was termed the divine puissance, or *potentia divina*, which did precede his act or emanation, no otherwise than the Father in time, order, and being, is justly said to exist before the Son, or the Creator before the creature: And thereupon the wise man hath it . . . *Wisdom was created before all things.*[3] And yet it is most apparent, that some of the Greekish and Ægyptian Philosophers, namely, *Plato, Pythagoras, Socrates, Hermes, &c.* did so instruct their understandings, partly by the observation of their predecessors doctrine, and partly through the experience, which in their long travails and peregrinations they had gathered, among the Æthiopians, Ægyptians, Hebrews, Armenians, Arabians, Babylonians, and Indians, (for, over all or most of these Countries did *Plato, Pythagoras, Hippocrates*, and others of them travell, for the augmentation and increase of their knowledge, as Historiographers, that are worthy of credit, have related) that without doubt they did discern, though afar off, and as it were in a cloud, the true light in the humid nature. And among the rest it is reported, as also it appeareth by his works, that *Plato* had the knowledge of the Word, and had read the Books of *Moses*; and for that reason he was called . . . *the divine Plato*. In like manner, the excellent Philosopher *Hermes*, otherwise termed *Mercurius Trismegistus*, expresseth plainly, that he was not onely acquainted with *Moses* his books, but also was made partaker of his mysticall and secret practise, as by his Sermons, which he calleth *Pymander*,[4] a man may plainly discern, where he doth mention the three Persons in Trinity, and sheweth the manner of the worlds creation, with the elements thereof, by the Word. And therefore of all other antient Philosophers, I may justly ascribe divinity unto these two: But in this I cannot much commend them, *viz.* in that they having had a view of *Moses* his labours, which were indited by the Spirit of God, did gather out, and confesse the truth of his doctrine, touching the principles of all things, and yet would not in open tearms acknowledge their Master, but altered the names of them; but as *Plato* served his Master *Moses*, even so was he dealt with by his schollar *Aristotle*, who knowing that his Masters three Mosaicall Principles of all things, masked under strange titles, were but truth, would nevertheless arrogate his doctrine unto himself,

---

[3] From the apocryphal book of Ecclesiasticus or The Wisdom of Jesus Son of Sirach 1:4.

[4] The first of the treatises, a creation account, contained in the *Corpus Hermeticum*; for Fludd and others, following Ficino's translation, *Pymander* could also designate the entire collection.

and for that cause did alter the assumed names of *Plato's* principles, gilding them over with new denominations, and did afterward rear up upon them a spurious philosophicall structure, carved and framed out after his own inventions... That Principle which *Moses* termed *darknesse, the darke Abysse*[5] or potentiall Principle, *Aristotle* doth call his *Materia prima, or first matter*, which he averreth to be something in puissance or potentially only, because it is not as yet reduced into act. Again, he seemeth to term it privation, but falsly, being that no position did precede it. On the other side *Plato* calleth it *Hyle*, which is esteemed to be nothing, forasmuch as it is invisible and without form. Also he compareth it to a dark body, in respect of the soul and spirit. As for *Hermes*, he intitleth it by the name of *umbra horrenda, or fearfull shadow*. *Pythagoras* maketh it his Symbolicall Unity: From in this its estate, it hath relation unto nothing else but it self, which is mere Unity, and consequently it acquireth not so much as the name of a Father, because it doth not by an emanation respect or attempt the production of a Son... Is not this therefore a notable kind of Robbery amongst the choisest Ethnick Philosophers, thus falsly to ascribe and attribute the Principles and Doctrine unto themselves, which were revealed by God's Spirit, unto the wise Prophet *Moses*, and that of purpose to make themselves great and eminent, not only in the eies of the Gentiles,[6] but also by subtill allurements, or false and fading suggestions, laid on those foundations, to distract Christian men from the Truth? And yet as for *Plato* and *Hermes*, I must excuse them, being that they do both of them acknowledg in express terms with *Moses*, that the matter or substance whereof the heavens and the earth were made, was a humid nature, and the internall form or act, which did dispose of it into diversity of figures or forms, was the divine Word, as you may find most plainly expressed in *Plato's* works, and in the *Pimander* of *Hermes* or *Mercurius Trismegistus*.

From Bk. 4, Sec. 1, Chap. 5: How the lower waters, or catholick sublunary element, were distinguished, ordered, and shaped out into sundry distinct sphears, which are called particular Elements, and that by the foresaid all-working Spirit, or divine Word.

Since that it is most certainly proved already, that the universall substance of the world's machine was made but of one onely thing, namely, of a matter that was produced out of the potentiall bowells of the dark chaos or abyss, by the spagerick vertue of the divine Word: the which matter *Moses* tearmed Waters, and *Hermes* the humid nature, of the which in generall (as both *Moses* and St. *Peter* aver) the heavens and the earth were made of old, it must needs follow, that out of this catholic masse of waters, the universall sublunary element was derived, which is commonly termed by the name of *Aer*, as all that humid substance in the celestiall orbe is called *Æther*. Now this generall element is by the breath of the divine Spirit *Ruach Elohim*, altered and changed from one shape unto another; for that which is the visible waters, was made first of the aire, which is an invisible water, as again the visible water by condensation is made earth. And this is proved, first, by the words of St. *Paul* [Heb. 11:3 cited]. But besides these proofs, we are taught by chymicall experience, that earth is nothing else but coagulated waters; nor visible water anything else, but invisible air, reduced by condensation to a visibility; nor fire anything else but

---

[5] "And the earth was without form, and void; and darkness was upon the face of the deep" (Gen. 1:2). Cf. the selection from Aristotle's *Meteorology*.

[6] Another term for the "Ethnick Philosophers."

rarified aire. And, in conclusion, all the sublunary waters were in the beginning, but an invisible, humid, or watry spirit, which we call by a common name, *Aire*.

From Bk. I, Sec. 2, Chap. 4: Where it is evidently proved, as well by the ancient Ethnick Philosophers, as by the authority of Holy Scriptures, that there is a soul of the world: Herein also is expressed what this catholick Soul is, and whereof it is composed or made.

In like manner the Platonists did call the generall vertue, which did engender and preserve all things the *Anima mundi*, or *the soul of the world*.[7] And to this their opinions, the *Arabick Astrologians* do seem to adhere: forasmuch as they did maintain, that every particular thing in the world hath his distinct and peculiar soul from this vivifying Spirit. To this opinion also *Mercurius Trismegistus, Theophrastus, Avicenna, Algazel*,[8] and as well all the Stoicks and Peripateticks, do seem wholly to consent or agree. Again, *Zoroaster* and *Heraclitus*, the *Ephesian*, conclude that the soul of the world is that catholick invisible fire, of which and by the action whereof, all things are generated and brought forth from puissance unto act. *Virgil*, that excellent Latine Poet, calleth it that mentall Spirit, which is infused through every joint and member of the world, whereby the whole Mass of it, namely the heaven and the earth, or spirit and body, are after an abstruse manner agitated and moved...

The wiser sort of Alchymists do make the Soul a certain infinite nature, or power in all things, which doth procreate like things of their like: for this nature doth engender all things, yea, and multiplieth, and nourisheth, or sustaineth them: and they also style it the *Ligament*, or *bond of the elements*, since by it they are fastned together with the Symphoniacal accords of peaceable harmony, although of themselves, that is in regard of their matter, they are dissonant. Also it is termed the true virtue, that mingleth and proportionateth every thing in this sublunary world, allotting unto each specifick creature a convenient and well agreeing form, that thereby one thing might be distinguished and made to vary from another: and, in conclusion, the mysticall *Rabbies* do averre, that this occult fire is that Spirit of the Lord, or fiery love, which when it moved upon the waters, did impart unto them, a certain harmonious and hidden fiery vertue, without whose lovely assistance and favorable heat, nothing could be generated of them, or multiplied in them.

Thus you may discern the manifold opinions, as well of Christian as Heathen Philosophers touching this *Anima mundi*, or *soul of the world*, which will appear to vary little or nothing at all from the tenet of Holy Scripture in sense, but in words onely...

From Bk. 1, Sec. 2, Chap. 5: How all particular Souls are said to spring forth or proceed, and then afterwards to have their preservation and multiplication, from this generall Anima Mundi, or Soul of the World.

Hermes (called also for another reason *Mercurius Trismegistus*) said rightly, that the world was made after the similitude or Type of God, and therefore as the one is termed *Archetypus*, so also the other is said to be *Typus*: For this reason therefore in another place he saith[9]...
God is the Father of the World, the world is the father of them that are in the world, and the world is the off-spring of God, and it is rightly called Cosmos, because it adorneth with verity every kind

---

[7] Cf. the "Body and Soul" sec. from Plato's *Timaeus* in this collection.

[8] Al-Gazzali or Algazel was an early Arabic writer on magic, fascination, and the occult (see *HMES*, vols. 2 and 3 passim).

[9] I.e., in Discourse 9 of the *Hermetica*.

of generation, and also with a never ceasing operation of life, and a perpetuall celerity of necessity in the commixtion of the Elements, which by order are brought forth, &c. In all this he varieth not from Scriptures: For that in the beginning, God is said to have made the world of a matter without a form, and to have adorned his humid nature or the heavens with his vivifying Spirit, which filleth and operateth all in all … and that from the breath of the self-same Spirit of life, all the creatures of the world are animated, and from the substantiall Elements in the world they receive their matter. So that as God by the pouring forth of his bright vivifying and all-acting Spirit, did make the humid and passive nature of the world to operate, and that so animated Spirit which is mixed, *secundum totum & in qualibet ejus parte, in all and every part*, with his increated Animatour, is rightly called the Soul of all the Universe; So we ought to make no question at all, but that every particular Soul in this vaulted machine of the world, doth depend and is procreated, preserved, and multiplied from that catholick Soul, because it is an axiom infallible among Philosophers, that the whole doth comprehend each part, and again, each particular hath his existence and being from the whole … And therefore *Hermes* spake not amiss, when he said that the world was the Image of God, and man the image of the world: being that as God created and vivifyed the watery Spirit of the world, by adding unto it his creating Spirit of life, so that Spirit of life (which is all one in essence with the Father) being sent into the world, and filling the Spirit of the world doth vivify, multiply, and preserve, not onely man, but also every other animal, vegetable, and minerall, that is in the world …

The spirit of life was by God so inspired into man, that he was made a living creature, no otherwise then when *Elohim Ruach*[10] was breathed on the waters, they were animated and vivified, and became a great world, which the Platonists for that reason called, *Magnum animal, A great living creature.*[11] But as the world was made after the image of God, before man was made, and afterwards man by the same Spirit in the world, was framed by the Word, after the pattern of that Spirit of life, and the substance of the waters, which were in the great world. Therefore we must conceive that man hath the vivifying means of his sustentation, preservation, and multiplication, by generation from the soul of the world, and his elements. Wherefore *Hermes* doth not unadvisedly expresse the descent and ingression of the worlds vivifying spirit into man, after this manner, *Aer est in corpore, anima in aere, mens in anima, in mente verbum; Verbum vero est eorum pater. The aire is in the body, the soul or life is in the aire, the mentall Spirit is in the soul, the Word is in the mentall Spirit; and the Word is the Father of them all* … Whereby we may discern, the admirable tie, which every portion of each dignity in the great world hath unto other, in the composition of the little world …

From Bk. 2, Sec. 2, Chap. 1: That Sympathy is the off-spring of Light, as Antipathy hath its beginning from Darkness.

Since the radical and essential Unity, with its two opposite branches or properties, which are the characters of his *Nolunty* and *Volunty*,[12] have in generall terms been thus evidently described unto you, with the two catholick effects thereof, namely love and hatred, and all

---

[10] The previously-mentioned breath of the divine Spirit.

[11] Cf. Plato's "the world came into being – a living creature truly endowed with soul and intelligence by the providence of God," ("The Creator" sec. from the *Timaeus*).

[12] *Volunty* is "Will, desire, pleasure; that which one wishes or desires" (*OED*). *Nolunty* is the opposite, as the following discussion makes clear.

those passions as well spirituall as corporall, which are derived from them, whether they be good or bad, in respect of the creature that suffereth: I think it now most fit, to enter into our main discourse, and to anatomise the secret bowels of that Sympathy and Antipathy, which is not onely seen and made manifest in naturall but also supernaturall creatures by effect. For no man of learning can be so ignorant and blind, being instructed by daily experience, (which is the mother even of very fools) as not to discern the hidden miracles both of heavenly and earthly things, daily shining forth in Sympathy and Antipathy, that is, in concords and discords, which are caused by reason of a secret league or friendship, which is betwixt them, even from their very mixtion in their first creation? But before we presume to enter into this profound discovery, it will be requisite to lay open the signification or Etymology of them both, that thereby we may the better conceive their distinct natures and essences.

[Sympathy] imports a passion, bred of unity, concord, and love, tearmed more properly compassion; and the other [i.e. Antipathy] an odible passion, mooved by two resisting and fighting natures, of a contrary fortitude: I may therefore rightly define Sympathy to be a consent, union, or concord, between two spirits, shining forth, or having their radical emanation from the self-same or the like divine property. As for example: All creatures that participate of those benigne emanations or beams, which are sent out from God, by his Angelicall Organs into the orbe of *Jupiter*, are from thence emitted down to the earth, and are conferred upon a multitude of creatures, that were created under this property; which, for that reason, do shine forth and emit their beams unto one another here upon earth, lovingly and joyfully, namely because they proceed all from one root; which descendeth unto *Jupiter*; also such as are friends to *Jupiter*, or like unto him in condition, send down influences in creatures, which are acceptable unto such as live, from their nativities, and are sustained and have their complexionary faculties from *Jupiter*, and therefore they send forth beams of friendship or benignity unto one another, as are also *Venus*, &c. But contrariwise, where the influences which are adverse in property, or of an opposite divine emanation, are sent down unto the Planet *Mars*, which is enemy to *Jupiter*, and from thence are poured out on creatures beneath, there will be ill and unwelcome encounters made between the secret emissions of those creatures beams: So that one by a naturall instinct doth seek to fly and escape the encounters of the other, or to resist and fight against the other...

From Bk. 3, Sec. 2, Chap. 6: How the feisibility and possibility of the Magneticall manner of cure by the Weapon-salve is produced and demonstrated to be naturall.

If after the wound is made, a portion of the wound's externall blood, with his inward spirits, or of his internall spirits onely, that have penetrated into the weapon, or any other thing, which hath searched the depth of the wound, be conveyed from the wound, at any reasonable, but unlimited or unknown distance, unto an Ointment, whose composition is Balsamick,[13] and agreeing specifically with the nature of the creature so wounded, and be in a decent and convenient manner adapted, and, as it were, transplanted or grafted into it; the oyntment so animated by those spirits will become forthwith magneticall, and apply with a magneticall aspect or regard unto the beamy spirits, which stream forth invisibly from the wound, being directed thereunto by those spirituall bloody spirits in the weapon,

[13] "Having the healing properties of balsam; soothing, restorative, health-giving" (*OED*).

or other thing, which hath received or included them; and the lively and southern beams streaming and flowing from the wound, will with the northern attraction of the oyntment, so magnetically animated, concur and unite themselves with the northern and congealed, or fixed bloody spirits contained in the oyntment, and stir them to act southernly, that is, from the center to the circumference; so that by this reciprocall action, union, or continuity, the lively southern beams will act and revive the chill, fixt, or northern beams, which do animate the oyntment with a magneticall vertue, and quickned spirits of the oyntment, animated by the spirits of them both, and directed by the spirits which were first transplanted into it, doth impart by the said union or continuity, his balsamick and sanative vertue unto the spirits in the wound, being first magnetically attracted; and they afterwards by an unseperable harmony, transfer it back again unto the wound. And this is the reason of that sympatheticall and antipatheticall reference or respect, which is by experience observed to be between the oyntment and the wound, so that if the whole space of the weapon that made the wound, be covered and annointed with the unguent, and the unguent be well wrapped and kept warm, the wound will find consolation, and be at ease; but if a part of the oyntment be pared away, or wiped off from the weapon, it hath been often tryed, that pain or dolour will immediately ensue and afflict the wound. Moreover, if the place anoynted be kept temperately warm, the wound will also rest in temper; but if it be uncovered and left in the open cold aire, then will it happen, that the wound will also be distempered and vexed with cold.

The particulars of the foresaid Proposition are easily proved and maintained by such ocular demonstrations, as may be produced from the vertuous operation of the mineral Load-stone, unto the which we may rightly compare all magneticall bodies, with their actions, because they have their denominations from the mineral magnet, and therefore this weapon-salve is tearmed by some men, *Unguentum magneticum*, and the cure is also called Magneticall.

22 Gabriel Plattes (first half of seventeenth century)

A Caveat for Alchymists

In 1655, Samuel Hartlib, the educational reformer and friend of Milton and Pepys, published a small collection of miscellaneous tracts entitled *Chymical, Medicinal, and Chyrurgical Addresses*. One exception to the general anonymity of the nine works he included is Gabriel Plattes's short piece bearing the long title, *A Caveat for Alchymists, or, a Warning to all ingenious Gentlemen, whether Laicks or Clericks, that study for the finding out of the Philosophers Stone; shewing how that they need not to be cheated of their Estates, either by the perswasion of others, or by their own idle conceits.* Very little is known about Plattes, other than that he, like Hartlib, was interested in improving the practical arts of agriculture and mining and published a few titles on these topics before the Restoration. He is said to have died in poverty and neglect (see the *DNB*, s.v. "Plattes, Gabriel"). Plattes makes his didactic purpose in writing the *Caveat* abundantly clear at the beginning and end of the tract; we suspect, however, that entertainment – including a wholly unsatisfactory summary of Chaucer's *Canon's Yeoman's Tale* in the "fourth Cheat" – was no less important. The text, slightly abbreviated and modernized, is taken from Hartlib's collection.

The first Chapter

Whereas I am shortly to demonstrate before the High and Honourable Court of Parliament in *England*, that there is such a thing feisible as the Philosophers Stone; or to speak more properly, an Art in the transmutation of Mettals, which will cause many a thousand men to undo and begger themselves, in the searching for the same: I cannot chuse but to publish these advertisements, for that is a fundamental point in my Religion, to do good to all men, as well enemies as friends: If I could be satisfied, that the publishing thereof, would do more good than hurt; then the world should have it in plain terms, and as plain as an Apothecaries receit: But in regard that I have often vowed to God Almighty upon my knees, to do the greatest good with it, that my understanding could perswade me unto, I have craved the advice of the Honourable Parliament, for that I have strongly conceived an opinion, that by the well contriving of the use of it, the worlds ill manners may be changed into better: if this can be done, then I should break my vow to God, if I should not do my best endeavours, and therefore I dare not to cheat God Almighty (having obtained this blessed science of his free gift) and go into a corner, and there eat, drink and sleep like a swine, as many have done before me, upon whom this blessed knowledge, hath been unworthily bestowed: but had rather improve it to his glory, if my counsel craved shall so think fit. But howsoever my meaning is to do some considerable good with it howsoever, that is, to make my self a sea-mark, to the end, that no ingenious Gentleman shall from henceforth be undone by the searching for this noble Art, as many have heretofore been.

Therefore my first Caveat shall be to shew, that no man needs to be damnified[1] above the value of 20.s. to try whether he be in a right way to it, or not?

The second Caveat shall be, to shew a way how to try whether any wandring Alchymist, that promiseth golden mountains, know any thing or not?

The third Caveat shall be, to shew how any mans Judgement ought to be grounded by a Concordance of the best books, before he fall to practice?

The fourth Caveat shall be, to shew which are false books, and which are true ones, to the end that every student in this excellent Art may trouble himself with fewer books, till he hath made a Concordance, and hath gathered the same out of the aenigmatical discourses, and hieroglifical figures, wherein this Art is hidden, and never to be found in plain terms, nor written plainly in any receipt.

Well for the first Caveat, that no man needs to be damnified above 20.s. to know whether he be in a right way, or not, let him be pleased to consider, that without *putrefactio unius*, there can be no *generatio alterius*;[2] as in all other sublunary bodies, as well Animals as Vegetables, right so in Minerals and Metals.

Therefore he that cannot take one ounce of the filings of copper, or any other base Mettal, and by an ingenious addition of a Mineral moisture of the same kind, putrefie the same in a few moneths, and make it totally volatil, except a few faeces of no considerable weight, then he is out of the way, and is not to meddle with gold or silver, or any thing of great price: for he shall never obtain his desire (though he spend his whole life, time and estate).

Also he that hath not gathered a Concordance, by reading of books, which cannot be controlled by humane wit, is not fit to begin to practice this noble Art, and not in one part thereof, but in six several parts, which are these that follow.

First, it is clear that he must have a Mineral spirit, before he can dissolve a Mineral body, or else he will work out of kind; and if he think that Quicksilver, which is sold at the Apothecaries shops, is this Mineral spirit, then he is deceived, and will find it to be so; but the truth is, that if nature had not created quicksilver, this Art could never have been found; not that it can be made the Philosophical dissolvent, by any preparation whatsoever, but without it the first dissolvent (for there are three) cannot be gotten: for it only hath power to separate this Mineral spirit, from a crude Mineral, taken from the mine, which the fire hath never touched, and no other thing under heaven can do it else, no more than any creature besides a Bee, can extract hony out of a flower.

Secondly, that he must know the secret of dissolution, which is not by the common way used by Alchymists, but by the way meant by *Bernardus Comes Trevisanus*, where he saith *hujus dissolutionis via paucissimis est nota*:[3] and I know not one Alchymist this day, nor ever did, to whom, if I should have given him the true dissolvent in one hand, which is a ponderous bright water, and the dissolvend in the other hand, which is a powder or filings of mettal: yet he knew not how to dissolve it.

---

[1] Suffer the loss of (*OED*).   [2] "Without putrefaction of one there can be no generation."
[3] "The way of this dissolution is known to very few."

Thirdly, he must know what is meant by the hollow Oak, a comparison not very unfit for the furnace, wherein this secret of dissolution, is to be accomplished.

Fourthly, he must know the reason and manner of refixing his bodies when he hath made them volatil, by this secret way of dissolution.

Fifthly, he must know the secret of projection, which hath beguiled many, when by their great charges, study and labour, they have made the Philosophers Stone, so that they could make no use it. For when it is mingled with the imperfect metals, yea, though prepared philosophically, not vulgarly, yet there is another thing to be done, before the mettal transmuted goeth to the test, or else all is lost: and if any one will not believe me, let him read the books of *Raymundus Lullius*, and he shall finde in three several places, in several books, that after projection, the matter must be put in *cineritio*, in *vasi longo*, but he saith also, *non intelligas quod ponas plumbum in cineritio*:[4] for there is something to be separated by the Art of the Philosopher, before the lead come to do its duty, or else all will be gone according to the saying: *totum vertitur in fumum, quicquid ineptus agit*.[5]

Sixthly, he must know the fire and the regiment thereof; and also the nature, which is to be gentle, continual, compassing round about the matter, and not burning it.

And now that I have shewed what an Artist must know, or else all his labour and charge is lost, I wish every man to consider what a hazard he undergoeth, if he meddle without the knowledge of these six secrets, for so much as he may very well faile, though he have them, I mean, though he have the Theorick, yet he may fail in the Practick.

Therefore if any smoak seller, or wandring Alchymist, shall come to any ingenious Gentleman that studieth this Art, though he bring with him a recipe that promiseth golden mountains, and maketh affidivit, I mean that searcheth never so deeply, that he hath done it, or seen it done, which is a common trick amongst wandring Alchymists: believe him not, unless he can satisfie you concerning all the six former mentioned secrets, for, if you do believe him having not that knowledge, I will give my word for him, that he shall cozen you. For there is but *unica via, unica operatio*,[6] to accomplish any work in Alchymie, which is as hard to be found, as the way to heaven in this world, where there are an hundred Religions, or rather an hundred Sects of Religion, wherein the true Religion is smothered and bemisted, even as the way to make the Philosophers Stone is, by the idle conceits of men that are ruled by opinion, more than by knowledge.

As for example, one *Petrus Bonus ferrariensis*,[7] a great learned man, and a Doctor of the chair of an University, wrote a book called *Margarita Pretiosa*, and penned it most admirably, concerning the Philosophers stone, and the way to make it; and when he had done, confessed that he never had made it, yet he guessed indifferent well, but all his directions are not worth a button. I would give an impression of his books away freely, that I had his School-learning, but as for his knowledge, I would not give two pence: whereby it may be seen how easily wise men may be deceived, and therefore let fools look about them before they attempt this noble science.

---

[4] "... after projection, the matter must be put in *cineritio* [cupel or test], in a long vase or glass, but he saith also, note that you do not put the lead in an oven." On *cineritio*, see Roger Bacon, *Radix Mundi*, n. 5.

[5] "Whatever a fool does turns to smoke."   [6] "One sole way, one sole procedure."

[7] Petrus Bonus's influential alchemical text, the *Pretiosa margarita novella* (*The Precious New Pearl*) was purportedly written about 1330 in Istria, rather than Ferrara as Plattes here notes. Little is known with certainty of the author, and the work was first edited by Janus Lacinius and published in Venice in 1546 (see *HMES* 3: chap. 9).

Also one *Gaston Dulco Clavens*, a great Champion that quarrelled with all opposers of this sacred Art, and wrote a book which is greatly esteemed by Alchymists, and seemeth very rational to all those which have not the practick, wherein he defendeth the truth of this Art by 32 Arguments and many experiments, which are all false, upon my certain knowledge, and if my purse could speak, it should swear it.[8]

And many others have written upon this subject, which knew nothing but what they had collected out of books, to what end, I know not, unless it were to draw other learned men unto them, thinking to gain some knowledge by their conference.

Also another, whose name I have forgotten (for it is a great while since I read any books) wrote a book intituled *De interitu Alchymie*,[9] which is as foolish as any of the other, unless that when all his hopes were at an end, he thought that some man would have come unto him, and confuted him, by shewing him the experience of it.

Well thus much for false books; now as for true ones, I could name many that could not be written but by those that had made certain trial of the work; but for brevity sake, *and to keep this book within the price promised, viz. two pence*, I will name onely four, viz. *The Compound of Alchymie*, written by *Georgius Ripleus Anglus*, *The Hierogliphical Figures of Nicholaus Tilamellus*,[10] whose body lieth buried in *Paris*: The works of *Raymundus Lullius*; The two books of *Bernardus Comes Trevisanus*. These four men shewed by their actions, that they had the Art of the transmutation of Mettals. For *Georgius Ripleus Anglus* maintained an Army of souldiers at *Rhodes* against the Turks, at his own charge: *Nicholaus Tilamellus* builded up seven Churches and seven Hospitals at *Paris*, and endowed them with good revenues, which may be easily proved: *Raymundus Lullius* made gold in the Tower of *London*, to furnish an *Army* to go against the Turks: *Bernardus Comes Trevisanus*, recovered his Earldome again, which he had formerly spent in the seeking of this Art. And now me thinks, I hear every one demanding, how shall we do to find out this great secret?

But *Geber*, an *Arabian* Prince and a famous Philosopher, shall answer in his own words, viz. *non per lectionem librorum, sed per immensam cognitionem, per profundam imaginationem, & per assiduam praxim*: and when all this is done, he concludeth that *est donum Dei Altissimi, qui cui vult, largitur, & subtrahit*.[11]

Well now me thinks I hear the cousening Alchymists saying, what shall we do now, we have no other living? To which I answer, that I would gladly rid the world of cheaters if I could: but if they must needs couzen, then let them trade with those that have so little love to art, that they cannot afford to read this book to defend themselves, and that will improve the wits of the world very much, so that it may possibly do more good than hurt: for the truth is that the world is unhappy, only for want of wit, which I have demonstrated in a little book lately printed,[12] which sheweth how any Kingdome may live in great plenty,

---

[8]   This work is Gastone Dulcone Claveo's *Philosophia chymica tribus tractatibus comprehensa* (Lugduni [Lyon]: Apud Johannem Vignon, 1612).

[9]   "On the Destruction of Alchemy": Nicolas Guibert was the author of *De interitu alchymiæ metallorum transmutatoriæ tractatus* (Toul: S. Phillippe, 1614).

[10]   I.e., Nicolas Flamel or Flammel.

[11]   "Not by the reading of books, but through immense thinking, through deep imagination & diligent practice . . . it is the gift of Highest God who bestows it or withholds it from whom he will."

[12]   Plattes appears to be referring to his *Profitable Intelligencer, communicating his knowledge for the generall good of the common-wealth and all posterity; containing many rare secrets and experiments*, printed in London, 1644.

prosperity, health, peace and happiness, and the King and Governours may live in great honour and riches, and not have half so much trouble, as is usual in these times: and if any one shall be cheated, and lay the fault upon me for discovering of cheats in this book, I cannot help it: for he that is willing to do good, must needs do some hurt, unless men were Angels. But in this case I see not but my action is justifiable: for first, I have given every one an antidote against cheating, and if they will not take it, let them be cheated, and then I will shew them a way to recover their losses, by an experiment tried upon my self: for till I was soundly cheated of divers hundred pounds, I thought my self to be a very knowing man: but then I found that I was a fool, and so disdained not to learn wit at any bodies hands that could teach me, whereby I attained a considerable quantity of knowledge, which I will not give or change, for any mans estate whatsoever; but though I sped so well by being cheated, yet I wish all others to take heed, for fear least that their fortunes prove not so good as mine.

The Second Chapter

Whereas I have professed my self to be an Anti-cheater, it behoveth me to discover the several ways whereby the world is so universally cheated by the cosening Alchymists: and therefore though I could discover fourscore cheats, yet at this time I will onely discover four grand ones, and so conclude.

The first shall be to discover the knavery of [Edward] *Kelly*,[13] the grand Impostor of the world, whom the Emperour of *Germany* kept prisoner in a Castle, and maintained him honourably, thinking either by fair means or by foule, to get the Philosophers Stone out of him, who God knows had it not, but made divers cosening projections before great men, which by the report thereof, have caused many to spend all that ever they had; and it cannot be well estimated, how many hundred thousand pounds have been spent in *Europe* about it, since that time, more than before.

And thus one of his projections was made before three great men sent over by Q *Elizabeth*, to see the truth of the business. He gave order to them to buy a warming panne, which they did accordingly, and brought it to him; he took a pair of compasses, and marked out a round plate in the middle of the cover thereof, and with a round chisel he took out the piece; then he put it in the fire, and when it was red hot, he put a little pouder upon it, which flowed all over it, and made it to look like to gold, which is an easie matter to be done: but when he came to fit it to the hole, he had a piece of good gold, taken out of a plate of gold by the compasses, not altered, and this by a trick of Legerdemain, or slight of hand (a thing common, for I have known a Porter that could have done it) he conveyed into the place, and delivered the warming panne into the hands of the spectators, who brought it into *England*, and the noise thereof made almost all mens ears to tingle, and their fingers to itch, till they were at the business, and raised the price of Alchymie books fearfully. Now if he had meant plain dealing, he would have given them some of his pouder home to their lodging, that they might have done the like again themselves at home, but he neither offered it, neither did they desire it, at which I marvel: for if he had denyed that, as it is like that he would, then the knavery had

---

[13] For a full and objective account of Kelly's adventures, see Michael Wilding, "Edward Kelly: A Life," *Cauda Pavonis: Studies in Hermeticism* 18, 1–2 (Spring and Fall 1999):1–26.

been presently discovered, so that this false news had not been brought into *England*, whereby many men have received great loss. Some have reported that he clipped out a sheard with a pair of Goldsmiths sheers, and then he took a little more time, and cast one of gold like to it, which is easily done: whethersoever he did, the whole scope of the business argueth cheating, and his meaning was nothing else, but by either of these wayes, to make the spectators to be less suspitious; like to a jugler that foldeth up his sleeves for the like purpose. But admit that he had the true Philosophers Stone, and that the body of a Mettal might be altered by it, and turned into true gold without reduction of it to the first matter, which is altogether unpossible: yet he was a detestable villain to publish it in such manner, to the great dammage of so many men as were thereby irritated to undoe themselves, and not to give them some Advertisements, like to these in this book, whereby they might be preserved from undergoing any considerable loss. But the old saying proved true, *qualis vita, finis ita*:[14] he lost his ears in *London* for cheating, when he was a young cousener; and when he was grown too skilfull to be discovered by men, then God Almighty took punishment of him; for he bought as much linnen cloth, pretending to make shirts and other things, as he thought would serve to let him down to the ground out at a window in the Tower of the Castle wherein he was a prisoner; and whether his hold slipped, or the cloth was too short, I could never learn certainly; but it is certain that he fell down and broke his bones and died, and there was an end of him . . .

The third Cheat

An Alchymist travelled with this cheat into many Kingdoms and Countries, and it may be done by one that hath not the Art of Legerdemain, or slight of hand; and thus it was done. He filed a twenty shilling piece of gold into dust, and put it into the bottom of a crucible, or a Goldsmiths melting pot, then he made a thin leaf of wax of a fit breadth, and rammed it down a little hollow in the middle, & with an hot iron sodered it, then he painted it over with a paint hereafter mentioned, and dried it, and painted it again, and thus did till it was like the crucible; and when he wanted mony, he would go to a rich hostess in some City, and take a chamber for a week, and when he had been there a day or two, and had payed royally, the next morning he would be sick, and keep his bed, and when his Hostess came to visit him, he would ask her, if she could help him to a Goldsmith, that would do some business for him, and he would pay him for his pains very largely, so she was ready, and brought one. He asked him if he could do him one hours work or two presently, the Goldsmith answered him, yes Sir, with all my heart: so he took his purse from under his pillow, and gave him half a crown, and prayed him to buy half an ounce of quicksilver, and bring it to him presently. The Goldsmith did so; then he gave him his key, and prayed him to open his portmantle, and take out a little box and open it, where he found a crucible, and a little Ivory box, filled with the red pouder of Vermillion; the Cheater prayed him to weigh out a grain of the red pouder, with his gold weights, which he did; then he bid him look well upon the crucible if it were a good one, and not cracked in the carryage; the Goldsmith said it was as sound an one as he had seen, and had a good strong bottom. Then he bid him to put it into the quicksilver, and the grain of red pouder, and set it

---

[14] "As the quality of life, so its end."

into the fire, and by degrees melt it down. The Goldsmith did so; when it was melted, he bid him set it by to cool, and then break it; then he lay down in his bed, and after a little while, he asked the Goldsmith what he found in the bottom, to which the Goldsmith answered that he found a little lump of gold, as good as ever he saw, so he prayed him to help him to money for it, for his money was almost all spent; that I will, said the Goldsmith presently, and went home, and weighed it, and brought him nineteen shillings in silver, and was desirous to know, how that red pouder was made; he said it was an extract out of gold, which he carried with him in his long travels, for ease of carriage, and that there was no other grain in it, or else he would tell it him. So the Goldsmith asked him how much he would have again of his half crown, and he should have all if he please; for he was well enough paid for his work, in seeing that rare piece of Art: no said the Alchymist, take it all, and I thank you too; so the Goldsmith took his leave, with great respect: then he laid down in his bed a little while, and by and by he knocked for his Hostess, who came immediately, and he prayed her to call for a porter; whilst that he wrote a note, she did so. When the porter came, he sent him to his fellow cheater, who lay in the other end of the Town, who presently brought him a letter formally framed betwixt them; upon the reading whereof, he called for his Hostess again, and desired her to fetch the Goldsmith again, she did so; when she brought him, he [the Alchymist] was rising, and gruntled[15] and groaned, and told the goldsmith, that though he was not well, yet necessity forced him to go about earnest business, and shewed him the Letter, and prayed him to read it whilst he put on his cloaths, and when the Goldsmith had read it, he said, you see what a strait I am in for twenty pounds, can you furnish me, and to morrow or next day you shall work for me, and pay your self, and I will leave you my box in pawn, which now you know how to make five hundred pounds of it, as well as I? The Goldsmith answered, it shall be done, and went down and told the Hostess all things; and also told her, that the Gentleman was in great distress for twenty pounds, and that he had promised to furnish him instantly, but he had but ten pounds by him; if she pleased to furnish him with the other ten pounds, she should be sure enough to have it with great advantage, for so short a time: for saith he, we shall have his box in pawn and will make bold with twice as much of his pouder, as our money comes to; and besides that, he will pay us royally I warrant you; and all the while I can do the work so well, that I should be glad never to hear of him more. So she agreed, and they brought him up twenty pounds presently, whereupon he delivered them the box, and made a motion to have it sealed up; but at length he said, that because they had furnished him in his necessity, and because he esteemed them to be honest people, in regard of his Host, he would not stay to seal it and so took his leave, and prayed the Goldsmith to be ready within a day or two, to help him to work, but from that day to this, they never saw him. So when he came not again within a week or fortnight, they concluded that some misfortune had happened to him, or that he had taken cold by going abroad so hastily, being not well, and so was dead, for else he would have sent about it before that time, if he were but sick; so they resolved to make use of it and fell to work with great alacrity; but when they could make no gold, their hearts were cold, and they found themselves to be miserably cheated.

[15] "To grumble, murmur, or complain" (OED).

The fourth Cheat

This Cheat is described in old Chawcer, in his *Canterbury* Tale;[16] but because everyone hath not that book, I will relate it briefly, and those that would see it more largely described, shall be referred to the said book.

And thus it was done: The Cheater took a charcoal about two inches long and one inch thick, and did cleave it through the middle, and made a little concavity in the middle thereof, and put in a little ingot of gold, weighing an ounce, into the middle of it, and glewed it up again, so that it seemed to be nothing, but a very coal. Then before [i.e. in the presence of] the cheated, he put in one ounce of quicksilver into a crucible, and a little red powder with it, and bid the cheated to set it into the fire, and when it began to smoak, oh saith he, I must stir it a little, to mingle the pouder with the Mercury, or else we shall have great loss; so he took up a coal from the heap with the tongs, like to his coal which he had prepared, and let it fall out of the tongs by the side of the heap, and dropped down his own coal by it, and took it up in room of the other, and stirred the quicksilver and the pouder together with it, and left the coal in the pot, and then bid the cheated to cover the pot with charcoals, and to make a good fire, and after a little space to blow it strongly with a pair of good hand bellows, til it was melted, for he assured him, that the quicksilver would be fixed and turned into gold, by the vertue of that small quantity of pouder; which the cheated found by experience, as he verily thought, and so was earnest with the cheater to teach him his Art, but what bargain they made I have forgotten, for it is twenty years since I read *Chawcers* book.

Now whereas I have received the reports of some of these Cheaters in divers manners, yet I am sure that they being wrought according to my prescription, will cheat almost any man that hath not read this book or *Chawcers*, unless a man should happen upon one that knoweth the great work, which is hardly to be found in ten Kingdoms; for he knoweth that none of these things can be done unless they be meer albifications or citrinations, but are nought else but sophistications and delusions, and will abide no triall, unless it be the eyes of an ignorant man that hath no skill in mettals.

Well now I will adde some more Caveats to fill up my book, and so make a short conclusion.

And first, To sum up all, Let men beware of all books and receipts that teach the multiplication of gold or silver with common quicksilver by way of animation or *minera*,[17] for they cannot be joyned inseparably by any *medium*, or means whatsoever. 2. Let all men beware of any books or receipts which teach any dissolutions into clear water like unto gold or silver dissolved in *aqua fortis*, or *aqua regis*, or spirit of salt, made by any way whatsoever, or any dissolution whatsoever, which is not done *cum congelatione spiritus*, according to the manner used in the great work. 3. Let all men take heed of books that teach any operations in vegetable, or animals, be they never so gloriously penned; for it is as possible for a bird to live in the water, or for a fish to live in the air, as for any thing that is not radically mettallical, to live in the lead upon the test.

And lastly, let all men beware of his own conceit of wisdom, for that hath undone many a man in this Art. Therefore let every one take notice that though it be a thousand to

---

[16] Plattes's summary of Chaucer's *Canon's Yeoman's Prologue* and *Tale* is pathetically inadequate; fortunately for the modern reader, the original is readily available.

[17] "Animation" probably means "the imparting of any physical quality or virtue" (*OED* 7); the *minera* is the "matrix in which a metal or a precious stone was supposed to grow" (*OED*).

one odds, that any seeker shal not obtain his desire, that is because many men being unfit and not quallified sufficiently to take in hand this great business; let these remember what *Salomon*, the wisest of men saith, *into a wicked heart wisdom shall not enter*,[18] and he saith not great wisdom, not much wisdom, but ordinary wisdom; then how can any wicked or foolish man hope to find out this great secret, which being the most sublime knowledge that God hath given to men, requireth the greatest wisdome to accomplish it, that God hath bestowed upon men.

Therefore if any man attempteth this Art, which hath not attained to such a perfection in the knowledge of nature, especially in minerals, that by his own speculation and practice, without the help of books, he can write a rational discourse of either animals, vegetables, or minerals, in such a solid way that no man can contradict it, without shame upon fair tryal, the questions being rightly stated, then his labour and charge is the cause why so many men fail and undo themselves in this Art; for if the search be quallified sufficiently, then it is ten to one odds, that he speedeth . . . I did not write this book with an intent to teach the Art absolutely, but onely to preserve men from undoing themselves foolishly; which if it be well considered of, will be found to be large charity.

[18] The apocryphal Wisdom of Solomon (1:4) reads, "Wisdom will not enter a shifty soul, nor make her home in a body that is mortgaged to sin," *The New English Bible with the Apocrypha* (New York: Oxford Univ. Press, 1971).

23 John French (1616?–1657)

Preface to *The Divine Pymander of Hermes Mercurius Trismegistus in XVII Books*

John French, holder of degrees from Oxford University (BA 1637, MA 1640), was a Paracelsian physician who practiced his profession with the Parliamentary army during the Civil War. He wrote the popular *Art of Distillation; or, a treatise of the choicest spagyricall preparations* that appeared in several editions beginning in 1651, and another treatise on medicinal spas in Yorkshire. Besides espousing Paracelsian iatrochemistry, French's works often reveal a strong mystical and millenarian emphasis, along with a bias against the "tyranny" of Aristotle and Galen. French was also a notable translator of alchemical and medical works; we have already seen that *A New Light of Alchymie*, the Sendivogian work included in this collection, was "faithfully translated out of the Latin into the English tongue. By J. F. M. D."

Further confirmation of French's belief in the truth of alchemy appears in his brief address "To the Reader," prefixed to the first edition of John Everard's English translation of *The Divine Pymander*[1] *of Hermes Mercurius Trismegistus*, published in 1650. He categorically affirms the authenticity of the translation's original, which can "justly challenge the first place for antiquity, from all the Books in the World, being written some hundreds of yeers before *Moses* his time." French's assertion appeared nearly forty years after Isaac Casaubon's correct dating of the Hermetic writings. The text of French's preface is from the 1650 edition of *The Divine Pymander*.

[John French] To the Reader.
This Book may justly challenge the first place for antiquity, from all the Books in the World, being written some hundreds of yeers before *Moses* his time, as I shall endevor to make good. The Original (as far as is known to us) is *Arabick*, and several Translations thereof have been published, as *Greek, Latine, French, Dutch, &c.* but never *English* before. It is pity the Learned Translator[2] had not lived, and received himself, the honor, and thanks

---

[1] Or *Pimander*, the name given to the first of the treatises, a creation account, in the *Corpus Hermeticum*; also, following the practice of Marsilio Ficino's Latin translation published in 1471, the name for the collection itself.

[2] John Everard (?1575–?1650), a non-conforming London preacher, scholar, and mystic, for whom accusations of heresy, familism, antinomianism and anabaptism brought frequent imprisonment. His was the first English translation of the *Pymander*, published the year of his death (*DNB*).

due to him from *Englishmen*; for his good will to, and pains for them, in translating a Book of such infinite worth, out of the Original, into their Mother-tongue.

Concerning the Author of the Book it self, Four things are considerable, *viz.* His Name, Learning, Countrey, and Time. 1. The name by which he was commonly stiled is, *Hermes Trismegistus*, i.e. *Mercurius ter Maximus*, or, The thrice greatest Intelligencer. And well might he be called *Hermes*, for he was the first Intelligencer in the World (as we read of) that communicated Knowledg to the sons of Men, by Writing, or Engraving. He was called *Ter Maximus*, for some Reasons, which I shall afterwards mention. 2. His Learning will appear, as by his Works; so by the right understanding the Reason of his Name. 3. For his Countrey, he was King of *Egypt*. 4. For his Time, it is not without much Controversie, betwixt those that write of this Divine, ancient Author, what time he lived in. Some say he lived after *Moses* his time, giving this slender Reason for it, *viz.* Because he was named *Ter Maximus*; for being preferred (according to the *Egyptian* Customs) being chief Philosopher, to be chief of the Priesthood; and from thence, to be chief in Government, or King. But if this be all their ground, you must excuse my dissent from them, and that for this reason, Because according to the most learned of his followers, he was called *Ter Maximus*; for having perfect, and exact Knowledg of all things contained in the World; which things he divided into Three Kingdoms (as he calls them), *viz. Mineral, Vegetable, Animal*; which Three, he did excel in the right understanding of; also, because he attained to, and transmitted to Posterity (although in an Ænigmatical and obscure stile) the Knowledge of the Quintessence of the whole Universe (which Universe, as I said before, he divided into Three Parts) otherwise called, The great *Elixir* of the Philosophers; which is the Receptacle of all Celestial and Terrestial Vertues; which Secret, many ignorantly deny, many have chargeably sought after, yet few, but some, yea, and *Englishmen*, [marginal note: "*Ripley, Bacon, Norton, &c.*"] have happily found. The Description of this great Treasure, is said to be found ingraved upon a *Smaragdine* Table,[3] in the Valley of *[H]ebron*, after the Flood. So that the Reason before alleaged to prove this Author to live after *Moses*, seems invalid; neither doth it any way appear, that he lived in *Moses* his time, although it be the opinion of some, as of *John Functius*,[4] who saith in his Chronology, That he lived Twenty one yeers before the *Law* was given by *Moses* in the Wilderness: But the Reasons that he, and others, give are far weaker then those that I shall give, for his living before *Moses* his time. My reasons for that are these; First, because it is received amongst the Ancients, that he was the first that invented the Art of communicating Knowledg to the World, by Writing or Engraving. Now if so, then in all probability he was before *Moses*; for it is said of *Moses* that he was from his childehood skilled in all the *Egyptian* Learning,[5] which could not well have been without the help of Literature, which we never read of any before that invented by *Hermes*. Secondly, He is said by himself, to be the son of *Saturn*, and by others to be Scribe of *Saturn*. Now *Saturn* according to Historians, lived in the time of *Sarug, Abrahams* great Grand-Father.[6] I shall but take in *Suidas* his judgment, and so rest

---

[3] I.e., the *Emerald Table* of Hermes Trismegistus.

[4] The name of Joannes Functius Norimberge in the *Index Librorum Prohibitorum* suggests that he was a Reformist theologian and author. He also calculated the time between the Creation and the birth of Christ as 3963 years.

[5] See Acts 7:22.   [6] On the genealogy of Abraham stemming from Serug, see Gen. 11:20–26.

satisfied that he did not live onely before, but long before *Moses*: His words are these, *Credo Mercurium Trismegistum sapientem Egyptium floruisse ante Pharaonem.*[7]

In this Book, though so very old, is contained more true knowledg of God and Nature, then in all the Books in the World besides, I except onely Sacred Writ: And they that shall judiciously read it, and rightly understand it, may well be excused from reading many Books; the Authors of which pretend so much to the knowledg of the Creator and Creation. If God ever appeared in any man, he appeared in him, as it appears by this Book. That a man who had not the benefit of his Ancestors knowledg, being as I said before, the first inventer of the Art of Communicating Knowledg to Posterity by writing, should be so high a Divine, and so deep a Philosopher, seems to be a thing more of God, then of Man; and therefore it was the opinion of some, that he came from Heaven, not born upon Earth. There is contained in this Book, that true Philosophy, without which, it is impossible ever to attain to the height and exactness of Piety and Religion. According to this Philosophy, I call him a Philosopher that shall learn and study the things that are, and how they are ordered and governed, and by whom, and for what cause, or to what end; and he that doth so, will acknowledg thanks to, and admire the Omnipotent Creator, Preserver, and Director of all these things. And he that shall be thus truly thankful, may truly be called Pious and Religious; and he that is Religious, shall more and more, know where, and what the Truth is: And learning that, he shall yet be more and more Religious.

The glory and splendor of Philosophy is an endevoring to understand the chief Good, as the Fountain of all Good: Now how can we come neer to, or finde out the Fountain, but by making use of the Streams as a conduct to it? The operations of Nature are Streams running from the Fountain of Good, which is God. I am not of the ignorant and foolish opinion of those that say, the greatest Philosophers are the greatest Atheists; as if to know the Works of God, and to understand his goings forth in the Way of Nature, must necessitate a man to deny God. The Scripture disapproves of this as a sottish tenet, and experience contradicts it: For behold! Here is the greatest Philosopher, and therefore the greatest Divine.

Read understandingly this ensuing Book (and for thy help, thou mayest make use of that voluminous Commentary written upon it [marginal note: "Hannibal Rosseli Calabar"][8] then it will speak more for its Author, then can be spoken by any man, at least by me.

Thine in the love of the Truth,

J[ohn] F[rench]

---

[7] The *Lexicon* of Suidas was a historical and literary encyclopedia dating from the tenth century, commonly cited as authoritative on early alchemy: "I believe that the wise Mercury Trismegistus lived before the Egyptian Pharaoh."

[8] French refers to the *Pymander Mercurii Trismegisti, cum commento Fratris Hannibalis Rosseli* (Krakow, 1585).

24 George Starkey/Eirenaeus Philalethes (1628–1665?)

The Admirable Efficacy, and almost incredible Virtue of true Oyl; From *An Exposition Upon Sir George Ripley's Epistle to King Edward IV*

From the start, George Starkey's career has been marked by controversy and uncertainty. Born in Bermuda and holder of BA and MA degrees from Harvard College, Starkey (or Stirk) practiced medicine for a time in America before relocating to London about 1650; there he became active in the scientific circle of Samuel Hartlib and an associate of Robert Boyle. At some point, probably before his arrival in England, he began to promote the work of a mysterious adept who wrote under the pseudonym "Eirenaeus Philalethes," with whom Starkey is usually, but not universally, identified. He published prolifically under both names until the time of his death, which perhaps resulted from exposure during the Great Plague of London. Publications continued to be issued under his name even after his death, and his influence on the development of chemistry is reflected in positive references by both Boyle and Newton.

Starkey's orientation toward healing and the formulation of new medicines is Paracelsian and iatrochemical (he often styles himself a "Philosopher by Fire"), and he was thus deeply engaged in disputes that were part of the politics of medicine in the seventeenth century. For example, an argumentative edge is often present even in the titles of his works, as in *Pyrotechny Asserted and Illustrated, to be the surest and safest means for Arts Triumph over Natures Infirmities* (1658). In the *Admirable Efficacy . . . of true Oyl*, reprinted below, Starkey argues for his own special formulation of this chemical medicine, in opposition to the false claims of his competitors. (At this time, "universal medicines" like Starkey's, along with weapon salves and potions of "drinkable gold," were staples of Paracelsian pharmacology.) In the pseudonymous *Exposition Upon Sir George Ripley's Epistle to King Edward IV*, Philalethes provides a detailed commentary on Ripley's popular dedicatory letter; the passages he cites are included in the Ripley section of this collection and should be referred to.

The text of *The Admirable Efficacy* is from the *Collectanea Chymica: A Collection of Ten Several Treatises in Chymistry*, edited by William Cooper (London, 1684); *An Exposition* is taken from Philalethes's *Ripley Reviv'd: or, an Exposition upon Sir George Ripley's Hermetico-Poetical Works*, edited by William Cooper (London, 1678). Additional readings: William R. Newman, *Gehennical Fire: The Lives of George Starkey, an American Alchemist in the Scientific Revolution* (Cambridge: Harvard Univ. Press, 1994).

The Admirable Efficacy, and almost incredible Virtue of true Oyl

Of this most noble Liquor, and not vulgar Medicine, the noble *Helmont*[1] writeth thus in his excellent Discourse concerning the Tree of Life.

In the year 1600, a certain man belonging to the Camp, whose Office was to keep account of the Provision of Victuals which was made for the Army, being charged with a numerous Family of small Children, unable to shift for themselves, himself being then 58 years of Age, was very sensible of the great care and burden which lay upon him to provide for them, while he lived, and concluded, that should he dye, they must be inforced to beg their bread from door to door, whereupon he came (saith *Helmont*) and desired of me something for the preservation of his life. I then (being a young man) pitied his sad condition, and thus thought with my self, the fume of burning *Sulphur*, is by experience found powerfully effectual, to preserve Wines from corruption. Then I recollecting my thoughts, concluded that the acid liquor or Oyl, which is made of Sulphur Vive,[2] set on fire, doth of necessity contain in it self this fume, yea, and the whole odor of the Sulphur, in as much as it is indeed nothing else, but the very Sulphurous fume imbibed, or drunk up in its Mercurial Salt, and so becomes a condensed liquor. Then I thought with my self, Our blood being (to us) no other then as it were the Wine of our life, that being preserved, if it prolong not the life, at least it will keep it sound from those many Diseases which proceed originally from corruption, by which means the life being sound, and free from diseases, and defended from pains and grief, might be in some sort spun out to a further length than otherwise. Upon which meditated resolution, I gave him a Viol glass, with a small quantity of this Oyl, distilled from Sulphur Vive burning, and taught him (moreover) how to make it as he should afterward need it; I advised him of this liquor, he should take two drops before each Meal in a small draught of Beer, and not ordinarily to exceed that Dose, nor to intermit the use of it, taking for granted, that two drops of that Oyl contained a large quantity of the fume of Sulphur, the man took my advice, and at this day in the year 1641 he is lusty and in good health, walks the Streets at *Brussels*, without complaint, and is likely longer to live, and that which is most remarkable, in this whole space of forty one years, he was not so much as ill, so as to keep his Bed, yea, although (when of great age) in the depth of Winter, he broke his Leg, near to his Ancle-Bone, by a fall upon the Ice, yet with the use of this Oyl, he recovered without the least Symptome of a Fever, and although in his old age, poverty had reduced him to great straits, and hardship, and made him feel much want of things necessary for the comfort and conveniency of Life; yet he lives healthy and sound, though spare and lean. The old mans name is *John Mass*, who waited upon *Rithovius* Bishop of *Ypre*,[3] in his Chamber, where the Earls of *Horne*, and *Egmondon* were beheaded by the Duke of *Alva*, and he was then 25 years of age, so that now he is compleat 99 years of age, healthy and lusty, and still continues the use of that liquor daily.

---

[1] Johannes Baptista van Helmont (1577–1644) has been called "the most original alchemical or iatrochemical writer of the first half of the seventeenth century" (*HMES* 7:218).

[2] The basis of Starkey's preparation is *sulphur vivum*, i.e., "Native or virgin sulphur; also, in a fused, partly purified form" (*OED*). William R. Newman refers to it as "dilute sulfuric acid" (*Gehennical Fire*, 192).

[3] A town in northwestern Belgium, near the French border.

Thus far *Helmont*, which relation as it is most remarkable, so it gives the Philosophical reason of his advice, on which it was grounded: And elsewhere the same Author relates how by this liquor he cured many dangerous deplorable Fevers, which by other Doctors had been given over for desperate. And in other places he commends it as a peerless remedy to asswage the insatiable thirst which accompanies most Fevers.

To which relation and testimony of this most learned Doctor, and acute Philosopher, I shall add my own experience.

I find it a rare preservative against corruption, not only in living Creatures, but even in dead flesh, Beer, Wine, Ale &c. a recoverer of dying Beer, and Wines that are decayed, a cure for Beer, when sick and roping;[4] Flesh by this means may be preserved so incorruptible, as no embalming in the World can go beyond it, for the keeping of a dead Carcase, nor Salting come near its efficacy, as to the conserving Meat, or Fowles, or Fish, which by this means, are not only kept from corruption, but made a mumial Balsome, which is itself a preservative from corruption, of such as shall eat thereof, which being a curious rarity and too costly for to be made a vulgar experiment, I shall pass it over, and come to those uses which are most beneficial and desirable.

It is an excellent cleanser of the Teeth, being scoured with it, they will become as white as the purest Ivory, and the mouth being washed with Oyl dropped in water or white-Wine, so as to make it only of the sharpness of Vinegar, it prevents the growing of that yellow scale which usually adheres to the Teeth, and is the forerunner of their putrefaction. It prevents their rottenness for future, and stops it (being begun) from going farther, takes away the pain of the teeth, diverts Rheums, and is a sure help for the strong favour of the Breath, making it very sweet. In a word, there is not a more desireable thing can be found, for such who would have clean or sound Teeth, or sweet Breath, or to be free from Rheums: for which use let the water be made by dropping this Oyl into it, as sharp as Vinegar, as I said before.

Against a tickling cough and hoarsness, it is a rare remedy, not only taken two or three drops, twice a day inwardly, in the usual drink one useth before each meal, but also by gargling the Throat with it, and (so used) it is excellent against swelled Throats, *Angina's*, *Struma's*,[5] Palates of the mouth inflamed, or the *Uvula* of the Throat, or the *Almonds* of the Ears,[6] which are (usually said then to be) fallen; It is excellent also against the Head-ach, and to divert Rheums from the Eyes, to wash the Temples therewith, likewise to take away *Tetters*, *Morphew*,[7] *Itch*, or *Scabs*, this dropped in water is a pleasant, safe, and effectual remedy.

Besides which outward applications, it is a Lord[8] internally taken, preventing corruption, rooting out the seeds thereof, though never so deeply concealed in the body, and upon that score opening inveterate obstructions, eradicating old pains, and preventing otherwise usual relapses into Stranguretical,[9] Colical, or Arthritical pains: it is abstersive,[10]

---

[4] "A viscid or gelatinous stringy formation in beer or other liquid" (*OED* 7.a).

[5] *Angina* is *quinsy*, an inflammatory disease of the throat; *struma* is *scrofula*, also goitre (*OED*).

[6] The tonsils (*OED* 6).

[7] *Tetters* are skin diseases marked by itching; *morphew* is a "leprous or scurfy eruption" (*OED*).

[8] In the sense of a preeminent remedy.   [9] Probably producing a strangulating effect.

[10] "Having the quality of purging, cleansing, scouring, or washing away impurities" (*OED*).

cleansing all Excrementitian setlings in the Mesaraick or Mesenterial Vessels, and so cutting off the original sourse, and taking away the cause of putrefactive corruption, which is the productive beginner of very many diseases.

On this score it lengthens the life, and frees the body from many Pains and Ailes, to which otherwise it would be subject.

It is a pleasant remedy, having only a little sharpness, which to the Palate is most gratefull, and yet this Acidity is contradistinct from that Acidity which is the forerunner of putrefaction, which it kills and destroys, as the Acidity of Spirit of Vitriol is destroyed by the fixed Acrimony of its own *Caput mortuum*,[11] or that of Vinegar, by the touch of *Cerusse* or *Minium*.

Præternatural heat and thirst in Fevers is no way allayed so speedily and easily, as by this, nor is there any thing that for a constant continuance may be more safely and profitably taken; Spirit of Salt (such as the noble *Helmont* speaks of) alone may be joyned with this, for its safety, and continual use with profit, especially in Nephritical distempers and the heat or sharpness of Urine.

Now as this is so noble a medicine, so there is none in the World more basely adulterated and counterfeited, our wise Doctors commending for it (*quid pro quo*) an adulterated mineral acidity of Vitriol, distilled in a Retort from vulgar Sulphur, which the Apostate Chemists prepare, and sell for, and the Knavish Apothecarries use, and give to their Patients instead of this true Spirit, which if sincere is clear as water, ponderous, and exquisitely acide, made of Sulphur Vive only, set on Fire without any other mixture, and the fumes received in a broad Glass, fitted for the purpose, vulgarly called a *Campana* or *Bell*, from its shape or likeness.

Most sottish is that Maxime of the Doctors, that Spirit of Sulphur and Vitriol are of one nature, when experience teacheth, that the meer Acetosity of Vitriol (which brings over nothing of its excellent vertue) will dissolve Argent Vive, which the strongest Spirit of Sulphur, truly, and not sophistically made, will not touch, nor will that recover Beer or Wines, or preserve them, as this will do, one therefore is an unripe Esurine Acetosity,[12] of little vertue: the other a Balsom of an Antidotary vertue, a preservative against corruption, and upon that score nothing can be used more effectually as a preservative against, or a remedy in, *Contagious Fevers*, *Small-Pox*, *Measles*, or *Pestilence* than this, nor more ridiculously than the other, which being drawn from the vulgar Sulphur, that hath an infection of malignity mixed with it (which it took from the Arsenical nature of the Minerals from which it was melted) adds nothing of vertue to the *crude vitriolate* Spirits, but only that which was before of little vertue, to become a Medicine of more danger and hazard, but not a jot more goodness, than it was when first drawn from the Vitriol; which being of it self clear and crude, is for to deceive the ignorant (by its Colour) tincted with some Root or Bark. Thus the credulous world is imposed on and cheated, while instead of most noble remedies (in name promised) adulterated trifles are produced, to the Disparagement of Art, and the scandal and reproach of the professors [of] Medicine.

To discover which abuses, and vindicate true Art, I have made my Præludium, concerning this Oyl or Spirit of Sulphur, the vertues of which (if truly and faithfully made) are so eminently remarkable, and almost incredibly efficatious, that I thought it not unworthy

---

[11] Literally, "death's head," the residue after sublimation or distillation of a substance is completed.
[12] A corrosive sourness or acidity.

my pains, in a few lines to communicate to the studious Reader, both what real benefit is to be expected from the true, and what injury is done to deluded (at least) if not destroyed Patients, by the Sophisticate Oyl of Sulphur.

From *An Exposition Upon Sir George Ripley's Epistle to King Edward IV*

This Epistle as it was immediately written to a King, who was in his Generation, both wise and valiant; so it doth comprize the whole secret, both learnedly described, and yet artificially vailed. Yet as the Author testifieth, that in this Epistle he doth plainly untie the main knot; So I can, and do testifie with him, that there is nothing desirable for the true attaining of this Mystery, both in the Theory and Practick of it, which is not in this short Epistle fully taught. This then I intend as a Key to all my former writings, and assure you on my faithful word, that I shall not speak one word doubtfully or Mystically, as I have in all my other writings, seeming to aver some things, which taken without a Figure, are utterly false, which we did only to conceal this Art. This Key therefore we intend not to make common; and shall intreat you to keep it secret to your self, and not to communicate it, except it be to a sure friend, who you are confident will not make it publick: And this request we make upon very good grounds, knowing that all our writings together, are nothing to this, by reason of the contradictions, which we have woven into them, which here is not done in the least measure. I shall therefore in this Epistle take up a new Method, and that different from the former, and shall first draw up the substance of the Philosophy couched in this Epistle, into several conclusions, and after elucidate the same.

The first Conclusion is drawn from the Ninth Stave [i.e. stanza] of this Epistle, the eight first Staves being only complementall; and that is, That as all things are multiplied in their kind, so may be Metalls, which have in themselves a capacity of being transmuted, the imperfect into perfect.

The second Conclusion in the Tenth Stave is, That the main ground for the possibility of transmutation, is the possibility of reduction of all Metalls, and such Minerals as are of metallick principles, into their first Mercurial matter.

The third Conclusion is in the Eleventh Stave, that among so many Metaline and *Mineral Sulphurs*, and so many *Mercuries* there are but two *Sulphurs* that are related to our work, which *Sulphurs* have their *Mercuries* essentially united to them.

The fourth Conclusion from the same Stave is, That he who understands these two *Sulphurs* & *Mercuries* aright, shal find that the one is the most pure red *Sulphur of Gold*, which is *Sulphur in manifesto*, and *Mercurius in occulto*, and that other is most pure white *Mercury*, which is indeed true *Quicksilver in manifesto*, and *Sulphur in occulto*, these are our two Principles.

The fifth Conclusion from the Twelfth Stave is, That if a mans Principles be true, and his Operations regular, his Event will be certain, which Event is no other then the true Mystery.

These Conclusions are but few in number, but of great weight or concernment; the Amplification, Illustration and Elucidation therefore of them, will make a son of Art truly glad.

Stave IX.[13]

For the First; Forasmuch as it is not for our purpose here to invite any to the Art, only intending to lead and guide the sons of Art; We shall not prove the possibility of *Alchymy*, by many Arguments, having done it abundantly in another Treatise. He then that will be incredulous, let him be incredulous; he that will cavil, let him cavil; But he whose mind is perswaded of the truth of this Art and of its Dignity, let him attend to what is in the Illustration of these Five Conclusions discovered, and his heart shall certainly rejoyce. We shall therefore briefly illustrate this 1st Conclusion, and insist there more largely, where the secrets of the Art are most couched.

For this first, which concludes in effect the truth of the Art, and its validity; he that would therein be more satisfied in it, let him read the *Testimony of the Philosophers*: And he that will not believe the Testimony of so many men, being most of them men of renown in their own times, he will cavil also against all other Arguments.

We shall only hold to *Ripley's* Testimony in this our Key, who in the Fourth Stave, assures the King that at *Lovain* he first saw the greatest and most perfect secrets, namely, the two *Elixirs*; and in his following Verses, craved his confident credit, that he himself hath truly found the way of secret *Alchymy*, and promiseth the discovery of it to the King, only upon condition of secrecy.

And in the Eighth Stave, though he protests never to write it by Pen, yet proffers the King at his pleasure, to shew him occularly the Red and White *Elixir*, and the working of them, which he promiseth will be done for easie costs in time. So then, he that will doubt the truth of this Art, must account this Famous Author for a most simple mad Sophister, to write and offer such things to his Prince, unless he were able in effect to do what he promised; from which imputation, his Writings, and also the History of him, of his Fame, Gravity, and Worth, will sufficiently clear him.

Stave X quoted; selections from commentary

We come to the second Conclusion; the substance of which is, *that all Metalls, and Bodies of Metalline Principles, may be reduced to their first Mercurial Matter*; And this is the main and chief ground for the possibility of Transmutation. On this we must insist largly and fully, for (trust me) this is the very hinge on which our secrets hang.

First, Then know that all *Metalls*, and several *Minerals* have *Mercury* for their next matter, to which (for the most part, nay indeed always) there adheres, and is Con–coagulated an external *Sulphur*, which is not *Metalline*, but distinguishable from the internal Kernal of the *Mercury*.

This *Sulphur* is not wanting even in common *Argent Vive*, by the Mediation of which, it may be precipitated into the form of a drie Powder: Yea, and by a Liquor well known to us, (though nothing helping the Art of Transmutation) it may be so fixed, that it may endure all Fires, the Test and Coppel, and this without the addition of any thing to it, but the Liquor (by virtue whereof it is fixed) coming away intire, both in its *Pondus*[14] and

---

[13] For the passages that Philalethes cites, see the corresponding stanzas of Ripley's *Epistle written to King Edward the 4*, in this volume. My text occasionally varies slightly from that included in Philalethes's *Ripley Reviv'd*.

[14] I.e., weight.

Virtue. This *Sulphur* in Gold and Silver is pure, in the other Metalls less pure; Therefore in Gold and Silver it is fixed, in others it is fugitive: in all the Metalls it is coagulated, in *Mercury* or *Argent Vive*, it is coagulable; in *Gold, Silver* and *Mercury* this *Sulphur* is so strongly united, that the Antients did ever judge *Sulphur* and *Mercury* to be all one; but we by the help of a Liquor, the Invention of which in these parts of the world we owe to *Paracelsus*, (though among the *Moors* and *Arabians*, it hath been, and is (at this day) commonly known to the acuter sort of *Chymists*). By this I say, we know that the *Sulphur* which is in *Mercury* coagulable, and in the *Metals* coagulated, is external to the Internal nature of *Mercury*, and may be separated in the form of a tincted Metallick Oyl, the remaining *Mercury* being then void of all *Sulphur*, save that which may be called its Inward or Central *Sulphur*, and is now incoagulable of it self, (though by our *Elixir* it is to be coagulated) but of itself, it can neither be fixt nor precipitated, nor sublimed, but remains un–altered in all corrosive waters, and in all digestions of heat... There is then but one only humidity, which is applicable unto our Work, which certainly is neither of *Saturn* nor *Venus*, nor is drawn from any thing, which nature hath formed, but from a substance compounded by the Art of the Philosopher...

Our Art therefore is to compound two Principles (one in which the *Salt*, and another in which the *Sulphur* of Nature doth abound), which are not yet perfect, nor yet totally imperfect, and (by consequence) may therefore (by our Art) be changed or exalted... and then by Common *Mercury* to extract not the *Pondus*, but the Coelestial virtue out of the compound; which virtue (being Fermental) begets in the common *Mercury* an Offspring more noble then it self, which is our true *Hermaphrodite*,[15] which will congeal it self, and dissolve the Bodies: Observe but a grain of Corn, in which, scarce a discernable part is Sprout, and this Sprout, if it were out of the Grain, would die in a moment; the whole grain is sown, yet the Sprout only produceth the Herb: So is it in our Body, the Fermental Spirit that is in it, is scarce a third part of the whole, the rest is of no value, yet all is joyned (in the composition) and the *faeculent corporeous* parts of the Body come away with the dregs of the *Mercury*... In all truth I tell you, that if you should take our imperfect compound Body, *per se*, and *Mercury per se*, and Ferment them alone, though you might bring out of the one a most pure *Sulphur*, and out of the other *Mercury of Mercury*, which is the Nut of Mercury,[16] yet with these thou couldest effect nothing, for Fermental virtue is the wonder of the world, and it is by it, that water becomes Herbs, Trees, and Plants, Fruits, Flesh, Blood, Stones, Minerals, and every thing; seek then for it only, and rejoyce in it, as in a deservedly invaluable treasure... We conclude then, that all operations for our *Mercury*, but by common *Mercury*, and our Body according to our Art, are erroneous, and will never produce our Mysterie, although they be otherwise, *Mercuries* never so wonderfully made. For as the Author of the *New Light*,[17] saith, *No Water in any Island of the Philosophers was wholsom, but that which was drawn out of the reigns of* Sol *and* Luna. Wilt thou know what

---

[15] One of the most famous of all alchemical symbols, the hermaphrodite is the offspring of the union of "masculine" sulphur and "feminine" mercury, and signifies the philosopher's stone. Its dual sexual nature made it a favorite subject in alchemical art. Throughout this section Philalethes draws heavily on the Paracelsian *tria prima* of salt, sulphur, and mercury (body, soul, and spirit).

[16] I.e., the very essence or kernel of Mercury.   [17] Michael Sendivogius.

that means, *Mercury* in its *pondus* and incombustibility is *Gold fugitive*,[18] our Body in its purity is called the *Philosophers Luna*, being far more pure than the imperfect Metals, and its *Sulphur* also as pure as the *Sulphur* of *Sol*, not that it is indeed *Luna*, for it abides not in the fire ...

Stave XII Quoted

Thus come we to the last Conclusion, which is, that if a Mans Operations be Regular and his Principles true, his end will be certain, (*viz.*) the Mastery.

O Fools and Blind that do not consider how each thing in the world hath his proper Cause and Progress in Operation; Think you, if a Seaman should with a gallant Coach, intend to Sail to any place beyond Sea, he would not find his attempt to be foolish; Or if with a Ship gallantly furnished, he should Row at Random, he may not sooner stumble on an infortunate Rock, then arrive at the golden Coast: Such fools are they who seek our secret in trivial matters, and yet hope to find the Gold of *Ophir*.[19]

For the more exact Guiding of your practice, take notice of these Twenty Rules following.

1. Whatever any Sophister may suggest unto you, or you may read in any Sophistical Author; yet let none take you from this ground, (*viz.*) That as the end you look for is Gold: so let Gold be the subject on which you work, and none other.

2. Let none deceive you with telling you, that our *Gold* is not common, but Philosophical; for *common Gold* is dead, which is true: But as we order it, there is made a quickening of it, as a grain of Corn in the Earth is quickened.[20]

    So then in our work, after six Weeks, *Gold* that was dead, becomes quick, living, and spermatical; and in our composition, it may be called *Our Gold*, because it is joyn'd with an Agent that will certainly quicken it: So a Condemned Man, is called a Dead Man, though at present living.

3. Besides Gold, which is the Body or Male, you must have another Sperm, which is the Spirit and Soul, or Female, and this is *Mercury*, in Flux and Form like to common *Argent Vive*, yet more clean and pure.

    There are many, who instead of *Mercury,* will have strange Waters or Liquors, which they stile by the name of *Philosophical Mercury*; Be not deceived by them, for what a Man sows, that he must look to reap: If thou shalt sow thy Body in any Earth, but that which is Metalline and Homogeneal to it; thou shalt instead of a *Metalline Elixir*, reap an unprofitable *Calx*, which will be of no value.

4. Our *Mercury* is in substance one with common *Argent Vive*, but far different in Form; For it hath a Form Coelestial, Fiery, and of excellent Virtue: and this is the Nature which it receives by our Artificial Preparation.

5. The whole Secret of our Preparation, is, that thou take that Mineral which is next of kin to Gold, and to *Mercury*; Impregnate this with Volatile Gold, which is found in the reins of *Mars*, with this purifie your *Mercury* until seaven times are past, then it is fitted for the Kings Bath.

7. This *Mercury* thus actuated, is after to be distilled in a Glass retort twice or thrice; and that for this reason, because some Atoms of the Body may be in it, which were insensibly

---

[18] Like mercury in its "escaping from or eluding the grasp, slippery" (*OED*); cf. Sendivogius's characterization of Mercury in his *Dialogue* in this edition.

[19] See 1 Kings 10:11.   [20] See John 12:24.

left in the Preparation of the *Mercury*, afterwards it is to be cleansed well with Vinegar and *Sal-armoniack*,[21] then is it fit for the work.

10. ...Our Sophism[22] lies only in the two kinds of Fire in our work: the Internal secret Fire, which is Gods Instrument, hath no qualities perceptible to man, of that Fire we speak often, and seem yet to speak of the External heat; and hence arise among the unwary many Errours. This is our Fire which is graduated, for the External heat, is almost linear all the work, to the white work, it is one without alteration, save that in the seaven first days we keep the heat a little slack for certainty and security sake, which an experienced Philosopher need not do.

But the Internal governing heat is insensibly graduated hourly, and by how much that is daily vigorated by the continuance of Decoction, the Colours are altered, and the Compound maturated: I have unfolded a main knot unto you; take heed of being insnared here again.

11. Then you must provide a Glass Tun, in which you may perfect your work, without which you could never do any thing; Let it be either Oval or Spherical, so big in reference to your Compound, that it may hold about twelve times the quantity of it within its Sphere, let your Glass be thick and strong, clear, and free of flaws, with a neck about a Span or Foot long; In this Egg put your matter, sealing the neck carefully, without flaw, or crack, or hole, for the least vent will let out the subtile Spirit, and destroy the work...

12. You must then provide your self with a Furnace, by wise men called an *Athanor*, in which you may accomplish your work; nor will any one serve in your first work; But such a one in which you may give a heat obscurely red at your pleasure, or lesser, and that in its highest degree of heat, it may endure twelve hours at the least.

This if you would obtain; Observe, First, that your nest be no bigger then to contain your dish with about an Inch vacancy at the side where the Vent-hole of your *Athanor* is for the Fire to play.

Secondly, Let your Dish be no bigger then to hold one Glass with about an inch thickness of Ashes between the Glass and side, remembring the word of the Philosopher,[23] One Glass, One Thing, One Furnace; for such a Dish standing with the bottom level to the vent-hole, which in such a Furnace ought to be but one, about three Inches Diameter, sloping upwards, will with the stream of Flame, which is always playing to the top of the Vessel, and round about the bottom, be kept always in a glowing heat...

Fifthly, Let the top of your Furnace be closed to an hole which may but just serve for casting in of Coals about three Inches Diameter or Square, which will keep down the heat powerfully.

13. ...Since then you know that your work appertains all to the Mineral Kingdom, you must know what heat is fit for Mineral Bodies, and may be called a gentle heat, and what violent; First, now consider, where Nature leaves you, not only in the Mineral

---

[21] I.e., sal ammoniac or ammonium chloride.

[22] "A specious but fallacious argument, either used deliberately in order to deceive or mislead, or employed as a means of displaying ingenuity in reasoning" (*OED*).

[23] "Philosopher" may refer to Geber, whose writings on furnaces and fires were widely cited, or to Aristotle as author of many supposititious alchemical works.

Kingdom, but in it to work on Gold and *Mercury*, which are both incombustible: Yet *Mercury* being tender, will break all Vessels, if the Fire be over extreme; Therefore though it be incombustible, and so no Fire can hurt it, yet also it must be kept with the Male Sperm in one Glass, which if the Fire be too big, cannot be, and by consequence the work cannot be accomplished. So then from the degree of heat that will keep Lead or Tin constantly molten, and higher, so high as the Glass will endure without danger of breaking, is a temperate heat; and so you begin your degrees of heat according to the Kingdom in which Nature hath left you . . .

14. Know, that all your progress in this Work is to ascend in *Bus & Nubi*,[24] from the Moon up to the Sun; that is in *Nubibus*, or in *Clouds*: Therefore I charge thee to sublime in a continual vapour, that the Stone may take Air, and live.

15. Nor it this enough, but for to attain our permanent Tincture, the water of our Lake must be boyled with the Ashes of *Hermes Tree*;[25] I charge thee then to boyl night and day without ceasing, that in the troubles of the stormy Sea, the Heavenly Nature may ascend, and the Earthly descend.

　　For verily, if we did not Boyl, we would never name our work Decoction, but Digestion; For where the Spirits only Circulate silently, and the Compound below moves not by an Ebullition, that is only properly to be named Digestion.

16. Be not over hasty, expecting Harvest too soon, or the end soon after the beginning: For if thou be patiently supported, in the space of fifty days at the farthest, thou shalt see the Crows Bill[26] . . . Dost think then, that Gold, the most solid Body in the world, will change its Form in a short time? Nay, thou must wait and wait until about the 40th day utter blackness begins to appear; when thou seest that, then conclude thy Body is destroy'd, that is, made a living Soul, and thy Spirit is dead, that is Coagulated with the Body; But till this sign of Blackness, both the Gold and the *Mercury* retain their Forms and Natures.

17. Beware that thy Fire go not out, no not for a moment, so as to let thy Matter be cold, for so Ruine of the Work will certainly follow.

　　By what has been said, thou mayst gather that all our work is nothing else but an uncessant boyling of thy Compound in the first degree of liquifying heat, which is found in the Metalline Kingdom, in which the Internal Vapours shall go round about thy matter, in which fume it shall both die and be revived.

18. Know, that when the White appears, which will be about the end of Five Months, that then the accomplishment of the White Stone approacheth; Rejoyce then, for now the King hath overcome Death, and is rising in the East with great Glory.[27]

19. Then continue your Fire until the Colours appear again, then at last you shall see the fair Vermillion, the Red Poppy; Glorifie God then, and be thankful.

---

[24] Philalethes repeats the cloud imagery used in st. 27 of Ripley's *Epistle* to suggest the "heavenly" ascent of the liquids and vapors during distillation.

[25] The image of "Hermes' tree" or the "philosophical tree" appears frequently in the *Compound*. Philalethes's gloss on Ripley's *Preface* states that "our Tree is at his periods of [several] colours, and in this form, which Tree by the heat of the Fire is dryed to a Calx, is called the Ashes of Hermes Tree" (*Ripley Reviv'd* 66).

[26] A symbol of putrefaction and the *nigredo* (blackness) stage in the preparation of the philosopher's stone.

[27] The emergence of the white stone and red stone in sts. 18 and 19, betokening transmutations into silver and gold, is, as here, often figured forth in images of the resurrection and millenium.

20. Lastly, you must boyl this Stone in the same water, in the same proportion, with the same Regimen, (only your Fire shall then be a little slacker) and so you shall increase Quantity and Goodness at your pleasure.

Now the only God the Father of light, bring you to see this Regeneration of the light, and make us to rejoyce with him for ever hereafter in light. Amen.

25 Elias Ashmole (1617–1692)
From the "Prolegomena" to the *Theatrum Chemicum Britannicum*

Like the somewhat older Robert Fludd (1574–1637), the close contemporary Robert Boyle (1627–91), and the slightly younger Isaac Newton (1642–1727), Elias Ashmole's interests and achievements bridge the often invisible boundaries of seventeenth-century English magic and science. While Ashmole's genius did not lead him in the more specialized paths taken by these contemporaries, his accomplishments in many fields are noteworthy. He is best known, of course, as an antiquarian and collector whose remarkable assemblage of curiosities, bequeathed to him by John Tradescant the son (1608–63), was given to Oxford University and became the foundation of the Ashmolean Museum; likewise, his papers became central to the Bodleian Library's manuscript collection. Ashmole wrote *The Institution, Laws and Ceremonies of the Order of the Garter* (1672). He was a member of both the Royal Society and the Learned Society of Astrologers, thus finding a place amongst the champions of the "New Philosophy" and with London's leading astrologers, including William Lilly. Ashmole was himself a notable practitioner of astrology and a student of Rosicrucianism. Most, if not all, of these interests are reflected in the "Prolegomena" to the *Theatrum Chemicum Britannicum*.

As its full title suggests, the *Theatrum Chemicum Britannicum, Containing Severall Poeticall Pieces of our Famous English Philosophers, who have written the Hermetique Mysteries in their owne Ancient Language* is Ashmole's major contribution to the preservation of early *English* alchemical texts written in poetic form. It is a monument to Ashmole's interest in alchemy and an expression of his nationalistic fervor: a means of paying tribute to Thomas Norton, George Ripley, Chaucer, John Dastin, Edward Kelly and John Dee – more than thirty identified and anonymous pieces in all – that have their Englishness in common. In addition, Ashmole, the antiquarian, provides richly detailed "Annotations and Discourses" upon the texts he includes, along with the "Prolegomena" printed below. The latter tells us much about the state of alchemy in mid-seventeenth century England as seen through the eyes of a leading magician-scientist.

The following selections, with modernized capitalization and typography, are taken from the original edition of the *Theatrum Chemicum Britannicum* (London 1652). Additional readings: Allen G. Debus's introduction to his facsimile edition of the *Theatrum Chemicum Britannicum* (New York and London: Johnson Reprint Corp., 1967); C. H. Josten, ed., *Elias Ashmole (1617–1692)*, 5 vols., esp. vol. I, Biographical Introduction.

The subject of this ensuing worke is a philosophicall account of that eminent secret treasur'd up in the bosome of nature; which hath been sought for of many, but found by a few, notwithstanding experience'd antiquity hath afforded faithfull (though not frequent) discoveries thereof. Past ages have like rivers conveied downe to us, (upon the floate) the more light and sophisticall pieces of learning; but what were profound and misterious, the weight and solidity thereof, sunke to the bottome; whence every one who attempts to dive, cannot easily fetch them up: so, that what our Saviour said to his disciples, may (I hope without offence) be spoken to the Elected Sons of Art; unto you it is given to know the mysteries of the Kingdome of God; but to others in parables, that seeing they might not see, and hearing they might not understand.

Our English philosophers generally (like prophets) have received little honour (unlesse what hath beene privately paid them) in their owne countrey; nor have they done any mighty workes amongst us, except in covertly administring their medicine to a few sick, and healing them. (For greater experiments then what it performes in physick, they never publikely made shew of.) This did I. O. (one of the first foure Fellowes of the Fratres R. C.) in curing the young Earle of Norfolke, of the leprosie;[1] and Doctor B. in carrying off the virulency of the small-pox, twice, from Queen Elizabeth;[2] insomuch that they never appeared. But in parts abroad they have found more noble reception, and the world greedy of obteyning their workes; nay, (rather then want the sight thereof) contented to view them through a translation, though never so imperfect. Witnesse what Maierus, Hermannus, Combachius, Faber,[3] and many others have done; the first of which came out of Germanie, to live in England; purposely that he might so understand our English tongue, as to translate Norton's *Ordinall* into Latin verse, which most judiciously and learnedly he did; Yet (to our shame be it spoken) his entertainment was too too coarse for so deserving a scholler.

How great a blemish is it then to us, that refuse to reade so famous authors in our naturall language, whilst strangers are necessitated to read them in ours, to understand them in their own, yet think the dignity of the subject, much more deserving, then their paines.

If this we do but ingeniously consider, we shall judge it more of reason that we looke back upon, then neglect such pieces of learning as are native of our owne countrey, and by this inquisition, finde no nation hath written more, or better, although at present

[1] Ashmole draws this information directly from the *Fama Fraternitatis*, the first of the Rosicrucian manifestoes, dated 1614. Members of the Fraternity of the Rosy Cross were thought to possess various kinds of secret and magical knowledge, especially those related to medicine and healing. For the text of the *Fama* and its companion tract, the *Confessio Fraternitatis* (1615), see Frances A. Yates, *The Rosicrucian Enlightenment*, Appendix, esp. 244.

[2] Queen Elizabeth's life was seriously threatened by smallpox in October 1562; she was cured through the efforts of a "skillful though extremely irascible German physician," Dr. Burcot (see Christopher Hibbert, *The Virgin Queen: Elizabeth I, Genius of the Golden Age*, 86–7).

[3] Michael Maier (1568–1622) was a German alchemist, Rosicrucian, sometime physician to Emperor Rudolph II in Prague, and author of several alchemical books notable for their illustrations (see especially the *Atalanta Fugiens* of 1618). His Latin translation of Thomas Norton's fifteenth-century poem, *Ordinall of Alchimy,* appeared in 1618. Hermannus Condeesyanus (one of the pseudonyms of the German alchemical author, Johann Grasshoff) also published works by Rhazes in 1625. Ludwig Combach (b. 1590) edited alchemical works by Edward Kelly, John Isaac Holland, and, in 1649, the *Opera omnia* of George Ripley. Albert Otto Faber (d. 1678), widely travelled German physician, achieved notoriety as author of a work on *aurum potabile* and also as physician in the court of Charles II; or, Ashmole may be referring to Pierre Jean Fabre (d. 1650), physician of Languedoc and author and editor of alchemical works (see *Bibl. Chem.* I: 259–60).

(as well through our owne supinenesse, as the decrees of fate,) few of their workes can be found. John Leland tooke very much paines, even at the yeilding up of the ghost, of our English learning, to preserve its latest (but weakest, 'cause almost spent) breath; and from him John Bale, with John Pitts[4] (who indeed is but Bale's plagiary) hath left us a Catalogue of the Writers of this Nation, and that's neere all. Yet posterity for this is deeply obliged. What punishment then did their pestilent malice deserve, who rob'd us of their whole workes?

A juditious author speaking of the Dissolution of our Monasteries, saith thus: Many manuscripts, guilty of no other superstition then red letters in the front, were condemned to the fire; and here a principall key of antiquity was lost to the great prejudice of posterity. Indeed (such was Learnings misfortune, at that great devastation of our English libraries, that) where a red letter or a mathematicall diagram appeared, they were sufficient to intitle the booke to be popish or diabolicall.

Our English nation hath ever beene happy for learning and learned men, and to illustrate this, I hope it will not prove distastfull.

As first, the Druydæ (the famous and mysterious Druydæ) that were priests, diviners, and wise men: and took their originall and name from Druys Sarronyus[5] the fourth king of the Celts, (styled Sapientum & Augurum Doctor) who dyed Anno Mundi, 2069.

Next the Bardi, who celebrated the illustrious deeds of famous men, which they ingeniously dispos'd in heroique verse, and sung them to the sweete melody of the harpe: amongst other testimonies hereof receive Chaucer's:

> The old gentle Brittons in her dayes
> Of divers aventures maden Layes,
> Rymed erst in her Mother Tongue,
> Whych Layes, with her Instruments they songe.[6]

These philosophers had their name from Bardus Druydus (the 5th King of the Celts) who was the first inventor of verses, as Berosius[7] tells us; and dyed An. Mundi 2138. Neither of these sects of philosophers used any writing (indeed it was not lawfull) for such was the policy and curiosity of elder ages (to defend their learning and mysteries from the injury of ignorant interpretations) that they delivered them to posterity by tradition only.

Cæsar testifies (and tis a noble testimony) that the learning of the Druydi was first invented in Britaine and thence transferr'd into France; and that, in all his time, those of France came over hither to be instructed.[8] Agricola (in Tacitus) preferrs the Britaines before the Students of France (nothwithstanding that they were of a docible wit, and apt to learne) in that they were curious in attaining the eloquence of the Latin tongue.[9]

---

[4] John Leland (c. 1503–52), John Bale (1495–1563) and John Pits (Joannis Pitseus, 1561–1616) were important sources of information on early English writers.

[5] Here and in the following reference to Bardus Druydus, Ashmole follows the Celtic royal chronology given in Holinshed's *Chronicles of England*: beginning with Samothes, followed by Magus, Sarron, Druiyus and Bardus. See A. L. Owen, *The Famous Druids*, 6–7.

[6] Ashmole quotes ll. 709–12 from the opening of *The Franklin's Prologue* in *The Canterbury Tales*.

[7] Berosus or Berossus (fl. c. 290 BC), priest of Bel and author of a history of Babylon (*OCD*).

[8] Caesar discusses the druids in the *Gallic War* 6: 13, 14, 16, 18, 21.

[9] From the *Life* of Agricola (AD 40–93), the Roman general and governor of Britain, written by Tacitus.

As for magick, Pliny tells us, it flourished in Britaine, and that the people there were so devoted to it (yea, with all complements of ceremony) a man would think that even the Persian learned his magick thence.

A German poet sayes that when the World was troubled with Pannonick invasions,[10] England flourished in the knowledge of all good arts; and was able to send of her learned men into other countries to propagate learning; and instances Winifrid (alias Boniface the Devonshire man) and Willebroad (the Northerne man) that were sent into Germany.

Nay more, England was twice schoole-mistress to France (for so saith Peter Ramus)[11] *viz.* First by the Druydæ (who taught them their discipline) and afterwards by Alcunius,[12] in Charles the Great's time, through whose perswasions the Emperour founded the University of Paris.

For the Saxons, it is not to be denied but that many of them, after their conversion to Christianity, were exceedingly learned, and before that, much addicted to soothsaying, augury, divination by the neighing of horses, &c. And tis worth the enquiry (there being more in it then we ordinarily apprehend) why they in generall worshipped Herthus [i.e. Dame Earth] for a goddess, and honoured Mercury above all the gods of the Germanes, whom they called Wooden,[13] (hence Wodensday now our Wednesday). For, they believed that this Dame Herthus intermediated in humane affaires and relieved the poore; whose image was made armed, standing among flowers, having in its right hand a staffe, and in it a banner wherein was painted a rose; in the other hand a ballance, and upon the head thereof a cock; on the brest a carved beare, and before the midle, a fixed scutchion; in chiefe whereof was also a ballance; in face, a lion; and in point, a rose. And for their god Wooden they esteemed him as their god of battaile, representing him by an armed man. Insomuch that wee to this very day retaine the word "wood" [i.e., "wode"] among us, to signifie fierce, furious, raging, [as when one is in a great rage, we usually say he is wode:] So the Mercury of the philosophers[14] is shaddowed under the fierce and terrible names of lion, dragon, poyson, &c. But this is not all, although it be something.

And now to come yet neerer to our selves; we must needs say that of later times (since the Conquest) our nation hath produced such famous and eminently learned men, as have equall'd (if not surpast) the greatest schollers of other nations, and happy were we if now we could but partake of those legacies they left, and which envy and ignorance has defrauded us of: Howsoever the small remainder which is left, we have good reason to prize,

> For out of olde Fields as Men saythe,
> Cometh alle this new Corne from yeare to yeare;
> And out of olde Bokes in good faythe
> Cometh all this Scyence, that Men leare.

That England hath been successively enrich'd with such men our country man John Leland (and I never heard he was partiall) abundantly testifies; who avers, that generally

---

[10] I.e., those involving ancient Pannonia, corresponding to modern Hungary (*OED*).

[11] Peter Ramus (Pierre de la Ramée) 1515–72, influential French humanist and grammarian, wrote on the druids in his *Liber de Moribus veterum Gallorum* (Paris, 1559).

[12] Alcuin (735–804), a leading theologian, writer, and educational reformer in the reign of Charlemagne.

[13] I.e., Wotan or Odin, the chief of the Germanic gods and god of war.

[14] The universal agent of transmutation.

we have had a great number of excellent wits and writers, learned with the best as times served, who besides their knowledge in the four tongues, in which part of them excelled, there was no liberall science or any feate concerning learning, in which they have not shewed certaine arguments of great felicity and wit. And thus much for the generality of learning.

Now for a particular account of the hermetique science, vouchsafe (Ingenious Reader) to accept the ensuing collections, yet not so, as if therein were contained all the workes of our English hermetique philosophers, (for more are design'd in a second part to follow and compleate this a full Theatrum; the which God allowing me further time and tranquility to run through it, as I have already this, I intend shortly to make ready for the presse). Whereby yet more to manifest what men we have had, no lesse famous for this kinde of philosophy, then for all other commendable arts and sciences.

To adde any thing to the praise thereof, were but to hold a candle before the sunne; or should I here deliver a full account of the marvellous operations and effects thereof, it would be as far beyond the limits of a preface, as remote from the beliefe of the generality of the world. Nor doe I expect that all my readers should come with an engagement, to believe what I here write, or that there was ever any such thing *in rerum natura* as what we call a Philosophers Stone, nor will I perswade them to it, (though I must tell them I have not the vanity to publish these sacred and serious mysteries and arcana, as Romances) tis enough that I know incredulity is given to the world as a punishment. Yet Ile tell them what one of our ancient poeticall philosophers sayes,

If yow wyl lysten to my Lay,
Something thereby yow maie finde,
That may content your minde:
I will not sweare to make yow give credence,
For a Philosopher will finde, here in Evidence
Of the Truth; and to Men that be Lay,
I skill not greatly what they say.[15]

I must professe I know enough to hold my tongue, but not enough to speake; and the no lesse reall then miraculous fruits I have found in my diligent enquiry into these arcana, lead me on to such degrees of admiration, they command silence, and force me to lose my tongue. Yet, as one greatly affecting my native countrey, and the satisfaction of all ingenious artists, I have published (for their use) these ensuing collected antiquities; and shall here say something more then they speak of.

He who shall have the happiness to meet with S. Dunstans worke *De Occulta Philosophia*,[16] (a booke which E. G. A. I. made much use of, and which shall chiefly back what here I am about to say) may therein reade such stories as will make him amaz'd to think what stupendious and immense things are to be performed by vertue of the Philosophers Mercury, of which a taste onely and no more.

---

[15] From "The Hunting of the Greene Lyon. Written by the Viccar of Malden," in Ashmole's *TCB* 280.

[16] St. Dunstan (924 or 925–988) was an abbot of Glastonbury and archbishop of Canterbury, to whom a treatise on the philosopher's stone was attributed (see *HMES* 1:773, and *Bibl. Chem.* 1:171–72). "E. G. A. I." is unidentified.

And first, of the Minerall Stone, the which is wrought up to the degree onely that hath the power of transmuting any imperfect earthy matter into its utmost degree of perfection; that is, to convert the basest of metalls into perfect gold and silver; flints into all manner of precious stones; [as rubies, saphirs, emeralds, and diamonds, &c.] and many more experiments of the like nature. But as this is but a part, so it is the least share of that blessing which may be acquired by the philosophers materia, if the full vertue thereof were knowne. Gold I confesse is a delicious object, a goodly light, which we admire and gaze upon *ut Pueri in Junonis avem*,[17] but, as to make gold (saith an incomparable authour) is the cheifest intent of the alchimists, so was it scarce any intent of the ancient philosophers, and the lowest use the adepti made of this materia.

For they being lovers of wisdome more then worldly wealth, drove at higher and more excellent operations: and certainly he to whom the whole course of nature lyes open, rejoyceth not so much that he can make gold and silver, or the divells to become subject to him, as that he sees the heavens open, the angells of God ascending and descending, and that his own name is fairely written in the book of life.

Next, to come to the Vegitable, Magicall, and Angelicall Stones; the which have in them no part of the Minerall Stone (Quatenus a stone, fermented with metalline and earthy nature) for they are marvelously subtile, and each of them differing in operation and nature, because fitted and fermented for severall effects and purposes. Doubtlesse Adam (with the Fathers before the Flood, and since) Abraham, Moses, and Solomon, wrought many wonders by them, yet the utmost of their vertues they never fully understood, nor indeed any but God the Maker of all things in Heaven and Earth, blessed for evermore.

For, by the Vegitable [stone] may be perfectly known the nature of man, beasts, foules, fishes, together with all kinds of trees, plants, flowers, &c. and how to produce and make them grow, flourish & beare fruit; how to encrease them in colour and smell, and when and where we please, and all this not onely at an instant, *Experimenti gratia*, but daily, monethly, yearly, at any time, at any season; yea, in the depth of winter. And therefore not unlike, but the Wall-nut Tree which anciently grew in Glastenbury church-yard, and never put forth leaves before S. Barnabies Day,[18] yet then was fully loaded with them, as also the Hawthorne there, so greatly fam'd for shooting forth leaves and flowers at Christmas, together with the oake in New-Forrest in Hampshire that bore greene leaves at the same season; may be some experiments made of the Vegitable Stone.

Besides the masculine part of it which is wrought up to a solar quality, and through its exceeding heat will burne up and destroy any creature, plant, &c. That which is lunar & feminine (if immediately applyed) will mitigate it with its extreme cold: and in like manner the lunar quality benums and congeals any animall, &c. unlesse it be presently helped and resolved by that of the Sun; for though they both are made out of one natural substance; yet in working they have contrary qualities: neverthelesse there is such a naturall assistance between them, that what the one cannot doe, the other both can, and will perform.

Nor are their inward vertues more then their outward beauties; for the solar part is of so resplendent, transparent lustre, that the eye of man is scarce able to indure it; and if the

---

[17] "Like boys [gazing at] the bird of Juno."

[18] Ashmole's account of the miraculous walnut tree and the "oake in New Forrest" is closely related to the legend of Joseph of Arimathea's staff and the famous Glastonbury Thorn (see the *Cath. Ency.*, s.v. "Glastonbury Abbey," by G. Roger Hudleston).

lunar part be expos'd abroad in a dark night, birds will repaire to (and circulate about) it, as a fly round a candle, and submit themselves to the captivity of the hand: And this invites mee to believe, that the stone which the ancient Hermet (being then 140 years old) tooke out of the wall in his cell, and shewed Cornelius Gallus, Ann. 1602 was of the nature of this Vegitable Stone: For, (upon the opening his Golden Box wherein it was inclosed) it dilated its beames all over the roome, and that with so great splendor, that it overcame the light that was kindled therein; besides the Hermet refused to project it upon metall (as being unworthy of it) but made his experiment upon Veronica and Rue.[19]

By the Magicall or Prospective Stone it is possible to discover any person in what part of the world soever, although never so secretly concealed or hid; in chambers, closets, or cavernes of the Earth: for there it makes a strict inquisition. In a word, it fairely presents to your view even the whole world, wherein to behold, heare, or see your desire. Nay more, it enables man to understand the language of the creatures, as the chirping of birds, lowing of beasts, &c., to convey a spirit into an image, which by observing the influence of heavenly bodies, shall become a true oracle; And yet this as E. A.[20] assures you, is not any wayes necromanticall or devilish; but easy, wonderous easy, naturall and honest.

Lastly, as touching the Angelicall Stone, it is so subtill, saith the aforesaid author, that it can neither be seene, felt, or weighed; but tasted only. The voyce of man (which bears some proportion to these subtill properties) comes short in comparison; nay the air itself is not so penetrable, and yet (Oh mysterious wonder!) a stone, that will lodge in the fire to eternity without being prejudiced. It hath a Divine power, celestiall, and invisible, above the rest; and endowes the possessor with Divine gifts. It affords the apparition of angells, and gives a power of conversing with them, by dreames and revelations: nor dare any evill spirit approach the place where it lodgeth. Because it is a quintessence wherein there is no corruptible thing; and where the elements are not corrupt, no devill can stay or abide.

S. Dunston calls it the Food of Angels, and by others it is tearmed The Heavenly Viaticum; The Tree of Life; and is undoubtedly (next under God) the true Alchochodon, or Giver of Years; for by it mans body is preserved from corruption, being thereby inabled to live a long time without foode: nay 'tis made a question whether any man can dye that uses it. Which I doe not so much admire, as to think why the possessors of it should desire to live, that have those manifestations of glory and eternity, presented unto their fleshly eyes; but rather desire to be dissolved, and to enjoy the full fruition, then live where they must be content with the bare speculation.

After Hermes had once obtained the knowledge of this stone, he gave over the use of all other stones, and therein only delighted: Moses and Solomon (together with Hermes)

---

[19] A letter from Ashmole to a "Mr. Allestrey," dated Jan.1656, provides a partial gloss on this incident. Ashmole recounts reading a piece, written in Dutch, in which one Frederick Gallus (not Cornelius), while travelling in the Thuringian Forest in 1603, discovers an old alchemical book by Paracelsus in a "ruind chapell." At St. Michael's Hermitage, he finds a 140-year-old hermit who explicates this work and reveals "many rare secrets of Transmutation." See C. H. Josten, ed., *Elias Ashmole*, 2: 685–86.

[20] Acquiring the "language of the birds" and beasts is confirmation of the magus's wisdom and profound understanding of creation. For Milton's pre-lapsarian Adam, such wisdom is also manifest in his naming of the birds and animals: ". . . each Bird stoop'd on his wing. / I nam'd them, as they pass'd, and understood / Thir Nature, with such knowledge God endu'd / My sudden apprehension" (*Paradise Lost*, 8:351–54). "E. A." is perhaps Ashmole himself.

were the only three that excelled in the Knowledge thereof, and who therewith wrought wonders.

That there is a gift of prophesie hid in the Red-stone, Racis [Rhazes] will tell you; for thereby (saith he) philosophers have foretold things to come: And Petrus Bonus avers, that they did prophesie, not only generally but specially; having a fore-knowledge of the Resurrection, Incarnation of Christ, Day of Judgement, and that the world should be consumed with fire: and this not otherwise, then from the insight of their operations.

In briefe, by the true and various use of the philosophers prima materia (for there are diversities of gifts, but the same spirit) the perfection of liberall sciences are made known, the whole wisdome of nature may be grasped: and (nothwithstanding what has been said, I must further adde) there are yet hid greater things then these, for we have seen but few of his workes.

Howbeit, there are but a few Stocks that are fitted to inoculate the grafts of this science on: they are mysteries incommunicable to any but the adepti, and those that have beene devoted even from their cradles to serve and waite at this altar: and how rarely such have been heard of, may appear by Norton:

> For few (saith he) or scarsely One
> In fifteene kingdomes had our Red Stone.[21]

And they perhaps were (with S. Paul) caught up into Paradice, and as he, heard unspeakeable words, so they wrought unoperable workes such as it is not lawfull to utter.

Of such as these therefore will I glory, yet of my selfe I will not glory, but of mine infirmities. And truly whether such were in the body or out of the body I cannot tell, God knoweth, doubtlesse they were not far from the kingdom of God.

But I feare I have waded too farre; and therefore now to give some particular account, as well touching the publication of this worke, as also the disposition thereof, and the nature of the obsolete language wherein tis written: I shall in the first place acquaint the reader, that the kinde acceptance my former endeavours received at the hands of candid artists, in publishing some chemicall collections, very earnestly invited me to finde out a seconde piece wherewith to present those gratefull persons. Whereupon I intended to rally up some of my own conceptions in this science, and expose them also to the test: but (to this end, reviewing the philosophers) I found that many (assuming that name) wrote what their fancies, not their hands had wrought, and further then in apprehension had not seene Projection; (amongst whom our Ripley was sometimes one, as appears by his ingenious Retraction, hereafter mentioned:)[22] and being truly sensible of the great injury such workes have done young students (at the first not able to distinguish, who have written upon their undeceveable experience, who not; and consequently, not which to follow, or which to avoyde) I withdrew my thoughts (having never as yet set my selfe effectually upon the manuall practise) lest I should adde to the many injuries the world has already suffered, by delivering the bare medley of my dubious apprehensions, without

---

[21] From chap. 5 of Thomas Norton's *Ordinall of Alchimy* (written 1477), the alchemical poem which Ashmole included in *TCB*, 88.

[22] George Ripley (1415–90) appended "An Admonition, wherein the Author declareth his erronious Experiments" to his famous poem, *The Compound of Alchymy*.

the confident attestation of practise: and be justly esteemed as indiscreete as those whom Ripley mentions, that prate

Of Robin Hode and of his Bow,
Which never shot therein I trow.[23]

Yet still casting about what to make choyce of, at length (by the incouragement of some that are industrious after publique benefit) centred my thoughts, and fix'd them on this designe of collecting all (or as many as I could meet with) of our own English hermetique philosophers, and to make them publique.

Nor did I change this resolution with my clothes, notwithstanding the difficulties I saw, ready to encounter and obstruct the undertaking: for besides the paines and care that was thereunto requisite, the feare of not meeting with, or obtaining the originall manuscripts, or authentique copies of this nature (which I knew to be in some mens hands, yet wanting them my selfe) shrewdly beset, though nothing discourag'd me: yet was I therewith freely and plentifully supplyed by some worthy and intimate friends, whom I would gladly here mention, but that I well know they delight not to see their names in print. These had, my care was next to dispose them in such a series as might be answerable to the respective times, wherein each author flourished; and withall to the best advantage of the laborious student: the which I have manag'd with so just an adequation, as (I hope) will neither detract from the due honour of the one, nor yet disturbe or darken the direct path of the other.

But whilst I was doing this, I made a question (in regard some philosophers had writ in verse, others in prose) which of these should take precedency; and after some consideration adjudged it to the poetique part: and that, not only because its originall may probably anticipate the time of Orpheus, (although he be noted by Maierus, Primus Antistes, Sacerdos, Theologus, VATES, & Doctor totius Græcorum nationis) because that Linus is said to be the most perite[24] of any lyrick poet, and so ancient that some suppose him master to Orpheus, who writ that admirable allegory of the Golden Fleece, and was the first of all the Grecians that brought the chemick learning (with other sciences) out of Ægipt, as the other the first that brought the Phœnician learning to the Grecians: I say not only for that it is the ancientest, and prose but of latter use with other nations: but because poetry hath bin most anciently used with us, and (as if from a grant of Nature) held unquestionable.

Again, the excellent melody thereof is so naturall and universall, as that it seemes to be borne with all the nations of the world, as an hereditary eloquence proper to all mankinde: nor was this all, for I considered that it claimes a generall succession, and reception, in all nations, all ages, who were never without a Homer, a Virgil, or an Ovid: No not this small segment of the world [England] without a Rasis Cestrensis and an Hortulanus; for the first of these, his *Liber Luminum*, and his *Lumen de Luminum* are the ancientest now extant in Latine verse:[25] in the latter of which, I cannot omit this title of his, [*Responsio*

---

[23] From st.10 of the "ninth Gate" (Of Firmentation) of Ripley's *Compound*.

[24] According to Greek myth, Linus was a very ancient musician and singer; "perite" means "expert" and "skilful" (*OED*).

[25] Ashmole here refers to Rhazes' *Liber Luminum Rasis Cestrensis. Rasis Cestrensis . . . liber qui dicitur Lumen Luminum in expositione compositionis Alchimi* (both in verse), published in Hermannus Condeesyanus's (pseud.) *Harmoni . . . Chymico-Philosophic* (Frankfurt 1625).

Rasis Cestrensis Filio suo Merlino;] whereby it appeares he was Merlin's contemporary (at least) if not his master, in this abstruse mystery. These workes of his are both published by Hermannus, but very imperfectly, as I found by comparing them with a manuscript, as ancient as King John's time. And for the second [i.e. Hortulanus],[26] he was the first Christian philosopher after Morienus, who (travelling abroad, and returning hither in the raigne of William the Conqueror) because he was the first that transplanted the Chemicall Muses from remotest parts into his own country; is called Garland, *ab Coronam Hermeticam & Poeticam*. But to return to our matter.

If neither its antiquity, nor the naturall ratification, generall succession, and reception thereof, were enough to allow it the right hand of fellowship, yet I suppose the effects thereof, (which so affect and delight the eare, rejoyce the heart, satisfie the judgement and indulge the hearers) justly may: in regard poesy has a life, a pulse, and such a secret energy, as leaves in the minde, a far deeper impression, then what runs in the flow and evenlesse numbers of prose: whereby it won so much upon the world, that in rude times, and even amongst barbarous nations, when other sorts of learning stood excluded, there was nothing more in estimation. And for that we call Rythme, the custome of divers of our Saxon and Norman poets, shewes the opinion they had thereof; whilst the Latine (notwithstanding its excellency) could not sufficiently delight their eares, unlesse their verses (in that language) were form'd with an harmonicall cadence, and brought into rythme: nor did the Ancients wrap up their chiefest mysteries, any where else, then in the parobolical & allusive part of poetry, as the most sacred, and venerable in their esteeme, and the securest from prophane and vulgar wits. For such was the goodnesse of our fathers, that they would not willingly hazard (much lesse throw) their childrens bread among dogs; and therefore their wisdome and policy was, first, to finde out a way to teach, and then an art (which was this) to conceale. In a word, to prefer prose before poetry, is no other, or better, then to let a rough-hewen-clowne, take the wall of a rich-clad Lady-of-Honour: or to hang a presence chamber[27] with tarpalin, instead of tapestry.

And for these reasons, and out of these respects, the poeticall (as I conceiv'd) deserved the precedency.

Howbeit probably some of these pieces (now brought to publique light) had welnigh perish'd in a silent ruine; and destruction got a complete victory over them, but that my diligence and laborious inquisition rescued them from the jawes thereof; being almost quite shrouded in the dust of antiquity, and involv'd in the obscurity of forgotten things, with their leaves halfe worm-eaten. And a wonder it is, that (like the creatures in Noahs Arke) they were hitherto so safely preserved from that universall deluge, which (at the Dissolution of abbies) overflowed our greatest libraries.

And in doing this, I presume it no arrogance to challenge the reputation of performing a worke, next that of a mans own: and something more, in that (as if having the Elixir it selfe) I have made old age become young and lively, by restoring each of the ancient writers not only to the Spring of their severall beauties, but to the Summer of their strength and perfection.

---

[26] Hortulanus or Ortolanus is the name – real or pseudonymous – of a mysterious but widely-cited alchemical author, perhaps of the fourteenth century, best known for his commentary on the *Emerald Table* of Hermes Trismegistus. Ashmole and others identified him with John of Garland (see *HMES* 3:176ff.).

[27] "The reception-room in a palace" (*OED*).

As for the whole worke it selfe, it is sheav'd up from a few gleanings in part of our English fields; where though I have bestowed my industry to pick up here and there, what I could finde in my way, yet I believe there are many other pieces of this nature in private hands, which if any are pleas'd (out of the same ingenious score that I have published these) to communicate to me: I shall set thereon a value sutable to the worth of their favours, and let the world know its obligation to them besides.

The style and language thereof, may, I confesse (to some) seeme irksome and uncouth, and so it is indeed to those that are strangers thereunto; but withall very significant: old words have strong emphasis; others may look upon them as rubbish or trifles, but they are grossly mistaken: for what some light braines may esteem as foolish toys; deeper judgements can and will value as sound and serious matter.

We English have often varied our fashions (such is the levity of our fancies) and therefore if you meet with spellings different from those in use; or uncouth words as strangely ridiculous, as a maunch, hood, cod-piece, or trunke hose, know; as they were the fashionable attyres, so these the usuall dialects of those times: and posterity will pay us in our own coyne, should we deride the behaviour and dresse of our ancestors. For we must consider that languages which are daily used in our discourse, are in as continuall mutation; what custome brings into habit, is best lik'd for the present, whether it be to revive what is lost, or introduce something new; or to piece up the present, with the retained shreds of what preceded; but learned tongues (which are contain'd in books) injoy a more immutable fate, because not subject to be washt away with the daily tyde and current of times. They are like the fashion and drapery wrought on marble statues which must ever be retained without alteration.

And therefore that the truth and worth of their workes might receive no diminution by my transcription, I purposely retain'd the old words and manner of their spelling, as I found them in the originalls (except only some palpable mistakes and blemishes of former transcribers, which I took upon me to correct and purge as litle more then litterall imperfections:) yet not to leave the reader unsatisfied, have added a compendious table, for the interpretation of old, unusuall, and obsolete words, and thereby smooth'd (as I suppose) the passage for such as have not hitherto bin conversant in these ancient rough-hew'd expressions.

Wherefore you that love to converse with the dead, or consult with their monuments, draw near: perhaps you may find more benefit in them, then the living; there you may meet with the genii of our hermetique philosophers, learne the language in which they woo'd and courted Dame Nature, and enjoy them more freely, and at greater command, (to satisfie your doubts) then when they were in the flesh; for, they have written more then they would speake; and left their lines so rich, as if they had dissolved gold in their inke, and clad their words with the soveraign moysture.

My annotations are limited within the bounds of what is historicall, or what occasion-ally must needs intrench on the confines of other arts, and all glosses upon the philosophicall worke purposely omitted, for the same reasons that I chose to send forth other mens chil-dren into the world, rather then my own. And what presumptuous mistaks, or errors, the candid reader shall meet with, will (I hope) be censured with no lesse favour and charity, then that whereby they are wont to judge the faults of those they esteem their friends and well-wishers.

And now to conclude: May the God of Nature be gratiously pleased (out of the immense treasury of his goodness) to vouchsafe all such (whose good angells direct them to, or have already religiously engaged them in this mysterious knowledge) the full and entire accomplishments of a true and pious philosopher, [To wit, learning, humility, judgement, courage, hope, patience, discretion, charity & secrecie:] That so they may enjoy the fruits of their labours, which otherwise will be but vain, and unpleasant: and causelessly render the Divine Science and secret it selfe, contemptible.

Farewell (Industrious Students) and let your goodnesse still invite me to accomplish the end I have proposed: in doing which, (I presume) you may one day esteeme me, better deserving your patronage; at least-wise, your charitable censure: which is all the recompence expected or merited, by him, who is.

Yours Really Devoted,
E. Ashmole
26 Jan. 1651/2

26 Robert Boyle (1627–1691)

From *An Historical Account of a Degradation of Gold Made by an Anti-Elixir: A Strange Chymical Narative*

Like Sir Isaac Newton whose work concludes this collection, the alchemical interests and writings of Robert Boyle have undergone major reevaluation in recent years. For more than two and a half centuries following his death in 1691, Boyle's alchemical pursuits were conveniently overlooked by scientists and historians alike, who preferred to see him in a more rational, progressive, "mechanistic" light that precluded attention to such antiquated "occult" thought systems as alchemy. Consequently, beginning with the eighteenth century, little serious concern was shown for the *Sceptical Chymist* (1661) and the work included here, *An Historical Account of a Degradation of Gold* (1678), which were deemed unsuitable pastimes for the "Father of Modern Chemistry."

This stereotypical portrait of a "Newtonized," "Enlightenment" Boyle began to evaporate in the last decades of the twentieth century through the efforts of a new generation of scholars and editors, led by Michael Hunter and Lawrence M. Principe. The thesis of Principe's recent book, *The Aspiring Adept: Robert Boyle and his Alchemical Quest*, for example, is that Boyle's alchemical interests "were serious and persistent, constituting a significant and influential dimension of his life, thought, and works" (12). Moreover, his alchemy was of a distinctly traditional type, grounded in *chrysopoeia* or gold-making through use of the philosopher's stone. In short, Boyle the alchemist writes as an "adept," including use of secret codes, and – most remarkable of all – he displays keen interest in connections between alchemy and the supernatural world (Principe 188–213).

The *Anti-Elixir* tract was printed anonymously, a fact that, along with its highly implausible narrative and lightly ironic tone, makes it easy to interpret as a kind of alchemical jest. Nonetheless, the dialogue's nominal setting is a meeting of the Royal Society (of which Boyle was a prominent member), and it contains serious commentary on how alchemical knowledge is to be gained, how it can be recognized, and, most of all, how it is to be used.

The text is derived from [*An Historical Account*] *of a Degradation of Gold Made by an Anti-Elixir: A Strange Chymical Narative* (London 1678), and modernized by reducing the capitalization and italics of the original and occasionally regularizing spelling and punctuation. Additional readings: Lawrence M. Principe, *The Aspiring Adept: Robert Boyle and his Alchemical Quest* (Princeton: Princeton University Press, 1998); Michael Hunter, ed., *Robert Boyle Reconsidered* (Cambridge: Cambridge University Press, 1984).

"The Publisher to the Reader"

Having been allowed the liberty of perusing the following paper at my own lodging, I found myself strongly tempted by the strangeness of the things mention'd in it, to venture to release it: the knowledge I had of the author's inclination to gratifie the Virtuosi,[1] forbidding me to despair of his pardon, if the same disposition prevail'd with me, to make the curious partakers with me of so surprising a piece of philosophical news. And, though it sufficiently appear'd that the insuing conference was but a continuation of a larger discourse;[2] yet, considering that this part consists chiefly, not to say only, of a narrative, which (if I may so speak) stands upon its own legs, without any need of depending upon any thing that was deliver'd before; I thought it was no great venture, nor incongruity, to let it come abroad by itself. And, I the less scrupled to make this publication because I found that the Honorable Mr. Boyle confesses himself to be fully satisfied of the Truth,[3] of as much of the matter of fact, as delivers the phoenomena of the tryal; the truth whereof was further confirm'd to me, by the testimony and particular account, which that most learned and experience'd physitian, who was assistant to Pyrophilus in making the experiment, and with whom I have the honor to be acquainted (being now in London) gave me with his own mouth, of all the circumstances of the tryal. And, where the truth of that shall be once granted, there is little cause to doubt that the novelty of the thing will sufficiently indear the relation: especially to those that are studious of the higher arcana of the Hermetick Philosophy. For most of the phoenomena here mentioned will probably seem wholly new, not only to vulgar Chymists, but also to the greatest part of the more knowing Spagyrists[4] and Natural Philosophers themselves: none of the orthodox authors, as far as I can remember, having taken notice of such an Anti-Elixir. And, though Pyrophilus's scrupulousness (which makes him very unwilling to speak the utmost of a thing) allowes it to be a deterioration into an imperfect mettal onely; yet, to tell the truth, I think it was more imbas'd than so; for the part left of it (and kept for some farther discoveries) which I once got a sight of, looks more like a mineral, or Marchasite, then like any imperfect mettal: and therefore this degradation is not the same, but much greater, than that which Lullius[5] doth intimate in some places. These considerations make me presume it will easily be granted, that the effects of this Anti-Philosophers Stone, as I think it may not unfitly be call'd, will not only seem very strange to Hermetick, as well as other Philosophers, but may prove very instructive to speculative wits; especially if Pyrophilus shall please to acquaint them with that more odd Phoenomenon, which he mentions darkly in the close of his discourse.

[1] "One who has a general interest in arts and sciences, or who pursues special investigations in one or more of these; a learned person; a scientist, savant, or scholar" (*OED*). In Boyle's time, the term was frequently used of members of the Royal Society of London (established 1662), of which Boyle was one. A Royal Society meeting provides the fictional setting for this dialogue.

[2] The entire "larger discourse" is printed in Lawrence M. Principe, *The Aspiring Adept: Robert Boyle and His Alchemical Quest.*

[3] Here and elsewhere Boyle wittily writes himself into the dialogue through the anonymous persona's appeal to the authority and veracity of "the Honorable Mr. Boyle."

[4] An alchemist, in this case a knowledgeable and respectable one.

[5] Raymond Lull (b. *c.*1232–36, d. 1315) was an influential Spanish philosopher, theologian, mystic and missionary to whom many alchemical treatises were falsely attributed.

An Historical Account of the Degradation of Gold by an Anti-Elixir

After the whole Company had, as it were by common consent, continued silent for some time, which others spent in reflections upon the preceding conference, and *Pyrophylus*, in the consideration of what he was about to deliver; this *Virtuoso* at length stood up, and addressing himself to the rest, "I hope, *Gentlemen*," sayes he, "that what has been already discoursed, has inclin'd, if not perswaded you to think, that the exaltation or change of other metals into Gold is not a thing absolutely impossible; and, though I confess, I cannot remove all your doubts, and objections, or my own, by being able to affirm to you, that I have with my own hands made projection (as *Chymists* are wont to call the sudden transmutation made by a small quantity of their admirable *Elixir*) yet I can confirm much of what hath been argued for the possibility of such a sudden change of a metalline body, by a way, which, I presume, will surprize you. For, to make it more credible, that other metals are capable of being graduated, or exalted into gold by way of projection; I will relate to you that by the like way, Gold has been degraded, or imbased."

The novelty of this Preamble having much surprised the auditory, at length, *Simplicius*, with a disdainful smile, told *Pyrophilus*, "that the Company would have much thanked him, if he could have assured them, that he had seen another mettal exalted into Gold; but that to find a way of spoiling Gold, was not onely an useless discovery, but a prejudicial practice."

Pyrophilus was going to make some return to this animadversion, when he was prevented by *Aristander*, who, turning himself to *Simplicius*, told him, with a countenance and tone that argued some displeasure, "If *Pyrophilus* had been discoursing to a company of goldsmiths or of merchants, your severe reflection upon what he said would have been proper: but, you might well have forborn it, if you had considered, as I suppose he did, that he was speaking to an assembly of *Philosophers* and *Virtuosi*, who are wont to estimate experiments, not as they inrich mens purses, but their brains, and think knowledge especially of uncommon things very desirable, even when 'tis not accompanyed with any other thing, than the light that still attends it and indears it. It hath been thought an useful secret, by a kind of retrogradation to turn Tin and Lead into brittle bodies, like the ores of those metals. And if I thought it proper, I could shew, that such a change might be of use in the investigation of the nature of those metals, besides the practical use that I know may be made of it. To find the nature of wine, we are assisted, not only by the methods of obtaining from it a spirit; but by the ways of readily turning it into vinegar; the knowledge of which ways hath not been despised by Chymists or Physitians, and hath at *Paris*, and divers other places, set up a profitable trade. 'Tis well known that divers eminent *Spagyrists* have reckon'd amongst their highest *Arcana* the ways by which they pretended (and I fear did but pretend) to extract the Mercury of Gold, and consequently destroy that metal; and 'twere not hard to shew by particular instances, that all the experiments wherein bodies are in some respects deteriorated, are not without distinction to be rejected or despis'd; since in some of them, the light they may afford may more than countervail the degradation of a small quantity of matter, though it be Gold itself. And indeed," continues he, "if we will consider things as philosophers, and look upon them as nature hath made them, not as opinion hath disguised them; the prerogatives and usefulness of Gold, in comparison of other metals, is nothing near so great as alchymists and usurers imagine. For, as it is true, that Gold is more ponderous, and more fix'd, and perhaps more difficult to be spoiled, than Iron; yet these qualities (whereof the first makes it burthensom, and the two others serve chiefly but to distinguish the true from counterfeit) are so balanced by the hardness, stiffness, springiness, and other useful qualities of Iron; that if those two metals I speak of, (Gold and Iron) were equally plentiful in the world, it is scarce to be doubted, but that men would prefer the more useful before the more splendid, considering how much worse it were for mankind to want hatchets and knives and swords, than coin and plate? Wherefore," concludes he, "I think *Pyrophilus* ought to be both desired and incouraged to go on with his intended discourse, since whether Gold be or not be the best of metals, an assurance that it may be degraded, may prove a novelty very instructive and perhaps more so than the transmutation of a baser metal into a nobler…"

Pyrophilus perceiving by several signs that he needed not add anything of apologetical to what *Aristander* had already said for him, resumed his discourse by saying, "I was going, Gentlemen, when *Simplicius* diverted me, to tell you that looking upon the vulgar objections that have been wont to be fram'd against the possibility of metalline transmutations, from the authority and prejudices of *Aristotle* and the School Philosophers, as arguments that in such an assembly as this need not now be solemnly discuss'd; I consider that the difficulties that really deserve to be call'd so, and are of weight even with Mechanical Philosophers, and judicious Naturalists, are principally these. *First*, that the great change that must be wrought by the *Elixir* (if there be such an agent) is effected upon bodies of so stable and almost immutable a nature as metals. *Next*, that this great change is said to be brought to pass in a very short time. *And thirdly* (which is yet more strange), that this great and suddain alteration is said to be effected by a very small, and perhaps inconsiderable proportion of the transmuting powder. To which three grand difficulties, I shall add another that to me appears, and perhaps will seem to divers of the new Philosophers, worthy to be lookt upon as a *fourth*, namely, the notable change that must by a real transmutation be made in the Specifick Gravity[6] of the matter wrought upon: which difficulty I therefore think not unworthy to be added to the rest, because upon several trials of my own and other men, I have found no known quality of Gold (as its colour, malleableness, fixity, or the like) so difficult, if not so impossible, to be introduc'd into any other metalline matter, as the great Specifick Gravity that is peculiar to Gold. So that, Gentlemen," concludes *Pyrophilus*, "if it can be made appear that Art has produc'd an *Anti-Elixir*, (if I may so call it) or agent that is able in a very short time, to work a very notable, though deteriorating, change upon a metal; in proportion to which, its quantity is very inconsiderable; I see not why it should be thought impossible that Art may also make a *true Elixir*, or powder capable of speedily transmuting a greater proportion of a baser metal into Silver or Gold; especially if it be considered, that those that treat of these *Arcana*, confess that 'tis not every matter which may be justly called the Philosophers Stone, that is able to transmute other metals in vast quantities; since several of these writers (and even *Lully* himself) make differing orders or degrees of the *Elixir*, and acknowledge that a Medicine or tincture of the first or lowest order will not transmute above ten times its weight of an inferior metal."

---

[6] I.e., the ratio of the density of any substance to the density of some other substance taken as a standard, e.g. water for liquids and solids.

Pyrophilus having at this part of his discourse made a short pawse to take breath, *Crattippus* took occasion from his silence to say to him, "I presume, *Pyrophilus*, I shall be disavowed by very few of these Gentlemen, if I tell you that the Company is impatient to hear the narrative of your experiment, and that if it do so much as probably make out the particulars you have been mentioning, you will in likelyhood perswade most of them, and will certainly oblige them all. I shall therefore on their behalf as well as my own, sollicite you to hasten to the historical part of a discourse that is so like to gratifie our curiosity."

The Company having by their unanimous silence testified their approbation of what *Crattippus* had said; and appearing more than ordinarily attentive,

"As I was one day abroad," saith *Pyrophilus*, "to return visits to my friends, I was by a happy providence (for it was beside my first intention) directed to make one to an ingenious foreigner, with whom a few that I had received from him, had given me some little acquaintance.

Whilst this gentleman and I were discoursing together of several matters, there came in to visit him a stranger, whom I had but once seen before; and though that were in a promiscuous company,[7] yet he addressed himself to me in a way that quickly satisfied me of the greatness of his civility; which he soon after also did of that of his curiosity. For the *Virtuoso*, in whose lodgings we met, having (to gratifie me) put him upon the discourse of his voyages, the curious stranger entertained us an hour or two with pertinent and judicious answers to the questions I askt him about places so remote, or so much within land, that I had not met with any of our English navigators or travellers that had penetrated so far as to visit them . . . I made the more haste to propose such questions to him, as I most desired to be satisfied about; and among other things, enquiring whether in the Eastern parts [of the world] he had travers'd, he had met with any Chymists; he answered me that he had; and that though they were fewer, and more reserved than ours, yet he did not find them all less skilful. And on this occasion, before he left the town to go aboard the ship he was to overtake; he in a very obliging way put into my hands at parting a little piece of paper, folded up, which he said contained all that he had left of a rarity he had received from an Eastern *Virtuoso*, and which he intimated would give me occasion both to remember him, and to exercise my thoughts in uncommon speculations.

The great delight I took in conversing with a person that had travelled so far, and could give me so good an account of what he had seen, made me so much resent the being so soon deprived of it, that though I judg'd such a *Vertuoso* would not, as a great token of his kindness, have presented me a trifle, yet the present did but very imperfectly consoal me for the loss of so pleasing and instructive a conversation.

Nevertheless, that I might comply with the curiosity he himself had excited in me, and know how much I was his debtor, I resolved to see what it was he had given me, and try whether I could make it do what I thought he intimated, by the help of those few hints rather than directions how to use it, which the parting haste he was in (or perhaps some other reason best known to himself) confin'd him to give me. But in regard that I could not but think the experiment would one way or other prove extraordinary, I thought fit to take a witness or two and an assistant in the trying of it; and for that purpose made choice

---

[7] I.e., an assembly of mixed and diverse types of people.

of an experienced Doctor of Physick, very well vers'd in the separating and copelling[8] of metals."

"Though the Company," says *Heliodorus*, "be so confident of your sincerity and wariness, that they would give credit even to unlikely experiments upon your single testimony; yet we cannot but approve your discretion in taking an assistant and a witness, because in nice and uncommon experiments we can scarce use too much circumspection, especially when we have not the means of reiterating the tryal: for in such new, as well as difficult cases, 'tis easie even for a clear-sighted experimenter to overlook some important circumstance, that a far less skilful bystander may take notice of."

"As I have ever judged," saith *Pyrophilus*, "that cautiousness is a very requisite qualification for him that would satisfactorily make curious experiments; so I thought fit to imploy a more than ordinary measure of it in making a tryal, whose event I imagined might prove odd enough. And therefore having several times observed that some men are prepossessed, by having a particular expectation rais'd in them, and are inclined to think that they do see that happen which they think they should see happen, I resolved to obviate this prejudication as much as innocently I could, and (without telling him any thing but the truth, to which philosophy as well as religion obliges us to be strictly loyal) I told him but thus much of the truth, that I expected that a small proportion of a powder presented me by a foreign *Virtuoso* would give a brittleness to the most flexible and malleable of metals, Gold itself. Which change I perceiv'd he judged so considerable and unlikely to be effected, that he was greedy of seeing it severely try'd.

Having thus prepared him not to look for all that I my self expected, I cautiously opened the paper I lately mentioned, but was both surprized and troubled (as he also was), to find in it so very little powder, that in stead of two differing tryals that I designed to make with it, there seem'd very small hope left that it would serve for one (and that but an imperfect one neither). For there was so very little powder that we could scarce see the colour of it (save that as far as I could judge it was of a darkish red) and we thought it not only dangerous but useless to attempt to weigh it, in regard we might easily lose it by putting it into, and out of the balance; and the weights we had were not small enough for so despicable a quantity of matter, which in words I estimated at an eighth part of a grain:[9] but my assistant (whose conjecture I confess my thoughts inclin'd to prefer) would allow it to be at most but a tenth part of a grain. Wherefore seeing the utmost we could reasonably hope to do with so very little powder was to make one tryal with it, we weighed out in differing balances two drams of Gold that had been formerly *English* coyn, and that I caused by one that I usually imploy to be *cupell'd* with a sufficient quantity of Lead, and *quarted*,[10] as they speak, with refin'd Silver, and purg'd *Aqua fortis*, to be sure of the goodness of the Gold: these two drams I put into a new crucible, first carefully annealed, and having brought them to fusion by the meer action of the fire, without the help of Borax, or any other Additament (which course, though somewhat more laborious than the most usual we took to obviate scruples) I put into the well-melted metal with my own hand the little parcel of powder lately mentioned, and continuing the vessel in the fire for about a quarter

---

[8] "The process of assaying or refining the precious metals in a cupel" (*OED*).

[9] In troy and apothecaries' ounces there are 480 grains; in the avoirdupois ounce, 437.5 grains.

[10] Quartation is "that operation in which gold is melted with thrice its weight of silver, and then in aqua fortis whatever is not gold is dissolved away" (*Aspiring Adept*, 283, note n).

of an hour, that the powder might have time to defuse itself every way into the metal, we poured out the well-melted Gold into another crucible that I had brought with me, and that had been gradually heated before to prevent cracking. But though from the first fusion of the metal, to the pouring out, it had turn'd in the crucible like ordinary Gold, save that once my assistant told me he saw that for two or three moments it lookt almost like an Opale; yet I was somewhat surpriz'd to find when the matter was grown cold, that though it appear'd upon the balance that we had not lost anything of the weight we put in, yet in stead of fine Gold, we had a lump of metal of a dirty colour, and as it were overcast with a thin coat, almost like half vitrified *Litharge*;[11] and somewhat to increase the wonder, we perceived that there stuck to one side of the crucible a little globule of metal that lookt not at all yellowish, but like coarse Silver, and the bottom of the crucible was overlaid with a vitrified substance whereof one part was of a transparent yellow, and the other of a deep brown, inclining to red; and in this vitrified substance I could plainly perceive sticking at least five or six little globules that lookt more like impure Silver than pure Gold. In short, this stuff look[ed] so little like refin'd, or so much as ordinary, Gold, that though my Friend did much more than I marvel at this change, yet I confess I was surpriz'd at it myself. For though in some particulars it answered what I lookt for, yet in others, it was very differing from that which the donor of the powder had, as I thought, give[n] me ground to expect. Whether the cause of my disappointment were that (as I formerly intimated) this *Virtuoso's* haste or design made him leave me in the dark; or whether it were that finding my self in want of sufficient directions, I happily pitcht upon such a proportion of materials, and way of operating, as were proper to make a new discovery, which the excellent giver of the powder had not design'd or perhaps thought of...

[Pyrophilus next descibes the testing of the newly transmuted metal.] And first, having rubb'd it upon a good touchstone, whereon we had likewise rubb'd a piece of *Coyn'd silver*, and a piece of *Coyn'd Gold*, we manifestly found that the mark left upon the stone by our mass between the marks of the two other metals, was notoriously more like the touch of the Silver than to that of the Gold. Next, having knockt our little lump with a hammer, it was (according to my prediction) found brittle, and flew into several pieces. Thirdly, (which is more) even the insides of those pieces lookt of a base dirty colour, like that of Brass or worse, for the fragments had a far greater resemblance to *Bell-metal*,[12] than either to Gold or to Silver. To which we added this fourth, and more considerable, examen; that having carefully weigh'd out one dram of our stuff (reserving the rest for trials to be suggested by *second thoughts*) and put it upon an excellent new and well-neal'd cupel, with about half a dozen times its weight of Lead, we found, somewhat to our wonder, that though it turn'd very well like good Gold, yet it continued in the fire above an hour and an half, (which was twice as long as we expected) and yet almost to the very last the fumes copiously ascended, which sufficiently argu'd the operation to have been well carried on..."

"There yet remain'd," saith *Heliodorus*, "one examen more of your odd metal, which would have satisfied me, at least as much as any of the rest, of its having been notably imbas'd: for if it were altered in its *specifick gravity*, that quality I have always observ'd

---

[11] "Protoxide of lead (PbO) prepared by exposing melted lead to a current of air" (*OED*).

[12] "The substance of which bells are made; an alloy of copper and tin" (*OED*).

(as I lately perceiv'd you also have done) to stick so close to Gold, that it could not by an additament so inconsiderable in point of bulk, be considerably altered without a notable and almost essential change in the texture of the metal."

To this pertinent discourse, *Pyrophilus*, with the respect due to a person that so worthily sustain'd the dignity he had of presiding in that choice Company, made this return: "I owe you, Sir, my humble thanks for calling upon me to give you an account I might have forgotten, and which is yet of so important a thing, that none of the other Phænomena of our experiment seem'd to me to deserve so much notice. Wherefore I shall now inform you, that having provided my self of all the requisites to make hydrostatical tryals (to which perhaps I am not altogether a stranger) I carefully weighed in the water the ill-lookt mass (before it was divided for the coupelling of the above-mentioned dram) and found, to the great confirmation of my former wonder and conjectures, that in stead of weighing about nineteen times as much as a bulk of water equal to it, its proportion to that liquor was but that of fifteen, and about two thirds to one: so that its *specifick gravity* was less by about 3 1/3 than if it had been pure Gold it would have been."

At the recital of this notable circumstance, superadded to the rest, the generality of the Company, and the President too, by looking and smiling upon one another, express'd themselves to be as well delighted as surpriz'd; and after the murmuring occasion'd by the various whispers that pass'd amongst them, was a little over, *Heliodorus* address'd himself to *Pyrophilus*, and told him, "I need not, and therefore shall not, stay for an express order from the Company to give you their hearty thanks: for as the obliging stranger did very much gratifie you by the present of his wonderful powder, so you have not a little gratified us by so candid and particular a narrative of the effects of it; and I hope," continues he, "that if you have not yet otherwise dispos'd of that part of your deteriorated Gold that you did not cupel, you will sometime or other favour us with a sight of it..."

[Crattippus then comments on the larger implications of Pyrophilus's report.] "And though I freely grant that some old copper metals are of good use in history, to keep alive by their inscriptions the memory of the taking of a town, or the winning of a battel; though these be but things that almost every day are somewhere or other done, yet I think *Pyrophilus's* imbas'd metal is much to be preferr'd, as not only preserving the memory, but being an effect of such a victory of Art over Nature, and the conquering of such generally believ'd insuperable difficulties, as no story that I know of gives us an example of..."

[Heliodorus then calls upon Pyrophilus to present "what Corrollaries he thinks fit to propose from what he hath already delivered."] Pyrophilus responds, "our experiment plainly shews that Gold, though confessedly the most homogeneous, and the least mutable of metals, may be in a very short time (perhaps not amounting to many minutes) exceedingly chang'd, both as to malleableness, colour, homogeneity, and (which is more) specific gravity; and all this by so very inconsiderable a proportion of injected powder, that since the Gold that was wrought on weighed two of our English drams, and consequently an hundred and twenty grains, an easie computation will assure us that the Medicine did thus powerfully act, according to my estimate, (which was the modestest) upon near a thousand times, (for 'twas above nine hundred and fifty times) its weight of Gold, and according to my assistants estimate, did (as they speak) go on upon twelve hundred; so that if it were fit to apply to this *Anti-Elixir* (as I formerly ventur'd to call it) what is said of the true *Elixir* by divers of the Chymical Philosophers, who will have the virtue of their Stone increas'd in such a proportion, as that at first 'twill transmute but *ten* times its weight; after the next rotation *an hundred* times, and after the next to that *a thousand times*,[13] our powder may in their language be stil 'd *a Medicine of the third order*."

[Aristander provides a final defense of pursuing the arcana of chemistry.] "The Computation," saith *Aristander*, "is very obvious, but the change of so great a proportion of metal is so wonderful and unexampled, that I hope we shall among other things learn from it this lesson, That we ought not to be so forward as many men otherwise of great parts are wont to be, in prescribing narrow limits to the power of Nature and Art, and in condemning and deriding all those that pretend to, or believe, uncommon things in Chymistry, as either Cheats or Credulous. And therefore I hope, that though (at least in my opinion) it be very allowable to call Fables, Fables, and to detect and expose the impostures or deceits of ignorant or vain-glorious pretenders to chymical mysteries, yet we shall not be too hasty and general censur[er]s of the sober and diligent indigators of the *Arcana* of chymistry, [to] blemish (as much as in us lies) that excellent Art itself, and thereby disoblige the genuine Sons of it, and divert those that are indeed possessors of noble secrets, from vouchsafing to gratifie our curiosity, as we see that one of them did *Pyrophilus's*, with the sight at least, of some of their highly instructive rarities."

---

[13] Pyrophilus here describes the Multiplication stage of the alchemical process.

27 Sir Isaac Newton (1642–1727)

The Key (Keynes MS 18); *The Commentary on the Emerald Tablet* (Keynes MS 28)

On 14 February 1727/28, Humphrey Newton wrote to John Conduitt:

> About 6 weeks at spring, and 6 at the fall, the fire in the elaboratory scarcely went out, which was well furnished with chemical materials as bodies, receivers, heads, crucibles, etc., which was made very little use of, the crucibles excepted, in which he fused his metals; he would sometimes, tho' very seldom, look into an old mouldy book which lay in his elaboratory, I think it was titled *Agricola de Metallis*, the transmuting of metals being his chief design . . . His brick furnaces, *pro re nata*, he made and altered himself without troubling a bricklayer. [Quoted in Betty Jo Dobbs, *Foundations* 8.]

The experimenter in question was not a deluded alchemist pursuing *ignes fatui* in a squalid workhouse, such as one finds in paintings by Brueghel or Teniers, but Sir Isaac Newton. Thanks to much pioneering study in the last quarter century, it is now widely known that this great investigator of light and optics, planetary motion, mathematics, and physics, was also a tireless experimenter in matters alchemical. The late Professor Dobbs has stated that "most of [Newton's] great powers were poured out upon church history, theology, 'the chronology of ancient kingdoms,' prophecy, and alchemy" (*Foundations* 6) – not upon "scientific" interests. Estimates are that Newton's alchemical studies comprise more than a million words in manuscript, examination of which has brought about a major reassessment of his thought and works. Of the two short manuscript pieces included here, the *Clavis* or *Key* (Keynes MS 18, King's College, Cambridge) has been called "the summit and crown of Newton's earliest alchemical efforts" (*Foundations* 134); and while its attribution to Newton is not beyond dispute, it is now generally accepted as his. The purpose of this experiment was to produce the "philosophical mercury" or universal solvent so prized by the alchemists as the necessary first step in preparation of the philosopher's stone.

It is fitting that the final reading in this collection should be Newton's *Commentary on the Emerald Tablet* of Hermes Trismegistus, thus – to reinscribe the ouroboros – ending at a point close to where it began, with the Father of Modern Science (or the "Last of the Magicians") commenting upon the best known work of the Father of Alchemy and the Hermetic Arts. Newton's *Commentarium* is recorded in Latin autograph in Keynes MS 28 (King's College, Cambridge), which also includes Latin and English versions of the *Emerald Table*. Composed in the early 1680s, it blends ideas and phrases from the *Emerald Table* with the Mosaic creation account, so as to illuminate the process of alchemical creation.

The translated text of Newton's *Clavis* or *Key* is reprinted from Betty Jo Dobbs's *The Foundations of Newton's Alchemy* (Cambridge: Cambridge University Press, 1975), 253–55; the translation of *The Commentary on the Emerald Tablet* is reproduced from Dobbs's *The Janus Faces of Genius: The Role of Alchemy in Newton's Thought* (Cambridge: Cambridge University Press, 1991), 276–77. Permission to reprint has been granted by Cambridge University Press.

The Key

[f. 1r] First of all know antimony[1] to be a crude and immature mineral having in itself materially what is uniquely metallic, even though otherwise it is a crude and indigested mineral. Moreover, it is truly digested by the sulfur that is found in iron and never elsewhere.

Two parts of antimony [combined] with iron give a regulus[2] which in its fourth fusion exhibits a star; by this sign you may know that the soul of the iron has been made totally volatile by the virtue of the antimony. If this stellate regulus is melted with gold or silver by an ash heat in an earthen pot, the whole regulus is evaporated, which is a mystery. Also, if this regulus is amalgamated with common mercury and is digested in a sealed vessel on a slow fire for a short time – two or three hours – and then ground for 1/8 of an hour in a mortar without moisture while being warmed moderately, until it spits out its blackness, then it may be washed to deposit the greatest part of its blackness, until the water, which in the beginning becomes quite black, is scarcely more tinged by the blackness. This can be done by flushing it with water many times. Let the amalgam be dried, again placed near the fire, and kept in the above-mentioned heat for three hours. Afterwards let it be ground again as before in a dry and warm mortar. It pushes out new blackness, which must be washed away again; this must be repeated continually until the whole amalgam becomes like shining and cupellated silver,[3] whereas at first it had a dark leaden color.

Then distill this mercury which has been so washed and amalgamate over again seven or nine times, and in each amalgamation see to the heating, grinding, and washing as many times as before, Distill the whole as before. On the seventh time you will have a mercury dissolving all metals, particularly gold.[4] I know whereof I write, for I have in the fire manifold glasses with gold and this mercury. They grow in these glasses in the form of

---

[1] The *OED*'s definition coincides with Newton's statement as to antimony's "crude and immature" original nature and its "digested" potential: "One of the elementary bodies, a brittle metallic substance, of bright bluish white colour and flaky crystalline texture. Its metallic characteristics are less pronounced than those of the metals generally."

[2] A *regulus* is "the metallic form of antimony, so called by early chemists, apparently on account of its ready combination with gold" (*OED*), when brought to a state of liquidity or fusion through the application of heat. But Newton also draws upon its astronomical sense (the bright star in the constellation Leo), in that a star pattern is revealed in the amalgam when it undergoes multiple fusion.

[3] I.e., silver that has been purified in a cupel.

[4] Thus the object of the process is production of "philosophical mercury" from common mercury. Dobbs notes that the alchemists' "attempts to dissolve gold seem to have been made with the same notion a modern chemist employs when he analyzes a compound before he attempts to synthesize it: if one knows what a substance is made of, then it is easy enough to make it" (*Foundations of Newton's Alchemy*, 184–85).

a tree,[5] and by a continued circulation the trees are dissolved again with the work into new mercury. I have such a vessel in the fire with gold thus dissolved, where the gold was visibly not dissolved by a corrosive into atoms, but extrinsically and intrinsically into a mercury as living and mobile as any mercury found in the world. For it makes gold begin to swell, to be swollen, and to putrefy, and to spring forth into sprouts and branches, changing colors daily, the appearances of which fascinate me every day. I reckon this a great secret in Alchemy, and I judge it is not rightly to be sought from artists who have too much wisdom to decide that common mercury ought to be attacked through reiterated cohobation[6] by the regulus of leo [that is, of iron or antimony]. That unique body, that regulus, however, is familial with mercury seeing that it is closest to that mercury you have known and recognized in the whole mineral kingdom, and hence most closely related to [f. 1v] gold. And this is the philosophical method of meliorating nature in nature, consanguinity in consanguinity.

With regard to this operation, look at the Letter responding to Thomas of Bologna,[7] and you will find this question fully solved.

Another secret is that you need the mediation of the virgin Diana [quintessence, most pure silver]; otherwise the mercury and the regulus are not united.

The regulus is made from antimony four ounces /nine parts/, iron two ounces /four parts/; this is a good proportion. Do not neglect to have a mass of antimony greater than that of iron, for if an error is made here you will be disappointed. Make the regulus by casting in nitre bit by bit; cast in between three and four ounces of nitre so that the matter may flow.

It is not a good idea to prepare in one crucible a greater quantity than the above measure of antimony. The antimony is ground, then cupelled together with iron, whatever others may say or write.

Little nails may be used and especially the ends of those broken from horn shoes. Let the fire be strong so that the matter may flow [like water], which is easily done. When it flows, cast in a spoonful of nitre; and when that nitre has been destroyed by the fire, cast in another. Continue that process until you have cast in three or four ounces. Then pile up the charcoals about the crucible, taking care that they do not fall into it. Increase the fire as much as the fusion of common silver requires, and keep it in that state for 1/8 of an hour. [The matter ought to be like a subtle water if you have labored correctly.] Then pour the matter out into a cone. The regulus will subside. Separate the ashy scoria from it. Keep the cooled material in a dry vessel.

It is a sign of a good fusion if the iron is completely fused and if the scoriae break up by themselves into powder.

Beat the regulus and add to it two, or at most $2\frac{1}{2}$, ounces of nitre. Grind the regulus and the nitre together completely and again melt. Throw away the arsenical and useless scoriae.

---

[5] The interactive phenomenon Newton describes closely resembles – perhaps is – the alchemists' well known "philosophical tree" or "tree of Hermes," previously noted in Ripley and Philalethes.

[6] Repeated distillation.

[7] A reference to *The Answer of Bernardus Trevisanus, to the Epistle of Thomas of Bononia, Physician to King Charles the Eighth* [sic], which exists in many manuscript copies and had been printed recently in *Aurifontina Chymica: or, A Collection of Fourteen small Treatises Concerning the First Matter of Philosophers*, trans. John Frederick Houpreght (London, 1680). Thomas of Bologna was a physician, alchemist, and astrologer in the courts of Charles V (1364–80) and Charles VI (1380–1422) of France and father of Christine de Pisan.

Grind the regulus a third and fourth time with at most one ounce of nitre and melt in a new crucible, and on the fourth time you will have scoriae tinged with a golden color and a stellate regulus.

NB In the last three times the scoriae must be thrown away because they are arsenical; however, they are useful in surgery.

NB In the last three fusions the regulus must be beaten, and ground and mixed with nitre. Some cast the nitre into the crucible, but this is not recommended, for, firstly, the fusion is as a result prolonged and the regulus is not without some loss of itself by exhalation. Secondly, nitre thrown in in this way stays on the surface and in time it cools the regulus. And since nitre flows easily, [f. 2r] it may flow at first and encrust so that it will not flow again without a large fire. If that happens, the best part of the regulus perishes in the conflagration, whence it is that sometimes a star perishes because it is falsely ascribed to a constellation. You will see that the regulus mixed with nitre in this way flows easily with it; and you will not see it become hard in any manner, except for the difference in the depuration, which is far greater if it is mixed than if the nitre is just tossed in.

Take of this regulus one part, of silver two parts, and melt them together until they are like fused metal. Pour out, and you will have a friable mass of the color of lead.

NB If the regulus is joined with the silver, they flow more easily than either one separately and they remain fused as long as lead even though there are thus two parts of silver, which is then changed into the nature of antimony, friable and leaden.

Beat this friable mass, this lead, and cast it together with the mercury of the vulgar into a marble mortar. The mercury should be washed (say ten times) with nitre and distilled vinegar and likewise dried (twice), and the mortar should be constantly heated just so much as you are able to bear the heat of with your fingers. Grind the mercury 1/4 of an hour with an iron pestle and thus join the mercury, the doves of Diana mediating,[8] with its brother, philosophical gold, from which it will receive spiritual semen. The spiritual semen is a fire which will purge all the superfluities of the mercury, the fermental virtue intervening. Then take a little beaten sal ammoniac and grind with the mercury. When it is fully amalgamated, add just enough humidity to moisten it, and this one philosophical sign will appear to you: that in the very making of the mercury there is a great stink. Finally, wash your mercury by pouring on water, grinding, decanting, and again pouring on fresh water, until few feces appear.

The Commentary on the Emerald Tablet

The things that follow are most true. Inferior and superior, fixed and volatile, sulfur and quicksilver have a similar nature and are one thing, like man and wife. For they differ one from another only by the degree of digestion and maturity. Sulfur is mature quicksilver, and quicksilver is immature sulfur; and on account of this affinity they unite like male and

---

8 The "doves of Diana" are silver or the female principle that serves to mediate or join mercury with the regulus. Dobbs notes that "the common mercury is receiving 'spiritual semen' from the 'philosophical gold' or star regulus of antimony. Presumably, the 'spiritual semen' has been drawn into the regulus from the 'universal spirit' in the surrounding Neoplatonic 'aire'" (*Foundations of Newton's Alchemy*, 184).

female, and they act on each other, and through that action they are mutually transmuted into each other and procreate a more noble offspring to accomplish the miracles of this one thing. And just as all things were created from one Chaos by the design of one God, so in our art all things, that is the four elements, are born from this one thing, which is our Chaos, by the design of the Artificer and the skillful adaptation of things. And this generation is similar to the human, truly from a father and mother, which are the Sun and the Moon. And when the Infant is conceived through the coition of these, he is borne continuously in the belly of the wind until the hour of birth, and after birth he is nourished at the breasts of foliated Earth until he grows up. This wind is the bath of the Sun and the Moon, and Mercurius, and the Dragon, and the Fire that succeeds in the third place as the governor of the work; and the earth is the nurse, Latona washed and cleansed, whom the Egyptians assuredly had for the nurse of Diana and Apollo, that is, the white and red tinctures. This is the source of all the perfection of the whole world. The force and efficacy of it is entire and perfect if, through decoction to redness and multiplication and fermentation, it be turned into fixed earth. Thus it ought first to be cleansed by separating the elements sweetly and gradually, without violence, and by making the whole material ascend into heaven through sublimation and then through a reiteration of the sublimation making it descend into earth: by that method it acquires the penetrating force of spirit and the fixed force of body. Thus will you have the glory of the whole world and all obscurities and all need and grief will flee from you. For this thing, when it has through solution and congelation ascended into heaven and descended into earth, becomes the strongest of all things. For it will constrain and coagulate every subtle thing and penetrate and tinge every solid thing. And just as the world was created from dark Chaos through the bringing forth of the light and through the separation of the aery firmament and of the waters from the earth, so our work brings forth the beginning out of black Chaos and its first matter through the separation of the elements and the illumination of matter. Whence arise the marvellous adaptations and arrangements in our work, the mode of which here was adumbrated in the creation of the world. On account of this art Mercurius is called thrice greatest, having three parts of the philosophy of the whole world, since he signifies the Mercury of the philosophers, which is composed from the three strongest substances, and has body, soul, and spirit, and is mineral, vegetable, and animal, and has dominion in the mineral kingdom, the vegetable kingdom, and the animal kingdom.

Glossary

Ablution: the purification of matter through successive washings, usually with water.

Albedo or Albification: an intermediate stage of the alchemical process associated with whiteness and transmutation of base metals to silver (cf. Nigredo and Rubedo).

Alembic: the still-head, or upper part of the still; see Cucurbit.

Aludel: a pear-shaped vessel, open at both ends, which, when stacked one upon another, is used in sublimation.

Argent Vive: literally "quick" or "living" silver; mercury.

Assation: the process of roasting or baking.

Athanor: the alchemical furnace.

Balneum Mariae or bain-Marie: the alchemists' water-bath.

Calcination: the reduction of a metal or mineral to fine powder through the application of heat.

Chemical Wedding: the alchemists' metaphor for the combining of philosophical sulphur (male) and philosophical mercury (female), the two principle ingredients in the preparation of the philosopher's stone.

Cibation: the process of "feeding the matter" of the philosopher's stone to increase its potency.

Color Sequence: Black; Peacock's Tail ("Cauda Pavonis") or Rainbow; White; and Red.

Cucurbit: the gourd-shaped vessel forming the lower part of the still, in which liquid to be distilled is placed (cf. Alembic).

Decoction or Digestion: the use of heat, e.g. boiling, to bring a substance to maturity and perfection by breaking it down.

Elixir: a synonym for the philosopher's stone or universal medicine.

Fixation: the transformation of a volatile substance into a non-volatile substance.

Four Elements: earth, water, air, and fire; derived from the four humors (coldness, dryness, hotness, moistness), they are the basic constituents from which all sub-lunary substances are created.

Inceration: bringing a hard substance to the consistency of soft wax.

Lute: cement used in sealing a vessel, to prevent the "spirits'" escape.

Macrocosm and Microcosm: the "great world" and the "little world" of man, particularly as they mirror each other.

Mercury, or Quicksilver: with sulphur, the primary component of the philosopher's stone.

Multiplication: A late stage in the production of the philosopher's stone, in which its quality and quantity are augmented.

Mundification: the action of cleansing.

Nigredo: the initial stage of the alchemical opus associated with the putrefaction, death, decomposition, and blackening of the body of the base metal.

Philosopher's Stone: the alchemists' final goal; the secret preparation that, when cast upon imperfect metals, will transform them into silver and gold.

Projection: The final stage of the alchemical opus in which the completed philosopher's stone is cast upon base metals to effect their transmutation.

Quintessence: the "fifth essence," a perfect, harmonious substance from which all heavenly bodies are constituted but present in all things; a synonym for the philosopher's stone.

Rubedo or Rubification: the culmination of the alchemical process, associated with redness, completion of the philosopher's stone, and transmutation of base metals to gold (cf. Nigredo and Albedo).

Solve and Coagula: The alternating processes of Solution (dissolving) and Coagulation of the matter of the philosopher's stone, used to increase its quality and quantity (see Multiplication).

Sublimation: the process of converting a solid substance into a gas or vapor, by means of heat.

Bibliography

Abraham, Lyndy. *A Dictionary of Alchemical Imagery*. Cambridge: Cambridge University Press, 1998.
    Marvell and Alchemy. Aldershot, Hants.: Scolar Press, 1990.

Adams, Alison and Stanton J. Linden, eds. *Emblems and Alchemy*. Glasgow Emblem Studies 3. Glasgow: University of Glasgow, 1998.

[Albertus Magnus.] *Libellus de Alchimia, Ascribed to Albertus Magnus*. Translated by Sister Virginia Heines. Berkeley and Los Angeles: University of California Press, 1958.

Ambix: The Journal of the Society for the Study of Alchemy and Early Chemistry (published since 1937).

Aristotle. *The Complete Works of Aristotle*. Edited by Jonathan Barnes. Rev. Oxford trans. 2 vols. Princeton: Princeton University Press, 1984.

Ashmole, Elias. *Theatrum Chemicum Britannicum*. London, 1652.
    The Way to Bliss. London, 1658.

Aurifontina Chymica: or, A Collection of Fourteen small Treatises Concerning the First Matter of Philosophers. London, 1680.

Bacon, Francis. *The Works of Francis Bacon*. Edited by James Spedding, Robert L. Ellis, and Douglas D. Heath. 14 vols. 1872; reprint, New York: Garret Press, Inc., 1968.

Berthelot, Marcellin. *Collection des anciens alchimistes grecs*. 3 vols. Paris: Georges Steinheil, 1887–88.

Broek, R. van den, and Wouter J. Hanegraaff, eds. *Gnosis and Hermeticism from Antiquity to Modern Times*. Albany: State University of New York Press, 1998.

Caley, Earle Radcliffe. "The Leyden Papyrus X: An English Translation with Brief Notes." *Journal of Chemical Education* 3 (Oct. 1926): 1149–66.
    "The Stockholm Papyrus: An English Translation with Brief Notes." *Journal of Chemical Education* 4 (Aug. 1927): 979–1002.

Copenhaver, Brian P., trans. *Hermetica: The Greek "Corpus Hermeticum" and the Latin "Asclepius" in a new English translation, with notes and introduction*. Cambridge: University Press, 1992.

Coudert, Allison. *Alchemy: The Philosopher's Stone*. London: Wildwood House, 1980.

[Culpeper, Nicholas]. *The Complete Herbal by Nicholas Culpeper, A New Edition*. Facsimile. Birmingham: Kynoch Press, 1953.

Debus, Allen G. *The Chemical Philosophy: Paracelsian Science and Medicine in the Sixteenth and Seventeenth Centuries*. 2 vols. New York: Science History Publications, 1977.
    The English Paracelsians. New York: Franklin Watts, 1966.

[Democritus.] "The Treatise of Democritus on Things Natural and Mystical." Translated by Robert R. Steele. *Chemical News* 61 (1890): 88–125.

Dixon, Laurinda. *Alchemical Imagery in Bosch's Garden of Delights*. Ann Arbor, MI: UMI Research Press, 1980.

Dixon, Laurinda, ed. *Nicolas Flamel: His Exposition of the Hieroglyphicall Figures (1624)*. New York and London: Garland, 1994.

Dobbs, Betty Jo Teeter. *Alchemical Death & Resurrection: The Significance of Alchemy in the Age of Newton.* Washington, D.C.: Smithsonian Institution Libraries, 1990.

    The Foundations of Newton's Alchemy or "The Hunting of the Greene Lyon." Cambridge: Cambridge University Press, 1975.

    The Janus Faces of Genius: The Role of Alchemy in Newton's Thought. Cambridge: Cambridge University Press, 1991.

Duchesne, Joseph [Quersitanus]. *The Practise of Chymicall, and Hermetical Physicke . . . Translated by Thomas Timme, Minister.* London, 1605.

Evans, R. J. W. *Rudolf II and His World: A Study in Intellectual History, 1576–1612.* Oxford: Clarendon Press, 1973.

Ferguson, John, comp. *Bibliotheca Chemica.* 2 vols. Glasgow: J. Maclehose and Sons, 1906; reprint, London: Derek Verschoyle, 1954.

Fowden, Garth. *The Egyptian Hermes: A Historical Approach to the Late Pagan Mind.* Cambridge: Cambridge University Press, 1986.

French, John. Preface to *The Divine Pymander of Hermes Mercurius Trismegistus, In XVII. Books.* London, 1650.

Gillispie, Charles C., ed. *Dictionary of Scientific Biography.* New York: Charles Scribner's Sons, 1970. S.v. "Bolos of Mendes," by Jerry Stannard and "Zosimus of Panopolis," by M. Plessner.

Hibbert, Christopher. *The Virgin Queen: Elizabeth I, Genius of the Golden Age.* Reading, MA: Addison–Wesley, 1991.

Holmyard, E. J. *Alchemy.* Harmondsworth, Middlesex: Penguin, 1957.

Hopkins, Arthur John. *Alchemy: Child of Greek Philosophy.* Morningside Heights, NY: Columbia University Press, 1934.

Jonson, Ben. *Ben Jonson.* Edited by C. H. Herford and Percy and Evelyn Simpson. 11 vols. Oxford: Clarendon Press, 1925–52.

Josten, C. H., ed. *Elias Ashmole (1617–1692).* 5 vols. Oxford: Clarendon Press, 1966.

Jung, C. G. *Alchemical Studies.* Translated by R. F. C. Hull. Bollingen Series 20. Princeton: Princeton University Press, 1967.

    Psychology and Alchemy. Translated by R. F. C. Hull. 2nd edition. Bollingen Series 20. Princeton: Princeton University Press, 1968.

Kelly, L. G., ed. *Basil Valentine His Triumphant Chariot of Antimony with Annotations of Theodore Kirkringius (1678).* New York and London: Garland, 1990.

Klossowski De Rola, Stanislas. *The Golden Game: Alchemical Engravings of the Seventeenth Century.* London: Thames & Hudson, 1997.

Lennep, Jacques van. *Art & Alchimie.* Brussels: Éditions Meddens, 1971.

Linden, Stanton J. *Darke Hierogliphicks: Alchemy in English Literature from Chaucer to the Restoration.* Lexington: University Press of Kentucky, 1996.

Linden, Stanton J., ed. *George Ripley's Compound of Alchymy (1591).* Aldershot, Hants.: Ashgate, 2001.

    The Mirror of Alchimy Composed by the Thrice-Famous and Learned Fryer, Roger Bachon. New York and London: Garland Publishing, 1992.

Lindsay, Jack. *The Origins of Alchemy in Graeco-Roman Egypt.* London: Frederick Muller, 1970.

Luther, Martin. *The Table Talk of Martin Luther.* Translated by William Hazlitt. London: G. Bell, 1902.

Merkel, Ingrid and Allen G. Debus, eds. *Hermeticism and the Renaissance: Intellectual History and the Occult in Early Modern Europe.* Washington, D.C.: Folger Shakespeare Library, 1988.

Meulenbeld, G. Jan. *A History of Indian Medical Literature.* Vol. IIA (Text), IIB (Annotation). Groningen, Netherlands: Egbert Forsten, 2000.

Needham, Joseph. *Science and Civilisation in China*. Vol. 2, *History of Scientific Thought*. Cambridge: Cambridge University Press, 1956.

———. *Science and Civilisation in China*. Vol. 5, *Chemistry and Chemical Technology*, Pt. 2 *Spagyrical Discovery and Invention: Magisteries of Gold and Immortality*. Cambridge: Cambridge University Press, 1974.

Newman, William R. *Gehennical Fire: The Lives of George Starkey, an American Alchemist in the Scientific Revolution*. Cambridge, MA: Harvard University Press, 1994.

Owen, A. L. *The Famous Druids*. Oxford: Clarendon Press, 1962.

Pagel, Walter. *Paracelsus: An Introduction to Philosophical Medicine in the Era of the Renaissance*. 2nd (rev.) edn. Basel: Karger, 1982.

Philalethes, Eirenaeus [George Starkey]. *Ripley Reviv'd: or, an Exposition upon Sir George Ripley's Hermetico-Poetical Works*. London, 1678.

Pitai, Raphael. *The Jewish Alchemists: A History and Source Book*. Princeton: Princeton University Press, 1994.

Plato. *The Collected Dialogues of Plato*. Edited by Edith Hamilton and Huntington Cairns. Bollingen Series 71. New York: Bollingen Foundation, 1966.

Porto, Paulo Alves. "Michael Sendivogius on Nitre and the Preparation of the Philosophers' Stone." *Ambix* 48, 1 (March 2001): 3–7.

Priesner, Claus and Karin Figala, eds. *Alchemie: Lexicon einer hermetischen Wissenschaft*. Munich: C. H. Beck Verlag, 1998.

Principe, Lawrence. *The Aspiring Adept: Robert Boyle and his Alchemical Quest*. Princeton: Princeton University Press, 1998.

Read, John. *Prelude to Chemistry*. London: G. Bell and Sons, 1936.

Roberts, Gareth. *The Mirror of Alchemy: Alchemical Ideas and Images in Manuscripts and Books*. London: British Museum, 1994.

Roob, Alexander. *Alchemy and Mysticism*. Köln: Taschen, 1997.

Ruland, Martin the Elder. *A Lexicon of Alchemy*. Translated by A. E. Waite. London: Westminster Press, 1893; reprint, London: John Watkins, 1964.

Salmon, William. *Medicina Practica*. London, 1692.

Scholem, Gershom. *Kabbalah*. New York: New American Library, 1974.

Schuler, Robert M. *Alchemical Poetry 1575–1700: From Previously Unpublished Manuscripts*. English Renaissance Hermeticism. New York and London: Garland, 1995.

———. "Some Spiritual Alchemies of Seventeenth-Century England." *Journal of the History of Ideas* 41 (April-June 1980): 293–318.

Shumaker, Wayne. *The Occult Sciences in the Renaissance: A Study in Intellectual Patterns*. Berkeley: University of California Press, 1972.

Smith, Pamela. *The Business of Alchemy: Science and Culture in the Holy Roman Empire*. Princeton: Princeton University Press, 1994.

[Stephanos of Alexandria.] "The Alchemical Works of Stephanos of Alexandria." Translated by F. Sherwood Taylor. *Ambix* 1 (May 1937): 116–39.

Taylor, F. Sherwood. *The Alchemists: Founders of Modern Chemistry*. London: William Heinemann, 1951.

[Theophrastos.] "The Poem of the Philosopher Theophrastos upon the Sacred Art." Translated by C. A. Browne. *Scientific Monthly* 11 (Sept. 1920): 193–214.

Thorndike, Lynn. *A History of Magic and Experimental Science*. 8 vols. New York: Columbia University Press, 1923–58.

Vickers, Brian. "On the Function of Analogy in the Occult." In *Hermeticism and the Renaissance: Intellectual History and the Occult in Early Modern Europe*, ed. Ingrid Merkel and Allen G. Debus, 265–92. Washington, D.C.: Folger Shakespeare Library, 1988.

Vickers, Brian, ed. *Occult and Scientific Mentalities in the Renaissance*. Cambridge: Cambridge University Press, 1984.

Waite, Arthur Edward, ed. and trans. *The Hermetic and Alchemical Writings of . . . Paracelsus the Great*. 2 vols. London: James Elliott, 1894.

The Hermetic Museum, Restored and Enlarged. 2 vols. London: James Elliott and Co., 1893.

Waite, Arthur Edward, ed. *The Turba Philosophorum or Assembly of the Sages*. London: George Redway, 1896; reprint, New York: Samuel Weiser, 1976.

White, David Gordon. *The Alchemical Body: Siddha Traditions in Medieval India*. Chicago: University of Chicago Press, 1996.

"The Ocean of Mercury: An Eleventh-Century Alchemical Text." In *Religions of India in Practice*, ed. Donald S. Lopez, Jr., 281–87. Princeton: Princeton University Press, 1995.

Wilding, Michael. "Edward Kelly: A Life." *Cauda Pavonis: Studies in Hermeticism* 18, 1–2 (Spring and Fall 1999): 1–26.

Yates, Frances A. *Giordano Bruno and the Hermetic Tradition*. Chicago: University of Chicago Press, 1964.

The Rosicrucian Enlightenment. London: Routledge & Kegan Paul, 1972.

Index

Institution, Laws and Ceremonies of the Order of
the Garter 222; The Way to Bliss 13, 14
astrology, astronomy 8–10, 62, 146, 148, 151,
162, 168, 222
aurum potabile 148, 167, 170–173, 211
authority and tradition 21, 22, 41, 112–113
Avicenna 12, 13; Kitâb al-Shifâ' 95; De
Congelatione et Conglutinatione: 13, 95–98;
alchemy as imitation only 95, 97–98;
formation of metals 95–97; transmutation
rejected 95, 98, 100–102, 143

Bacon, Francis 13, 20, 111
Bacon, Roger 4, 12–14, 136; Excellent
Discourse . . . of Art and Nature 13, 111; black
magic 111; Radix Mundi: 111–122; authorities
112–113; colors (black, white, citrine, red)
117–119; elixir (powder) 120; four elements
111; laboratory equipment and practice:
115–116; alembic 115; balneum 117; cucurbit
115; degrees of fire 116–117; luting 116;
mercury 113; origin of metals 111–113;
philosopher's stone 113–114, 117; processes:
conjunction 115, 117; multiplication 119–120;
projection 120–121; purification of metals
114–115; requisite moral character 122
Bale, John 224
balneum mariae (bain-marie) 148, 170, 172
Berosius 224
Berthelot, Marcellin 1, 44
biblical references 16, 17, 123–135, 152,
157, 191
Bolos Democritus 8 (see also Pseudo-Democritus)
Bonus, Petrus, Pretiosa margarita novella 14,
201–202, 229
Book of Komarios 44
Bosch, Hieronymus 2, 19
Boyle, Sir Robert 1, 13, 19, 141, 211, 222,
234–242; An Historical Account of a Degradation
of Gold: anti-philosopher's stone 235, 237;
Aristander 236–237, 242; Art's victory over
Nature 241, 242; audience 236; chemical
philosophers 241; experiment described
239–240; outcome of 240; Pyrophilus's
summary of 241; specific gravity 237, 240–241;
testing results of 240–241; witnesses of
238–239; gold, properties of 236; Heliodorus
239, 241; hermetic philosophy 235; narrative

235, 238–241; mysterious stranger 238;
obstacles to transmutation summarized 237;
philosopher's stone (powder) 237, 239;
projection 236; Pyrophilus 235; Simplicius
236; transmutation, possibility of 236; wine
and vinegar 236; Sceptical Chymist 234
Bridlington (Yorkshire) 141
Browne, C. A. 61
Brueghel, Pieter, the Elder 2, 19, 243
Burcot, Dr. (physician to Queen Elizabeth I)
223

Caley, Earle R. 46
Carrington, Leonora 19
Casaubon, Isaac 11, 22, 27, 208
Chalcidius 29
Chaldeans 163
Chaucer, Geoffrey 19, 222; Canon's Yeoman's Tale
19, 199, 206; Franklin's Prologue 224
chemical wedding 17, 67, 74, 78, 115, 165
Chevalerie, P. Arnauld de la 123
China 6–7
Chou I Tshan Thung Chhi 6
Christ, God, Christian influences 11, 16, 22, 23,
54, 67, 124, 137 (see also biblical references)
Christine de Pisan 136
Christopher of Paris 137
Cleopatra 9; Cleopatra VII 44; Dialogue of
Cleopatra and the Philosophers: 44–46, 50, 54;
use of allegory and symbol 44–45
color symbols and sequences 8, 16, 58, 137, 181,
220
Combachius (Ludwig Combach) 223
Conduitt, John 243
Cooper, William (editor), Collectanea Chymica
136, 170, 211
Copenhaver, Brian 11
courtly practice of alchemy 83, 103, 174, 185
craft traditions 5, 8, 38, 46
creation theme 5, 28–30, 71

Dastin, John 222
De Alchemia 2
death-resurrection motif 17, 22, 44–45, 56, 152,
187, 218
Dee, John 222
Democritus of Abdera 8, 38, 58 (see also
Pseudo-Democritus)